Web Programming
for Beginners Series

Introduction
to JavaScript
(Volume 1)

Web Programming
for Beginners Series

Introduction
to JavaScript
(Volume 1)

First Edition

Randall Robertson MCSE, MCDBA, MCP
Broward College, Total Technical Institute

Web Programming for Beginners Series

**Programming
Language
Associates**

Ft Lauderdale   Pompano Beach   Boca Raton
West Palm Beach   Tampa   Miami
Jacksonville   Orlando

Preface

The primary purpose of this book is to provide an effective method for the student who knows nothing about JavaScript to learn the language in a gradual, easy-to-understand manner. The assumption that is held throughout this book is that the student knows absolutely nothing about JavaScript and must be led step-by-step through its basic principles from beginning to end. Starting with the basic concepts of JavaScript we slowly build on this foundation with brief text and an abundance of solved problems to illustrate the principles covered in that particular section.

The way this book is laid out allows for a gradual progression of knowledge and understanding of JavaScript. Just as missing rungs on a ladder make climbing difficult or impossible, no steps are skipped in building our ladder of knowledge for the JavaScript web programming language. Many books, in fact most books on JavaScript, start out by discussing just a few basic concepts with very few examples and then, after jumping over many necessary intermediate steps, the author goes into applications of the language that the student isn't ready for. It makes no sense that so many books on basic JavaScript assume background knowledge that the student rarely has. This only creates confusion and frustration on the part of the student who doesn't care about the advanced topics or obscure applications of the material that the author feels compelled to discuss.

That's definitely not the method that is used here. After a few pages of text (usually 2-6 pages), numerous solved problems are presented to the student so he/she can immediately apply what they've learned in gradual, step-by-step manner. There's absolutely no substitute for working through many problems that thoroughly clarify the material under discussion

This book features 764 solved problems - more than enough to assure that the student will get a clear, practical understanding of each subject and programming concept that's covered in this book. This volume contains 18 chapters and is the first in a series of three volumes on basic JavaScript. It covers a variety of subjects such as JavaScript variables, arithmetic operators, logical operators, data types, conditional statements, strings, loops and a wide variety of other subjects that the student needs to master in order to have a good understanding of the theory and practical application of the basic principles of JavaScript.

This volume (***Introduction to JavaScript - Volume 1***) is meant to be used in conjunction with the other two volumes (***Introduction to Basic JavaScript - Volume2,*** and ***Introduction to Basic JavaScript - Volume 3***). Together, the three volumes contain over 2000 solved problems which will help the student o acquire a thorough knowledge of the basic concepts of JavaScript. In the majority of cases this will produce a confident student who is ready to move on to a more in-depth study of intermediate and advanced JavaScript.

The real strengths of this 3-volume series is its abundance of solved problems and its brief, concise discussion of every topic of elementary JavaScript. We have complete confidence that you will find this book to be different from any other book on beginning JavaScript that you've ever read and that it will you give you an excellent foundation for successfully moving on to other more advanced facets of this practical and extremely useful programming language.

Randall Robertson

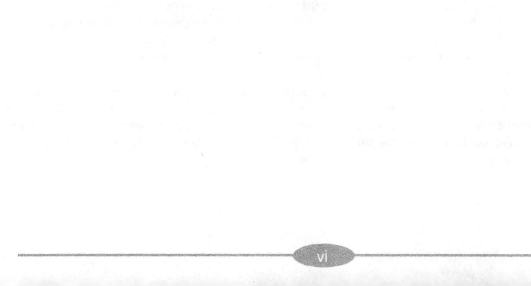

Contents

CHAPTER 6 — JavaScript Operators: Part 2 — 103

CHAPTER 7 — JavaScript Operators: Part 3 — 123

CHAPTER 8 — JavaScript Operators: Part 4 — 149

Chapter 1

Introduction to JavaScript

1.1 A BRIEF HISTORY OF JAVASCRIPT

JavaScript is one of the most useful and popular languages to have appeared in the relatively brief history of the world wide web. Its development and implementation has been almost single-handedly responsible for the web's tremendous growth and acceptance as the worldwide standard of information sharing and data transfer. JavaScript has also been responsible for the web's transition from a collection of static, non-interactive, one-way information-bearing pages to the dynamic, interactive environment that attracts, entertains and informs billions of people all over the world today.

JavaScript was created by software engineer Brendan Eich in May 1995 while he was working for Netscape Communications Corporation. Netscape was the creator of the proprietary web browser Netscape Navigator, which was the dominant web browser throughout the 1990's. The software engineers at Netscape soon realized that the web needed to become more dynamic (content such as text, images, form fields, etc. on a web page can change, in response to different contexts or conditions on a dynamic website) and interactive (an interactive site is a site that allows visitors to interact with the content in some way) if it was going to continue to attract a continually increasing stream of new users (and new buyers of Netscape Navigator).

Before that time, even if you wanted to do something as simple as checking to see if data had been entered into a form, you had to send the data back to the server in order to have it checked and/or validated. Clearly, an interpreted scripting language was needed that would allow these tasks to be accomplished by the web browser on the client computer.

Back in the 1960's when the internet got its start, its main use was to link collections of data in various separated locations together. After 20 years of gradual development and technological evolution the first modern web browser was invented by Tim Berners-Lee in 1991. The browser was called "worldwideweb" and it allowed users to transfer documents using HTTP hyper text language.

A few years later, a more advanced browser called Mosaic allowed web developers to go beyond plain text and include colors and simple graphics. In spite of these exciting and innovative breakthroughs in web technology, the web was still a very rudimentary and limited environment compared to the dynamic, interactive, media-rich web world we're familiar with today.

This began to change in the early 1990's when a group of web developers and engineers left the Mosaic project which was being developed at the NCSA (National Center for Supercomputing Applications) at the University of Illinois Urbana-Champaign. This led to the creation of the Netscape Communications Corporation (originally called Mosaic Communications Group) by Mark Andreesen and James Clark in 1994. The result of this was the birth of the Netscape browser.

It was soon after this that Brendan Eich, who was part of the team that developed Netscape Navigator, developed a new scripting language called JavaScript (originally called "Mocha" and then "Livescript") that would soon turn the world of web development on its head. Although JavaScript wasn't part of the first version of Netscape, it soon became an integral part of Netscape when its second version was released.

The JavaScript language is one of the most useful additions to the collection of web programming languages that have come along since the web was first introduced. Its main use has been to make web pages dynamic and interactive.

One of the areas that has caused some confusion and controversy with JavaScript is its name which is similar to the popular programming language Java. In spite of the similarity between the names of these languages there is no relationship between them. They are totally independent entities. JavaScript was developed by the Netscape Communications Corporation whereas Java was developed by Sun Microsystems.

Despite the confusion, JavaScript has become a very successful client-side scripting language. In response to JavaScript's success, Microsoft created its own similar client-side scripting language and called it Jscript which it released with Internet Explorer 3.0 in August, 1996.

In November of 1996, Netscape submitted JavaScript for standardization to ECMA (European Computer Manufacturers Association) International - an international standards organization. In June, 1997 JavaScript became the standard ECMA-262. The standardized language was officially named ECMAScript, although the language is still commonly referred to as JavaScript.

1.2 JAVASCRIPT VERSIONS

Version	Description
JavaScript 1.0	JavaScript was released as version 1.0 in March 1996 in Netscape Navigator 2.0 and Internet Explorer 2.0.
JavaScript 1.1	JavaScript version 1.1 was shipped in Netscape Navigator 3.0. Released on August 19, 1996.
JavaScript 1.2	JavaScript version 1.2 was shipped in Netscape Navigator 4.0 - 4.05. Released on June 11, 1997.
JavaScript 1.3	JavaScript version 1.3 was shipped in Netscape Navigator 4.06 - 4.7x. Released on October 19, 1998. Standardization work to be compliant with EMCA-262 1st and 2nd edition.
JavaScript 1.4	JavaScript version 1.4 was shipped in Netscape's server side JavaScript. Released in 1999.
JavaScript 1.5	JavaScript version 1.5 was shipped in Netscape Navigator 6. And Firefox 1.0. Released on November 14, 2000. Standardization work to be compliant with EMCA-262 3rd edition.
JavaScript 1.6	JavaScript version 1.6 was shipped in Firefox 1.5. Released in November, 2005. Includes ECMAScript for XML (E4X), new Array methods plus String and Array generics.
JavaScript 1.7	JavaScript version 1.7 was shipped in Firefox 2. Released in October, 2006. Includes generators, iterators, array comprehensions, let expressions, and destructuring assignment.
JavaScript 1.8	JavaScript version 1.8 was shipped in Firefox 3. Released in June, 2008. Includes closures, generator expressions and Array.reduce().
JavaScript 1.8.1	JavaScript version 1.8.1 was shipped in Firefox 3.5. Released on June 30, 2009. Includes the TraceMonkey JIT and supports native JSON.
JavaScript 1.8.2	JavaScript version 1.8.2 was shipped in Firefox 3.6. Released on June 22, 2009. Includes only minor changes.
JavaScript 1.8.5	JavaScript version 1.8.5 was shipped in Firefox 4. Released on July 27, 2010. Includes many new features for ECMA-262 Edition 5 compliance.

1.3 WHAT IS JAVASCRIPT?

JavaScript is a client-side scripting language that is used to add functionality and user interactivity to otherwise static HTML/CSS based web pages. JavaScript is also a lightweight programming language that's most commonly used as a part of web pages whose implementation allows client-side scripts to interact with the user. JavaScript is embedded directly into HTML pages and is interpreted directly by the web browser rather than being sent back to the server for processing.

While HTML markup language allows web developers to format the content of the web page, JavaScript lets them make the page changeable and dynamic and allows the user to interact with the web site. For example, HTML can be used to create bold text, list boxes, text boxes and buttons, whereas JavaScript can be written that allows for actions such as changing text on the page, moving images around the page, validating text that's been entered by the user in text boxes, creating pop-up messages and many other dynamic activities that can't be achieved with HTML and CSS alone.

From this we see that the main purpose of JavaScript, when used in web development, is to manipulate the web page elements and to make the page dynamic, controllable and changeable based on user input and a variety of other varying factors.

Imagine a web page that contains just text content. You can read it and you can click on any of the links in order to move to another page or website. There is some interaction here but it's on a very limited and rudimentary scale. What if you want to click on a button in order to replace one image with another image, check data in a form for validity, hide part of a page or move an image from one part of the page to another location. HTML doesn't have any provisions to create this kind of dynamic interactivity with the user but JavaScript allows you to do all these things.

JavaScript is written and placed inside of the HTML markup code using the opening `<script language='javascript'>` tag or just `<script>` without the language attribute. You can also link to an external JavaScript file using the `<script source='external_JSfile1.js'>` tag. When the browser encounters the `<script>` tag it reads the JavaScript code and then interprets it.

JavaScript is a very useful web programming tool that can be used to add many dynamic and interactive features on an otherwise static, one-way web page. It can turn a web page from a passive experience where the viewer simply looks at the page to an interactive experience that responds touser input. The following is a list of some the things that JavaScript can be used to accomplish:

- Display information based on user input
- Check validity and details that are entered into a form for compliance with certain criteria
- Perform arithmetic operations on numbers entered by the user
- Display the current date and time
- Play a game
- Check to see if the user has entered a valid e-mail address
- Respond to user-initiated events such as button clicks
- Add special effects such as changing colors, moving backgrounds, custom cursors, etc.
- Add text to an HTML page on-the-fly
- Detect what browser the visitor using and what features the browser does or doesn't support
- Create cookies
- Load new content or data onto the page without reloading the page
- Rollover effects
- Drop-down menus
- Playing audio and video
- Animating elements such as fading, resizing or relocating
- Change HTML form data
- Change HTML content, HTML styles, HTML attributes
- Perform calculations in forms

JavaScript is what's known as a client-side script or client-side language. This means that the code is downloaded from the server as part of the web page and executed on the end user's computer. This is in contrast to server-side languages (such s PHP, ASP and PERL) which run completely on the server and send only the finished output to the client/user computer.

The client-side environment that is used to run JavaScript is the browser. The processing takes place on the user's computer. The source code is transferred from the web server to the user/client's computer over the internet and run directly in the browser.

JavaScript is the main client-side scripting language used on the web. Client-side scripts are interpreted by the browser. The process for client-side scripting is as follows:

1. The user requests a web page from the server
2. The server finds the page and sends it to the user
3. The page is displayed on the browser with any scripts running during or after display

So, the purpose of client-side scripting is to make web page changes after they arrive at the browser. A client-side script performs its tasks entirely on the client's machine and doesn't need to interact with the server to function. All of the code needed to generate the current page has been sent to the client machine and since the code is interpreted and executed completely by the browser and the client computer, the user can still interact with the page after it's been loaded even if the client-server connection is severed.

Although JavaScript is primarily an interpreted language, it has optional JIT-compilation support. In older browser versions (Internet Explorer 8 and earlier, Firefox prior to 3.5) JavaScript was a purely interpreted language. This means that scripts execute without preliminary compilation, that is, without conversion of the script into system-dependent machine code. Instead, the user's browser interprets the script, analyzes and immediately executes it.

In newer browser versions, JavaScript code may be either interpreted or compiled using a just-in-time (JIT) compiler. At run time the browser decides what parts of the script code should be JIT-compiled for better performance. This makes JavaScript significantly faster and more stable for complex, high-performance web applications. New versions of all popular browsers have JavaScript JIT compilers.

Some of the advantages of JavaScript are:

- JavaScript is able to run dynamic sites on any browser
- JavaScript works fast and well without requiring a lot of memory
- JavaScript is easy to learn
- It has numerous extensions available for mobile app development
- Less server interaction - you can validate user input before sending it to the server. This saves server traffic which means less load on the server
- Immediate feedback to the users - they don't have to wait for a page reload to see if they have forgotten something
- Increased interactivity - you can create interfaces that react when the user hovers over them with a mouse or activates them via the keyboard
- Richer interfaces - you can use JavaScript to include such items as drag-and-drop components and sliders to a give a rich interface to your site users
- Speed. Being client-side, JavaScript is very fast because any code functions can be run immediately instead of having to contact the server and wait for an answer.
- Simplicity. JavaScript is relatively simple to learn and implement.
- Versatility. JavaScript plays nicely with other languages and can be used in a huge variety of applications. Unlike PHP or SSI scripts, JavaScript can be inserted into any web page regardless of the file extension.

JavaScript can't be treated as a full-fledged programming language because it lacks the following important features:

- Client-side JavaScript does not allow the reading or writing of files
- JavaScript can't be used for networking applications
- JavaScript doesn't have any multithreading or multiprocessor capabilities

1.4 WHERE DOES JAVASCRIPT GO IN YOUR HTML CODE?

1.4.1 The <script> tag

In HTML, JavaScript code must be inserted between <script> and </script> tags as follows:

```
Example:
<script>
    document.write ("Hello future JavaScript experts!");
</script>
```

1.4.2 JavaScript in the <head> section of an HTML file

You can place as many JavaScript scripts in an HTML document as you want. Scripts can be placed in either the <body> or in the <head> section of an HTML page, or you can put scripts in both sections. In the following example, JavaScript code is placed in the <head> section of an HTML page:

```
Example:
<!DOCTYPE html>
<html>
<head>
  <script>
    document.write("Hello future JavaScript experts!");
  </script>
</head>
<body>
  <h1>Demonstration of a script placed in the &lthead&gt section of an HTML page</h1>
</body>
</html>
```

Placing the script in the <head> section has the benefit of being a familiar and predictable location for scripts. They're easy to find this way . It also has the benefit of making sure that all JavaScript has been loaded and executed before the document is displayed.

The drawbacks are that the time taken to load your scripts delays the display of the document and that the script does not have access to the HTML in the document. Because of this you need to delay executiing any scripts that change the HTML of the document until the document has finished loading.

1.4.3 JavaScript in the <body> section of an HTML file

In the following example, JavaScript code is placed in the <body> section of an HTML page:

```
Example:
<!DOCTYPE html>
<html>
<head>
</head>
<body>
   <h1>Demonstration of a script placed in the
        &lthead&gt section of an HTML page</h1>
    <script>
     document.write ("Hello future JavaScript experts!");
    </script>
</body>
</html>
```

It is a good idea to place scripts at the bottom of the <body> element. This can improve page load, because HTML display is not blocked by scripts loading.

1.4.4 JavaScript in an external .js file

You can also put scripts in external files. If you want to run the same JavaScript on a variety of different pages in a web site, you should add an external JavaScript file instead of writing the same script over and over again on each individual HTML page. Save the script in a file with a .js extension, and then refer to it using the **src** attribute in the <script> tag:

```
<script src="externalScript.js"></script>
```

In the following example, a JavaScript code has been placed in placed in an external file called "externalScript.js". The code is referenced, called and executed using the **src** attribute of the <script> tag:

```
Example:
<!DOCTYPE html>
<html>
<head>
   <script src="externalScript.js"></script>
</head>
<body>
    <h1>Demonstration of a script placed in the
        &lthead&gt section of an HTML page</h1>
</body>
</html>
```

There are several advantages to placing JavaScript in external files:

- It creates a separation between HTML and JavaScript code
- Cached JavaScript files can speed up page loads because JavaScript doesn't have any multithreading or multiprocessor capabilities
- Once a .js file loads, it remains in browser memory for the duration of your session, so it does not need to be re-loaded as you navigate to different html pages - thus improving page-load performance
- If you need to make a change to your JavaScript that affects your entire website, you only need to make the change once, in your .js file, and not multiple times in each html file
- It makes HTML and JavaScript easier to read and maintain

Chapter 2

JavaScript Programs

2.1 JAVASCRIPT PROGRAM BASICS

2.1.1 What is a JavaScript program?

A JavaScript program is usually made up of many individual JavaScript statements, although it may contain just a few statements, depending on the purpose of the program. Each JavaScript statement ends with a semicolon. JavaScript statements that appear between <script> and </script> tags are executed in the order that they appear. When more than one script appears in a file, the scripts are executed in the order in which they appear.

If a script appears in the <head> section of an HTML document, none of the <body> section of the document has been defined yet. This means that the JavaScript objects that represent the contents of the document body have not been created yet and cannot be manipulated by that code. Your scripts should not attempt to manipulate objects that have not yet been created. For example, you can't write a script that manipulates the contents of an HTML form if the script appears before the form in the HTML file (more about this in later chapters).

In the following example, a and b are given the values 5 and 6, respectively, and c is set equal to the product of a * b and displayed on the page:

Example:
```
<script>
   var a = 5;
   var b = 6;
   var c = a * b;
   document.write (c);
</script>
```

Note:
- each statement ends with a semicolon
- each statement is put on a separate line for clarity and readability
- all of the statements are enclosed within one set of <script> tags
- this script could be in the <head> section, the <body> section or in an external .js file

2.1.2 JavaScript statements

In HTML, JavaScript statements are instructions to be executed by the web browser. JavaScript applications consist of statements with an appropriate syntax. A single statement may span multiple lines. Multiple statements may occur on a single line if each statement is separated by a semicolon. Best practice, though is to each statement on a separate line for clarity and ease of reading. All the JavaScript code that you will write will, for the most part, be comprised of many separate statements. A statement can set a variable equal to a value. A statement can also be a function call, i.e. document.write().

Statements define what the script will do and how it will be done. In addition to standard statements like changing a variable's value, assigning a new value, or calling a function, there are groups of statements that are distinct in their purpose. These distinct groups of statements include:

- Conditional statements
- Loop statements
- Object manipulation statements

- Comment statement statements
- Exception handling statements (more about all of these in later chapters)

Here are the most common types of statements:

var i;	variable declaration
i = 5;	value assignment
i = i + 1;	value assignment
var x = 9;	variable declaration and assignment
var fun = function() {...};	variable declaration, assignment and function definition
alert("hi");	function call

The following statement tells the browser to display the text "Goodbye cruel world" on the web page:

Example:
```
<script>
  document.write ( "Goodbye cruel world!");
</script>
```

2.1.3 Semicolons

Semicolons are used to separate JavaScript statements. Add a semicolon at the end of each executable statement. The semicolon in JavaScript is used to separate statements, but it can be omitted if the statement is followed by a line break (or there's only *one* statement in a {block}). In spite of this, it's recommended that you conclude every statement with a semicolon. It makes the code much easier to read and understand. The following statements all end with a semicolon (as should all statements):

Example:
```
<script>
  var animal1 = "cat";
  var animal2 = "dog";
  var animal3 = "mouse"
  var animal4 = "lion"
  var animal5 =  "raccoon";
</script>
```

Multiple statements are allowed on one line if each statement is separated by a semicolon:

Example:
```
<script>
  var animal1 = "cat"; var animal2 = "dog"; var animal3 = "mouse"; var animal4 = "lion"; var animal5 =  "raccoon";
</script>
```

2.1.4 Whitespace

A whitespace character is an empty space in the code (without any visual representation) on screen. Examples of whitespace characters include space characters, tabs, and line break characters. In JavaScript, use of excessive whitespace is ignored. For example, the following JavaScript code:

```
x   =   y   *   z   -    s;
```

is identical to and will execute in the same way as:

```
x = y * z - s
```

Both statements would be interpreted and executed in exactly the same way. So, why is whitespace important? Since whitespace is ignored in JavaScript and not taken into consideration when the script is being analyzed, you can use it to write code that is more readable and understandable. Consider the following JavaScript code:

```
If (num1 > num2) { document.write ("The first number is greater than the second number.") ; } else
{document.write ("The first number is greater than the second number.") ; }
```

This code is confusing and difficult to read. But the computer (to be more specific - the interpreter) has absolutely no problem with it. In fact it's better for the computer because most of the unnecessary whitespace has been eliminated. The following code adds whitespace (which is ignored by the interpreter) in order to make the code more readable and understandable:

```
If (num1 > num2) {
    document.write ("The first number is greater than the second number.") ;
}
else {
    document.write ("The first number is greater than the second number.") ;
}
```

So, remember that JavaScript ignores multiple spaces in the script code. You should add white space to your script to make it more readable. It's a good idea is to put spaces around operators (= + - * /):

```
var x = (num1 + num2) / (3.141 * num3);
```

2.1.5 Line length and line breaks

There are no hard and fast rules, but for easy readability, many programmers like to avoid code lines that are longer than 80 characters When a statement will not fit on a single line, it may be necessary to break it. Place the break after an operator, ideally after a comma. A break after an operator decreases the likelihood that a copy-paste error will be masked by semicolon insertion.

Example of a line break after an operator:

Example:

before

```
<script>
  var a = 6 + 5 + 4;
</script>
```

(continued on next page)

```
after
<script>
  var a = 6 +
    5 + 4;
</script>
```

2.1.6 Keywords

JavaScript statements often start with a keyword to identify the JavaScript action to be performed. These are words reserved for use by the JavaScript engine. You can not use these keywords as object, function names, variable names or methods. If you try to, more often than not, your script will fail.

The following is a list of some of the most important keywords used in JavaScript:

Keyword	Description
function	Declares a function
var	Declares a variable
debugger	Stops the execution of JavaScript, and calls (if available) the debugging function
do ... while	Executes a block of statements, and repeats the block, while a condition is true
if ... else	Marks a block of statements to be executed, depending on a condition
continue	Jumps out of a loop and starts at the top
switch	Marks a block of statements to be executed, depending on different cases
return	Exits a function
break	Terminates a switch or a loop
try ... catch	Implements error handling to a block of statements
for	Marks a block of statements to be executed, as long as a condition is true
default	Specifies the code to run if there is no case match in a switch statement
goto	Jump to another part of the program

JavaScript keywords are reserved words. Reserved words cannot be used as names for variables.

2.2 JAVASCRIPT SYNTAX

2.2.1 What is JavaScript syntax?

In computer science, the **syntax** of a computer language is the set of rules that defines the combinations of symbols that are considered to be a correctly structured document or fragment in that language. This applies both to programming languages, where the document represents source code, and markup languages, where the document represents data. The syntax of a language defines its surface form.

Computer language syntax is generally distinguished into three levels:

- Words – the lexical level, determining how characters form tokens;
- Phrases – the grammar level, narrowly speaking, determining how tokens form phrases;
- Context – determining what objects or variables names refer to, if types are valid, etc.

The syntax of JavaScript is the set of rules that define a correctly structured JavaScript program. JavaScript syntax refers to a set of rules that determine how the language will be written (by the programmer) and interpreted (by the browser).

2.2.2 Values

JavaScript contains two major types of values: **fixed** values and **variable** values. **Fixed** values are called **literals**. **Variable** values are called **variables**.

2.2.2.1 Literals

In any language, a **literal** is a data value that appears directly in the source code. Literals are distinct from variables because they are fixed and part of the program itself. Almost all programming languages have notations for fixed values such as integers, floating-point numbers, and strings, and usually for booleans and characters.

The following is a list of the primary literal types found in JavaScript:

- Integer
- Boolean
- Floating point
- Regular expression
- Null
- String
- Array
- Object

```
example
<script>
    var num1 = 105;              integer literal
    var num2 = 3.1416;          floating-point literal
    var str1 = "Hello my friend!";   string literal
</script>
```

2.2.2.2 Variables

In a programming language such as JavaScript, variables are used to store data values. JavaScript uses the **var** keyword to define variables. An equal sign is used to assign values to variables. JavaScript variables are containers for storing data values.

In this example, a, b, c and d, are variables:

example
```
<script>
  var a = 5;
  var b = 6;
  var c = 7;
  var d = a + b + c;
</script>
```

2.2.3 JAVASCRIPT OPERATORS

JavaScript operators are used to assign values, compare values, perform arithmetic operations, and more. The following is a list of some of the major operator types in JavaScript:

- Arithmetic operators
- Assignment operators
- String operators
- Comparison operators
- Logical operators

2.2.3.1 Arithmetic operators

An arithmetic operator takes numerical values (either literals or variables) as their operands and returns a single numerical value. The standard arithmetic operators are addition (+), subtraction (-), multiplication (*), and division (/). These operators work as they do in most other programming languages when used with floating point numbers. The following is a list of the major JavaScript arithmetic operators:

- Addition
- Subtraction
- Division
- Multiplication
- Remainder
- Increment
- Decrement

Addition (+)
The addition operator produces the sum of numeric operands.

Syntax
```
Operator:  x + y
```

Subtraction (-)
The subtraction operator subtracts the two operands, producing their difference.

Syntax
```
Operator:  x - y
```

Division (/)

The division operator produces the quotient of its operands where the left operand is the dividend and the right operand is the divisor.

Syntax

```
Operator:  x / y
```

Multiplication (*)

The multiplication operator produces the product of the operands.

Syntax

```
Operator:  x * y
```

Remainder (%)

The modulo (remainder) function is the integer remainder of dividing var1 by var2

Syntax

```
Operator:  var1 % var2
```

Increment (++)

The increment operator increments (adds one to) its operand and returns a value.

- If used **postfix**, with operator after the operand (for example, x++), then it returns the value before incrementing.
- If used **prefix** with operator before the operand (for example, ++x), then it returns the value after incrementing.

Syntax

```
Operator: x++ or ++x
```

Examples

```
Postfix
var x = 3;
y = x++;   results: y = 3, x = 4
```

```
Prefix
var x = 2;
y = ++x;   results: y = 3, x = 3
```

Decrement (--)

The decrement operator decrements (subtracts one from) its operand and returns a value.If used **postfix**, with operator after operand (for example, x--), then it returns the value before decrementing.

- If used **prefix** with operator before operand (for example, --x), then it returns the value after decrementing.

Syntax

Operator: **x-- or --x**

Examples

Postfix
var x = 3;
y = x--;   results: y = 3, x = 2

Prefix
var x = 2;
y = --x;   results: y = 3, x = 3

Table of Arithmetic operators:

Operator	Description	example	initial value of b	result value in a
+	Addition	a = b + 2	b = 9	a = 11
-	Subtraction	a = b - 2	b = 9	a = 7
*	Multiplication	a = b * 2	b = 9	a = 18
/	Division	a = b / 2	b = 9	a = 4.5
%	Modulus Division	a = b % 2	b = 9	a = 1
++	Increment	a = b++	b = 9	a = 9
++	Increment	a = ++b	b = 9	a = 10
--	Decrement	a = b--	b = 8	a = 8
--	Decrement	a = --b	b = 9	a = 8

2.2.3.2 Assignment operators

Assignment operators are used to assign values to JavaScript variables. An assignment operator assigns a value to its left operand based on the value of its right operand. The simple assignment operator is equal (=), which assigns the value of its right operand to its left operand. That is, x = y assigns the value of y to x.

The following is a list of the major JavaScript assignment operators:

- Simple assignment
- Add and assignment

- Subtract and assignment
- Multiply and assignment
- Divide and assignment
- Modulus and assignment

Simple Assignment (=)

Assigns values from the right side operand to the left side operand

Syntax

Operator: =

Example

z = y + x will assign the value of y + x to z

Add and Assignment (+ =)

Adds the right operand to the left operand and assigns the result to the left operand.

Syntax

Operator: +=

Example

z += y is equivalent to z = z + y

Subtract and Assignment (- =)

Subtracts the right operand from the left operand and assigns the result to the left operand.

Syntax

Operator: +=

Example

z -= y is equivalent to z = z - y

Multiply and Assignment (* =)

Multiplies the right operand with the left operand and assigns the result to the left operand.

Syntax

Operator: * =

Example

z *= y is equivalent to z = z * y

Divide and Assignment (/ =)

Divides the left operand with the right operand and assigns the result to the left operand.

Syntax

Operator: / =

Example

z /= y is equivalent to z = z / y

Modulus and Assignment (% =)

Takes modulus using two operands and assigns the result to the left operand.

Syntax

Operator: %=

Example

z %= y is equivalent to z = z + y

Table of Assignment operators:

Operator	Description	Example*	Equivalent To	Result value in a
=	Simple Assignment	a = b	a = b	a = 3
+=	Add and Assignment	a += b	a = a + b	a = 13
-=	Subtract and Assignment	a -= b	a = a - b	a = 7
*=	Multiply and Assignment	a *= b	a = a * b	a = 30
/=	Divide and Assignment	a /= b	a = a / b	a = 3.3333
%=	Modulus Assignment	a %=	a = a % b	a = 1

* assume that a = 10 and b = 3 as initial conditions

2.2.3.3 String operators

When working with JavaScript strings sometimes you need to join two or more strings together in order to form a single string. Joining multiple strings together is known as **concatenation**. The concatenation operator (+) concatenates two or more string values together and returns another string which is the union of the two operand strings. The += operator can also be used to concatenate (add) strings.

Examples

If text1 = "Hello " & text2 = "World!", **then text3 in the formula text3 = text1 + text2** will equal "Hello World!"

If text1 = "Hello " & text2 = "World!", **then text1 in the formula text1 += text2** will equal "Hello World!"

2.2.3.4 Comparison operators

A comparison operator compares its operands and returns a logical value based on whether the comparison is true. The operands can be numerical, string, logical, or object values. Strings are compared based on standard lexicographical ordering, using Unicode values. In most cases, if the two operands are not of the same type, JavaScript attempts to convert them to an appropriate type for the comparison. This behavior generally results in comparing the operands numerically. The sole exceptions to type conversion within comparisons involve the === and !== operators, which perform strict equality and inequality comparisons. These operators do not attempt to convert the operands to compatible types before checking equality. The following is a list of the major JavaScript arithmetic operators:

- Equal (==)
- Not equal (!=)
- Strict equal (===)
- Strict not equal (!==)
- Greater than (>)
- Greater than or equal to (>=
- Less than (<)
- Less than or equal to (<=)

Equal (==)

Returns true if the operands are equal.

Assume that x = 10 and y = 20 in this example:

Example

(x == y) is false

Not Equal (!=)

Returns true if the operands are not equal.

Assume that x = 10 and y = 20 in this example:

Example

(x != y) is true

Strict Equal (===)

Returns true if the operands are equal and of the same type.

Assume that x = 5 and y =5 in this example and that they are both integer data type:

Examples

```
(x === y) is true
```

Assume that x = 10 and is an integer and y = "10" and is a string in this example:

```
(x === y) is false
```

Strict Not Equal (!==)

Returns true if the operands are not equal and/or not of the same type.

Assume that x = 5 and is an integer and y =5.0 and is a floating-point number in this example:

Example

```
(x !== y) is true
```

Greater Than (>)

Returns true if the left operand is greater than the right operand.

Assume that x = 10 and y = 20 in this example:

Example

```
(x > y) is false
```

Greater Than Or Equal To (>=)

Returns true if the left operand is greater than or equal to the right operand.

Assume that x = 10 and y = 20 in this example:

Example

```
(x >= y) is false
```

Less Than (<)

Returns true if the left operand is less than the right operand.

Assume that x = 10 and y = 20 in this example:

Example

(x > y) is true

Less Than Or Equal To (<=)

Returns true if the left operand is less than or equal to the right operand.

Assume that x = 10 and y = 20 in this example:

Example

(x <= y) is true

Assume that x = 20 and y = 10 in this example:

(x <= y) is false

Table of Comparison operators:

Operator	Name	Description
==	Equal	Checks if the value of two operands are equal or not, if yes, then the condition becomes true.
+=	Not Equal	Checks if the value of two operands are equal or not, if the values are not equal, then the condition becomes true.
===	Strict Equal	Checks if the value and data type of the left operand is the same as the value and data type of the right operand, if yes, then the condition becomes true.
>	Greater Than	Checks if the value of the left operand is greater than the value of the right operand, if yes, then the condition becomes true.
>=	Greater Than or Equal To	Checks if the value of the left operand is greater than or equal to the value of the right operand, if yes, then the condition becomes true.
<	Less Than	Checks if the value of the left operand is less than the value of the right operand, if yes, then the condition becomes true.
<=	Less Than or Equal To	Checks if the value of the left operand is less than or equal to the value of the right operand, if yes, then the condition becomes true.

2.2.3.5 Logical operators

Logical operators are used when testing for Boolean (true and false) states. Usually when these operators are used, they are testing Boolean values and return a Boolean result. The following is a list of the major JavaScript arithmetic operators:

- AND
- OR
- NOT

AND (&&)

Returns true if two or more conditions are met. All comparisons must be true for the AND statement to equate to TRUE.

Assume that x = 8 and y = 3 in both examples:

Examples

(x < 10 && y > 1)   this statement is true

(x < 6 && y > 1)   this statement is false

(x > 6 && y > 2)   this statement is true

OR (||)

Returns true if one or more conditions are met. One or more of the comparisons must be true for the OR statement to equate to TRUE.

Assume that x = 8 and y = 3 in both examples:

Examples

(x == 5 || y == 7)   this statement is false

(x < 6 || y > 5)   this statement is false

(x < 6 || y < 2)   this statement is true

NOT (!)

Reverses the logical state of its operand. If a condition is true, then the Logical NOT operator will make it false.

Assume that x = 8 and y = 3 in both examples:

Examples

!(x == 5 || y == 7)   this statement is true

!(x < 6 || y < 5)   this statement is false

2.2.4 JAVASCRIPT CASE SENSITIVITY

JavaScript is a case-sensitive scripting language. This means that JavaScript considers capital letters as different from lowercase letters. JavaScript keywords, variables, function names, and any other identifiers must always be typed with a consistent capitalization of letters. For example, if you declare a variable called **timeOff** in JavaScript, you have to consistently use **timeOff** to refer to that variable not "TimeOff", "TIMEOFF", or some other variation. In the same way a keyword like **while**, for example, must be typed "while", not "While" or "WHILE". The same rules apply to variable names: "username", "Username", "UserName", and "USERNAME" are four distinct variable names.

In JavaScript the case sensitivity does not just apply to variable names but also to all JavaScript keywords, event handlers, and object properties or methods. Keywords in JavaScript are all lowercase, for example, "while", "for", "if", "else", "function", and so on.

Example of valid and invalid keyword use:

Example:

```
<script>
  function myFunction() {
    document.write("Hello World!");
  }
</script>
```

This statement is **valid** becausehe keyword **function** is written using all lower case letters

```
<script>
  Function myFunction() {
    document.write("Hello World!");
  }
</script>
```

This statement is **invalid** because the keyword **function** is written as "Function" with a capital "F".

2.2.5 JAVASCRIPT VARIABLE NAMING WITH CAMEL CASE

In general, programmers have used three ways of joining multiple words into one variable name:

- Hyphens:
    first-name, last-name, master-card, inter-city.
- Underscore:
    first_name, last_name, master_card, inter_city. main_text_element
- Camel Case:
    firstName, lastName, masterCard, interCity, mainTextElement

In JavaScript, usually either the camel case or underscore methods are used. The common practice is to use camel case in object-oriented programming and to use the underscore method when writing a program in the procedural/functional style. Because JavaScript is a flexible language both methods can be used depending on the programmer's preference, although the object-oriented approach using camel case variable naming is more widespread.

One of the advantages of using the camel case naming convention is that it results in shorter variable names because you don't have to use the extra underscore characters. Another advantage is that most built-in JavaScript methods use camel case, so, extending this use to variable names helps to maintain uniformity in naming.

2.3 JAVASCRIPT PROGRAM COMMENTS

Inserting comments into JavaScript is a way to tell the browser to ignore certain parts of the text which have been included for explanatory purposes within the body of the code. Comments are there to clarify the purpose of the code for human readers and not for the machine. Your comments will help you and others to understand when the time comes to revise or troubleshoot the code.

When writing code you may have some complex logic that can be confusing, especially when you're trying to troubleshoot the program or understand what the code is doing after it's been written. This is a good time to include some comments in the code that will explain what it's doing and trying to accomplish. Not only will this help you to understand it later on, but if someone else reads your code, they'll be aided to understand what's going on.

In general, JavaScript is harder to understand than either HTML or CSS so it's good to add detailed comments to the code, especially if you're working with a team of programmer's or if you plan on revising the code at some point in the future.

While there is only one way to add comments in HTML and CSS, there are two types of comments that can be added in JavaScript: single line comments and multi-line comments.

2.3.1 Single line comments

To create a single line comment in JavaScript, you place two slashes "//" in front of the code or text that you want to the JavaScript interpreter to ignore. When you place these two slashes, all text to the right of them will be ignored, until the next line.

The following is an example of 2 single line comments in a block of script:

Example:
```
<script>
    // This is a single line comment that will be ignored by the browser:
    document.getElementById("melem1").innerHTML = "Single line comment example";
    // This is also a single line comment that will not be displayed on the browser:
    document.write("Single line comments are great!");
</script>
```

2.3.2 Multi-line comments

Multi-line comments in JavaScript start with /* and end with */. Any text between /* and */ will be ignored by JavaScript.

The following is an example of a multi-line comments in a block of script:

Example:
```
<script>
    /* This is a multi-line comment. When your comment needs to be more than one
    line long a multi-line comment is definitely the way to go. Make sure to use the
    correct opening and closing tags*/
    document.getElementById("elem1").innerHTML = "Multiline comment example";
    document.write("Single line comments are good but multiline comments are better!");
</script>
```

Chapter 3

JavaScript Output

3.1 DISPLAYING JAVASCRIPT OUTPUT

There are several different ways that JavaScript can display data on a web page. For now, we're only going to consider three of these methods:

    1) Writing into an alert box, using the **alert()** function

    2) Writing into an prompt box, using the **prompt()** function

    3) Writing into the HTML output using the **document.write()** function

3.1.1 Alert box

The **alert()** method displays an alert box with a specified message and an "OK" button. The most common use of an alert box is to provide information or make a request to the user. **Alert** is a keyword - that is, a word that has special meaning for JavaScript. When you see an **alert()** function it means, "Display the following message in an alert box."

The **alert()** command pops up a message box that displays whatever you put in it. For example:

```
<!DOCTYPE html>
<html>
<body>
  <script>
    alert ("Hello World!");
  </script>
</body>
</html>
```

This code will display a popup box with the words "Hello World!" in it and an OK button:

The parentheses in **alert("Hello World!")** are required. The text "Hello World!" in the above example is called a text string. Variables can also be used in place of a text string but we're not going to cover that now. Since JavaScript ignores spaces **alert("Hello World!")** could also be written as:

    alert ("Hello World!"); or

    alert ("Hello World!");

SOLVED PROBLEMS

3.1 Write the code to create and display the following message: "When in the course of human events..." in an alert box:

Solution
```
<!DOCTYPE html>
<html>
 <body>
   <script>
     alert ( "When in the course of human events...!" );
   </script>
 </body>
</html>
```

3.2 Write the code to create and display the following alert box:

Solution
```
<!DOCTYPE html>
<html>
 <body>
   <script>
     alert ( "Is anybody out there? );
   </script>
 </body>
</html>
```

3.3 Write the code to create and display the following alert box with two lines of text:

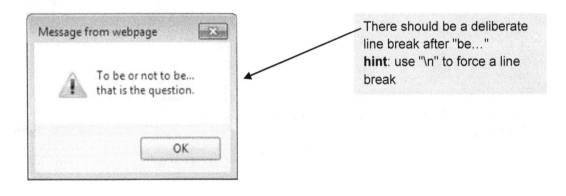

There should be a deliberate line break after "be..."
hint: use "\n" to force a line break

Solution

```
<!DOCTYPE html>
<html>
 <body>
   <script>
     alert ( "To be or not to be...\nthat is the question.");
   </script>
 </body>
 </html>
```

"\n" forces a line break in the text

3.4 Concatenate the following 3 phrases and display them on a single line in an alert box (**hint**: use "+" to concatenate the strings):

1) "The name"
2) " of this song"
3) " is 'Somewhere Over the Rainbow'."

Solution

```
<DOCTYPE html>
<html>
 <body>
   <script>
     alert ( "The name " + "of this song" + " is 'Somewhere Over the Rainbow'.");
   </script>
<body>
 </html>
```

"+" concatenates the individual strings together but doesn't force a line break.

Result displayed in alert box:

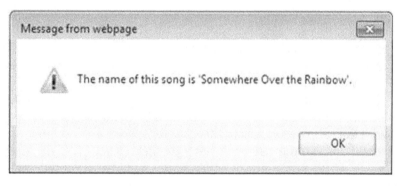

Message from webpage

⚠ The name of this song is 'Somewhere Over the Rainbow'.

OK

3.5 Concatenate the following 3 phrases and display them on 3 separate lines in an alert box (**hint**: use "+" to concatenate the strings and "\n" for force a line break):

1) "The name"
2) "of this song"
3) "is 'Somewhere Over the Rainbow'."

Solution

```
<DOCTYPE html>
<html>
<body>
  <script>
    alert ( "The name " + "\n" + "of this song" + "\n" + "is 'Somewhere Over the Rainbow'.");
  </script>
</body>
</html>
```

OR

```
DOCTYPE html>
html>
<body>
  <script>
    alert ( "The name " + "\nof this song" + "\nis 'Somewhere Over the Rainbow'.");
  </script>
</body>
</html>
```

The "\n"s (line breaks) can be concatenated separately or they can be incorporated into the individual strings

3.1.2 Prompt box

A **prompt box** asks the user for some information and then provides a response field for the user's response:

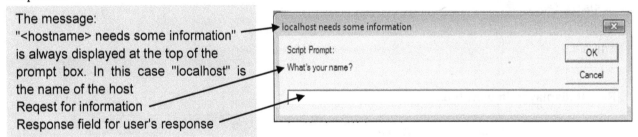

The message:
"<hostname> needs some information"
is always displayed at the top of the prompt box. In this case "localhost" is the name of the host
Reqest for information
Response field for user's response

The prompt box is created using JavaScript's built-in **prompt()** function. When the JavaScript **prompt()** function is triggered, a box will pop up and display a message to the user (supplied by you), a text field (for the user's input), an "OK" button, and a "Cancel" button.

If the user clicks the "OK" button, the value entered into the prompt box will be returned. If the user clicks the "Cancel" button, a null value (empty string) will be returned (we're not concerned with what the computer does with the returned values in this chapter - more on that later).

When a prompt box pops up, the user will have to click either "OK" or "Cancel" to proceed after entering an input value. If user clicks "OK" then input will be accepted and accepted input gets processed. If the user clicks "Cancel" then input will be rejected and popup window will be closed.

Example of code containing the **prompt()** function:

```
<DOCTYPE html>
  <html>
  <body>
    <script>
      prompt("What's your name?");
    </script>
  </body></html>
```

The preceding code produces the following output to the browser screen:

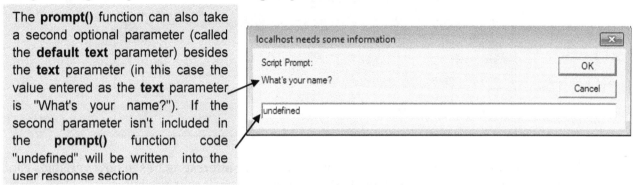

The **prompt()** function can also take a second optional parameter (called the **default text** parameter) besides the **text** parameter (in this case the value entered as the **text** parameter is "What's your name?"). If the second parameter isn't included in the **prompt()** function code "undefined" will be written into the user response section.

The following code will replace "undefined" in the default text section of the **prompt()** function with an empty string. It accomplishes this by putting an empty string ("") into the default text attribute:

```
<DOCTYPE html>
<html>
<body>
  <script>
    prompt ("What's your name?", "");
  </script>
</body>
  </html>
```

The first attribute in a **prompt()** function is the **text** attribute

The second (optional) attribute in a prompt() function is the default **text** attribute (an empty string in this case)

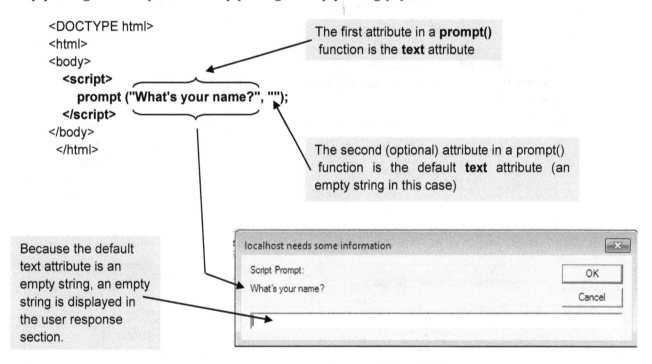

Because the default text attribute is an empty string, an empty string is displayed in the user response section.

The following code will replace the empty string ("") in the default text attribute of the **prompt()** function in the user response text area with an empty string. It accomplishes this by putting an empty string ("") into the default text attribute:

```
<DOCTYPE html>
<html>
<body>
  <script>
    prompt ("What's your name?", "Please enter your full name");
  </script>
</body>
  </html>
```

The default text that will be displayed in the user response section of the prompt box will be "**Please enter your full name**" rather than an empty string or "undefined" as in the above prompt box examples

The preceding code sends the following output to the browser screen:

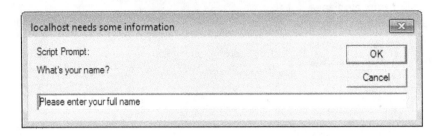

We'll be covering variables in depth in later chapters, but it's interesting to see how variables can be used with prompt boxes to supply both the **text** and optional default **text** attributes:

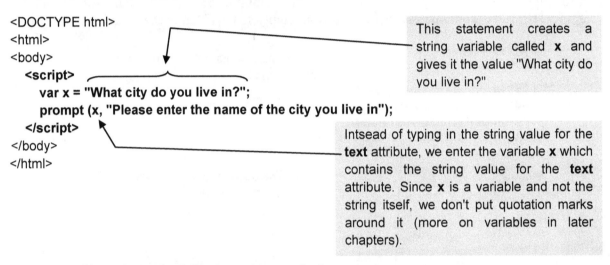

```
<DOCTYPE html>
<html>
<body>
    <script>
        var x = "What city do you live in?";
        prompt (x, "Please enter the name of the city you live in");
    </script>
</body>
</html>
```

This statement creates a string variable called **x** and gives it the value "What city do you live in?"

Intsead of typing in the string value for the **text** attribute, we enter the variable **x** which contains the string value for the **text** attribute. Since **x** is a variable and not the string itself, we don't put quotation marks around it (more on variables in later chapters).

The preceding code produces the following output to the browser screen:

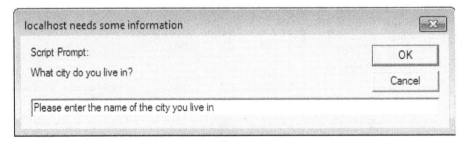

The following code uses variables to add both the **text** and default **text** attributes and produces the same prompt box as in the above example:

```
<DOCTYPE html>
<html>
<body>
    <script>
        var x = "What city do you live in?";
        var y = "Please enter the name of the city you live in";
        prompt (x, y);
    </script>
</body>
</html>
```

SOLVED PROBLEMS

3.6 Write the code to create and display the following prompt box:

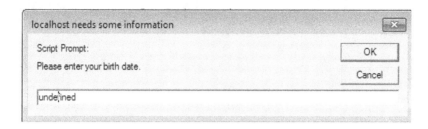

Solution

```
<DOCTYPE html>
<html>
<body>
  <script>
    prompt ("Please enter your birth date.");
  </script>
</body>
</html>
```

3.7 Write the code to create and display the following prompt box:

The two sentences in the **text** attribute should go on two separate lines. Force a line break using "\n" as in the alert box examples.

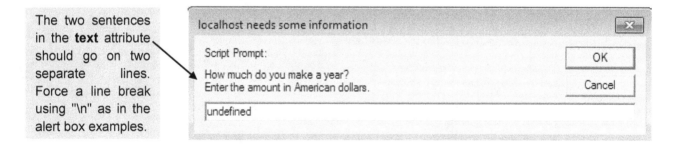

Solution

```
<html>
<body>
  <script>
    prompt ("How much do you make a year?\nEnter the amount in American dollars.");
  </script>
</body>
</html>
```

3.8 Write the code to create and display the following alert box:

The default text attribute should be blank. It should not say "undefined".

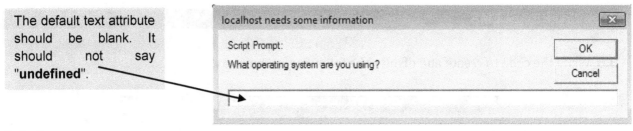

Solution

```
<DOCTYPE html>
<html>
<body>
  <script>
    prompt ("What operating system are you using?", "");
  </script>
</body>
</html>
```

3.9 Write the code to create and display the following prompt box. Instead of writing the text attribute value ("What planet is this?") as a text string in the code for the prompt box, put the text value into a variable called **txt**. Use a text string to define the value of the default **text** attribute.

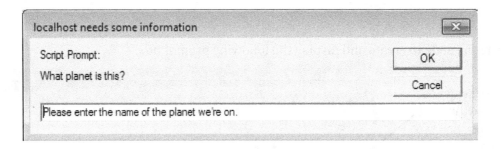

Solution

```
<DOCTYPE html>
<html>
<body>
  <script>
    var txt = "What planet is this?";
    prompt (txt, "Please enter the name of the planet we're on.");
  </script>
</body>
</html>
```

3.10 Write the code to create and display the following prompt box. Instead of writing the text attribute and the default text attribute as strings in the code for the prompt box, put the text value into a variable called **txt** and the default text value into a variable called **defaultTxt.**

```
localhost needs some information                                    [x]

Script Prompt:                                                  [  OK  ]
How long have you been a United States citizen?
                                                                [ Cancel ]

Please put your response in this box.
```

Solution

```
<DOCTYPE html>
<html>
<body>
  <script>
    var txt = "How long have you been a United States citizen?";
    var defaultTxt = "Please put your response in this box.";
    prompt (txt, defaultTxt);
  </script>
</body>
</html>
```

The default text that will be displayed in the user response section of the prompt box will be "Please put your response in this box" rather than an empty string or "**undefined**" as in the above prompt box examples.

3.1.3 document.write( )

The **document.write( )** methods outputs a string directly onto the browser page. It is used to write text directly to the HTML document. The **write( )** method writes HTML expressions or JavaScript code to a document. The code in the following example will display "Hello World!" on the browser page:

Example

```
document.write ("Hello World!");
```

The **write( )** function is a method of the **document** object. The **document** object is a property and sub-object of the **window** object. The **window** object is the top-level object in JavaScript and contains several other objects such as the **document** object, the **history** object, the **screen** object , the **navigator** object and the location object.

The **window** object represents the browser window. Since the **window** object is the highest level object in JavaScript, you don't have to explicitly specify it when accessing its properties such as the document object. For example, if you wanted to write "Hello World!" to the browser window using the **document.write( )** function you could code it in either one of the following ways:

    1) window.document.write ("Hello World!"); or

    2) document.write ("Hello World!")

The following code would not work because **write()** is not a method (function) of the windows object:

    window.write ("Hello World!");

We're going to cover JavaScript's object hierarchical structure and the **DOM** (Document Object Model) in more detail in later chapters but for now the following diagram will give you a simplified and partial understanding of the structural hierarchy of the JavaScript object model:

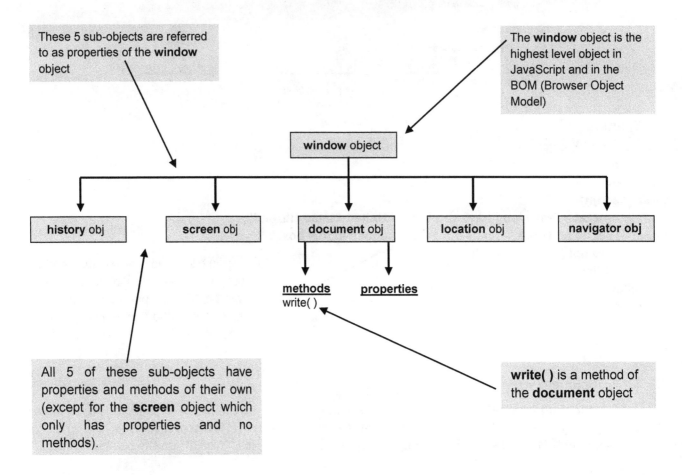

The following code writes "Have a nice day!" on the first line at the top left corner of the browser window:

```
<DOCTYPE html>
<html>
<body>
  <script>
    document.write ("Have a nice day!");
  </script>
</body>
</html>
```

Result displayed in browser:

```
Have a nice day!
```

The following code writes "Have a nice day!" two times (without a space between) on the first line at the top left corner of the browser window:

```
<DOCTYPE html>
<html>
<body>
  <script>
    document.write ("Have a nice day!");
    document.write ("Have a nice day!");
  </script>
</body>
</html>
```

Result displayed in browser:

```
Have a nice day!Have a nice day!
```

HTML formatting elements can be added to the text in the **document.write( )** function. The following code writes "Have a nice day!" two times. One time on the first line and one time on the second line at the top left corner of the browser window:

```
<DOCTYPE html>
<html>
<body>
  <script>
    document.write ("Have a nice day!<br>");
    document.write ("Have a nice day!");
  </script>
</body>
</html>
```

Result displayed in browser:

```
Have a nice day!
Have a nice day!
```

The following code writes "Have a nice day!" two times. Both expressions are on the same line. The first expression is in bold type and the second is in regular type with a space between it and the first expression:

```
<DOCTYPE html>
<html>
<body>
  <script>
    document.write("<b>Have a nice day!</b> ");
    document.write ("Have a nice day!");
  </script>
</body>
</html>
```

Result displayed in browser:

```
Have a nice day! Have a nice day!
```

To create a space between the expressions you need to add the ** ** (non-breaking space) character to the code. This creates a space without breaking to a new line.

The following code writes "Have a nice day!" one time. Instead of putting the text directly into the **document.write( )** function, the code puts the text into a variable called **exp1** and uses this variable in the **document.write( )** function:

```
<DOCTYPE html>
<html>
<body>
  <script>
    var exp1 = "Have a nice day!";
    document.write (exp1);
  </script>
</body>
</html>
```

Result displayed in browser:

```
Have a nice day!
```

As we learned earlier, JavaScript code can be placed in either the **<body>** or in the **<head>** section of an HTML file, or you can put scripts in both sections. Scripts that are directly in the head and/or body of the html file and not enclosed in functions or objects will run sequentially (in the order they appear in the html code) as soon as the file containing the code has loaded sufficiently for that code to be accessed. Basically this means that whatever code you have in the **<head>** and/or **<body>** of your page that is not inside a function or object will run as the page is loading once the page has loaded sufficiently for the line of code to be available to be run.

For example, the following html file has JavaScript code in the **<head>** and **<body>** sections. As we can see in the result, the JavaScript commands execute in the order that they're encountered by the browser:

```
<DOCTYPE html>
<html>
<head>
  <script>
    document.write("What's your name?<br>");
  </script>
</head>
<body>
  <script>
    document.write("My name is Johnny.<br>");
    document.write("Now tell me your name?");
  </script>
</body>
</html>
```

We haven't added a **<head>** section to the problems and examples before this but we will start adding one from here on.

Result displayed in browser:

```
What's your name?
My name is Johnny.
Now tell me your name.
```

SOLVED PROBLEMS

3.11 Write the code to create and display the following text in the browser window:

```
It's time for lunch.
```

Solution

```
<DOCTYPE html>
<html>
<head>
</head>
<body>
  <script>
    document.write ("It's time for lunch");
  </script>
</body>
</html>
```

3.12 Write the code to create and display the following text in the browser window. Use 2 separate **document.write()** functions to do this:

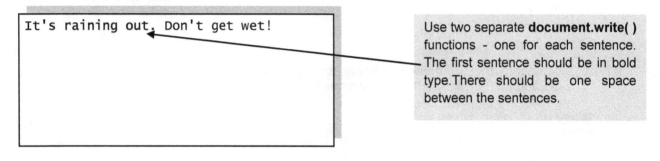

It's raining out. Don't get wet!

Use two separate **document.write( )** functions - one for each sentence. The first sentence should be in bold type. There should be one space between the sentences.

Solution

```
<DOCTYPE html>
<html>
<head>
</head>
<body>
  <script>
    document.write("<b>It's raining out.</b> ");
    document.write ("Don't get wet!");
  </script>
</body>
</html>
```

3.13 Write the code to create and display the following text in the browser window. Put the JavaScript into the **<head>** section instead of the **<body>** section :

What time is it?
Is it 5 o'clock yet?

Use two separate **document.write( )** functions - one for each sentence. The sentences should be on two separate lines. The first sentence should be in bold type and the second sentence should be in italics.

Solution

```
<DOCTYPE html>
<html>
<head>
  <script>
    document.write ("<b>What time is it?.</b><br>");
    document.write ("<i>Is it 5 o'clock yet?</i><br>");
  </script>
</head>
<body>
</body>
</html>
```

3.14 Write the code to create and display the following text in the browser window. Put the JavaScript into the **<head>** and **<body>** sections as described in the gray box:

```
The first sentence is located in the head section.
The second sentence is located in the head section.
The third sentence is located in the body section.
```

The first two sentences are coded in the **<head>** section of the html file and the third sentence is located in the **<body>** section. Each sentence should go on a separate line. Notice the words in **bold** in each sentence and code them appropriately.

Solution

```
<DOCTYPE html>
<html>
<head>
  <script>
    document.write ("The first sentence is located in the <b>head</b> section.<br>");
    document.write ("The second sentence is located in the <b>head</b> section.<br>");
  </script>
</head>
<body>
  <script>
    document.write ("The third sentence is located in the <b>body</b> section.");
  </script>
</body>
</html>
```

3.15 This problem will be the same as problem 2.14 but instead of using text strings as the arguments in the three **document.write( )** functions, assign each sentence to a separate variable ("sentence1", "sentence2" & "sentence3") and use the corresponding variable as the argument in each **document.write( )** function. Put the code to assign all three variables in the <head> section.

Solution

```
<DOCTYPE html>
<html>
<head>
  <script>
    var sentence1 = "The first sentence is located in the <b>head</b> section.<br>"
    var sentence2 = "The second sentence is located in the <b>head</b> section.<br>"
    var sentence3 = "The third sentence is located in the <b>body</b> section."
    document.write (sentence1);
    document.write (sentence2);
  </script>
</head>
<body>
  <script>
    document.write (sentence3);
  </script>
</body>
</html>
```

3.1.4 JavaScript order of program execution

Under normal circumstances, code statements in a JavaScript script program are executed one after the other, in the order in which they are written. Because of this, statements in the **<head>** section will be executed before statements in the **<body>.** This is called sequential execution, and is the default direction of program flow. As was mentioned in a previous section, any code that is located directly in the **<head>** and **<body>** sections of the web page and not enclosed in functions or objects will run in the order it's written as soon as the file containing the code has loaded sufficiently for that code to be accessed. What this means is that whatever code is in the **<head>** and **<body>** of the page and that is not inside a function or object will run while the page is loading as soon as the page has loaded to the point that the line of code is available to be run.

For example, the following code will run in the order that it was written in the html file with the code in the **<head>** section executing first followed by the code in the **<body>** section. Following this order of execution, the code will display the text string "It's a beautiful day out!" at the top left corner of the browser window

```
<DOCTYPE html>
<html>
<head>
  <script>
    var greeting1 = "It's a beautiful day out!";
  </script>
</head>
<body>
  <script>
    document.write (greeting1);
  </script>
</body>
</html>
```

Result in browser:

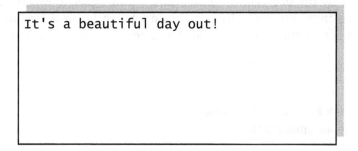

```
It's a beautiful day out!
```

However, if we put the **document.write( )** in the **<head>** section and the variable assignment in the **<body>** section, the **document.write( )** command can't execute because the variable hasn't been assigned a value yet:

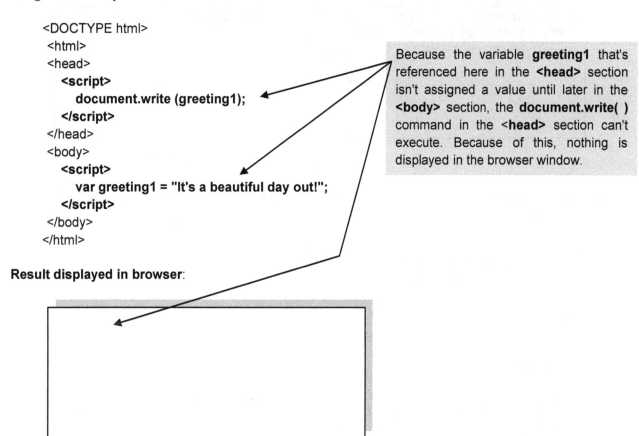

```
<DOCTYPE html>
 <html>
 <head>
   <script>
     document.write (greeting1);
   </script>
 </head>
 <body>
   <script>
     var greeting1 = "It's a beautiful day out!";
   </script>
 </body>
 </html>
```

Because the variable **greeting1** that's referenced here in the **<head>** section isn't assigned a value until later in the **<body>** section, the **document.write( )** command in the **<head>** section can't execute. Because of this, nothing is displayed in the browser window.

Result displayed in browser:

3.1.5 Multi-line JavaScript strings
If a string is long enough it can sometimes take up more than one line of code. For example:

```
<script>
    document.write ("If a cluttered desk is a sign of a cluttered mind,
                     of what, then, is an empty desk a sign?" );
 </script>
```

The above code will not produce any output to the browser. It's invalid and not recognized as a syntactically correct JavaScript statement by the browser. In order for the statement to be recognized as valid, a string that spans across more than one code line has to be broken up into two or more strings (depending on the number of lines that the string occupies) and concatenated to the next line with a "+" sign:

```
<script>
    document.write ("If a cluttered desk is a sign of a cluttered mind, " +
                    "of what, then, is an empty desk a sign? " );
</script>
```

Result displayed in browser:

```
If a cluttered desk is the sign of a cluttered mind, of what,
then, is an empty desk a sign?
```

Here is another example of the correct way to write a string that takes up more than one line of code - in this case, three lines:

```
<script>
    document.write ("This is the first part of the string. " +
                    "This is the second part of the string. " +
                    "This is the third part of the string.");
</script>
```

Result displayed in browser:

```
This is the first part of the string. This is the second part of the
string. This is the third part of the string.
```

The above example can also be written using backslashes ("\") instead of the quotation marks and plus signs that are used to concatenate the different parts of the string. The result is the same:

```
<script>
    document.write ("This is the first part of the string. \
                    This is the second part of the string. \
                    This is the third part of the string.");
</script>
```

In the previous example, each one of the 3 text lines was enclosed in quotation marks, but when you use backslashes instead of "+" signs you only have to put quotation marks at the beiginning and end of the string group.

Result displayed in browser:

```
This is the first part of the string. This is the second part of the
string. This is the third part of the string.
```

SOLVED PROBLEMS

3.16 Use a **document.write( )** command to display the following text on the browser screen:

> "When in the Course of human events, it becomes necessary for one people to dissolve the political bands which have connected them with another..."

The text should appear on one line in the browser window but the actual code for the **document.write()** command should be broken up into three lines with the second and third code lines starting after the words "becomes" and "political".

Remember to leave a space after the word at the end of each line (between the last letter in the word and the quotation marks) so you will get proper spacing in the browser display

Solution

```
<DOCTYPE html>
<html>
<head>
</head>
<body>
  <script>
    document.write ("When in the Course of human events, it becomes " +
                    "necessary for one people to dissolve the political " +
                    "bands which have connected them with another...");
  </script>
</body>
</html>
```

3.17 Same as problem 3.16 but use backslashes instead of plus signs to concatenate the text in the three code lines.

Solution

```
<DOCTYPE html>
<html>
<head>
</head>
<body>
    <script>
        document.write ("When in the Course of human events, it becomes \
                necessary for one people to dissolve the political \
                bands which have connected them with another...");
    </script>
</body>
</html>
```

The text to be displayed by the **document.write()** function in this problem will be displayed in the browser just like the text in the previous problem. The only difference is that instead of using the concatenation operator ("+") to tie the 3 strings together, along with two quotation marks for each line, we use backslashes ("/") at the end of each line and only two quotation marks total - one at the beginning at the end of the first line and one at the end of the last line.

3.18 Same as problem 3.16 - use plus ("+") signs to concatenate the multiline **document.write()** statement. But instead of displaying the text string, which appears in three separate lines in the code, on a single line in the browser window, display the text string in three separate lines in the browser window. The lines in the browser window should start and end at the same place as they do in the code. The result should be as follows:

```
when in the Course of human events, it becomes
necessary for one people to dissolve the political
bands which have connected them with another...
```

Solution

```
<DOCTYPE html>
<html>
<head>
</head>
<body>
    <script>
        document.write ("When in the Course of human events, it becomes<br>" +
                "necessary for one people to dissolve the political<br>" +
                "bands which have connected them with another...");
    </script>
</body>
</html>
```

You have to use a **
** character shere to create new lines. A new line character (**\n**) won't work in a document.write.( ) command. Also no spaces are needed after the last word in the first two lines because we skip to a new line here.

3.19 Write the code to create and display the following text in the browser window. Assign the text string ("This is text string 1. This is text string 2. This is text string 3.") to a variable called **txtString**. The variable assignment should span three lines with each individual sentence on a separate code line. Display the text string by using the variable as the parameter for the **document.write( )** command.

```
This is text string 1. This is text string 2. This is text string 3.
```

Solution

```
<DOCTYPE html>
<html>
<head>
</head>
<body>
  <script>
    var txtString = "This is text string 1. " +
                    "This is text string 2. " +
                    "This is text string 3.";
    document.write (txtString);
  </script>
</body>
</html>
```

<u>Chapter 4</u>

JavaScript Variables

4.1 WHAT IS A JAVASCRIPT VARIABLE?

In computer programming, a **variable** is a value that can change, depending on conditions internal to the program or on information passed to the program from an outside source. Usually, a program consists of a set of instructions or statements that tell the computer what to do along with the data that the program needs to function properly while it's running. An instruction is an order given to a computer processor under the direction of the program that's been written and loaded to the computer.

There are basically two types of data that the computer can work with: **constants** or fixed values that retain the same value throughout the program and **variables** whose values can change while the program is running due to changing circumstances and program inputs. Usually, both constants and variables are classified and defined as belonging to certain **data types**. Each data type sets limits on the form that the data can take and the type of actions that can be performed with it or to it.

A data type in JavaScript and other programming languages refers to a set of data (constants or variables) with values that have special characteristics designed specifically for the particular data type and the use and function that the data type usually performs. Some of the most common types found in most programming languages are: integer, floating point number, character, and string. Usually, a limited number of such data types come built into a language such as JavaScript. The particular language usually specifies the range of values of a given data type, how the values are processed and handled by the computer, and the method that's used to store them. We're going to cover JavaScript data types, particularly how they apply to variables, in greater depth later in this chapter.

Basically, JavaScript variables are just containers for storing various data values. In this first example, a, b, and c, are integer variables:

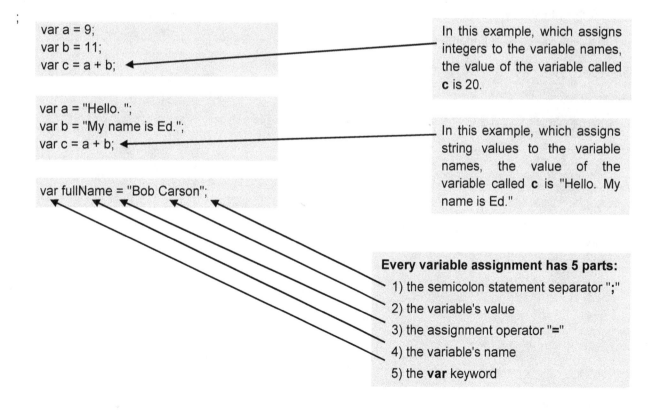

```
var a = 9;
var b = 11;
var c = a + b;
```

In this example, which assigns integers to the variable names, the value of the variable called **c** is 20.

```
var a = "Hello. ";
var b = "My name is Ed.";
var c = a + b;
```

In this example, which assigns string values to the variable names, the value of the variable called **c** is "Hello. My name is Ed."

```
var fullName = "Bob Carson";
```

Every variable assignment has 5 parts:
1) the semicolon statement separator ";"
2) the variable's value
3) the assignment operator "="
4) the variable's name
5) the **var** keyword

4.2 JAVASCRIPT VARIABLE NAMES / IDENTIFIERS

All JavaScript variables must be given unique names. These unique names are called **identifiers**. Identifiers can cover a wide range of names from short names such as **a**, **b** or **sum**, to longer, more descriptive names such as **firstName**, **lastKnownAddress** or **totalAssetValue**.

There are 10 basic rules for constructing JavaScript variable names that must be followed if the name is going to recognized as valid:

1) Variable names can only contain letters, digits, underscores, and dollar signs.
2) Variable names must begin with a letter, $ or _ .
3) Variable names cannot start with a number. You can, however, have numbers within a JavaScript variable name.
4) Variable names can include any letter, any number, or the underscore. You can't use any other characters, including spaces, symbols, and punctuation marks.
5) Variable names are case sensitive (y and Y are different variables).
6) Reserved words or JavaScript keywords (see list below) cannot be used as variable names.
7) Variable names cannot contain a mathematical or logical operator.
8) Variable names cannot contain any punctuation marks except for the underscore
9) Variable names cannot not contain spaces.
10) Variable names have no length limit.

4.2.1 JavaScript reserved words

In JavaScript, some identifiers are reserved words and cannot be used as variables or function names. The following is a list of JavaScript reserved words that can't be used as variable identifiers:

JavaScript Reserved Words

abstract	arguments	boolean	break	byte
case	catch	char	class	const
continue	debugger	default	delete	do
double	else	enum*	eval	export
extends	false	final	finally	float
for	function	goto	if	implements
import	in	instanceof	int	interface
let	long	native	new	null
package	private	protected	public	return
short	static	super	switch	synchronized
this	throw	throws	transient	true
try	typeof	var	void	volatile
while	with	yield		

SOLVED PROBLEMS

In each of the following problems (3.1 - 3.24) indicate whether the variable name given is a valid or an invalid identifier. If the variable name is invalid, give the variable naming rule number, or numbers, (from the variable naming list on page 42) that is being violated.

4.1 lastName

Solution

This is a **valid** identifier

4.2 function

Solution

This is an **invalid** identifier.
It violates Rule #6: "Reserved words or JavaScript keywords cannot be used as variable names."

4.3 total$cost

Solution

This is a **valid** identifier.

4.4 _myName

Solution

This is a **valid** identifier.

4.5 #lastName

Solution

This is an **invalid** identifier.
It violates Rule #2: "Variable names must begin with a letter, $ or _."

4.6 x

Solution

This is a **valid** identifier.

4.7 car name

Solution

This is an **invalid** identifier.

It violates Rule #9: "Variable names cannot not contain spaces."

4.8 3firstName

Solution

This is an **invalid** identifier.

It violates Rule #2: "Variable names must begin with a letter, $ or _ ."

It violates Rule #3: "Variable names cannot start with a number..."

4.9 /monthlyInterest

Solution

This is an **invalid** identifier.

It violates Rule #2: "Variable names must begin with a letter, $ or _ ."

4.10 boolean5

Solution

This is a **valid** identifier.

Although this identifier has the reserved word "boolean" embedded in it, it is valid because "boolean5" is not a reserved word.

4.11 a

Solution

This is a **valid** identifier.

It violates Rule #9: "Variable names cannot not contain spaces."

4.12 city@origin

Solution

This is an **invalid** identifier.

It violates Rule #1: "Variable names can only contain letters, digits, underscores, and dollar signs."

4.13 return

Solution

This is an **invalid** identifier.

It violates Rule #6: "Reserved words or JavaScript keywords cannot be used as variable names."

4.14 _departureTimeOrArrivalTimeOrTimeNeededToGoToRestRoom

Solution

This is a **valid** identifier

Rule #10: "Variable names have no length limit."

4.15 Continue

Solution

This is a **valid** identifier.

Even though "continue" is a reserved word and can't be used as a variable identifier, "Continue" is a totally different identifier because JavaScript variables are case sensitive.

Rule #5: "Variable names are case sensitive (y and Y are different variables)."

4.16 book, Author

Solution

This is an **invalid** identifier.

It violates Rule #1: " Variable names can only contain letters, digits, underscores, and dollar signs."

It violates Rule #8: "Variable names cannot contain any punctuation marks except for the underscore".

4.17 net&&Weight

Solution

This is an **invalid** identifier.

It violates Rule #1: " Variable names can only contain letters, digits, underscores, and dollar signs."

It violates Rule #7: "Variable names cannot contain a mathematical or logical operator."

4.18 while

Solution

This is an **invalid** identifier.
It violates Rule #6: "Reserved words or JavaScript keywords cannot be used as variable names."

4.19 _user_name

Solution

This is a **valid** identifier.

4.20 monthly||Interest

Solution

This is an **invalid** identifier.
It violates Rule #1: " Variable names can only contain letters, digits, underscores, and dollar signs."
It violates Rule #7: "Variable names cannot contain a mathematical or logical operator."

4.21 _$for

Solution

This is a **valid** identifier.

4.22 x1234567890

Solution

This is a **valid** identifier.

4.23 OFFICIALDATEOFHIRE

Solution

This is a **valid** identifier.

4.24 OfFiCiAldAtEoFhIrE

Solution

This is a **valid** identifier.

4.2.2 Variable case sensitivity in JavaScript

JavaScript is a **case-sensitive** programming language. As we've already seen to a limited extent, this means is that JavaScript considers and treats capital letters as completely different entities from their lowercase counterparts. For example, if you declare a variable called **monthlyInterest** in JavaScript, you have to use **monthlyInterest** to refer to that specific variable and not **MonthlyInterest**, **MONTHLYINTEREST**, **MONTHLYinterest** or some other combination of the same letters in their lowercase and uppercase forms. Programmers with backgrounds in other languages are often confused by this because some languages are not case sensitive with regard to variable names.

In JavaScript the case sensitivity does not just apply to variable names. It also applies to JavaScript keywords, event handlers, and object properties or methods (we'll be dealing with all these JavaScript entities in later chapters). JavaScript keywords are always written in lowercase, for example, **while**, **for**, **if**, **else**, and so on.

Because JavaScript is a case-sensitive programming language the following identifiers are all distinct and different variable names. Each one is stored in a separate memory location:

Examples

```
var firstName = "Ed";
```

```
var firstname = "Frank";
```

```
var FirstName = "John"
```

```
var FIRstName = "Bill";
```

```
var firstNAME = "Andy";
```

```
var fIRSTNAME = "Michael";
```

4.2.3 Under_score vs Camel Case Variable Naming Conventions

There are basically two ways of joining words into a variable name. The first is called **camel case**, and it looks like this:

```
var lastDayOfMonth;
```

The other one is called **underscore**:

```
var last_day_of_month;
```

> With some forms of camel case each word in the identifier starts with a capital letter. In this case the identifier would be **LastDayOfTheMonth**. But when camel case is used with JavaScript, the first word in the identifier begins with a small letter while the rest of the words begin with capital letters: **lastDayOfTheMonth**.

The common practice is to use the camel case variable naming convention in **object-oriented** programming and to use the underscore convention in **procedural/functional** style programming. Because of JavaScript's extreme flexibility, both conventions can be used to name variables. In spite of this, camel case is generally preferred by most JavaScript programmers.

One of the main advantages of using the camel case is shorter names, because you don't need to use extra underscores. Also, most of the methods that are built into JavaScript use camel-case, so it's recommended that you also use it. We will be using the camel case naming convention throughout this book rather than the underscore convention.

Examples

CAMEL CASE version	UNDER_SCORE version
daysInMonth	days_in_month
checkingAcountNumber	checking_account_number
carModel	car_model
monthlyFoodAllowance	monthly_food_allowance
countryOfOrigin	country_of_origin

4.3 DECLARING JAVASCRIPT VARIABLES

4.3.1 Declaring variables with the *var* keyword

Creating a variable in JavaScript is called "declaring" a variable. When you declare a variable you're letting the program know that that the variable exists. You declare a JavaScript variable with the **var** keyword:

```
var lastName;
```

The above declaration tells the program that a variable called **lastName** has just been created and will be given a value and used at some later point in the program.

Immediately after the variable has been declared, it has no value (technically its value at this point is **undefined**). The following code will result in "undefined" beng displayed on the browser screen:

```
<script>
    var lastName;
    document.write(lastName);
</script>
```

Because the variable **lastName** has only been declared but not given a value yet, the **document.write()** command is trying to display an undefined value. As a result, the message "**undefined**" will be displayed on the browser screen.

In order **assign** a value to the variable after it has been declared, you would use the assignment operator which is an equal sign:

```
lastName = "Jones";
```

The above declaration tells the program that the variable called **lastName** which was previously declared has been assigned the value "Jones". At this point, document.write(lastName) would display "Jones" on the browser screen.

You can also assign a value to the variable when you declare it:

```
var lastName = "Jones";
```

In many languages, such as **C**, you're required to declare a variable before you reference it in the program. However, JavaScript doesn't require you to declare a variable before you use it:

```
carMake = "Toyota";
```

is just as valid as

```
var carMake = "Toyota";
```

However, in this book, we will always use the **var** keyword when we declare a variable.

SOLVED PROBLEMS

4.25 Step 1: Declare a variable called **grossWeight.**
　　　　Step 2: Assign the value 125 to **grossWeight.**

Solution

```
<!DOCTYPE html>
<html>
<head>
</head>
<body>
  <script>
    var grossWeight;
    grossWeight = 125;
  </script>
</body>
</html>
```

4.26 Step 1: Declare a variable called **fullName.**
　　　　Step 2: Assign the value "Robert Allen" to **fullName.**

Solution

```
<!DOCTYPE html>
<html>
<head>
</head>
<body>
  <script>
    var fullName;
    grossWeight = "Robert Allen";
  </script>
</body>
</html>
```

4.27 Step 1: Declare a variable called **retailCost** and assign it the value **3000.**

Solution

```
<!DOCTYPE html>
<html>
<head>
</head>
<body>
  <script>
    var retailCost = 3000;
  </script>
</body>
</html>
```

4.28 Step 1: Declare a variable called **daysInMonth** and assign it the value **31.**

Solution

```
<!DOCTYPE html>
<html>
<head>
</head>
<body>
  <script>
    var daysInMonth = 31;
  </script>
</body>
</html>
```

4.29 Step 1: Declare a variable called **daysWorkedJanuary.**
       Step 2: Declare a variable called **daysSickJanuary.**
       Step 3: Declare a variable called **daysVacationJanuary.**
       Step 4: Assign the value 18 to **daysWorkedJanuary.**
       Step 5: Assign the value 3 to **daysSickJanuary.**
       Step 6: Assign the value 5 to **daysVacationJanuary.**

Solution

```
<!DOCTYPE html>
<html>
<head>
</head>
<body>
  <script>
    var daysWorkedJanuary;
    var daysSickJanuary;
```

```
      var daysVacationJanuary;
      daysWorkedJanuary = 18;
      daysSickJanuary = 3;
      daysVacationJanuary = 5;
    </script>
</body>
</html>
```

4.30 Step 1: Declare a variable called **firstChar** and assign it the value "a".
      Step 2: Declare a variable called **firstWord.**
      Step 3: Assign the value "when" to **firstWord**.

Solution
```
<!DOCTYPE html>
<html>
<head>
</head>
<body>
   <script>
     var firstChar = "a";
     var firstWord;
     firstWord = "when";
   </script>
</body>
</html>
```

4.31 Step 1: Declare a variable called **username** and assign it the value "fatboy".
      Step 2: Display the value of **username** on the browser screen.

Solution
```
<!DOCTYPE html>
<html>
<head>
</head>
<body>
   <script>
     var username = "fatboy";
     document.write (username);
   </script>
</body>
</html>
```

4.32 Step 1: Declare a variable called **password** and assign it the value "pepper".
      Step 2: Declare a variable called **sentenceFrag** and assign it the value "The password is: ".

Step 3: Use 2 **document.write( )** commands, with each **document.write( )** command using one of the variables as its parameter, to produce the following output:
"The password is: pepper"

Solution

```
<!DOCTYPE html>
<html>
<head>
</head>
<body>
   <script>
     var password = "pepper";
     var sentenceFrag = "The password is: ";
     document.write(sentenceFrag);
     document.write(password);
   </script>
</body>
</html>
```

Result displayed in browser:

```
The password is: pepper
```

4.33 Same as 3.32 but only use 1 **document.write( )** command to produce the same output. You will need to concatenate the 2 variables.

Solution

```
<!DOCTYPE html>
<html>
<head>
</head>
<body>
   <script>
     var password = "ginger";
     var sentenceFrag = "The password is: ";
     document.write(sentenceFrag + password);
   </script>
</body>
</html>
```

Result displayed in browser:

```
The password is: pepper
```

4.34 Step 1: Declare a variable called **lineOne** and give it the value "To be or not to be." ..
Step 2: Declare a variable called **lineTwo** and give it the value "That is the question.".
Step 3: Use three **document.write( )** commands to display the variable values on two lines.

Solution

```
<!DOCTYPE html>
<html>
<head>
</head>
<body>
   <script>
     var lineOne = "To be or not to be.";
     var lineTwo = "That is the question.";
     document.write(lineOne);
     document.write("<br>");
     document.write(lineTwo);
   </script>
</body>
</html>
```

Result displayed in browser:

```
To be or not to be.
That is the question.
```

4.35 Same as 3.34 but only use one **document.write( )** command to produce the same output.

Solution

```
<!DOCTYPE html>
<html>
<head>
```

```
</head>
<body>
  <script>
    var lineOne = "To be or not to be.";
    var lineTwo = "That is the question.";
    document.write(lineOne + "<br>" + lineTwo);
  </script>
</body>
</html>
```

"\n" won't work in a **document.write( )** command. You have to use
" to force a line break.

Result displayed in browser:

```
To be or not to be.
That is the question.
```

4.36 Step 1: Declare a variable called **poemLineOne** and give it the value "Shall I compare thee to a summer's day?"

Step 2: Display the value of **poemLineOne** in an Alert box.

Solution

```
<!DOCTYPE html>
<html>
<head>
</head>
<body>
  <script>
    var poemLineOne = "Shall I compare thee to a summer's day?";
    alert (poemLineOne);
  </script>
</body>
</html>
```

Result displayed in alert box:

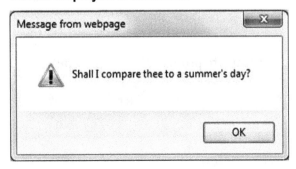

Message from webpage

Shall I compare thee to a summer's day?

OK

4.37 Same as 3.36 but add a second line to the poem. The value of the second line is: "Thou art more lovely and more temperate." Assign the second line to a variable called **poemLineTwo**. Display the values of the two variables on 2 separate lines in an Alert box.

Solution
```
<!DOCTYPE html>
<html>
<head>
</head>
<body>
  <script>
    var poemLineOne = "Shall I compare thee to a summer's day?";
    var poemLineTwo = "Thou art more lovely and more temperate.";
    alert(poemLineOne + "\n" + poemLineTwo);
  </script>
</body>
</html>
```

"<br>" won't work in an Alert box. You have to use "\n" to force a line break.

Result dislayed in alert box:

Message from webpage

⚠ Shall I compare thee to a summer's day?
Thou art more lovely and more temperate.

OK

4.38 Step 1: Declare a variable called **userRequest** and give it the value "state were you born in?"
        Step 2: Display the value of **userRequest** in a Prompt box. The user response section of the
                 Prompt box should say "undefined".

Solution
```
<!DOCTYPE html>
<html>
<head>
</head>
<body>
  <script>
    var userRequest = "What state were you born in?";
    prompt(userRequest);
  </script>
</body>
</html>
```

Result:

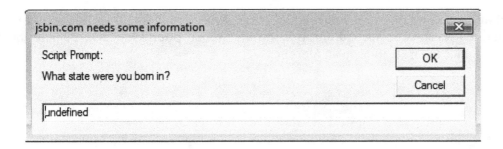

3.39 Step 1: Declare a variable called **userRequest** and give it the value "What's your name?" .
Step 2: Declare a variable called **userResponse** and give it the value "Enter your birth city here".
Step 3: Display the results in a Prompt box.

Solution

```
<!DOCTYPE html>
<html>
<head>
</head>
<body>
  <script>
    var userRequest = "What state were you born in?";
    var userResponse = "Enter your birth city here";
    prompt(userRequest, userResponse);
  </script>
</body>
</html>
```

Result displayed in prompt box:

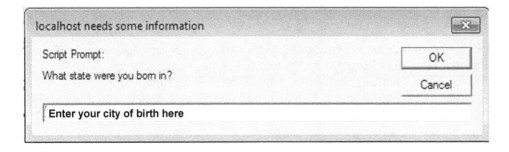

4.3.2 Declaring multiple variables with only one *var* keyword

In JavaScript, you can declare multiple variables in several ways. Like this:

```
var variable1 = "What's up, doc?";
var variable2 = "This is a test.";
var variable3 = 1543;
```

Or like this:

```
var variable1 = "What's up, doc?", variable2 = "Testing", variable3 = "1543";
```

SOLVED PROBLEMS

4.40 Step 1: Declare a variable called **var1** with the value "What's up, doc?".

Step 2: Declare a variable called **var2** with the value ""This is a test".

Step 3: Declare a variable called **var3** with the value 1543.

Step 4: Display the value of **var1** on the browser screen. Skip to the next line.

Step 5: Display the value of **var2** on the browser screen. Skip to the next line.

Step 6: Display the value of **var3** on the browser screen.

Solution

```
<!DOCTYPE html>
<html>
<head>
</head>
<body>
  <script>
    var var1 = "What's up, doc?";
    var var2 = "This is a test.";
    var var3 = 1543;
    document.write(var1 + "<br>");
    document.write(var2 + "<br>");
    document.write(var3);
  </script>
</body>
</html>
```

Result displayed in browser:

What's up, doc?
This is a test.
1543

4.41 Same as problem1 but declare all 3 variables on 1 line with one var keyword.

Solution

```
<!DOCTYPE html>
<html>
<head>
</head>
<body>
 <script>
```

```
    var var1 = "What's up, doc?", var2 = "This is a test.", var3 = 1543,var2 = "This is a test.", var3 =
           1543;
    document.write(var1 + "<br>");
    document.write(var2 + "<br>");
    document.write(var3);
  </script>
</body>
</html>
```

Result displayed in browser:
What's up, doc?
This is a test.
1543

4.3.3 Redeclaring variables

If you re-declare a JavaScript variable (without assigning a new value) it will not lose its value. For example, the variable **carName** will still have the value "Volvo" after the execution of these statements:

```
var carName = "Volvo";
var carName;
```

SOLVED PROBLEMS

4.40 Step 1: Declare a variable called **dogName1** with the value "Rover".
   Step 2: Display the value of **dogName1** on the browser screen.
   Step 3: Go to a new line.
   Step 4: Redeclare the variable **dogName1** with no value assigned.
   Step 5: Display the value of **dogName1** on the next line (Is it the same?).

Solution
```
<!DOCTYPE html>
<html>
<head>
</head>
<body>
  <script>
    var dogName1 = "Rover";
    document.write(dogName1);
    document.write("<br>");
    var dogName1;
    document.write(dogName1);
  </script>
</body>
</html>
```

Re-declaring **dogName1** without assigning it a new value assignment is **NOT** the same thing as writing **dogName1** = "". This would assign an empty string to **dogName1** and nothing would be printed to the browser screen.

The value of **dogName1** did not change when it was re-declared without a new value.

Result displayed in browser:
Rover
Rover

4.41 Step 1: Declare a variable called **dogName1** with the value "Rover".

Step 2: Display the value of **dogName1** on the browser screen.

Step 3: Start a new line.

Step 4: Redeclare the variable **dogName1** with the new value "Fido".

Step 5: Redeclare the variable **dogName1** with no value assigned.

Step 6: Display the value of **dogName1** (Is it the same?).

Solution
```
<!DOCTYPE html>
<html>
<head>
</head>
<body>
   <script>
      var dogName1 = "Rover";
      document.write(dogName1);
      document.write("<br>");
      var dogName1 = "Fido";
      var dogName1;
      document.write(dogName1);
   </script>
</body></html>
```

Since **dogName1** was assigned a new value ("Fido") when it was re-declared, this is the value that will be displayed on the browser screen. Usually a variable is not reassigned when it's given a new value. In this example, the new value ("Fido") should be assigned as follows: **dogName1 = "Fido"** not **var dogName1 = "Fido"**

Result displayed in browser:
Rover
Fido

4.3.4 JavaScript variable arithmetic

As with algebra, you can do arithmetic with JavaScript variables, using operators like "=" and "+":

Example:
```
var x = 5 + 2 + 3;
document.write(x);
```

Result displayed in browser:
10

You can also add strings, but strings will be concatenated (added end-to-end):

Example:
```
var x = "John" + " " + "Doe";
document.write(x);
```

Result displayed in browser:
John Doe

If you add a number to a string, the number will be treated as a string, and concatenated.

Example:
```
var x = "5" + 2 + 3;
document.write(x);
```

Result displayed in browser:
523

SOLVED PROBLEMS

4.42 Step 1: declare a variable called **num** and assign it the following value: 10 + 5.14 + 6.77
Step 2: display the value of **num** on the browser screen.

Solution
```
<!DOCTYPE html>
<html>
<head>
</head>
<body>
   <script>
      var num = 10 + 5.14 + 6.77
      document.write (num);
   </script>
</body>
</html>
```

Result displayed in browser:
21.91

4.43 Step 1: declare a variable called **num1** and assign it the following value: 7.
Step 2: declare a variable called **num2** and assign it the following value: 3 - 4 + num1.
Step 3: display the value of **num2** on the browser screen.

Solution

```
<!DOCTYPE html>
<html>
<head>
</head>
<body>
  <script>
      var num1 = 7
      var num2 = 3 - 4 + num1
      document.write (num2);
  </script>
</body>
</html>
```

Result displayed in browser:

6

4.44   Step 1: Declare a variable called **num1** and assign it the following value: 15.
       Step 2: Declare a variable called **num2** and assign it the following value: 3.
       Step 3: Declare a variable called **num3** and assign it the following value: num1 / num2.
       Step 4: Display the value of **num1** on the browser screen.

Solution

```
<!DOCTYPE html>
<html>
<head>
</head>
<body>
  <script>
      var num1 = 15;
      var num2 = 3;
      var num3 = num1 / num2
      document.write (num3);
  </script>
</body>
</html>
```

Result displayed in browser:

5

4.45   Step 1: declare a variable called **phrase1** and assign it the following value: "Hello" + " " + "World!"
       Step 2: display the value of **phrase1** on the browser screen.

Solution

```
<!DOCTYPE html>
```

```
<html>
<head>
</head>
<body>
  <script>
     var phrase1 = "Hello" + " " + "World!";
     document.write (phrase1);
  </script>
</body>
</html>
```

Result displayed in browser:

Hello World!

4.46 Step 1: Declare a variable called **sentenceFrag1** and assign it the following value: "Hello"
Step 2: Declare a variable called **sentenceFrag2** and assign it the following value: " ".
Step 3: Declare a variable called **sentenceFrag1** and assign it the following value: "World!".   .
Step 4: Display the value of **phrase1** on the browser screen.

Solution
```
<!DOCTYPE html>
<html>
<head>
</head>
<body>
  <script>
     var sentenceFrag1 = "Hello";
     var sentenceFrag2 = "";
     var sentenceFrag3 = "World!";
     var completeSentence = sentenceFrag1 + sentenceFrag2 + sentenceFrag3;
     document.write(completeSentence);
  </script>
</body>
</html>
```

Result displayed in browser:

Hello World!

4.4 JAVASCRIPT VARIABLE SCOPE

4.4.1 What is JavaScript variable scope?

Scope is the set of variables you have access to at any particular point in the program. Scope is also the environment that the function executes in. The scope of a variable is controlled by the location of the variable declaration, and defines the part of the program where a particular variable is accessible. Some variables are available to be used at any point in the program whereas other variables are only available to be used in specific parts in the program. All variables have a scope, which is the realm in which they exist. For example, variables that are created inside of functions (functions will be discussed in detail in a later chapter) do not exist and are not available to be used outside of that function, whereas variables created outside of functions are available to be used anywhere in the program, even inside of functions.

Each function has its own scope, and any variable declared within that function is only accessible from that function and any nested functions. Because local scope in JavaScript is created by functions, it's also called **function** scope.

Scoping rules vary from language to language. JavaScript has two scopes – **global** and **local**. A variable can be defined in either local or global scope, which establishes the variables' accessibility, existence and usability from different scopes during the time that the program is being executed (also called "runtime"). Scope refers to area of code where variables and functions are accessible, and in what context it is being executed. Basically, a variable or function can be defined in a global or local scope. Local variables exist only within the body of function in which they're defined and will have a different scope (always local and identical, but a different instance that local scope) every time that the function is called. A variable that is declared inside a function definition is local. It is created and destroyed every time the function is executed, and it cannot be accessed by any code outside the function. As far as any code outside of the function is concerned, the variable does not exist.

Any variable declared outside of a function belongs to the global scope, and is therefore accessible from anywhere in your code, even from within any function. Any defined global variable, meaning any variable that is declared outside of a function, will continue to exist throughout runtime and can be accessed and modified in any scope. A variable that is declared outside a function definition is a global variable and is accessible and alterable from anywhere in the program.

JavaScript, unlike many other languages, does not support **block** level scoping. This means that declaring a variable inside of a block structure like a **for**, **while** or **if** statement, does not restrict that variable's availability only to the loop. (More on **for**, **while** and **if** statements in later chapters).

4.4.2 Global scope / global variables

Any variables that are declared outside of a function (more on functions in a later chapter) are considered to be global variables in the global scope. When something is global it means that it is accessible from anywhere in your code. Any variable declared or initialized outside a function is a global variable, and it is therefore available to the entire application. Any statement, anywhere in a JavaScript program can access and use a global variable.

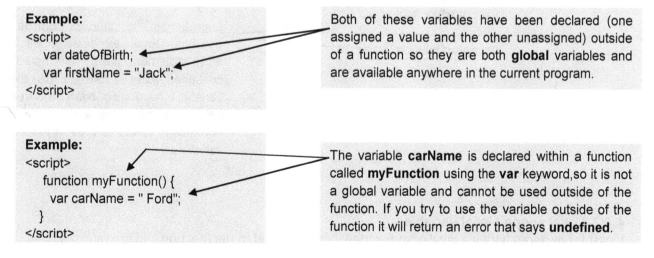

Example:
```
<script>
   var dateOfBirth;
   var firstName = "Jack";
</script>
```

Both of these variables have been declared (one assigned a value and the other unassigned) outside of a function so they are both **global** variables and are available anywhere in the current program.

Example:
```
<script>
   function myFunction() {
      var carName = " Ford";
   }
</script>
```

The variable **carName** is declared within a function called **myFunction** using the **var** keyword, so it is not a global variable and cannot be used outside of the function. If you try to use the variable outside of the function it will return an error that says **undefined**.

All scripts and functions on a web page can access a global variable. Any defined global variable, meaning any variable declared outside of a function body (or, as we will soon see, inside of a function but without the **var** keyword), will exist and be accessible as long as the program is running and the variable can be accessed and altered from any point in the program.

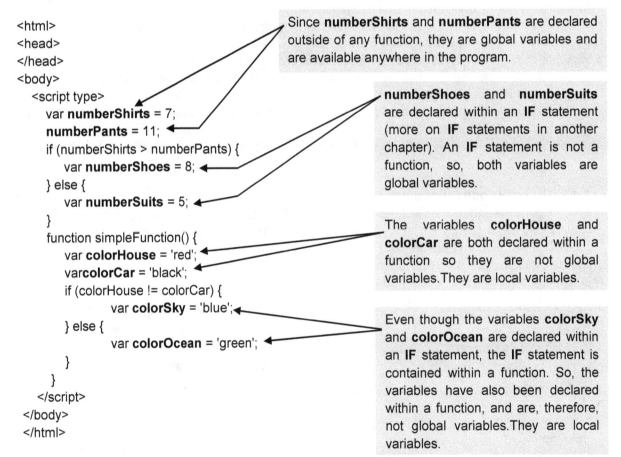

Example:
```
<script>
  var firstName = "Jack";
  function myFunction() {
    alert (firstName);
  }
</script>
```

Since the variable **firstName** was declared outside of any function it is a **global** variable and can be used by the **myFunction** function. In this case, when the function is called, it displays the value of **firstName** in an alert box. If **firstName** had been created in another function (other than **myFunction**) it would not be available to be used in **myFunction**. If another function (other than the function it was created in) tried to use **firstName**, an error would occur with the message: "undefined".

In the following code sample, we see examples of global and non-global variables (non-global variables are called **local** variables which we will discuss in the next section):

```
<html>
<head>
</head>
<body>
  <script type>
    var numberShirts = 7;
    numberPants = 11;
    if (numberShirts > numberPants) {
      var numberShoes = 8;
    } else {
      var numberSuits = 5;
    }
    function simpleFunction() {
      var colorHouse = 'red';
      varcolorCar = 'black';
      if (colorHouse != colorCar) {
        var colorSky = 'blue';
      } else {
        var colorOcean = 'green';
      }
    }
  </script>
</body>
</html>
```

Since **numberShirts** and **numberPants** are declared outside of any function, they are global variables and are available anywhere in the program.

numberShoes and **numberSuits** are declared within an **IF** statement (more on **IF** statements in another chapter). An **IF** statement is not a function, so, both variables are global variables.

The variables **colorHouse** and **colorCar** are both declared within a function so they are not global variables. They are local variables.

Even though the variables **colorSky** and **colorOcean** are declared within an **IF** statement, the **IF** statement is contained within a function. So, the variables have also been declared within a function, and are, therefore, not global variables. They are local variables.

4.4.3 Local scope / local variables
Variables declared within a JavaScript function, become **local** to the function and are referred to as

local variables. Local variables have local scope: They can only be accessed within the function in which they have been declared. Since local variables are only recognized inside their functions, variables with the same name can be used in different functions. Local variables are created when a function starts, and deleted when the function is completed. As opposed to the global scope, the local scope is when a variable is defined within a function and accessible only in that part of the code contained within the function or by sub-functions inside that function.

Example:
```
<script>
  function myFunction() {
    var carName = "Mustang";
  }
  alert (carName);
</script>
```

Because the variable **carName** is declared inside a function, it is a **local** variable and is not available for use outside of the function. When the command **alert (carName)** is encountered outside of the function, an error will occur and will display the error message: **undefined**.

Example:
```
<script>
  function displayFord() {
    var carName = "Mustang";
    alert (carName);
  }
  function displayChevy() {
    var carName = "Camaro";
    alert (carName);
  }
</script>
```

Because a local variable does not exist outside of the function that it's declared in, the same variable name can be used in two (or more) different functions without interfering with each other. The local variable **carName** which is declared in the **displayFord** function is totally independent of the the local variable **carName** which is declared in the **displayChevy** function. Neither one exists outside of the function that they were declared in so they can't interfere with one another.

Local variables have priority over global variables in functions. If you declare a global variable and a local variable with the same name, the local variable will have priority when you attempt to use the variable inside a function (local scope):

Example:
```
<script>
  var carName = "Buick";
  function carName() {
    var carName = "Mustang";
    alert (carName);
  }
</script>
```

Because the variable named **carName** is declared outside of the function as a global variable and within the function as a local variable, the local variable is the version that will be used inside the function. Because the local variable has priority over the global variable of the same name within a function, the value "Mustang" will be displayed in the alert box.

Any locally scoped items are not visible in the global environment. That is, if a variable is declared within a function, it will not exist outside of that function. If you try to use the variable within the global scope you will get the error message: **undefined**. Variables declared within a function are defined only within the body of that function. They are local variables and have local scope only. They do not exist outside the function they were declared in. They are not accessible from any other function, other than the one they were declared in.

4.4.4 Automatically global

If you declare a variable without using the **var** keyword, it automatically has global scope. This applies to variables declared inside a function also. Any variable declared within a function without the **var** keyword is also a global variable.

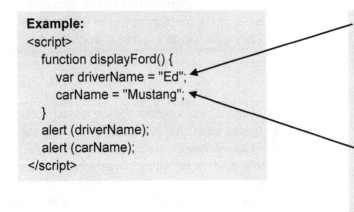

Example:
```
<script>
    function displayFord() {
        var driverName = "Ed";
        carName = "Mustang";
    }
    alert (driverName);
    alert (carName);
</script>
```

Because the variable **driverName** is declared inside the function using the **var** keyword it is a **local** variable and is only accesible inside the function. When the code outside of the function attempts to display the value of **driverName** in an alert box an error will be raised with the error message: **undefined**.

Because the variable **carName** is declared inside the function but without the **var** keyword, it automatically becomes a **global** variable and can be accessed outside of the function. When the code outside of the function attempts to display the value of **carName** in an alert box, the attempt is successful and "Mustang" displays in the alert box.

SOLVED PROBLEMS

4.47 Use the following script to answer the questions:

```
<!DOCTYPE html>
<html>
<head>
</head>
<body>
  <script>
      var dateOfHIre = "12/1/2010";
      alert (dateOfHire);
  </script>
</body>
</html>
```

Questions

a) What is the scope of the the variable called **dateOfHire**? Why?

b) What will appear in the alert box?

c) Where is **dateOfHire** available to be used?

Solution

a) global

   Because **dateOfHire** is declared outside of a function, it has global scope.

b) "12/1/2010"

c) Anywhere in the JavaScript code, including in a function.

4.48 Use the following script to answer the questions:

```
<!DOCTYPE html>
<html>
<head>
</head>
<body>
  <script>
      question1 = "What is your name?";
      prompt (question1);
  </script>
</body>
</html>
```

Questions

a) What is the scope of the variable called **question1**? Why?

b) What will appear in the dialog box section of the prompt box?

c) Where is **question1** available to be used?

Solution

a) global

Because **question1** is declared outside of a function, it has global scope. Also any variable declared without the **var** keyword (even if it's declared in a function) automatically has global scope.

b) "What is your name?"

c) Anywhere in the JavaScript code, including in a function.

4.49 Step 1: Declare a global variable called **phoneMsg** and assign it the following value: "No one is home right now."

     Step 2: Declare a second global variable called **timeOfCall** and assign it the following value: "14:25:10"

     Step 3: Use the **var** keyword to declare both variables

     Step 4: Display the value of **phoneMsg** and **timeOfCall** on two separate lines in the browser

Solution

```
<!DOCTYPE html>
<html>
<head>
</head>
<body>
   <script>
      var phoneMsg = "No one is home right now.";
      var timeOfCall = "14:25:10";
      document.write (phoneMsg);
      document.write ("<br>");
      document.write (timeOfCall);
   </script>
</body>
</html>
```

Result displayed in browser:

```
No one is home right now.
14:25:10
```

4.50 Step 1: Declare a global variable called **userPrompt** and assign it the following value: "How old are you?"

Step 2: Declare a second global variable called **userResponse** and assign it the following value: "Please enter your age here."

Step 3: Don't use the **var** keyword when you declare the variables.

Step 4: Display the value of **userPrompt** in the prompt section of a prompt box.

Step 5: Display the value of **userResponse** in the response section of the same prompt box.

Solution

```
<!DOCTYPE html>
<html>
<head>
</head>
<body>
   <script>
      userPrompt = "How old are you?";
      userResponse = "Please enter your age here.";
      prompt (userPrompt, userResponse);
   </script>
</body>
</html>
```

Result displayed in prompt box:

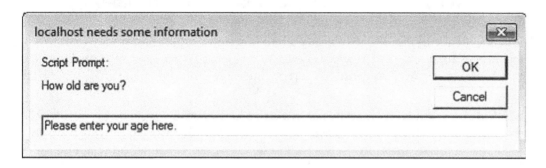

4.51 Use the following script to answer the questions:

```
<!DOCTYPE html>
<html>
<head>
</head>
<body>
  <script>
     var carName = "Toyota";
     function myFunction() {
        var carModel = "Corolla";
        document.write (carModel);
     }
     carYear = "2009";
  </script>
</body>
</html>
</html>
```

Questions

a) Which variables in the above code are global variables?

b) Where in the JavaScript program* can **carName** and **carYear** be used?

c) Where can the variable called **carModel** be used?

d) Will the value of **carModel** be displayed on the browser screen in response to the **document.write()** command (if the function is called from somewhere else in the program)?

Solution

a) **carName** and **carYear** are both global variables because they were both declared outside of a function (it doesn't matter if the **var** keyword is used or not). Any variable declared inside a function with the **var** keyword is a local variable and not a global variable.

---

*As a reminder, when we speak about the "JavaScript program", we're talking about any code between <script> tags that's embedded within the html code in the html file for the browser page.

b) Because **carName** and **carYear** are global variables, they're available to be used anywhere in any JavaScript code. That is, anywhere between **<script>** tags, regardless of whether they appear in the <head> section or the **<body>** section of the html file that contains the JavaScript code.

c) Because **carModel** is a local variable (it was declared in a function using the **var** keyword), it's only available to be used in the function that it was created in, which this case, is **myFunction**. If it's referenced anywhere outside of **myFunction**, an error message will be generated which says: **undefined**.

d) Yes. Although **carModel** is not a global variable, it is a valid local variable within the context of the function that it was created in, which, in this case, is **myFunction**. So, yes, it can be used in the **document.write()** command in **myFunction**. As the code is written now, the function won't be called and executed but if the function is called by some other part of the program the value of **carModel** will be displayed (more on function calls in later chapters).

4.52 Use the following script to answer the questions:

```
<!DOCTYPE html>
<html>
<head>
</head>
<body>
  <script>
     var numStudents = 100;
     numTeachers = 25;
     if (numStudents < numTeachers) {
       var numDesks = 50;
     } else {
       numBooks = 75;
     }
     function calcRatio() {
       var ratioStudentsToTeachers = numStudents / numTeachers;
       numSchools = 4;
     }
  </script>
</body>
</html>
</html>
```

Questions

a) Which of the 6 variables created in the code above (**numStudents, numTeachers, numDesks, numBooks, ratioStudentsToTeachers, numSchools**) is a global variable?

b) Which of the 6 variables created in the code above (**numStudents, numTeachers, numDesks, numBooks, ratioStudentsToTeachers, numSchools**) is a local variable?

Solution

a) **numStudents** - This variable is declared outside of a function so it is a global variable.

numTeachers - This variable is declared outside of a function so it is a global variable. Also, any variable declared without a **var** keyword is automatically a global variable.

numDesks - This variable was declared in an **if** statement, but not in a function, so, it is a global variable.

numBooks - This variable was declared in an **if** statement, but not in a function, so, it is a global variable.

numSchools - Even though this variable was declared inside a function, it was declared without a **var** keyword, so, it is automatically considered to be a global variable.

b) **ratioStudentsToTeachers** - This variable was declared within a function using the **var** keyword so it is a local variable and accessible only within the function itself.

4.53 Use the following script to answer the questions:

```
<!DOCTYPE html>
<html>
<head>
</head>
<body>
   <script>
     var x = 12;
     function displayValues() {
        alert (x);
        var y = 30;
        alert (y);
     }
   </script>
</body>
</html>
</html>
```

Questions

In the above code:

a) The statement **var x = 12** (line 7) is declaring what kind of variable?

b) What happens when the **alert(x)** command (line 9) is executed inside the function?

c) The statement **var y = 30** (line 10) is declaring what kind of variable?

d) What happens when the **alert(y)** command (line 11) is executed inside the function?

e) In what part of the code can variable **y** be used?

f) In what part of the code can variable **x** be used?

g) What is the scope of variable **y**?

h) What happens if you try to use variable **y** outside of the function that it was declared in (**displayValues**)?

i) Can you use variable **y** in another function besides **displayValues**?

Solution

a) **x** was declared outside of a function so it is a global variable.

b) **12** is displayed in an alert box. Even though **x** was declared and assigned outside of the function, it is a global variable, so, it's available for use by the function **displayValues** and anywhere else in the code.

c) **y** was declared inside of a function using the **var** keyword, so, it is a local variable.

d) **30** is displayed in an alert box. Because **y** was declared within a function using the **var** keyword, it is a local variable and can be used anywhere within the local context of the function it was declared in.

e) **y** can only be used within the function that it was declared in (**displayValues**).

f) **y** can only be used within the function that it was declared in (**displayValues**).

g) y has local scope. It only exists within the function it was declared in.

h) You will get an error message that says: **undefined**.

i) No

4.4.5 JavaScript variable lifetime

The lifetime of a JavaScript variable refers to the period of time during which a variable exists and can be used in some way by the program. When the lifetime of a JavaScript variable comes to an end, it isn't stored anywhere or kept in existence for later use. It's as if it never existed. All traces of it are gone forever. If you want to use a variable with the same name and scope at a later time, you have to declare it and create it from scratch. Even if the new variable has the same name, value and scope as a previous variable whose lifetime has come to an end, there is absolutely no connection between the two. No references can be made to the previous variable by using the name of the new variable. None of the "dead" variable's values, uses or contexts have been stored anywhere on the computer.

The lifetime of a global variable starts when it is declared (either with or without the **var** keyword), and ends when the page is closed.

If you declare a variable, using the **var** keyword, within a function, the variable has local scope and can only be accessed within that function. When you exit the function, the variable is destroyed (the variable will be created again and start a new lifetime if/when the function is called and executed again). These variables are called local variables. You can have local variables with the same name in different functions, because each is recognized only by the function in which it is declared. Local variables are deleted when the function is completed and the browser begins to execute code outside the function.

When a web page that contains a script (JavaScript code between **<script>** tags) is unloaded because the user has pointed the browser on to a new page, the script is unloaded along with the page that contains it. But what happens to the variables (global and local) that are declared and defined by the script on the page that's being unloaded? Since these variables are actually properties of the Window object (actually a local variable is a property of the **call** object, but more on that later) that contained the script, you might be inclined to consider them to still exist but in an undefined state. That is, the browser still remembers them, but they currently have no value. If that were the case, then, any new script that was loaded as the result of the user closing the old page and opening a new one, would have extra, unwanted baggage from the previous page. Obviously you want your scripts for a new page to start off fresh and unemcumbered with any baggage from the past.

In fact, all user-defined properties (which includes all global and local variables – actually at this point all local variables should have been destroyed since you should not be in the middle of executing a function when the jump to another page is made) are erased whenever a web page is unloaded. The scripts in a freshly loaded document start with no variables defined, and no properties in their **Window object**, except for the standard properties defined by the system. What this means is that the lifetime of scripts and of the variables they define is the same as the lifetime of the web page that contains the script. When the current page closes, all variables are destroyed – and their lifetime as useful, contributing members of the closed web page is gone forever.

4.4.6 No block scope in JavaScript

A programming language has **block scope** if a variable which is declared inside some block of code enclosed by curly braces is only visible within that block of code, and that variable is **not** visible outside of that particular block of code. In JavaScript, a "block" of code enclosed by curly braces could be an **if** statement, **switch** statement, **for** loop, **while** loop, etc. (more on all these statements in a later chapter). If a variable declared within a block of code is still visible outside of that block, then the programming language does **not** have block scope. If the variable created within a block of code which is enclosed by curly braces is not available outside of that code block, then, the language **does** have block scope. There is no block scope in JavaScript.

The following are examples which demonstrate that JavaScript does **not** recognize block scope (don't worry if you're not familiar with the **if** statement and for loop that are used here – more on them in later chapters):

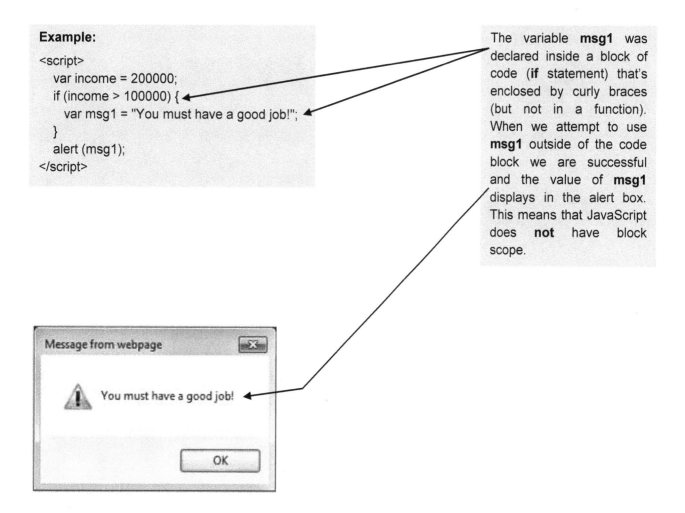

Example:
```
<script>
   var income = 200000;
   if (income > 100000) {
      var msg1 = "You must have a good job!";
   }
   alert (msg1);
</script>
```

The variable **msg1** was declared inside a block of code (**if** statement) that's enclosed by curly braces (but not in a function). When we attempt to use **msg1** outside of the code block we are successful and the value of **msg1** displays in the alert box. This means that JavaScript does **not** have block scope.

Message from webpage

⚠ You must have a good job!

OK

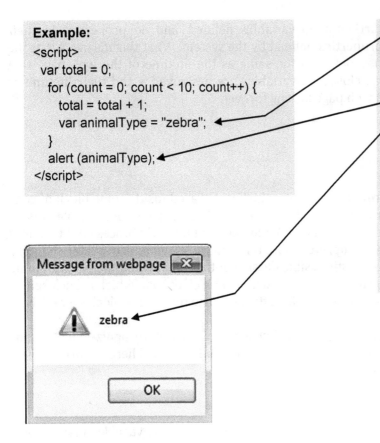

Example:
```
<script>
  var total = 0;
    for (count = 0; count < 10; count++) {
      total = total + 1;
      var animalType = "zebra";
    }
    alert (animalType);
</script>
```

The variable **animalType** was declared inside a block of code (for loop) that's enclosed by curly braces (but not in a function). When we attempt to use **animalType** outside of the code block we are successful and the value of **animalType** displays in the alert box. This means that JavaScript does **not** have block scope. We could do this for every type of code block that's enclosed by curly braces in JavaScript, but the fact is, JavaScript does not recognize block scope. Only variables declared with the **var** keyword in functions are not recognized outside a set of curly braces.

Chapter 5

JavaScript Operators: Part 1

5.1 WHAT IS A JAVASCRIPT OPERATOR?

JavaScript operators are used to assign values, compare values, perform arithmetic operations, and more. We briefly considered JavaScript operators in chapter 1 but we want to cover them more deeply here in CHAPTER 5. The following is a list of some of the major operator types in JavaScript:

- Arithmetic operators
- Assignment operators
- Increment operators
- String operators
- Comparison operators
- Logical operators

5.2 JAVASCRIPT ARITHMETIC OPERATORS

An arithmetic operator takes numerical values (either literals or variables) as their operands and returns a single numerical value. The standard arithmetic operators are addition (+), subtraction (-), multiplication (*), and division (/). These operators work as they do in most other programming languages when used with floating point numbers. The following is a list of the 7 major JavaScript arithmetic operators:

- Addition
- Subtraction
- Division
- Multiplication
- Remainder
- Increment
- Decrement

5.2.1 Addition operator (+)

The addition operator produces the sum of numeric operands.

Syntax

Operator: x + y

The following examples show the addition operator in action:

Example 1:

```
<script>
    var x = 200 + 150;
    document.write(x);
</script>
```

Result displayed in browser:

350

In this example, **x** is set equal to the sum of 200 + 150. The result is 350..

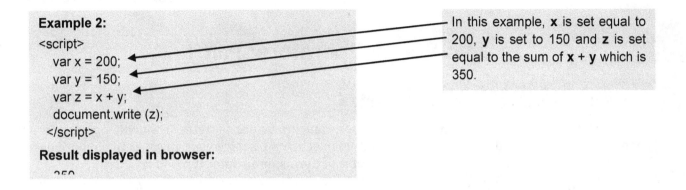

Example 2:
```
<script>
  var x = 200;
  var y = 150;
  var z = x + y;
  document.write (z);
</script>
```
Result displayed in browser:

In this example, **x** is set equal to 200, **y** is set to 150 and **z** is set equal to the sum of **x** + **y** which is 350.

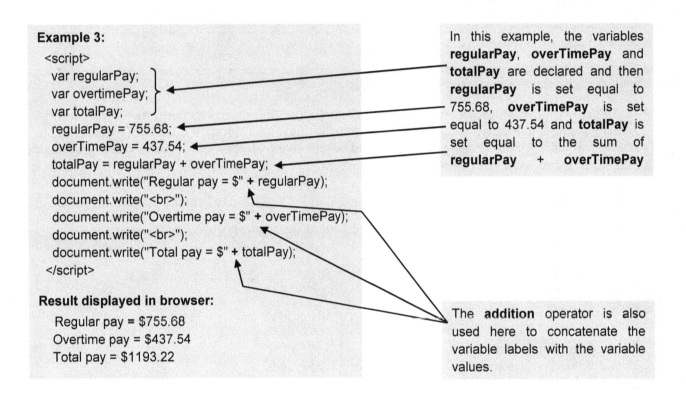

Example 3:
```
<script>
  var regularPay;
  var overtimePay;
  var totalPay;
  regularPay = 755.68;
  overTimePay = 437.54;
  totalPay = regularPay + overTimePay;
  document.write("Regular pay = $" + regularPay);
  document.write("<br>");
  document.write("Overtime pay = $" + overTimePay);
  document.write("<br>");
  document.write("Total pay = $" + totalPay);
</script>
```
Result displayed in browser:

Regular pay = $755.68
Overtime pay = $437.54
Total pay = $1193.22

In this example, the variables **regularPay**, **overTimePay** and **totalPay** are declared and then **regularPay** is set equal to 755.68, **overTimePay** is set equal to 437.54 and **totalPay** is set equal to the sum of **regularPay** + **overTimePay**

The **addition** operator is also used here to concatenate the variable labels with the variable values.

5.2.2 Subtracton operator (-)

The subtraction operator subtracts the two operands, producing their difference.

Syntax

Operator: x - y

The following examples show the subtraction operator in action:

Example 1:

```
<script>
   var a = 425 - 150;
   document.write(a);
</script>
```

Result displayed in browser:

275

In this example, **a** is set equal to the difference between 425 and 150. The result is 275.

Example 2:

```
<script>
   var a = 425;
   var b = 150;
   var c = a - b;
   document.write (a);
</script>
```

Result displayed in browser:

275

In this example, **a** is set equal to 425, **b** is set to 150 and **c** is set equal to the difference between **a** and **b** which gives the following result: 275.

Example 3:

```
<script>
   var grossYearIncome;
   var incomeTaxesPaid;
   var netYearPay;
   grossYearIncome = 56600;
   incomeTaxesPaid = 18450;
   netYearPay = grossYearIncome - incomeTaxesPaid;
   document.write("Gross income for year = $" +
               grossYearIncome);
   document.write("<br>");
   document.write("Income taxes paid = $" +
               incomeTaxesPaid);
   document.write("<br>");
   document.write("Net income for year = $" +
               netYearPay);
</script>
```

Result displayed in browser:

Gross income for year = $56600
Income taxes paid = $18450
Net income for year = $38150

In this example, the variables **grossYearIncome**, **incomeTaxesPaid** and **netYearPay** are declared and then **grossYearIncome** is set equal to 56600, **incomeTaxesPaid** is set equal to 18450 and **grossYearIncome** is set equal to the difference between **grossYearIncome** and **incomeTaxesPaid** which is 38150.

Statements can be written across several lines in JavaScript without any problem. JavaScript ignores all spaces between the different parts of the statement and executes it as if it were all written on one line. **Note**: This doesn't apply to strings. For information on how to code multiline strings see section: **2.1.5 Multi-line JavaScript strings.**

5.2.3 Division operator (/)

The division operator produces the quotient of its operands where the left operand is the dividend and the right operand is the divisor.

Syntax

Operator: x / y

The following examples show the division operator in action:

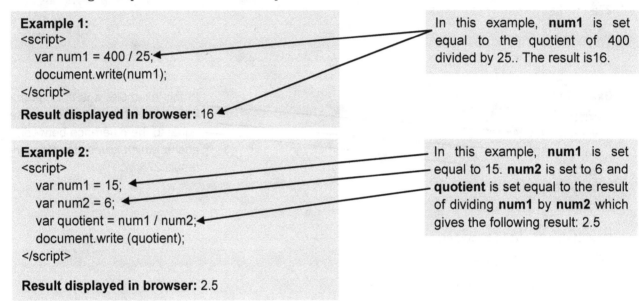

Example 1:
```
<script>
   var num1 = 400 / 25;
   document.write(num1);
</script>
```
Result displayed in browser: 16

In this example, **num1** is set equal to the quotient of 400 divided by 25.. The result is16.

Example 2:
```
<script>
   var num1 = 15;
   var num2 = 6;
   var quotient = num1 / num2;
   document.write (quotient);
</script>
```
Result displayed in browser: 2.5

In this example, **num1** is set equal to 15. **num2** is set to 6 and **quotient** is set equal to the result of dividing **num1** by **num2** which gives the following result: 2.5

Example 3:
```
<script>
   var numberAtBats;
   var numberHits;
   var battingAvg;
   numberAtBats = 360;
   numberHits = 90;
   battingAvg = numberHits / numberAtBats;
   battingAvg = battingAvg.toFixed(3);
   document.write("Number of at bats = "
                  + numberAtBats);
   document.write("<br>");
   document.write("Number of hits = "
                  + numberHits);
   document.write("<br>");
   document.write("Batting average = "
                  + battingAvg);
</script>
```

In this example, the variables **numberAtBats**, **numberHits** and **battingAvg** are declared and then **numberAtBats** is set equal to 360, **numberHits** is set equal to 90 and **battingAvg** is set equal to the result of dividing **numberHits by** which gives the following result: 0.250.

The **toFixed()** method determines the number of decimal places to the right of the decimal point for a given variable. In this case we've set the variable **battingAvg** to three decimal places (more on this in a later chapter).

Result displayed in browser:

Number of at bats = 360
Number of hits = 90
Batting average = 0.250

5.2.4 Multiplication operator (*)

The multiplication operator produces the product of the operands.

Syntax

Operator: x * y

The following examples show the multiplication operator in action:

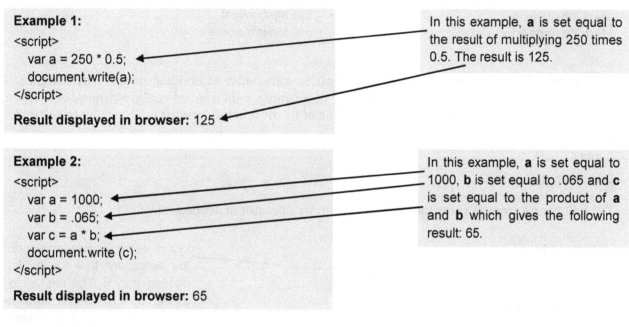

Example 1:
```
<script>
   var a = 250 * 0.5;
   document.write(a);
</script>
```
Result displayed in browser: 125

In this example, **a** is set equal to the result of multiplying 250 times 0.5. The result is 125.

Example 2:
```
<script>
   var a = 1000;
   var b = .065;
   var c = a * b;
   document.write (c);
</script>
```
Result displayed in browser: 65

In this example, **a** is set equal to 1000, **b** is set equal to .065 and **c** is set equal to the product of **a** and **b** which gives the following result: 65.

Example 3:
```
<script>
   var salePrice;
   var percentCommission;
   var totalCommission;
   salePrice = 100000;
   percentCommission = 8.5;
   totalCommission = salePrice * (percentCommission/100);
   document.write("Sale price = $"
               + salePrice);
   document.write("<br>");
   document.write("Percent Commission = "
               + percentCommission + "%";);
   document.write("<br>");
   document.write("Total commission = $"
               + totalCommission);
</script>
```

Result displayed in browser:

Sale price = $100000
Percent Commission = 8.5%
Total commission = $8500

In this example, the variables **salePrice**, **percentCommission** and **totalCommission** are declared and then **salePrice** is set equal to 100000, **percentCommission** is set equal to 8.5 and **totalCommission** is set equal to the product of **salePrice** times **percentCommission** divided by **100** which gives the following result: 8500.

In order to give the correct value for **totalCommission**, **percentCommission** has to be divided by 100 as part of the calculation for **totalCommission**.

5.2.5 Remainder operator (%)

When we divide two integers (with a remainder) the result will be an equation that looks like the following:

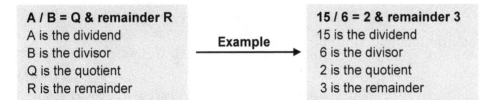

The **modulo** (remainder) function is the integer remainder of dividing integer1 by integer2. The result of a modulo division is the remainder of an integer division of the given numbers. Modulus division produces the remainder value only. One of its most helpful uses if for checking to see if values are divisible by a specified number.

Syntax

Operator: var1 % var2

The following examples show the modulo remainder operator in action:

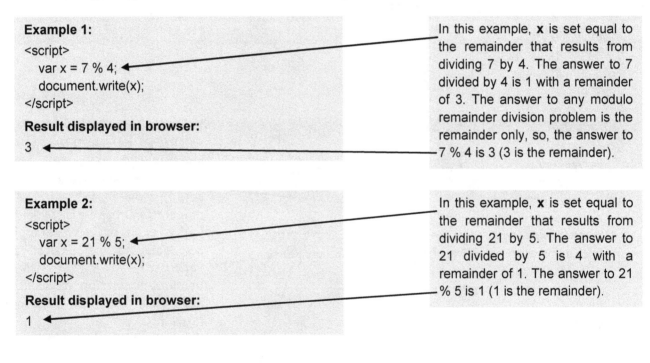

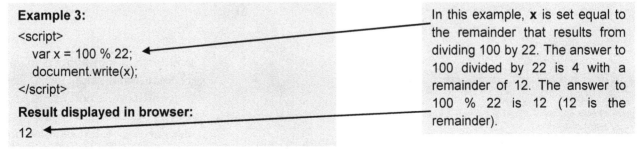

5.2.6 Increment operator (++)

The increment operator increments (adds one to) its operand and returns a value. If the operator appears before the variable, the value is modified before the expression is evaluated. If the operator appears after the variable, the value is modified after the expression is evaluated. In other words, if x = ++y; , the value of x is the original value of y plus one; given x = y++; , the value of x is the original value of y , which is incremented after its value is assigned to x.

- If used **postfix**, with operator after operand (for example, x++), then it returns the value before incrementing.
- If used **prefix** with operator before operand (for example, ++x), then it returns the value after incrementing.

Syntax

Operator: x++ or ++x

The following examples show the increment operator in action:

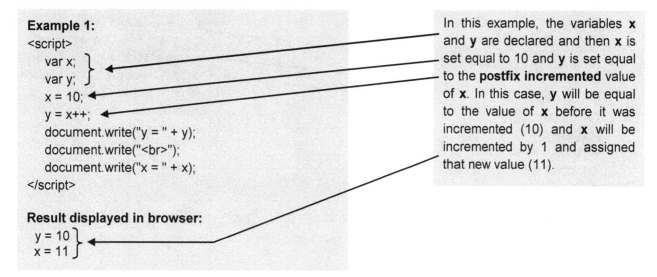

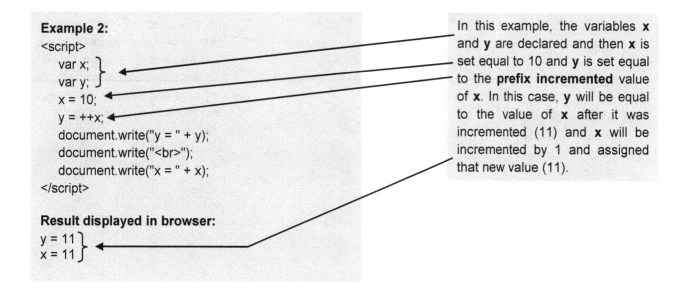

5.2.7 Decrement operator (++)

The decrement operator decrements (subtracts one from) its operand and returns a value. If the operator appears before the variable, the value is modified before the expression is evaluated. If the operator appears after the variable, the value is modified after the expression is evaluated. In other words, if x = --y; , the value of x is the original value of y minus one; given x = y--; , the value of x is the original value of y , which is decremented after its value is assigned to x.

- If used **postfix**, with operator after operand (for example, x--), then it returns the value before decrementing.
- If used **prefix** with operator before operand (for example, --x), then it returns the value after decrementing.

Syntax

Operator: x-- or --x

The following examples show the decrement operator in action:

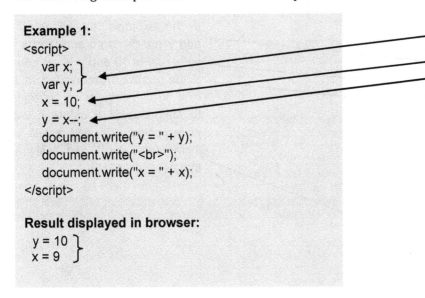

Example 1:
```
<script>
    var x;
    var y;
    x = 10;
    y = x--;
    document.write("y = " + y);
    document.write("<br>");
    document.write("x = " + x);
</script>
```

Result displayed in browser:
```
y = 10
x = 9
```

In this example, the variables **x** and **y** are declared and then **x** is set equal to 10 and **y** is set equal to the **postfix decremented** value of **x**. In this case, **y** will be equal to the value of **x** before it was decremented (10) and **x** will be decremented by 1 and assigned that new value (9).

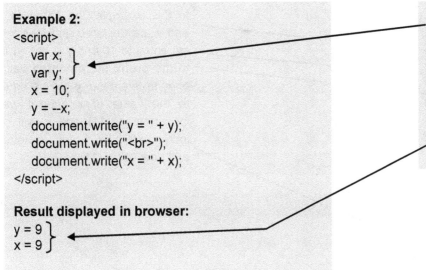

Example 2:
```
<script>
    var x;
    var y;
    x = 10;
    y = --x;
    document.write("y = " + y);
    document.write("<br>");
    document.write("x = " + x);
</script>
```

Result displayed in browser:
```
y = 9
x = 9
```

In this example, the variables **x** and **y** are declared and then **x** is set equal to 10 and **y** is set equal to the **prefix decremented** value of **x**. In this case, **y** will be equal to the value of **x** after it was decremented (9) and **x** will be decremented by 1 and assigned that new value (9).

SOLVED PROBLEMS

5.1 What will be displayed in the browser window when the following JavaScript code executes?

```
<!DOCTYPE html>
<html>
<head>
</head>
<body>
   <script>
      var m = 50 + 25;
      document.write (m);
   </script>
</body>
</html>
```

Result in browser window:

75

For problems **4.2** thru **4.16**, we're only going to show the JavaScript code between the **<script>** tags and omit the surrounding html code. Assume that the JavaScript within the **<script>** tags is in the **<body>** section of the html code as in all of the previous examples.

5.2 What will be displayed in the browser window when the following JavaScript code executes?

```
<script>
   var a = 35;
   var b = 15;
   var c = 22;
   document.write (a + b + c);
</script>
```

Result in browser window:

72

5.3 What will be displayed in the browser window when the following JavaScript code executes?

```
<script>
   var h = 5;
   var i = 7;
   var j = 3;
   document.write (h + I + j);
</script>
```

Result in browser window:

15

5.4 What will be displayed in the browser window when the following JavaScript code executes?

```
<script>
   var regularWeeksPay = 500;
   var overtimeWeeksPay = 350;
   var totalWeeksPay = regularWeeksPay + overtimeWeeksPay;
   document.write (totalWeeksPay);
</script>
```

Result in browser window:

850

5.5 What will be displayed in the browser window when the following JavaScript code executes?

```
<script>
   var x = 225 - 50;
   document.write (x);
</script>
```

Result in browser window:

175

5.6 What will be displayed in the browser window when the following JavaScript code executes?

```
<script>
   var q = 47;
   var r = 15;
   var s = 2;
   document.write (q - r - s);
</script>
```

Result in browser window:

30

5.7 What will be displayed in the browser window when the following JavaScript code executes?

```
<script>
   var x = 100;
   var y = 33;
   var z = x - y;
   document.write (z);
</script>
```

Result in browser window:

67

5.8 What will be displayed in the browser window when the following JavaScript code executes?

```
<script>
    var grossIncome = 2500;
    var totalExpenses = 325;
    var netIncome = grossIncome - totalExpenses;
    document.write (netIncome);
</script>
```

Result in browser window:

2175

5.9 What will be displayed in the browser window when the following JavaScript code executes?

```
<script>
    var d = 100 * 4;
    document.write (d);
</script>
```

Result in browser window:

400

5.10 What will be displayed in the browser window when the following JavaScript code executes?

```
<script>
    var f = 25;
    var g = 2;
    var h = 3;
    document.write (f * g * h);
</script>
```

Result in browser window:

150

5.11 What will be displayed in the browser window when the following JavaScript code executes?

```
<script>
    var x = 33;
    var y = 3;
    var z = x * y;
    document.write (z);
</script>
```

Result in browser window:

99

5.12 What will be displayed in the browser window when the following JavaScript code executes?

```
<script>
   var hoursWorked = 40;
   var hourlyPayRate = 20;
   var totalPay = hoursWorked * hourlyPayRate;
   document.write (totalPay);
</script>
```

Result in browser window:

800

5.13 What will be displayed in the browser window when the following JavaScript code executes?

```
<script>
   var a = 140 / 4;
   document.write (a);
</script>
```

Result in browser window:

35

5.14 What will be displayed in the browser window when the following JavaScript code executes?

```
<script>
   var i = 500;
   var j = 125;
   var k = i / j;
   document.write (k);
</script>
```

Result in browser window:

4

5.15 What will be displayed in the browser window when the following JavaScript code executes?

```
<script>
   var x = 900;
   var y = 300;
   document.write (x / y);
</script>
```

Result in browser window:

3

5.16 What will be displayed in the browser window when the following JavaScript code executes?

```
<script>
   var totalStockValue = 50000
   var totalShares = 1000;
   var perShareValue = totalStockValue / totalShares;
   document.write (perShareValue);
</script>
```

Result in browser window:

50

5.17 Step 1: Declare a variable called **a** and set it equal to the sum of 75 and 50.
      Step 2: Display the value of **a** in the browser window.

Solution

```
<script>
   var a = 75 + 50;
   document.write (a);
</script>
```

Result in browser window:

125

5.18 Step 1: Declare a variable called **num1** and set it equal to 85.
      Step 2: Declare a variable called **num2** and set it equal to 110.
      Step 3: Declare a variable called **num3** and set it equal to 50.
      Step 4: Display the value of **num1 + num2 + num3** in an alert box.

Solution

```
<script>
   var num1 = 85;
   var num2 = 110;
   var num3 = 50;
   alert (num1 + num2 + num3);
</script>
```

Result in alert box:

245

5.19 Step 1: Declare a variable called **x** and set it equal to 410.
      Step 2: Declare a variable called **y** and set it equal to 590.
      Step 3: Declare a variable called **z** and set it equal to the sum of **x** and **y**.

Step 4: Display the value of z in the browser window.

Solution
```
<script>
   var x = 410;
   var y = 590;
   var z = x + y;
   document.write (x + y);
</script>
```

Result in browser window:

1000

5.20 Step 1: Declare a variable called **a** and set it equal to 600.
          Step 2: Declare a variable called **b** and set it equal to 325.
          Step 3: Display the value of **a - b** in the browser window.

Solution
```
<script>
   var a = 600;
   var b = 325;
   document.write (a - b);
</script>
```

Result in browser window:

275

5.21 Step 1: Declare a variable called **endMileage** and set it equal to 55100.
          Step 2: Declare a variable called **startMileage** and set it equal to 52800.
          Step 3: Declare a variable called **milesTraveled** and set it equal to **endMileage - startMileage**.
          Step 4: Display the value of **milesTraveled** in an alert box.

Solution
```
<script>
   var endMileage = 55100;
   var startMileage = 52800
   var milesTraveled = endMileage - startMileage;
   alert (milesTraveled);
</script>
```

Result in browser window:

2300

5.22 Step 1: Declare a variable called **totalStudents** and set it equal to 1500.

Step 2: Declare a variable called **maleStudents** and set it equal to 850.

Step 3: Declare a variable called **femaleStudents** and set it equal to **totalStudents - maleStudents**.

Step 4: Display the value of **femaleStudents** in an alert box.

Solution

```
<script>
   var totalStudents = 1500;
   var maleStudents = 850;
   var femaleStudents = totalStudents - maleStudents;
   alert (femaleStudents);
</script>
```

Result in browser window:

650

5.23 Step 1: Declare a variable called **i** and set it equal to 3.5.

Step 2: Declare a variable called **j** and set it equal to 10.25.

Step 3: Display the product of **i** times **j** in the browser window.

Solution

```
<script>
   var i = 3.5;
   var j = 10.25;
   document.write (i * j);
</script>
```

Result in browser window:

35.875

5.24 Rewrite the code from problem **5.23** so that the value displayed has 5 places to the right of the decimal.

Solution

```
<script>
   var i = 3.5;
   var j = 10.25;
   document.write ((i * j).toFixed(5));
</script>
```

Result in browser window:

35.87500

5.25 Step 1: Declare a variable called **milesPerHour** and set it equal to 3.

Step 2: Declare a variable called **hoursWalked** and set it equal to 5.

Step 3: Declare a variable called **milesWalked** and set it equal to **milesPerhour** times **hoursWalked.**

Step 4: Display the value of **milesWalked** in an alert box.

Solution

```
<script>
   var milesPerHour = 3;
   var hoursWalked =5;
   var milesWalked = milesPerHour * hoursWalked;
   alert (milesWalked);
</script>
```

Result in alert box:

15

5.26 Step 1: Declare a variable called **a** and set it equal to 600.

Step 2: Declare a variable called **b** and set it equal to 120.

Step 3: Display the result of **a** divided by **b** in the browser window.

Solution

```
<script>
   var a = 600;
   var b = 120
   document.write (a / b);
</script>
```

Result in browser window:

5

5.27 Step 1: Declare a variable called **milesPerHour** and set it equal to 60.

Step 2: Declare a variable called **milesDriven** and set it equal to 240.

Step 3: Declare a variable called **hoursDriven** and set it equal to **milesDriven** divided by **milesPerHour**

Step 4: Display the value of **hoursDriven** in the browser window.

Solution

```
<script>
   var milesPerHour = 60;
   var milesDriven = 240;
   var hoursDriven = milesDriven / milesPerHour;
```

```
    document.write (hoursDriven);
</script>
```

Result in browser window:

4

5.28 Give the answer to each of the following modulo division problems:

a) 10 % 3

b) 15 % 4

c) 21 % 3

d) 45 % 8

e) 100 % 9

f) 80 % 7

g) 14 % 3

h) 500 % 110

i) 17 % 7

j) 42 % 7

Solution

a) 1 ⟶ 10 divided by 3 is 3 with a remainder of 1

b) 3 ⟶ 15 divided by 4 is 3 with a remainder of 3

c) 0 ⟶ 21 divided by 3 is 7 with a remainder of 0

d) 5 ⟶ 45 divided by 8 is 5 with a remainder of 4

e) 1 ⟶ 100 divided by 9 is 11 with a remainder of 1

f) 3 ⟶ 80 divided by 7 is 11 with a remainder of 3

g) 2 ⟶ 14 divided by 3 is 4 with a remainder of 2

h) 60 ⟶ 500 divided by 110 is 4 with a remainder of 60

i) 3 ⟶ 17 divided by 7 is 2 with a remainder of 3

j) 0 ⟶ 42 divided by 7 is 6 with a remainder of 0

5.29 Step 1: Declare a variable called **num1** and set it equal to 24.

　　　 Step 2: Declare a variable called **num2** and set it equal to 5.

　　　 Step 3: Declare a variable called **modRemainder** and set it equal to **num1 % num2**.

　　　 Step 4: Display the product of **modRemainder** in the browser window.

Solution

```
<script>
    var num1 = 24;
    var num2 = 5;
    var modDivision = num1 % num2;
    document.write (modDivision);
</script>
```

Result in browser window:

4

5.30 Step 1: Declare a variable called **x** and set it equal to 18.

Step 2: Declare a variable called **y** and set it equal to 7.

Step 3: Display the result of **x % y** in the browser window.

Solution

```
<script>
    var x = 18;
    var y = 7;
    document.write (x % y);
</script>
```

Result in browser window:

4

5.31 What is displayed in the browser window when this code executes:

```
<script>
    var x = 12;
    x++;
    document.write (x);
</script>
```

Result in browser window:

13

5.32 What is displayed in the browser window when this code executes:

```
<script>
    var x = 12;
    ++x;
    document.write (x);
</script>
```

Result in browser window:

13

5.33 What is displayed in the browser window when this code executes:

```
<script>
  var x = 5;
  var y = x++;
  document.write (y);
</script>
```

This is a **postfix** increment (the increment operator comes **after** the variable). In this case, **y** is set equal to the value of **x** before **x** is incremented and then **x** is incremented.

Result in browser window:
5

5.34 What is displayed in the browser window when this code executes:

```
<script>
  var x = 14;
  var y = ++x;
  document.write (y);
</script>
```

This is a **prefix** increment (the increment operator comes **before** the variable). In this case, **x** is incremented and then **y** is set equal to the value of **x** after **x** has been incremented.

Result in browser window:
15

5.35 Step 1: Declare a variable called **h** and set it equal to 13.
　　　 Step 2: Declare a variable called **i** and set it equal to 4.
　　　 Step 3: Declare a variable called **j** and set it equal to h % i.
　　　 Step 4: Display the result of **h** in an alert box.

Solution
```
<script>
  var h = 13;
  var i = 4;
  var j = h % i;
  document.write (j);
</script>
```

Result in browser window:
1

5.36 Step 1: Declare a variable called **a** and set it equal to 25.
　　　 Step 2: Declare a variable called **b** and set it equal to ++a.
　　　 Step 3: Display the value of **a** in the browser window.
　　　 Step 4: go to a new line
　　　 Step 5: Display the value of **b** in the browser window.

Solution

```
<script>
    var a = 25;
    var b = ++a;
    document.write (a);
    document.write ("<br>");
    document.write (b);
</script>
```

Result in browser window:

26
26

5.37 Step 1: Declare a variable called **x** and set it equal to 31.

Step 2: Declare a variable called **y** and set it equal to **x++**.

Step 3: Display the value of **x** in the browser window as follows: **x = <value of x>**.

Step 4: New line

Step 5: Display the value of **y** in the browser window as follows: **y = <value of y>**.

Solution

```
<script>
    var x = 31;
    var y = x++;
    document.write ("x = " + x);
    document.write ("<br>");
    document.write ("y = " + y);
</script>
```

Result in browser window:

x = 32
y = 31

5.38 What is displayed in the browser window when this code executes:

```
<script>
    var num1 = 19;
    num1--;
    document.write (num1);
</script>
```

Result in browser window:

18

5.39 What is displayed in the browser window when this code executes:

```
<script>
   var a = 47;
   --a
   document.write (a);
</script>
```

Result in browser window:

46

5.40 What is displayed in the browser window when this code executes:

```
<script>
   var i = 20;
   var j = i--;
   document.write (j);
</script>
```

This is a **postfix** decrement (the decrement operator comes **after** the variable). In this case, **j** is set equal to the value of **i** before **i** is decremented and then **i** is decremented.

Result in browser window:

20

5.41 What is displayed in the browser window when this code executes:

```
<script>
   var x = 38;
   var y = --x;
   document.write (y);
</script>
```

This is a **prefix** decrement (the decrement operator comes **before** the variable). In this case, **x** is decremented and then **y** is set equal to the value of **x** after **x** has been decremented.

Result in browser window:

37

5.41 Step 1: Declare a variable called **a** and set it equal to 55.
        Step 2: Declare a variable called **b** and set it equal to --**a**.
        Step 3: Display the value of **a** in the browser window.
        Step 4: go to a new line
        Step 5: Display the value of **b** in the browser window.

Solution

```
<script>
   var a = 55;
   var b = --a;
   document.write (a);
   document.write ("<br>");
   document.write (b);
```

</script>

Result in browser window:

54
54

4.42 Step 1: Declare a variable called **x** and set it equal to 16.

Step 2: Declare a variable called **y** and set it equal to **x--**.

Step 3: Display the value of **x** in the browser window as follows: **x = \<value of x>**.

Step 4: New line

Step 5: Display the value of **y** in the browser window as follows: **y = \<value of y>**.

Solution

```
<script>
   var x = 31;
   var y = x--;
   document.write ("x = " + x);
   document.write ("<br>");
   document.write ("y = " + y);
</script>
```

Result in browser window:

x = 30
y = 31

Chapter 6

JavaScript Operators: Part 2

6.1 JAVASCRIPT ASSIGNMENT OPERATORS

Assignment operators are used to assign values to JavaScript variables. An assignment operator assigns a value to its left operand based on the value of its right operand. The simple assignment operator is equal (=), which assigns the value of its right operand to its left operand. That is, x = y assigns the value of y to x.

The other assignment operators are usually shorthand for standard operations, as shown in the following definitions and examples.

The following is a list of the major JavaScript assignment operators:

- Simple assignment
- Add and assignment
- Subtract and assignment
- Multiply and assignment
- Divide and assignment
- Modulus and assignment

6.1.1 Simple assignment operator (=)

The **simple assignment operator** assigns values from the right side operand to the left side operand. The basic assignment operator is equal (=), which assigns the value of its right operand to its left operand. That is, x = y assigns the value of y to x. For example:

```
var a = 3;         // assign the value 3 to a
var b = 75;        // assign the value 75 to b
var c = b + 32;    // assign the value b + 32 to c
```

Syntax

Operator: =

The following examples show the assignment operator in action:

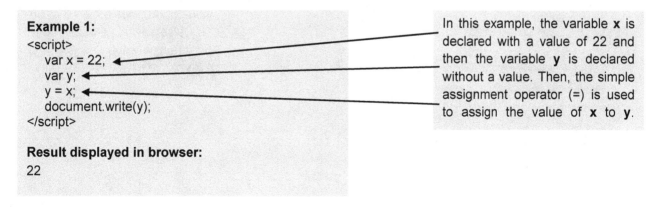

Example 1:
```
<script>
  var x = 22;
  var y;
  y = x;
  document.write(y);
</script>
```

In this example, the variable **x** is declared with a value of 22 and then the variable **y** is declared without a value. Then, the simple assignment operator (=) is used to assign the value of **x** to **y**.

Result displayed in browser:

22

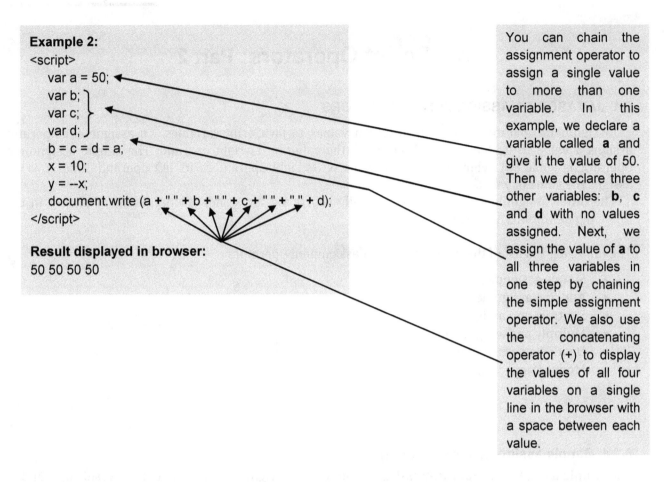

Example 2:
```
<script>
    var a = 50;
    var b;
    var c;
    var d;
    b = c = d = a;
    x = 10;
    y = --x;
    document.write (a + " " + b + " " + c + " " + " " + d);
</script>
```

Result displayed in browser:
50 50 50 50

You can chain the assignment operator to assign a single value to more than one variable. In this example, we declare a variable called **a** and give it the value of 50. Then we declare three other variables: **b**, **c** and **d** with no values assigned. Next, we assign the value of **a** to all three variables in one step by chaining the simple assignment operator. We also use the concatenating operator (+) to display the values of all four variables on a single line in the browser with a space between each value.

6.1.2 Add and assignment operator (+ =)

Adds the right operand to the left operand and assigns the result to the left operand. Using this operator is exactly the same as specifying: **result = result + expression**.

Syntax

Operator: +=

The following examples show the **add and assignment** operator in action:

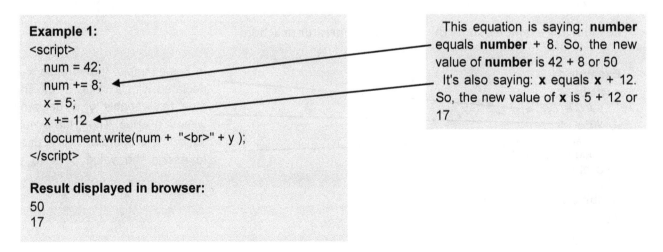

Example 1:
```
<script>
    num = 42;
    num += 8;
    x = 5;
    x += 12
    document.write(num +  "<br>" + y );
</script>
```

Result displayed in browser:

50
17

This equation is saying: **number** equals **number** + 8. So, the new value of **number** is 42 + 8 or 50
It's also saying: **x** equals **x** + 12. So, the new value of **x** is 5 + 12 or 17

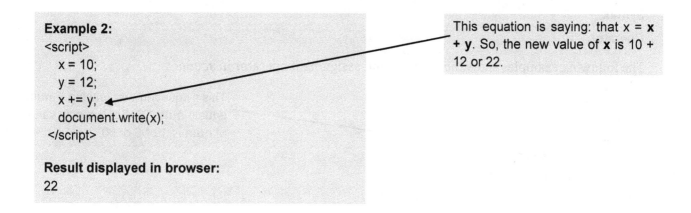

Example 2:
```
<script>
   x = 10;
   y = 12;
   x += y;
   document.write(x);
</script>
```

Result displayed in browser:
22

This equation is saying: that x = **x** **+ y**. So, the new value of **x** is 10 + 12 or 22.

6.1.3 Subtract and assignment operator (- =)

Subtracts the right operand to the left operand and assigns the result to the left operand.

Syntax

Operator: -=

The following examples show the subtract and assignment operator in action:

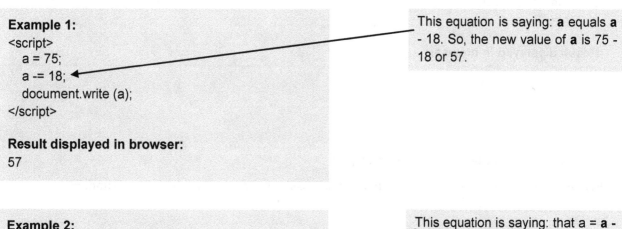

Example 1:
```
<script>
   a = 75;
   a -= 18;
   document.write (a);
</script>
```

Result displayed in browser:
57

This equation is saying: **a** equals **a** - 18. So, the new value of **a** is 75 - 18 or 57.

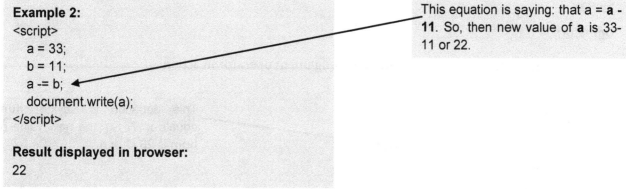

Example 2:
```
<script>
   a = 33;
   b = 11;
   a -= b;
   document.write(a);
</script>
```

Result displayed in browser:
22

This equation is saying: that a = **a** - **11**. So, then new value of **a** is 33-11 or 22.

6.1.4 Multiply and assignment operator (* =)

Multiplies the right operand by the left operand and assigns the result to the left operand.

Syntax

Operator: *=

The following examples show the multiply and assignment operator in action:

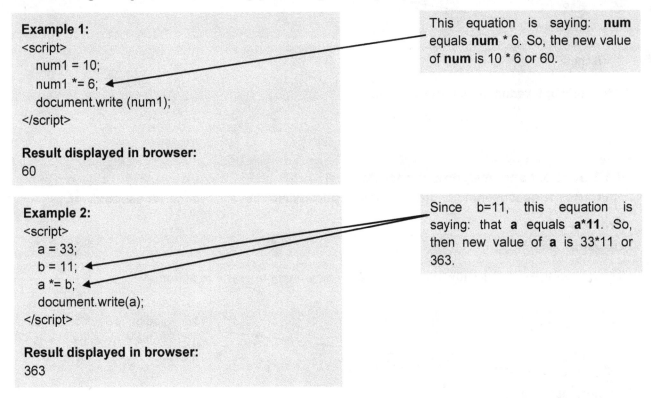

Example 1:
```
<script>
   num1 = 10;
   num1 *= 6;
   document.write (num1);
</script>
```

Result displayed in browser:
60

This equation is saying: **num** equals **num** * 6. So, the new value of **num** is 10 * 6 or 60.

Example 2:
```
<script>
   a = 33;
   b = 11;
   a *= b;
   document.write(a);
</script>
```

Result displayed in browser:
363

Since b=11, this equation is saying: that **a** equals **a*11**. So, then new value of **a** is 33*11 or 363.

6.1.5 Divide and assignment operator (/=)

Divides the right operand by the left operand and assigns the result to the left operand.

Syntax

Operator: /=

The following examples show the divide and assignment operator in action:

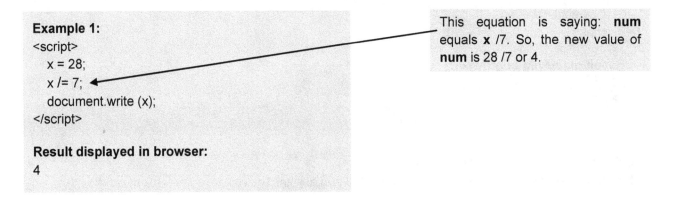

Example 1:
```
<script>
   x = 28;
   x /= 7;
   document.write (x);
</script>
```

Result displayed in browser:
4

This equation is saying: **num** equals **x** /7. So, the new value of **num** is 28 /7 or 4.

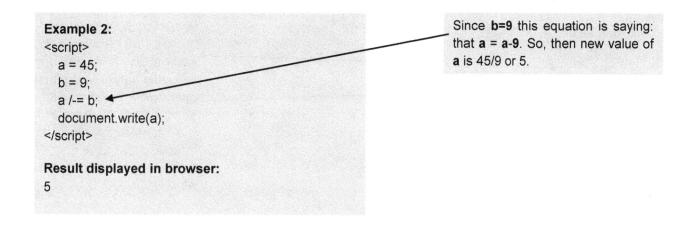

Example 2:
```
<script>
    a = 45;
    b = 9;
    a /-= b;
    document.write(a);
</script>
```

Result displayed in browser:
5

Since **b=9** this equation is saying: that **a** = **a-9**. So, then new value of **a** is 45/9 or 5.

6.1.6 Modulus and assignment operator (%=)

Takes modulus using two operands and assigns the result to the left operand.

Syntax

Operator: %=

The following examples show the modulus and assignment operator in action:

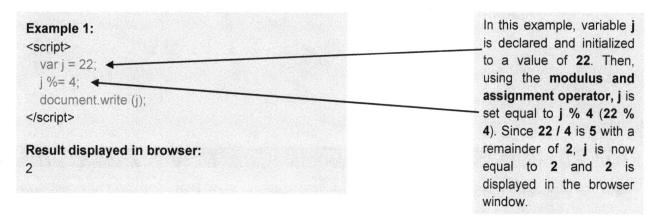

Example 1:
```
<script>
    var j = 22;
    j %= 4;
    document.write (j);
</script>
```

Result displayed in browser:
2

In this example, variable **j** is declared and initialized to a value of **22**. Then, using the **modulus and assignment operator, j** is set equal to **j % 4** (**22 % 4**). Since **22 / 4** is **5** with a remainder of **2**, **j** is now equal to **2** and **2** is displayed in the browser window.

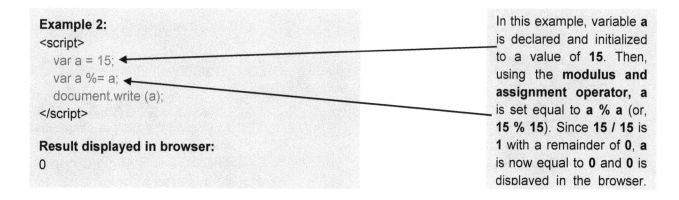

Example 2:
```
<script>
    var a = 15;
    var a %= a;
    document.write (a);
</script>
```

Result displayed in browser:
0

In this example, variable **a** is declared and initialized to a value of **15**. Then, using the **modulus and assignment operator, a** is set equal to **a % a** (or, **15 % 15**). Since **15 / 15** is **1** with a remainder of **0**, **a** is now equal to **0** and **0** is displayed in the browser.

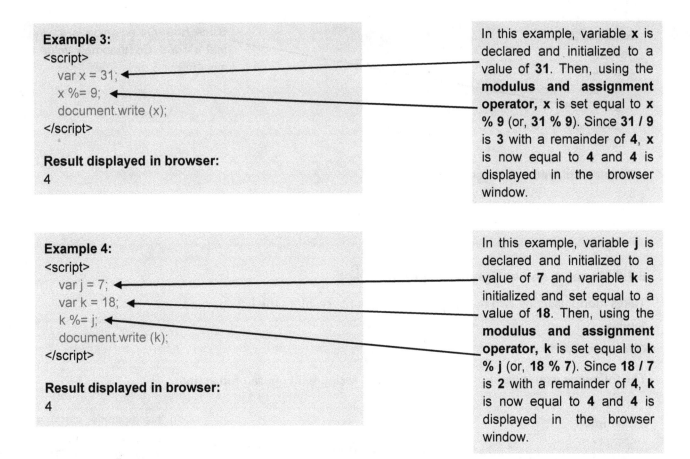

Example 3:
```
<script>
    var x = 31;
    x %= 9;
    document.write (x);
</script>
```

Result displayed in browser:
4

In this example, variable **x** is declared and initialized to a value of **31**. Then, using the **modulus and assignment operator, x** is set equal to **x % 9** (or, **31 % 9**). Since **31 / 9** is **3** with a remainder of **4**, **x** is now equal to **4** and **4** is displayed in the browser window.

Example 4:
```
<script>
    var j = 7;
    var k = 18;
    k %= j;
    document.write (k);
</script>
```

Result displayed in browser:
4

In this example, variable **j** is declared and initialized to a value of **7** and variable **k** is initialized and set equal to a value of **18**. Then, using the **modulus and assignment operator, k** is set equal to **k % j** (or, **18 % 7**). Since **18 / 7** is **2** with a remainder of **4**, **k** is now equal to **4** and **4** is displayed in the browser window.

SOLVED PROBLEMS

Give the value of **x** that's displayed in the browser window in each of the following code snippets in problems 4.43 - 4.71 (assume that each snippet is preceded by <script> and followed by </script>):

6.1
```
var x = 35;
    document.write (x);
```

Value of x displayed in browser:
35

Since **x** is assigned the numeric value of **35** using the **simple assignment operator** (=), **35** is displayed in the browser window.

6.2
```
var a = 15;
    var x = a;
    document.write (x);
```

Value of x displayed in browser:
15

Variable **a** is given the value **15** and then, using the **simple assignment operator** (=), **x** is set equal to **a**, so, **x**'s final value is **15**. **15** is displayed in the browser window.

6.3
```
var y = 12;
var z = 18;
var x = y + z;
document.write (x);
```

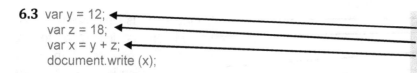

Variable **y** is assigned the value **12** and **z** is assigned the value **18**. **x** is then assigned the value of **y + z** using the **simple assignment operator** (=). This sets **x** equal to **30** which is displayed in the browser window.

Value of x displayed in browser:
30

6.4
```
var x = 15;
var x += 20;
document.write (x);
```

The Variable **y** is assigned the value **12** and **z** is assigned the value **18**. **x** is then assigned the value of **y + z** using the **simple assignment operator** (=). This sets **x** equal to **30** which is displayed in the browser window

Value of x in browser:
35

6.5
```
var x = 42;
var x += x;
document.write (x);
```

The value of **x** is initially set to **42**. In the next step **x** is set equal to **x + x** using the **add and assignment operator** (+=). The final value of **x** is **42 + 42**, or **84**, which is displayed in the browser window.

Value of x displayed in browser:
84

6.6
```
var x = 10;
x += 15;
x += 12;
document.write (x);
```

Variable **x** is initially assigned the value **10**. Next, using the **add and assignment operator**, **x** is set equal to **x + 15** which is **25**. Next, using **the add and assignment operator** once again, **x**, which at this point equals **25**, is set equal to **x + 12**, or **25 + 12**, which is **37**. This is the value of **x** that is displayed in the browser window.

Value of x displayed in browser:
37

6.7
```
var y = 20;
var x = 10
x += y;
document.write (x);
```

Variable **y** is assigned the value **20** and **x** is assigned the value **10**. Then, using the **add and assignment operator**, **x** is set equal to **x + y**, which is **10 + 20**. So, **30** is the value for **x** that's displayed in the browser window.

Value of x displayed in browser:
30

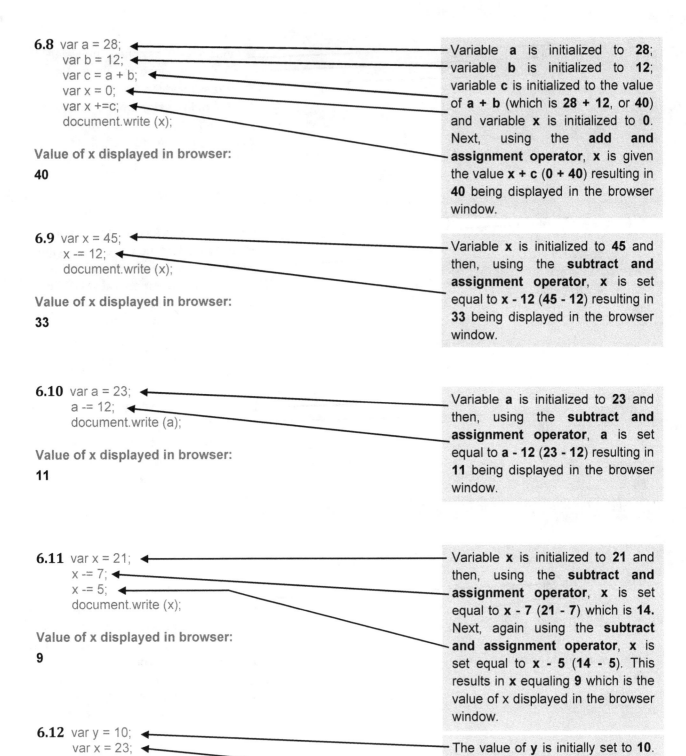

6.8   var a = 28;
      var b = 12;
      var c = a + b;
      var x = 0;
      var x +=c;
      document.write (x);

Value of x displayed in browser:
40

Variable **a** is initialized to **28**; variable **b** is initialized to **12**; variable **c** is initialized to the value of **a + b** (which is **28 + 12**, or **40**) and variable **x** is initialized to **0**. Next, using the **add and assignment operator**, **x** is given the value **x + c** (**0 + 40**) resulting in **40** being displayed in the browser window.

6.9   var x = 45;
      x -= 12;
      document.write (x);

Value of x displayed in browser:
33

Variable **x** is initialized to **45** and then, using the **subtract and assignment operator**, **x** is set equal to **x - 12** (**45 - 12**) resulting in **33** being displayed in the browser window.

6.10   var a = 23;
      a -= 12;
      document.write (a);

Value of x displayed in browser:
11

Variable **a** is initialized to **23** and then, using the **subtract and assignment operator**, **a** is set equal to **a - 12** (**23 - 12**) resulting in **11** being displayed in the browser window.

6.11   var x = 21;
      x -= 7;
      x -= 5;
      document.write (x);

Value of x displayed in browser:
9

Variable **x** is initialized to **21** and then, using the **subtract and assignment operator**, **x** is set equal to **x - 7** (**21 - 7**) which is **14.** Next, again using the **subtract and assignment operator**, **x** is set equal to **x - 5** (**14 - 5**). This results in **x** equaling **9** which is the value of x displayed in the browser window.

6.12   var y = 10;
      var x = 23;
      x -= y;
      document.write (x);

Value of x in browser:
13

The value of **y** is initially set to **10**. In the next step, **x** is declared and set equal to **23**. Next, using the **subtract and assignment operator**, **x** is set equal to **x - y** (**23 - 10**) which results in giving **x** a value of **13**, which is displayed in the browser.

6.13 var i = 6;
      var j = 7;
      var k = i + j;
      var x = 38;
      x -= k;
      document.write (x);

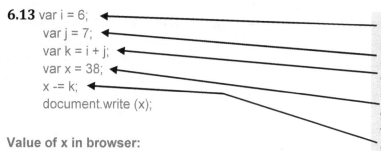

First of all, variable **i** is declared and initialized to a value of **6**. Next **j** is declared and initialized to a value of **7**. Then **k** is declared and set to the value of **i + j** (6 + 7 = 13). Next variable **x** is declared and given an initial value of **38**. Next **x**, using the **subtract and assignment operator**, is set equal to **x - k** (38 - 13 = 25). The resulting value of **x** is **25** which is written to the browser window.

Value of x in browser:
25

6.14 var x = 32;
      x *= 3;
      document.write (x);

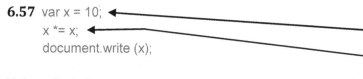

x is declared and initialized to a value of **32**. Next, using the **multiply and assignment operator**, **x** is set to **x * 3** which is **96**. **96** is then displayed in the browser window as the final value of **x**.

Value of x in browser:
96

6.57 var x = 10;
      x *= x;
      document.write (x);

x is declared and initialized to a value of **10**. Next, using the **multiply and assignment operator**, **x** is set to **x * x** which is **100**. **100** is then displayed in the browser window as the final value of **x**.

Value of x in browser:
100

6.15 var x = 5;
      x *= 3;
      x *= 4;
      document.write (x);

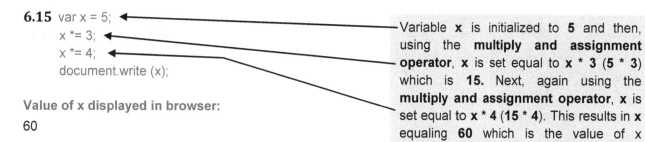

Variable **x** is initialized to **5** and then, using the **multiply and assignment operator**, **x** is set equal to **x * 3** (5 * 3) which is **15**. Next, again using the **multiply and assignment operator**, **x** is set equal to **x * 4** (15 * 4). This results in **x** equaling **60** which is the value of x displayed the browser.window.

Value of x displayed in browser:
60

6.16 var y = 3;
      var x = 8;
      x *= y;
      document.write (x);

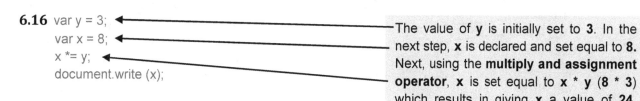

The value of **y** is initially set to **3**. In the next step, **x** is declared and set equal to **8.** Next, using the **multiply and assignment operator**, **x** is set equal to **x * y** (8 * 3) which results in giving **x** a value of **24**, which is displayed in the browser window.

Value of x in browser:
24

6.17 var a = 2;
      var b = 4;
      var c = a + b;
      var x = 7;
      x* = c;
      document.write (x);

Value of x in browser:
42

The value of **a** is initially set to **2**. In the next step, **b** is declared and set equal to **4**. Next, variable **c** is declared and initialized to a value of **a + b**. Next, **x** is declared and initialized to a value of **7**. After that, the **multiply and assignment** operator is used to set **x** equal to **x** **x * c** (**7 * 6**). The value of **x**, which is now **42**, is then written to the browser window.

6.18 var x = 9;
      x /= 3
      document.write (x);

Value of x in browser:
3

x is initialized with a value of **9**. Then, using the **divide and assignment operator**, **x** is set equal to **x / 3** (**9 / 3**). This results in assigning a value of **3** to **x** which is displayed in the browser window.

6.19 var x = 15;
      x /= x
      document.write (x);

Value of x in browser:
1

x is initialized with a value of **15**. Then, using the **divide and assignment operator**, **x** is set equal to **x / x** (**15 / 15**). This results in assigning a value of **1** to **x** which is displayed in the browser window.

6.20 var x = 60;
      x /= 5;
      x /= 3;
      document.write (x);

Value of x displayed in browser:
4

Variable **x** is initialized to **60** and then, using the **divide and assignment operator**, **x** is set equal to **x / 5** (**60 / 5**) which is **12**. Next, again using the **subtract and assignment operator**, **x** is set equal to **x / 3** (**12 / 3**). This results in **x** equaling **4** which is the value of **x** displayed the browser window.

6.21 var y = 2;
      x = 10;
      x /= y;
      document.write (x);

Value of x in browser:
5

y is declared and initialized to a value of **2**. Next, **x** is declared and initialized to a value of **10**. Next, using the **divide and assignment operator**, **x** is set to **x /= x** which is **5**. **5** is then displayed in the browser window as the final value of **x**.

6.22
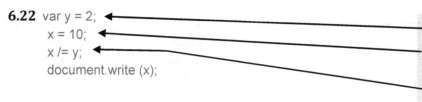
```
var y = 2;
x = 10;
x /= y;
document.write (x);
```

Value of x in browser:
5

y is declared and initialized to a value of **2**. Next, **x** is declared and initialized to a value of **10**. Next, using the **divide and assignment operator**, **x** is set to **x /= x** which is **5**. **5** is then displayed in the browser window as the final value of **x**.

6.23
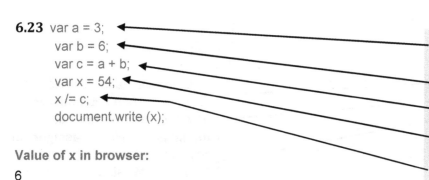
```
var a = 3;
var b = 6;
var c = a + b;
var x = 54;
x /= c;
document.write (x);
```

Value of x in browser:
6

First, variable **a** is declared and initialized to a value of **3**. Next, **b** is declared and initialized to a value of **6**. Then, **c** is declared and initialized to a value of **a + b**. Next, **x** is declared and set to an initial value of **54**. Then, using the **divide and assignment operator**, **x** is set to **x / c** (**54 / 9**) which results in a value of **6** for **x**.. **6** is then displayed in the browser window as the final value of **x**.

6.24
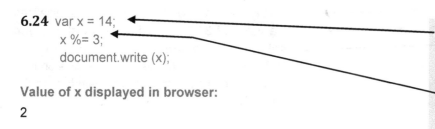
```
var x = 14;
x %= 3;
document.write (x);
```

Value of x displayed in browser:
2

Variable **x** is declared and initialized to a value of **14**. Then, using the **modulus and assignment operator**, **x** is set equal to **x % 3** (**14 % 3**). Since **14 / 3** is **4** with a remainder of **2**, **x** is now equal to **2** and 2 is displayed in the browser window.

6.25
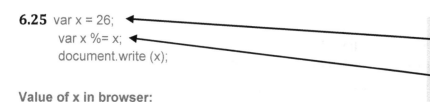
```
var x = 26;
var x %= x;
document.write (x);
```

Value of x in browser:
0

x is declared and initialized to a value of **26**. Next, using the **modulus and assignment operator**, **x** is set to **x %= x** (**26 % 26**) which is **0**. **0** is then displayed in the browser window as the final value of **x**.

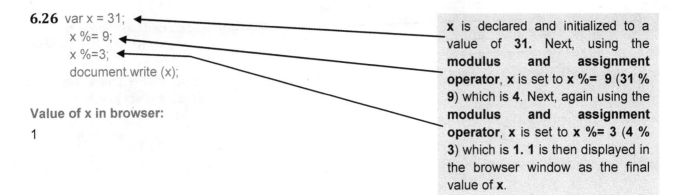

6.26 var x = 31;
        x %= 9;
        x %=3;
        document.write (x);

Value of x in browser:

1

x is declared and initialized to a value of **31**. Next, using the **modulus and assignment operator**, x is set to **x %= 9** (**31 % 9**) which is **4**. Next, again using the **modulus and assignment operator**, x is set to **x %= 3** (4 % 3) which is **1**. **1** is then displayed in the browser window as the final value of **x**.

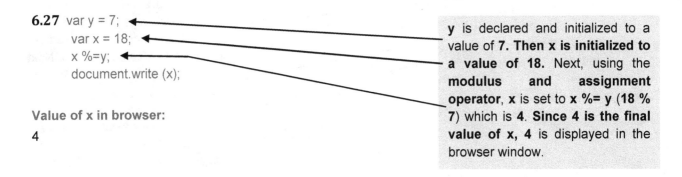

6.27 var y = 7;
        var x = 18;
        x %=y;
        document.write (x);

Value of x in browser:

4

y is declared and initialized to a value of **7**. **Then x is initialized to a value of 18**. Next, using the **modulus and assignment operator**, x is set to **x %= y** (**18 % 7**) which is **4**. **Since 4 is the final value of x, 4** is displayed in the browser window.

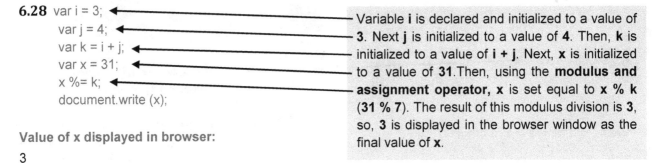

6.28 var i = 3;
        var j = 4;
        var k = i + j;
        var x = 31;
        x %= k;
        document.write (x);

Value of x displayed in browser:

3

Variable **i** is declared and initialized to a value of **3**. Next **j** is initialized to a value of **4**. Then, **k** is initialized to a value of **i + j**. Next, **x** is initialized to a value of **31**. Then, using the **modulus and assignment operator, x** is set equal to **x % k** (**31 % 7**). The result of this modulus division is **3**, so, **3** is displayed in the browser window as the final value of **x**.

6.1.7 Arithmetic operator precedence

The order in which operators are evaluated in an arithmetic expression is referred to as **operator precedence**. Take a look at the following arithmetic equation:

var x = 200 + 75 * 2:

Just as in algebra, multiplication and division have higher **precedence** than addition and subraction. Also, as in algebra, the precedence can be changed by using parentheses:

var x = (200 + 75) * 2:

Look at the following simple arithmetic equations and how operator precedence decides the order in which the calculations are performed:

5 + 8 + 2 * 2

Because multiplication has higher operator precedence than addition, the multiplication is performed first, That makes this equation equivalent to:

5 + 8 + (2 * 2)   **step 1**   Perform the multiplication operation first.
              4

(5 + 8) + 4   **step 2**   Because all of the remaining operators have equal precedence, start executing the operators from left to right.
    13

(13 + 4)   **step 3**   Make the final left to right calculation.

    17   **result = 17**

If we had performed the calculations from left to right, without taking operator precedence into consideration, the result would have been different:

(5 + 8) + 2 * 2   **step 1**   Perform the first left to right calculation.
    13

(13 + 2) * 2   **step 2**   Perform the next left to right calculation
    15

(15 * 2)   **step 3**   Perform the final left to right calculation.
    30   **result = 30**

Parentheses are used to alter the order of evaluation determined by operator precedence. This means an expression within parentheses is fully evaluated before its value is used in the remainder of the expression.

Example:
6 * 5 + 3 + 8 + 2

In this example, the first step is to multiply **6 * 5** (because multiplication has higher operator precedence than addition) and then perform the rest of the calculations from left to right. The result is 30 + 3 + 8 + 2 = **43**.

Example:
6 * (5 + 3) + 8 + 2

In this example, the first step is to evaluate the expression within the parentheses (**5 + 3**) and replace it with **8** in the equation. After this first step, the equation becomes:
      6 * 8 + 8 + 2
The next step is to multiply **6 * 8** (because multiplication has higher operator precedence than addition). Now the equation becomes:
      48 + 8 + 2
The next step is to add **48 + 8**. Now the equation becomes:.
      56 + 2
The final step is to add **56 + 2** with the result being **58**. This is a different result from what we calculated in the above example where no parentheses were used.

The following table shows JavaScript arithmetic operators from highest to lowest precedence:

Operator	Precedence
( )	Expression grouping
* / %	Multiplication, division and modulo division
+ -	Addition and subtraction

The evaluation of expressions is also influenced by the operator **associativity**. Associativity refers to the direction (usually left to right) in which entire expression is evaluated. Arithmetic operators with the same level of precedence are always evaluated from left to right. Consider the following equation and in what order it should be evaluated:

```
var x = 7 + 5 - 3 + 25 - 9 - 17:
```

All of the operators in the above equation have the same precedence so the equation is evaluated from left to right. Consider another equation:

```
var x = 7 * 5 - 3 / 25 - 9 - 17:
```

In this example, we have different levels of operator precedence with *, /, + and - operators mixed together. In this case, the numbers connected by higher precedence operators have to be grouped together and evaluated first, so, the equation becomes equivalent to:

```
var x = (7 * 5) - (3 / 25) - 9 - 17:
```

So far, we've seen that operator precedence describes the order in which operations are performed when an expression is evaluated. Operations with a higher precedence are performed before those with a lower precedence. For example, multiplication or division is performed before addition or subtraction. Parentheses are used to alter the order of evaluation determined by operator precedence. This means an expression within parentheses is fully evaluated before its value is used in the remainder of the expression.

Examples of evaluating equations using operator precedence:

```
var x = 25 - 8 + 14 * 3 + 8 / 2 - 6;
        = 25 - 8 + (14 * 3) + (8 / 2) - 6
        = 25 - 8 + 42 + 4 - 6
        = 57
```

```
var x = 3 * 8 - 12 + 20 + 9 / 3 - 6;
        = (3 * 8) - 12 + 20 + (9 / 3) - 6
        = 24 -12 + 20 + 3 - 6
        = 29
```

var x = 2 * 4 * 3 - 7 - 2 + 5;

= (2 * 4) * 3 - 7 - 2 + 5
= (8 * 3) - 7 - 2 + 5
= 24 - 7 - 2 + 5
= 20

var x = 8 * 5 + 7 - 4 + 3 * 2;

= (8 * 5) + 7 - 4 + 3 * 2
= 40 + 7 - 4 + (3 * 2)
= 40 + 7 - 4 + 6
= 49

var x = (4 + 3) * 6 - 1 - 2 * 4;

= (7 * 6) - 1 - (2 * 4)
= 42 - 1 - (2 * 4)
= 42 - 1 - 8
= 33

var x = 15 - 8 + 3 * 4 / 4 + 10;

= 15 - 8 + (3 * 4) / 4 + 10
= 15 - 8 + (12 / 4) + 10
= 15 - 8 + 3 + 10
= 20

var x = 4 * 3 / 4 * 6 * 5;

= (4 * 3) / 4 * 6 * 5
= (12 / 4) * 6 * 5
= (3 * 6) * 5
= (18 * 5)
= 90

var (15 - 8) * 4 - (3 + 7) / 5;

= (7 * 4) - (3 + 7) / 5
= 28 - (3 + 7) / 5
= 28 - (10 / 5)
= 26

SOLVED PROBLEMS

Calculate the final value of **x** in problems 4.71-4.80 after operational precedence rules have been applied to the equations.

6.29 var x = 4 + 7 + 2 * 3;

Solution

Step 1: 4 + 7 + (2 * 3);   - group and evaluate the operators with the highest precedence

                    6

Step 2: 4 + 7 + 6   - calculate equal precedence level operators from left to right
Step 3: 17   - final result

Result:

x = 17

6.30 var x = 3 * 8 + 3 + 6 -2;

Solution

Step 1: (3 * 8) + 3 + 6 - 2   - group and evaluate the operators with the highest precedence

            24

Step 2: 24 + 3 + 6 - 2   - calculate equal precedence level operators from left to right
Step 3: 31   - final result

Result:

x = 31

6.31 var x = 6 + 4 - 2 + 13 - 10;

Solution

Step 1: 6 + 4 - 2 + 13 - 10   - calculate equal precedence level operators from left to right
Step 2: 17   - final result

Result:

x = 11

6.32 var x = 12 / 2 - 6 / 3 + 8;

Solution

Step 1: (12 / 2) - (6 / 3) + 8   - group and evaluate the operators with the highest precedence

            6   2

Step 2: 6 - 2 + 8   - calculate equal precedence level operators from left to right
Step 3: 11   - final result

Result:

x = 12

6.33 var x = 13 - 3 + 12 * 2 + 16 / 4 - 2;

Solution

Step 1: 13 - 3 + (12 * 2) + (16 / 4) - 2   - group and evaluate the operators with the highest precedence

                        24   4

Step 2: 13 - 3 + 24 + 4 - 2   - calculate equal precedence level operators from left to right
Step 3: 36   - final result

Result:

x = 36

6.34 var x = 4 * 4 - 9 + 16 + 10 / 5 - 3;

Solution

Step 1: (4 * 4) - 9 + 16 + (10 / 5) - 3   - group and evaluate the operators with the highest precedence

              16   2

Step 2: 16 - 9 + 16 + 2 - 3   - calculate equal precedence level operators from left to right
Step 3: 22   - final result

Result:

x = 22

6.35 var x = 4 * 2 * 5 - 3 - 4 + 8;

Solution

Step 1: (4 * 2 * 5) - 3 - 4 + 8   - group and evaluate the operators with the highest precedence

                  40

Step 2: 40 - 3 - 4 + 8   - calculate equal precedence level operators from left to right
Step 3: 41   - final result

Result:

x = 41

6.36 var x = 12 / 3 / 2 + (6 - 3) * 3;

Solution

Step 1: (12 / 3 / 2) + (6 - 3) * 3   - group and evaluate the operators with the highest precedence

                2   3

Step 2: 2 + (3 * 3)   - group and evaluate the operators with the highest precedence

                  9

Step 3 2 + 9   - calculate equal precedence level operators from left to right
Step 4: 11   - final result

Result:

x = 11

6.37 var x = (5 + 4) * 8 - 4 - 3 * 6;

Solution

Step 1: (5 + 4) * 8 - 4 - (3 * 6)   - group and evaluate the operators with the highest precedence
              9   18
Step 2: (9 * 8) - 4 - 18   - group and evaluate the operators with the highest precedence
              72
Step 3   72 - 4 - 18   - calculate equal precedence level operators from left to right
Step 4: 50   - final result

Result:

x = 11

6.38 var x = (3 + 6) * 4 - (10 - 2) * 4;

Solution

Step 1: (3 + 6) * 4 - (10 - 2) * 4   - group and evaluate the operators with the highest precedence
              9   8
Step 2: (9 * 4) - (8 * 4)   - group and evaluate the operators with the highest precedence
              36   32
Step 3   36 - 32   - calculate equal precedence level operators from left to right
Step 4: 4   - final result

Result:

x = 4

6.2 JAVASCRIPT STRING OPERATORS

The most common operation performed with strings is **concatenation**. Concatenation is the process of combining and putting together two strings into one longer string. Along with serving as the arithmetic addition operator, the + operator can also be used to concatenate (combine) strings. When the + sign is used on strings, the + operator is called the **concatenation** operator. The concatenation operator (+) concatenates two or more string values together and return another string which is the union of the two operand strings. For example, considering the following 2 examples:

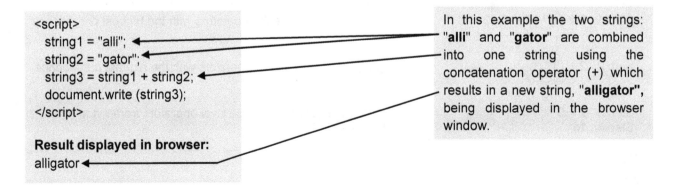

```
<script>
    string1 = "alli";
    string2 = "gator";
    string3 = string1 + string2;
    document.write (string3);
</script>

Result displayed in browser:
alligator
```

In this example the two strings: **"alli"** and **"gator"** are combined into one string using the concatenation operator (+) which results in a new string, **"alligator"**, being displayed in the browser window.

```
<script>
  string1 = "Hello";
  string2 = "World!";
  string3 = string1 + " " + string2;
  document.write (string3);
</script>
```

Result displayed in browser:
Hello World!

The shorthand assignment operator **+=** can also be used to concatenate strings as in the following example:

```
<script>
  string1 = "Hello ";
  string2 = "World!";
  string1 += string2;
  document.write (string1);
</script>
```

Result displayed in browser:
Hello World!

SOLVED PROBLEMS

6.39 Display the message "**What's up doc?**" in the browser window by concatenating three string variables: **x**, **y** and **z**. Put one of the three words in each string and then concatenate them together and then display the results in the browser window. There should be a space between each word.

Solution
```
<script>
  var x = "What's";
  var y = "up,";
  var z = "Doc?";
  document.write(x + " " + y + " " + z);
</script>
```

Result displayed in browser:
What's up, Doc?

6.40 Display the message "**Welcome to Florida**" in the browser window by concatenating three string variables: **str1**, **str2** and **str3**. Put one of the three words in each string and then concatenate them together and assign the result to a variable called **message.** There should be a space between each word. Display the resulting value of **message** in the browser window.

Solution

```
<script>
   var str1 = "Welcome";
   var str2 = "To";
   var str3 = "Florida!";
   var message = str1 + " " + str2 + " " + str3;
   document.write (message);
</script>
```

Result displayed in browser:

Welcome to Florida!

Chapter 7

JavaScript Operators: Part 3

7.1 JAVASCRIPT COMPARISON OPERATORS

We have already considered JavaScript comparison operators briefly in chapter 1 but now we're going to cover them in more depth. A comparison operator compares its operands and returns a logical/Boolean value (true or false) based on whether the comparison is true or false. The operands can be numerical, string, logical, or object values. Strings are compared based on standard lexicographical ordering, using Unicode values. In most cases, if the two operands are not of the same type, JavaScript attempts to convert them to an appropriate type for the comparison. This behavior generally results in comparing the operands numerically. The sole exceptions to type conversion within comparisons involve the === and !== operators, which perform strict equality and inequality comparisons. These operators do not attempt to convert the operands to compatible types before checking equality. The following is a list of the major JavaScript arithmetic operators:

- Equal
- Not equal
- Strict equal
- Strict not equal
- Greater than
- Greater than or equal to
- Less than
- Less than or equal to

Table of Comparison operators:

Operator	Name	Description
==	Equal	Checks if the value of two operands are equal or not, if yes, then the condition becomes true.
!=	Not Equal	Checks if the value of two operands are equal or not, if the values are not equal, then the condition becomes true.
===	Strict Equal	Checks if the value and data type of the left operand is the same as the value and data type of the right operand, if yes, then the condition becomes true.
!==	Strict Not Equal	Checks if the value and/or data type of the left operand is a different value and/or data type than the right operand. If, yes, then he condition becomes true.
>	Greater Than	Checks if the value of the left operand is greater than the value of the right operand, if yes, then the condition becomes true.
>=	Greater Than or Equal To	Checks if the value of the left operand is greater than or equal to the value of the right operand, if yes, then the condition becomes true.
<	Less Than	Checks if the value of the left operand is less than the value of the right operand, if yes, then the condition becomes true.
<=	Less Than or Equal To	Checks if the value of the left operand is less than or equal to the value of the right operand, if yes, then the condition becomes true.

7.1.1 Equal (==)

Returns true if the operands are equal.

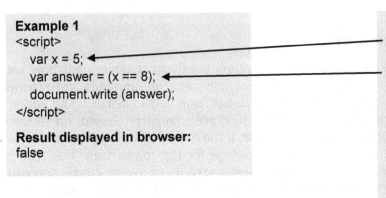

Example 1
```
<script>
   var x = 5;
   var answer = (x == 8);
   document.write (answer);
</script>
```

Result displayed in browser:
false

In this example, the variable **x** is given the initial value of **5** and then the variable **answer** is set equal to the result of the comparison: **x == 8**. This comparison is asking the question: "Does **x** equal **8**?" or "Does **5** equal **8**?". Any comparison will return one of two values: **true** or **false**. Because the actual value of **x**, at this point, is **5** the result of the comparison is **false** (5 does not equal **8**). As a result, **answer** is set to **false** and **false** being displayed in the browser window.

Example 2
```
<script>
   var y = 10;
   var z = 10;
   var answer = (y == z);
   document.write (answer);
</script>
```

Result displayed in browser:
true

In this example, the variable **y** is given the initial value of **10** and the variable **z** is given the initial value of **10**. Next, the variable **answer** is set equal to the result of the comparison: **y == z**. This comparison is asking the question: "Does **y** equal **z**?" or "Does **10** equal **10**?". Because the actual value of **y**, at this point, is **10** and the value of **z** is **10**, the result of the comparison is **true** (**10** is equal to **10**). This results in **answer** being set to **true** and **true** being displayed in the browser window.

Example 3
```
<script>
   var x = true;
   var answer = (x == 1);
   document.write(answer);
</script>
```

Result displayed in browser:
true

In this example, the variable **x** is given the initial value of **true**. Next, the variable **answer** is set equal to the result of the comparison: **x == 1**. This comparison is asking the question: "Does **x** equal **1**?". When a Boolean value (**true** or **false**) is compared with a number, the Boolean value is first converted to a number before the comparison is made. **True** is converted to **1** and **false** is converted to **0**. At this point the value of **x** is **true**, which will converted to a **1** before the comparison is made. Since **1 = 1**, the result of the comparison will be **true**. This results in **answer** being be set to **true** and **true** being displayed in the browser window.

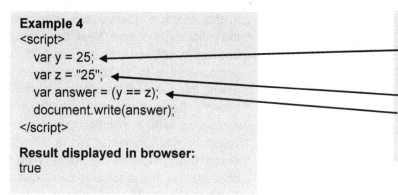

Example 4
```
<script>
    var y = 25;
    var z = "25";
    var answer = (y == z);
    document.write(answer);
</script>
```

Result displayed in browser:
true

When a non-string (in this case, **y = 25**) is compared with a string (in this case **z = "25"**) it results in the non-string first being converted to a string (in this case **y = 25** is converted to **y = "25"**) and then the comparison is made. Since, **"25" = "25"** the result is **true** which is displayed in the browser window.

7.1.2 Not Equal (!=)

Returns true if the operands are not equal.

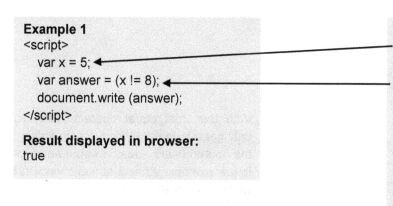

Example 1
```
<script>
    var x = 5;
    var answer = (x != 8);
    document.write (answer);
</script>
```

Result displayed in browser:
true

In this example, the variable **x** is given the initial value of **5** and then the variable **answer** is set equal to the result of the comparison: **x != 8**. This comparison is asking the question: "Is **x** not equal to **8**?" or "Is **5** not equal to **8**?". Any comparison will return one of two values: **true** or **false**. Because the actual value of **x**, at this point, is **5,** the result of the comparison is **true** (**5** does not equal **8**). This results in **answer** being set to **true** and **true** being displayed in the browser window.

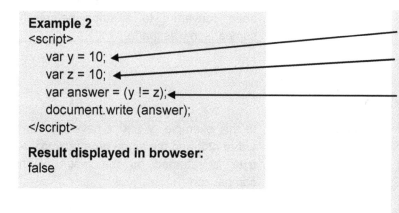

Example 2
```
<script>
    var y = 10;
    var z = 10;
    var answer = (y != z);
    document.write (answer);
</script>
```

Result displayed in browser:
false

In this example, the variable **y** is given the initial value of **10** and the variable **z** is given the initial value of **10**. Next, the variable **answer** is set equal to the result of the comparison: **y != z**. This comparison is asking the question: "Is **y** not equal to **z**?" or "Is **10** not equal to **10**?". Because the actual value of **y**, at this point, is **10** and the value of **z** is **10**, the result of the comparison is **false** (**10** is not not equal to **10).** This results in **answer** being set to **false** and **false** being displayed in the browser window.

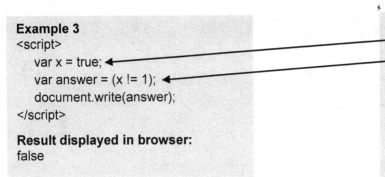

Example 3
```
<script>
    var x = true;
    var answer = (x != 1);
    document.write(answer);
</script>
```

Result displayed in browser:
false

In this example, the variable **x** is given the initial value of **true**. Next, the variable **answer** is set equal to the result of the comparison: **x != 1**. This comparison is asking the question: "Is **x** not equal to **1**?" When a Boolean value (true or false) is compared with a number the Boolean value is first converted to a number before the comparison is made. **True** is converted to **1** and **false** is converted to **0**. At this point the value of **x** is **true**, which will be converted to a **1** before the comparison is made. Since **1 = 1**, the result of the comparison will be **false**. This results in **answer** being be set to **false** and **false** being displayed in the browser window.

7.1.3 Strict Equal (===)

Returns true if the operands are equal and of the same type.

Example 1
```
<script>
    var y = 25;
    var z = "25";
    var answer = (y === z);
    document.write(answer);
</script>
```

Result displayed in browser:
false

With the strict equal operator **===**, you only get a **true** result for the comparison if the operands are equal in **value** and **type**. In this example **y** has a numeric value (**25**) while **z** has a string value (**"25"**), so, even though the value is the same, the operands are of different types, so, a **false** is returned as the result of the comparison. If we had used the equal comparison operator **==**, the result would have been **true** because **y** would have automatically been converted to a string before the comparison was made.

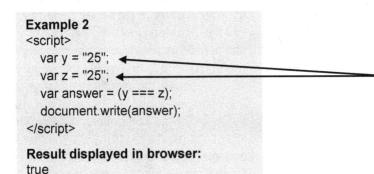

Example 2
```
<script>
    var y = "25";
    var z = "25";
    var answer = (y === z);
    document.write(answer);
</script>
```

Result displayed in browser:
true

In this example, **y** and **z** have the same **value (25)** and the same **type (string)**, so, **true** is returned as the result of the comparison.

7.1.4 Strict Not Equal (!==)

Returns true if the operands are not equal and/or not of the same type.

Example 1
```
<script>
   var a = 12;
   var b = "12";
   var answer = (y !== z);
   document.write(answer);
</script>
```

Result displayed in browser:
true

With the strict not equal comparison operator **!==**, you only get a **true** result for the comparison if the operands are not equal in **value** and/or the data **types** are not equal. In this example **a** has a numeric value (**12**) while **b** has a string value (**"12"**), so, even though the value is the same, the operands are of different data types, so, a **true** is returned as the result of the comparison.

Example 2
```
<script>
   var a = "12";
   var b = "12";
   var answer = (a !== b);
   document.write(answer);
</script>
```

Result displayed in browser:
false

In this example, **a** and **b** have the same **value (12)** and the same **type (string)**, so, **false** is returned as the result of the comparison. You only get a **true** result from a comparison with the **strict not equal** comparison operator **!==** if the operands are not equal in value and/or not of the same data types.

Example 1
```
<script>
   var a = 50;
   var b = 48;
   var answer = (a !== b);
   document.write(answer);
</script>
```

Result displayed in browser:
true

In this example, var **a** and var **b** have different values but the same data type. You only get a **true** result from a comparison with the **strict not equal** comparison operator **!==** if the operands are not equal in value and/or not of the same data types. Since, the two variables have different values and are not strictly equal the result of the comparison is **true**.

7.1.5 Greater Than (>)

Returns true if the left operand is greater than the right operand.

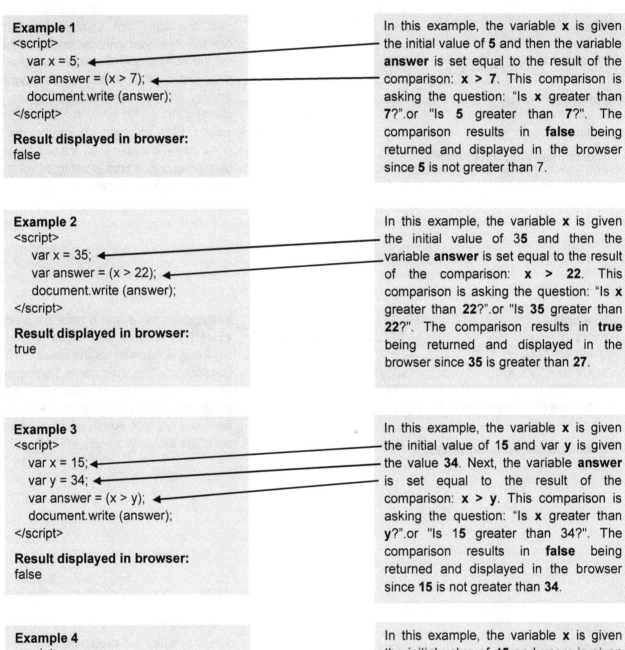

Example 1
```
<script>
  var x = 5;
  var answer = (x > 7);
  document.write (answer);
</script>
```
Result displayed in browser:
false

In this example, the variable **x** is given the initial value of **5** and then the variable **answer** is set equal to the result of the comparison: **x > 7**. This comparison is asking the question: "Is **x** greater than **7**?".or "Is **5** greater than **7**?". The comparison results in **false** being returned and displayed in the browser since **5** is not greater than 7.

Example 2
```
<script>
  var x = 35;
  var answer = (x > 22);
  document.write (answer);
</script>
```
Result displayed in browser:
true

In this example, the variable **x** is given the initial value of 3**5** and then the variable **answer** is set equal to the result of the comparison: **x > 22**. This comparison is asking the question: "Is **x** greater than **22**?".or "Is **35** greater than **22**?". The comparison results in **true** being returned and displayed in the browser since **35** is greater than **27**.

Example 3
```
<script>
  var x = 15;
  var y = 34;
  var answer = (x > y);
  document.write (answer);
</script>
```
Result displayed in browser:
false

In this example, the variable **x** is given the initial value of **15** and var **y** is given the value **34**. Next, the variable **answer** is set equal to the result of the comparison: **x > y**. This comparison is asking the question: "Is **x** greater than **y**?".or "Is **15** greater than 34?". The comparison results in **false** being returned and displayed in the browser since **15** is not greater than **34**.

Example 4
```
<script>
  var x = 45;
  var y = 19;
  var answer = (x > 22);
  document.write (answer);
</script>
```
Result displayed in browser:
true

In this example, the variable **x** is given the initial value of **45** and var **y** is given the value **19** Next, the variable **answer** is set equal to the result of the comparison: **x > 22**. This comparison is asking the question: "Is **x** greater than **22**?". The comparison results in **true** being returned and displayed in the browser since **45** is greater than **22**.

7.1.6 Greater Than Or Equal To (>=)

Returns true if the left operand is greater than or equal to the right operand.

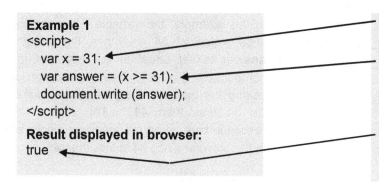

Example 1
```
<script>
  var x = 31;
  var answer = (x >= 31);
  document.write (answer);
</script>
```
Result displayed in browser:
true

In this example, the variable **x** is given the initial value of **31** and then the variable **answer** is set equal to the result of the comparison: **x >= 31**. This comparison is asking the question: "Is **x** greater than **or equal to 31**?" or "Is **31** greater than or equal to **31**?". The comparison results in **true** being returned and displayed in the browser since **31** is greater than or equal to **31**.

Example 2
```
<script>
  var x = 48;
  var answer = (x >= 66);
  document.write (answer);
</script>
```
Result displayed in browser:
false

In this example, the variable **x** is given the initial value of **48** and then the variable **answer** is set equal to the result of the comparison: **x >= 66**. This comparison is asking the question: "Is **x** greater than or equal to **66**?" or "Is **48** greater than or equal to **66**?". The comparison results in **false** being returned and displayed in the browser since **48** is not greater than or equal to **66**.

Example 3
```
<script>
  var x = 55;
  var y = 55;
  var answer = (x >= y);
  document.write (answer);
</script>
```
Result displayed in browser:
true

In this example, the variable **x** is given the initial value of **55** and var **y** is given the value **55**. Next, the variable **answer** is set equal to the result of the comparison: **x >= y**. This comparison is asking the question: "Is **x** greater than **y**?" or "Is **55** greater than or equal to **55**?". The comparison results in **true** being returned and displayed in the browser since **55** is greater than or equal to **55**.

Example 4
```
<script>
  var x = 55;
  var y = 54;
  var answer = (x >= y);
  document.write (answer);
</script>
```
Result displayed in browser:
true

In this example, the variable **x** is given the initial value of **55** and var **y** is given the value **54**. Next, the variable **answer** is set equal to the result of the comparison: **x >= y**. This comparison is asking the question: "Is **x** greater than or equal to **y**?" or "Is **55** greater than or equal to **54**?". The comparison results in **true** being returned and displayed in the browser since **55** is greater than or equal to **54**.

7.1.7 Less Than (<)

Returns true if the left operand is less than the right operand.

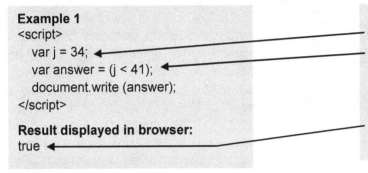

Example 1
```
<script>
   var j = 34;
   var answer = (j < 41);
   document.write (answer);
</script>
```
Result displayed in browser:
true

In this example, the variable **j** is given the initial value of **34** and then the variable **answer** is set equal to the result of the comparison: **j < 41**. This comparison is asking the question: "Is **j** less than **41**?".or "Is **34** less than **41**?". The comparison results in **true** being returned and displayed in the browser since **34** is less than **41**.

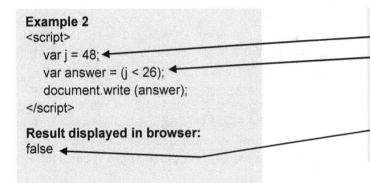

Example 2
```
<script>
   var j = 48;
   var answer = (j < 26);
   document.write (answer);
</script>
```
Result displayed in browser:
false

In this example, the variable **j** is given the initial value of **48** and then the variable **answer** is set equal to the result of the comparison: **j < 26**. This comparison is asking the question: "Is **j** less than **26**?".or "Is **48** less than **26**?". The comparison results in **false** being returned and displayed in the browser since **48** is not less than **26**.

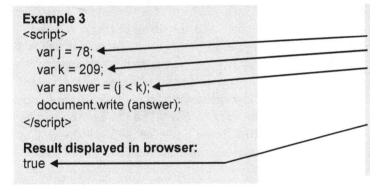

Example 3
```
<script>
   var j = 78;
   var k = 209;
   var answer = (j < k);
   document.write (answer);
</script>
```
Result displayed in browser:
true

In this example, the variable **j** is given the initial value of **78** and var **k** is given the value **209**. Next, the variable **answer** is set equal to the result of the comparison: **j < k**. This comparison is asking the question: "Is **j** less than **y**?" or "Is **78** less than **209**?". The comparison results in **true** being returned and displayed in the browser since **78** is greater than or equal to **209**.

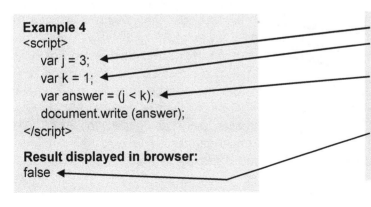

Example 4
```
<script>
   var j = 3;
   var k = 1;
   var answer = (j < k);
   document.write (answer);
</script>
```
Result displayed in browser:
false

In this example, the variable **j** is given the initial value of 3 and var **k** is given the value 1. Next, the variable **answer** is set equal to the result of the comparison: **j < k**. This comparison is asking the question: "Is **x** lessr than **y**?" or "Is **3** less than **1**?". The comparison results in **false** being returned and displayed in the browser since **3** is not less than **1**.

7.1.8 Less Than Or Equal To (<=)

Returns true if the left operand is less than or equal to the right operand.

Example 1
```
<script>
   var a = 57;
   var answer = (a <= 91);
   document.write (answer);
</script>
```
Result displayed in browser:
true

In this example, the variable **a** is given the initial value of **57** and then the variable **answer** is set equal to the result of the comparison: **x <= 91**. This comparison is asking the question: "Is **x** greater than **or equal to 91**?" or "Is **31** less than or equal to **91**?". The comparison results in **true** being returned and displayed in the browser since **57** is less than or equal to **91**.

Example 2
```
<script>
   var a = 16;
   var answer = (a <= 15);
   document.write (answer);
</script>
```
Result displayed in browser:
false

In this example, the variable **a** is given the initial value of **16** and then the variable **answer** is set equal to the result of the comparison: **a <= 15**. This comparison is asking the question: "Is **x** less than or equal to **15**?" or "Is **16** less than or equal to **15**?". The comparison results in **false** being returned and displayed in the browser since **16** is not less than or equal to **15**.

Example 3
```
<script>
   var a = 53;
   var b = 53;
   var answer = (a <= b);
   document.write (answer);
</script>
```
Result displayed in browser:
true

In this example, the variable **a** is given the initial value of **53** and var **b** is given the value **53**. Next, the variable **answer** is set equal to the result of the comparison: **a <= b**. This comparison is asking the question: "Is **a** less than or equal to **b**?" or "Is **53** less than or equal to **53**?". The comparison results in **true** being returned and displayed in the browser since **53** is less than or equal to **53**.

Example 4
```
<script>
   var a = 110;
   var b = 111;
   var answer = (a <= b);
   document.write (answer);
</script>
```
Result displayed in browser:
true

In this example, the variable **a** is given the initial value of **110** and var **b** is given the value **111**. Next, the variable **answer** is set equal to the result of the comparison: **a <= b**. This comparison is asking the question: "Is **a** less than or equal to **b**?" or "Is **110** less than or equal to **111**?". The comparison results in **true** being returned and displayed in the browser since **110** is less than or equal to **111**.

7.1 Match the comparison operator symbols (#1 - #8) in the left-hand column with the comparison operator names (a - h) in the right-hand column:

1) ==   a) less than or equal to
2) !=   b) strict not equal
3) ===   c) greater than
4) >   d) equal
5) <   e) not equal
6) >=   f) less than
7) !==   g) strict equal
8) <=   h) greater than or equal to

Solution
1) d
2) e
3) g
4) c
5) f
6) h
7) b
8) a

7.2 Match the comparison operator names (#1 - #8) in the left-hand column with the comparison operator symbols (a - h) in the right-hand column:

1) equal   a) !==
2) strict equal   b) >
3) greater than or equal to   c) ==
4) strict not equal   d) <
5) greater than   e) >=
6) less than or equal to   f) !=
7) less than   g) ===
8) not equal

Solution
1) c
2) g
3) e
4) a
5) b
6) h
7) d
8) f

7.3 Match the comparison operator descriptions (#1 - #8) in the left-hand column with the comparison operator symbols (a - h) in the right-hand column:

1) Checks to see if the value of two operands are equal or not, if yes, then the condition becomes true.

2) Checks to see if the value of the left operand is greater than or equal to the value of the right operand, if yes, then the condition becomes true.

3) Checks to see if the value and data type of the left operand is the same as the value and data type of the right operand, if yes, then the condition becomes true.

4) Checks to see if the value of two operands are equal or not, if the values are not equal, then the condition becomes true.

5) Checks to seeif the value of the left operand is greater than the value of the right operand, if yes, then the condition becomes true.

6) Checks to see if the value of the left operand is less than or equal to the value of the right operand, if yes, then the condition becomes true.

7) Checks to see if the value and/or data type of the left operand is a different value and/or data type than the right operand. If, yes, then he condition becomes true.

8) Checks to see if the value of the left operand is less than the value of the right operand, if yes, then the condition becomes true.

a) !=
b) ===
c) <=
d) !==
e) >=
f) <
g) =
h) >

Solution

1) g		5) h	
2) e		6) c	
3) b		7) d	
4) a		8) f	

7.4 Step 1: Declare a variable called **x** with an initial value of **15**.

   Step 2: Use a comparison operator to see if **x** is equal to **15** and put the **true/false** value returned by the comparison into a variable called **comparisonResult.**

   Step 3: Display the value of **comparisonResult** in the browser window.

Solution

```
<!DOCTYPE html>
```

```
<html>
<head>
</head>
<body>
   <script>
      var x = 15;
      var comparisonResult = (x==15);
      document.write(comparisonResult);
   </script>
</body>
</html>
```

Result displayed in browser:
True

Give the final value of the Boolean comparison that's displayed in the browser window in each of the following JavaScript code snippets in problems 7.5 - 7.33. In order to save space we're going to leave out the html code and assume that each code snippet is preceded by **<script>** and followed by **</script>** and is located in the **<body>** section of the main html code.

7.5 Step 1: Declare a variable called **x** with a value of **15**.

Step 2: Use a comparison operator to see if **x** is equal to **12** and put the **true/false** Boolean value that's returned by the comparison into a variable called **comparisonResult**.

Step 3: Display the value of **comparisonResult** in the browser window.

Solution
```
<script>
   var x = 15;
   var comparisonResult = (x == 15);
   document.write(comparisonResult);
</script>
```

Result displayed in browser:
true

In this problem, the variable **x** is given the initial value of **15**. Next, the **equal** comparison operator is used to check to see if **x** is equal to **15**. The **true/false** Boolean result that is returned by the comparison is then stored in the variable called **comparisonResult**. Because **x** equals **15**, the comparison results in **true** being returned and stored in the variable **comparisonResult** and then displayed in the browser window.

7.6 Step 1: Declare a variable called **j** with a value of **33**.

Step 2: Use a comparison operator to see if **j** is equal to **27** and put the **true/false** Boolean value that's returned by the comparison into a variable called **comparisonResult**.

Step 3: Display the value of **comparisonResult** in the browser window.

Solution

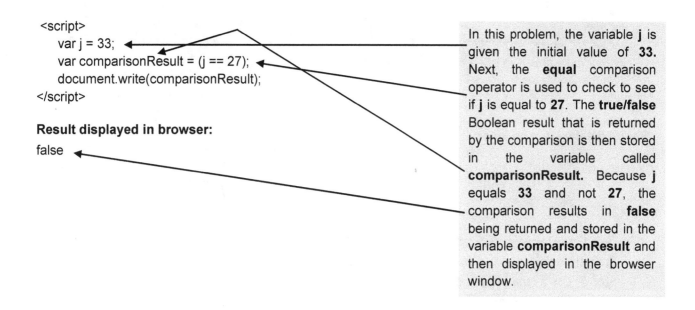

```
<script>
    var j = 33;
    var comparisonResult = (j == 27);
    document.write(comparisonResult);
</script>
```

Result displayed in browser:

false

In this problem, the variable **j** is given the initial value of **33**. Next, the **equal** comparison operator is used to check to see if **j** is equal to **27**. The **true/false** Boolean result that is returned by the comparison is then stored in the variable called **comparisonResult**. Because **j** equals **33** and not **27**, the comparison results in **false** being returned and stored in the variable **comparisonResult** and then displayed in the browser window.

7.7 Step 1: Declare a variable called **x** with a value of **45**.

Step 2: Use a comparison operator to see if **x** is not equal to **59** and put the **true/false** Boolean value that's returned by the comparison into a variable called **comparisonResult**.

Step 3: Display the value of **comparisonResult** in the browser window.

Solution

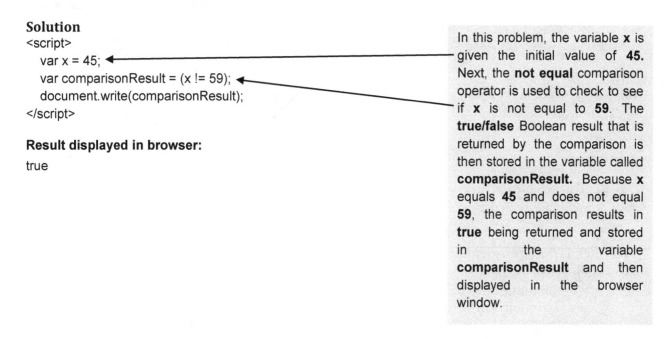

```
<script>
    var x = 45;
    var comparisonResult = (x != 59);
    document.write(comparisonResult);
</script>
```

Result displayed in browser:

true

In this problem, the variable **x** is given the initial value of **45**. Next, the **not equal** comparison operator is used to check to see if **x** is not equal to **59**. The **true/false** Boolean result that is returned by the comparison is then stored in the variable called **comparisonResult**. Because **x** equals **45** and does not equal **59**, the comparison results in **true** being returned and stored in the variable **comparisonResult** and then displayed in the browser window.

7.8 Step 1: Declare a variable called **i** with a value of **18**.

Step 2: Use a comparison operator to see if **i** is not equal to **18** and put the **true/false** Boolean value that's returned by the comparison into a variable called **comparisonResult**.

Step 3: Display the value of **comparisonResult** in the browser window.

Solution

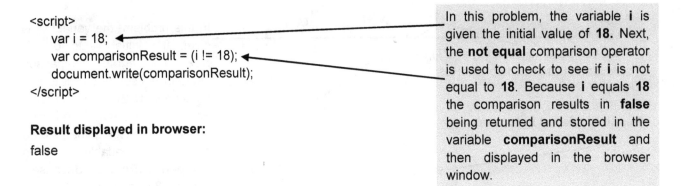

```
<script>
    var i = 18;
    var comparisonResult = (i != 18);
    document.write(comparisonResult);
</script>
```

Result displayed in browser:

false

In this problem, the variable **i** is given the initial value of **18**. Next, the **not equal** comparison operator is used to check to see if **i** is not equal to **18**. Because **i** equals **18** the comparison results in **false** being returned and stored in the variable **comparisonResult** and then displayed in the browser window.

7.9 Step 1: Declare a numeric variable called **m** with a value of **47.**

Step 2: Declare a string variable called **n** with a value of **"47".**

Step 3: Use a comparison operator to see if **m** is strictly equal to **n** and put the **true/false** Boolean value that's returned by the comparison into a variable called **comparisonResult**.

Step 4: Display the value of **comparisonResult** in the browser window.

Solution

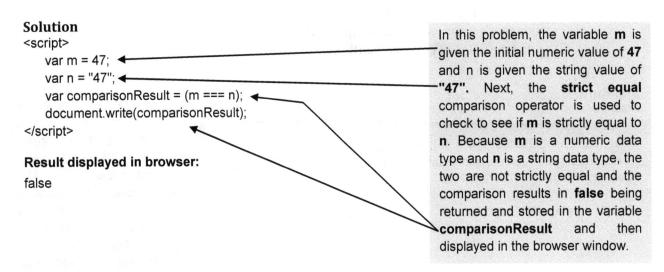

```
<script>
    var m = 47;
    var n = "47";
    var comparisonResult = (m === n);
    document.write(comparisonResult);
</script>
```

Result displayed in browser:

false

In this problem, the variable **m** is given the initial numeric value of **47** and n is given the string value of **"47"**. Next, the **strict equal** comparison operator is used to check to see if **m** is strictly equal to **n**. Because **m** is a numeric data type and **n** is a string data type, the two are not strictly equal and the comparison results in **false** being returned and stored in the variable **comparisonResult** and then displayed in the browser window.

7.10 Step 1: Declare a numeric variable called **q** with a value of **8.**

Step 2: Use a comparison operator to see if **q** is greater than **10** and put the **true/false** Boolean value that's returned by the comparison into a variable called **comparisonResult**.

Step 3: Display the value of **comparisonResult** in the browser window.

Solution

```
<script>
    var q = 8;
    var comparisonResult = (q > 10);
    document.write(comparisonResult);
</script>
```

Result displayed in browser:

false

> In this problem, the variable **q** is given the initial value of **8.** Next, the **greater than** comparison operator is used to check to see if **q** is greater than **10.** Because **q** is equal to **8** which is not greater than **10,** the comparison results in **false** being returned and stored in the variable **comparisonResult** and then displayed in the browser window.

7.11 Step 1: Declare a numeric variable called **q** with a value of **38.**

Step 2: Declare a string variable called **r** with a value of **41.**

Step 3: Use a comparison operator to see if **q** is greater than **r** and put the **true/false** Boolean value that's returned by the comparison into a variable called **comparisonResult.**

Step 4: Display the value of **comparisonResult** in the browser window.

Solution

```
<script>
    var q = 38;
    var r = 41
    var comparisonResult = (q > r);
    document.write(comparisonResult);
</script>
```

> In this problem, the variable **q** is given the initial value of **38** and r is given the value of **41** Next, the **greater** **than** comparison operator is used to check to see if **q** is greater than **r.** Because **q** is equal to **38** which is not greater than **41,** the comparison results in **false** being returned and stored in the variable **comparisonResult** and then displayed in the browser window.

Result displayed in browser:

false

7.12 Step 1: Declare a numeric variable called **x** with a value of **89.**

Step 2: Use a comparison operator to see if **x** is less **57** and put the **true/false** Boolean value that's returned by the comparison into a variable called **comparisonResult.**

Step 3: Display the value of **comparisonResult** in the browser window.

Solution

```
<script>
    var x = 89;
    var comparisonResult = (x < 57);
    document.write(comparisonResult);
```

```
</script>
```

Result displayed in browser:

false

In this problem, the variable **x** is given the initial value of **89**. Next, the **less than** comparison operator is used to check to see if **x** is less than **57**. Because **x** is equal to **89** which is not less than **57**, the comparison results in **false** being returned and stored in the variable **comparisonResult** and then displayed in the browser window.

7.13 Step 1: Declare a numeric variable called **m** with a value of **47.**

Step 2: Declare a string variable called **n** with a value of **"47".**

Step 3: Use a comparison operator to see if **m** is strictly equal to **n** and put the **true/false** Boolean value that's returned by the comparison into a variable called **comparisonResult**.

Step 4: Display the value of **comparisonResult** in the browser window.

Solution

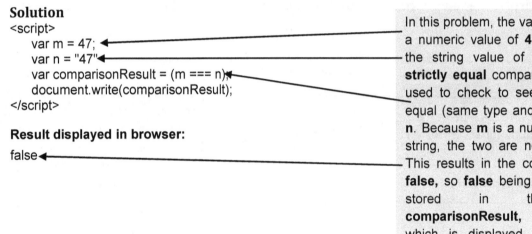

```
<script>
    var m = 47;
    var n = "47";
    var comparisonResult = (m === n);
    document.write(comparisonResult);
</script>
```

Result displayed in browser:

false

In this problem, the variable **m** is given a numeric value of **47** and **n** is given the string value of **"47"**. Next, the **strictly equal** comparison operator is used to check to see if **m** is strictly equal (same type and same value) to **n**. Because **m** is a number and n is a string, the two are not strictly equal. This results in the comparison being **false,** so **false** being is returned and stored in the variable **comparisonResult,** the value of which is displayed in the browser window.

7.14 Step 1: Declare a numeric variable called **a** with a Boolean value of **true.**

Step 2: Use a comparison operator to see if **a** is equal to **0** and put the **true/false** Boolean value that's returned by the comparison into a variable called **comparisonResult**.

Step 3: Display the value of **comparisonResult** in the browser window.

Solution

```
<script>
    var a = true;
    var comparisonResult = (a == 0);
    document.write(comparisonResult);
</script>
```

Result displayed in browser:

false

In this example, the variable **a** is given the initial value of **true**. Next, the variable **comparisonResult** is set equal to the result of the comparison: **a==0.** This comparison is asking the question: "Does **a** equal **0?**".

When a Boolean value (**true** or **false**) is compared with a number, the Boolean value is first converted to a number before the comparison is made. **True** is converted to **1** and **false** is converted to **0**. At this point the value of **a** is **true**, which will converted to a **1** before the comparison is made. Since **1** does not equal **0**, the result of the comparison will be **false**. This value will be stored in the variable **comparisonResult** and displayed in the browser window.

7.15 Step 1: Declare a variable called **num1** with a value of **147.**

Step 2: Declare a variable called **num2** with a value of **85.**

Step 3: Use a comparison operator to see if **num1** is not equal to **num2** and put the **true/false** Boolean value that's returned by the comparison into a variable called **comparisonResult**.

Step 4: Display the value of **comparisonResult** in the browser window.

Solution

```
<script>
    var num1 = 147;
    var num2 = 85;
    var comparisonResult = (num1 != num2);
    document.write(comparisonResult);
</script>
```

In this problem, the variable **num1** is given the initial value of **147** and **num2** is given the value of **85**. Next, the **not equal** comparison operator is used to check to see if **num1** is not equal to **num2**. Because **num1** is equal to **147** and **num2** is equal to **85**, **num1** is not equal to **num2** and the comparison results in **true** being returned This value will be stored in the variable **comparisonResult** and displayed in the browser window.

Result displayed in browser:

true

7.16 Step 1: Declare a string variable called **m** with a value of **"55".**

Step 2: Declare a string variable called **n** with a value of **"55".**

Step 3: Use a comparison operator to see if **m** is strictly equal to **n** and put the **true/false** Boolean value that's returned by the comparison into a variable called **comparisonResult**.

Step 4: Display the value of **comparisonResult** in the browser window.

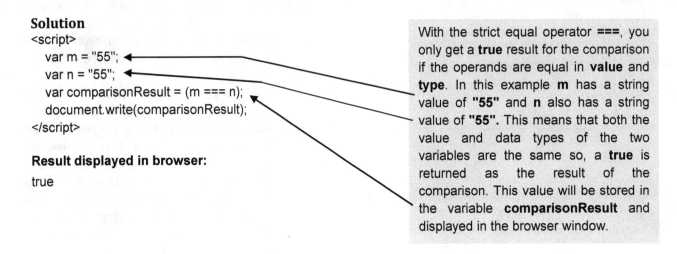

Solution
```
<script>
    var m = "55";
    var n = "55";
    var comparisonResult = (m === n);
    document.write(comparisonResult);
</script>
```

Result displayed in browser:

true

> With the strict equal operator **===**, you only get a **true** result for the comparison if the operands are equal in **value** and **type**. In this example **m** has a string value of **"55"** and **n** also has a string value of **"55"**. This means that both the value and data types of the two variables are the same so, a **true** is returned as the result of the comparison. This value will be stored in the variable **comparisonResult** and displayed in the browser window.

7.17 Step 1: Declare a numeric variable called **i** with a value of **65.**

Step 2: Declare a string variable called **j** with a value of **"65".**

Step 3: Use a comparison operator to see if **i** is not strictly equal to **j** and put the **true/false** Boolean value that's returned by the comparison into a variable called **comparisonResult**.

Step 4: Display the value of **comparisonResult** in the browser window.

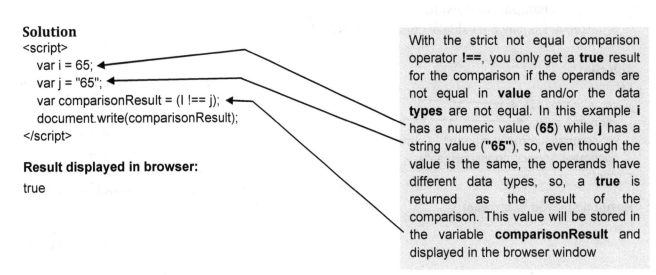

Solution
```
<script>
    var i = 65;
    var j = "65";
    var comparisonResult = (I !== j);
    document.write(comparisonResult);
</script>
```

Result displayed in browser:

true

> With the strict not equal comparison operator **!==**, you only get a **true** result for the comparison if the operands are not equal in **value** and/or the data **types** are not equal. In this example **i** has a numeric value (**65**) while **j** has a string value (**"65"**), so, even though the value is the same, the operands have different data types, so, a **true** is returned as the result of the comparison. This value will be stored in the variable **comparisonResult** and displayed in the browser window

7.18 Step 1: Declare a numeric variable called **x** with a value of **250.**

Step 2: Use a comparison operator to see if **x** is less than **300** and put the **true/false** Boolean value that's returned by the comparison into a variable called **comparisonResult**.

Step 3: Display the value of **comparisonResult** in the browser window.

Solution
```
<script>
   var x = 250;
   var comparisonResult = (x < 300);
   document.write(comparisonResult);
</script>
```

In this problem, the variable **x** is given the initial value of **250**. Next, the **less than** comparison operator is used to check to see if **x** is less than **300**. Because **x** is equal to **250** which is less than **300**, the comparison results in **true** which is store din the variable **comparisonResult** and displayed in the browser window.

Result displayed in browser:

true

7.19 Step 1: Declare a numeric variable called **m** with a value of **true**.

Step 2: Declare a string variable called **n** with a value of **1**.

Step 3: Use a comparison operator to see if **m** is equal to n**j** and put the **true/false** Boolean value that's returned by the comparison into a variable called **comparisonResult**.

Step 4: Display the value of **comparisonResult** in the browser window.

Solution
```
<script>
   var m = true;
   var n = 1;
   var comparisonResult = (m == n);
   document.write(comparisonResult);
</script>
```

In this example, the variable **m** is given the initial value of **true** and variable **n** is given the initialvalue **1**. Next, the variable **comparisonResult** is set equal to the result of the comparison: **m == n**. This comparison is asking the question: "Does **m** equal **n**?" or "does **true** = **1**?". When a Boolean value (**true** or **false**) is compared with a number, the Boolean value is first converted to a number before the comparison is made. **True** is converted to **1** and **false** is converted to **0**. At this point the value of **m** is **true**, which will be converted to a **1** before the comparison is made. Since **1** = **1**, the result of the comparison will be **true**. This results in **answer** being be set to **true** and **true** being displayed in the browser window.

Result displayed in browser:

true

7.20 Step 1: Declare a variable called **num1** with a value of **100**.

Step 2: Declare a variable called **num2** with a value of **4**.

Step 3: Declare a variable called **num3** with a value of **25**.

Step 4: Use a comparison operator to see if **num1** minus **num2** is equal to **num3** and put the **true/false** Boolean value that's returned by the comparison into a variable called **comparisonResult**.

Step 5: Display the value of **comparisonResult** in the browser window.

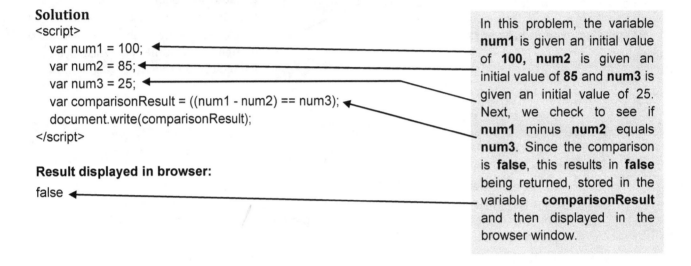

Solution
```
<script>
   var num1 = 100;
   var num2 = 85;
   var num3 = 25;
   var comparisonResult = ((num1 - num2) == num3);
   document.write(comparisonResult);
</script>
```

In this problem, the variable **num1** is given an initial value of **100, num2** is given an initial value of **85** and **num3** is given an initial value of 25. Next, we check to see if **num1** minus **num2** equals **num3**. Since the comparison is **false**, this results in **false** being returned, stored in the variable **comparisonResult** and then displayed in the browser window.

Result displayed in browser:

false

7.21 Step 1: Declare a numeric variable called **num1** with a value of **41.**

Step 2: Use a comparison operator to see if **num1** is greater than or equal to **52** and put the **true/false** Boolean value that's returned by the comparison into a variable called **comparisonResult**.

Step 3: Display the value of **comparisonResult** in the browser window.

Solution
```
<script>
   var num1 = 41;
   var comparisonResult = (num1 >= 52);
   document.write(comparisonResult);
</script>
```

In this problem, the variable **num1** is given the initial value of **41**. Next, the **greater than or equal to** comparison operator is used to check to see if **num1** is greater than or equal to **52**. Because **num1** is equal to **41** and **num1** is not greater than or equal to **52,** the comparison results in **false** being returned, stored in the variable **comparisonResult** and then displayed in the browser window.

Result displayed in browser:
false

7.22 Step 1: Declare a numeric variable called **num1** with a value of **63.**

Step 2: Use a comparison operator to see if **num1** is greater than or equal to **47** and put the **true/false** Boolean value that's returned by the comparison into a variable called **comparisonResult**.

Step 3: Display the value of **comparisonResult** in the browser window.

Solution

```
<script>
    var num1 = 63;
    var comparisonResult = (num1 >= 47);
    document.write(comparisonResult);
</script>
```

In this problem, the variable **num1** is given the initial value of **63**. Next, the **greater than or equal to** comparison operator is used to check to see if **num1** is greater than or equal to **47**. Because **num1** is equal to **63** and **num1** is greater than or equal to **47** the comparison results in **true** being returned, stored in the variable **comparisonResult** and then displayed in the browser window.

Result displayed in browser:

true

7.23 Step 1: Declare a numeric variable called **a** with a value of **27.**

Step 2: Declare a string variable called **b** with a value of **27**

Step 3: Use a comparison operator to see if **a** is strictly equal to **b** and put the **true/false** Boolean value that's returned by the comparison into a variable called **comparisonResult**.

Step 4: Display the value of **comparisonResult** in the browser window.

Solution

```
<script>
    var a = 27;
    var b = 27;
    var comparisonResult = (a === b);
    document.write(comparisonResult);
</script>
```

With the strict equal operator **===**, you only get a **true** result for the comparison if the operands are equal in **value** and **data type**. In this example **a** has a numeric value of **27** and **b** also has a numeric value of **27**. This means that both the value and data types of the two variables are the same so, **true** is returned, stored in the variable **comparisonResult** and then displayed in the browser window.

Result displayed in browser:

true

7.24 Step 1: Declare a variable called **x** with a value of **125.**

Step 2: Declare a variable called **y** with a value of **100.**

Step 3: Use a comparison operator to see if **x** is less than **y** and put the **true/false** Boolean value that's returned by the comparison into a variable called **comparisonResult**.

Step 4: Display the value of **comparisonResult** in the browser window.

Solution

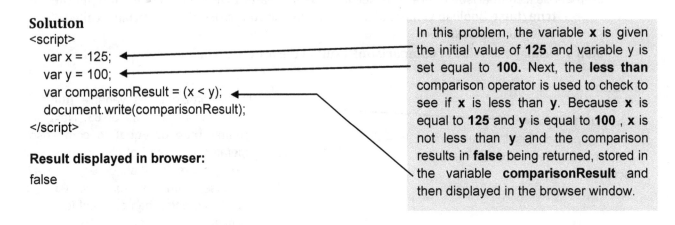

```
<script>
    var x = 125;
    var y = 100;
    var comparisonResult = (x < y);
    document.write(comparisonResult);
</script>
```

In this problem, the variable **x** is given the initial value of **125** and variable y is set equal to **100**. Next, the **less than** comparison operator is used to check to see if **x** is less than **y**. Because **x** is equal to **125** and **y** is equal to **100** , **x** is not less than **y** and the comparison results in **false** being returned, stored in the variable **comparisonResult** and then displayed in the browser window.

Result displayed in browser:

false

7.25 Step 1: Declare a numeric variable called **a** with a value of **4** ; **b** with a value of **2** and **c** with a value of **a * b**.

Step 2: Use a comparison operator to see if **c** is less than or equal to **a** and put the **true/false** Boolean value that's returned by the comparison into a variable called **comparisonResult**.

Step 3: Display the value of **comparisonResult** in the browser window.

Solution

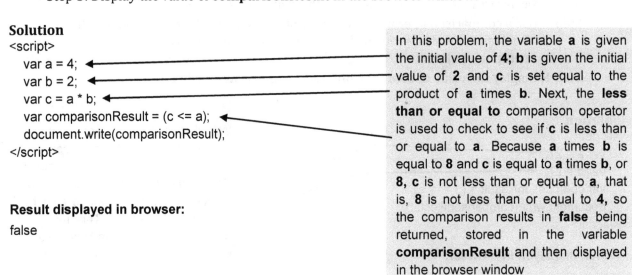

```
<script>
    var a = 4;
    var b = 2;
    var c = a * b;
    var comparisonResult = (c <= a);
    document.write(comparisonResult);
</script>
```

In this problem, the variable **a** is given the initial value of **4; b** is given the initial value of **2** and **c** is set equal to the product of **a** times **b**. Next, the **less than or equal to** comparison operator is used to check to see if **c** is less than or equal to **a**. Because **a** times **b** is equal to **8** and **c** is equal to **a** times **b**, or **8, c** is not less than or equal to **a**, that is, **8** is not less than or equal to **4,** so the comparison results in **false** being returned, stored in the variable **comparisonResult** and then displayed in the browser window

Result displayed in browser:

false

7.26 Step 1: Declare a variable called **x** with a value of **100.**

Step 2: Declare a variable called **y** with a value of **200.**

Step 3: Declare a variable called **z** with a value of **300.**

Step 4: Use a comparison operator to see if **x + y** is equal to **z** and put the **true/false** Boolean value that's returned by the comparison into a variable called **comparisonResult**.

Step 5: Display the value of **comparisonResult** in the browser window

Solution

```
<script>
    var x = 100;
    var y = 200;
    var z = 300;
    var comparisonResult = ((x + y) = z);
    document.write(comparisonResult);
</script>
```

In this problem, the variable **x** is given an initial value of **100;** variable **y** is set equal to **200** and variable **z is** set to **300.** Next, the equal comparison operator is used to check to see if **x + y** is equal to **z**. Because **x + y** is equal to **300** and **z** is equal to **300**, **x + y** is equal to **z** and the comparison results in **true** being returned, stored in the variable **comparisonResult** and then displayed in the browser window

Result displayed in browser:

true

7.27 Step 1: Declare a string variable called **i** with a value of **"32"**.

Step 2: Declare a string variable called **j** with a value of **"32"**.

Step 3: Use a comparison operator to see if **i** is not strictly equal to **j** and put the **true/false** Boolean value that's returned by the comparison into a variable called **comparisonResult**.

Step 4: Display the value of **comparisonResult** in the browser window.

Solution

```
<script>
    var i = "32";
    var j = "32";
    var comparisonResult = (i== j);
    document.write(comparisonResult);
</script>
```

With the strict equal comparison operator **===**, you only get a **true** result for the comparison if the operands are not equal in **value** and/or the data **types** are not equal. In this example **i** has a string value of **"32"** while **j** also has a string value of **"32"**. So, both the values and data types of the operands are the same. This results in **true** being returned, stored in the variable **comparisonResult** and then displayed in the browser window

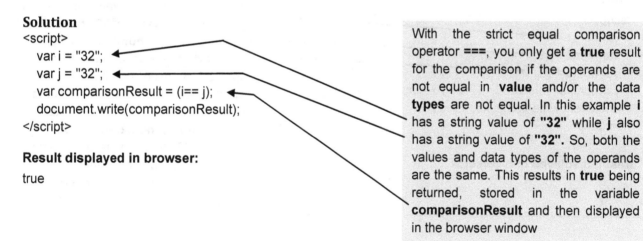

Result displayed in browser:

true

7.28 Step 1: Declare a numeric variable called **q** with a value of **12.**

Step 2: Declare a numeric variable called **r** with a value of **19.**

Step 3: Declare a numeric variable called **s** with a value of **30.**

Step 4: Use a comparison operator to see if **q + r** is greater than **s** and put the **true/false** Boolean value that's returned by the comparison into a variable called **comparisonResult**.

Step 5: Display the value of **comparisonResult** in the browser window.

Solution

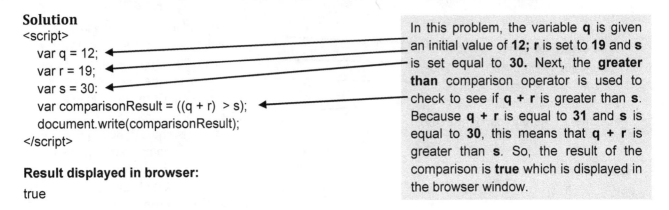

```
<script>
    var q = 12;
    var r = 19;
    var s = 30:
    var comparisonResult = ((q + r)  > s);
    document.write(comparisonResult);
</script>
```

In this problem, the variable **q** is given an initial value of **12; r** is set to **19** and **s** is set equal to **30**. Next, the **greater than** comparison operator is used to check to see if **q + r** is greater than **s**. Because **q + r** is equal to **31** and **s** is equal to **30**, this means that **q + r** is greater than **s**. So, the result of the comparison is **true** which is displayed in the browser window.

Result displayed in browser:

true

7.29   Step 1: Declare a variable called **num1** with a value of **17**; a variable called **num2** with a value of 19 and a variable called **num3** with a value of 36.

Step 2: Use a comparison operator to see if **num1 + num2** is not equal to **num3** and put the **true/false** Boolean value that's returned by the comparison into a variable called **comparisonResult**.

Step 3: Display the value of **comparisonResult** in the browser window.

Solution

```
<script>
    var num1 = 17;
    var num2 = 19;
    var num3 = 36;
    var comparisonResult = ((num1 + num2) != num3);
    document.write(comparisonResult);
</script>
```

In this problem, the variable **num1** is given an initial value of **17; num2** is set equal to **19** and **num3** is set equal to **36**. Next, the **not equal** comparison operator is used to check to see if **num1 + num2** is not equal to **num3**. If **num1** equals **17** and **num2** equals **19**, then, **num1 + num2** equals **36**. Since **num3 = 36,** this means that **num1 + num2** is equal to **num3**, so, the comparison results in **false** being returned and displayed in the browser window.

Result displayed in browser:

false

7.30   Step 1: Declare a variable called **w** with a value of **25.**

Step 2: Declare a variable called **x** with a value of **34.**

Step 3: Declare a variable called **y** with a value of **10.**

Step 4: Declare a variable called **z** with a value of **x - y.**

Step 5: Use a comparison operator to see if **z** is less than **w** and put the **true/false** Boolean value that's returned by the comparison into a variable called **comparisonResult**.

Step 6: Display the value of **comparisonResult** in the browser window.

Solution

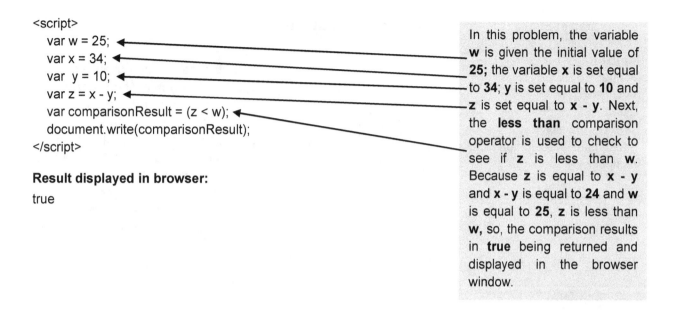

```
<script>
    var w = 25;
    var x = 34;
    var  y = 10;
    var z = x - y;
    var comparisonResult = (z < w);
    document.write(comparisonResult);
</script>
```

In this problem, the variable **w** is given the initial value of **25;** the variable **x** is set equal to **34**; y is set equal to **10** and **z** is set equal to **x - y**. Next, the **less than** comparison operator is used to check to see if **z** is less than **w**. Because **z** is equal to **x - y** and **x - y** is equal to **24** and **w** is equal to **25**, **z** is less than **w,** so, the comparison results in **true** being returned and displayed in the browser window.

Result displayed in browser:

true

7.31   Step 1: Declare a variable called **x** with a value of **60.**

        Step 2: Declare a string variable called **y** with a value of **50.**

        Step 3: Declare a string variable called **z** with a value of **x - y.**

        Step 4: Use a comparison operator to see if **z** is strictly equal to **10** and put the **true/false** Boolean value that's returned by the comparison into a variable called **comparisonResult.**

        Step 4: Display the value of **comparisonResult** in the browser window.

Solution

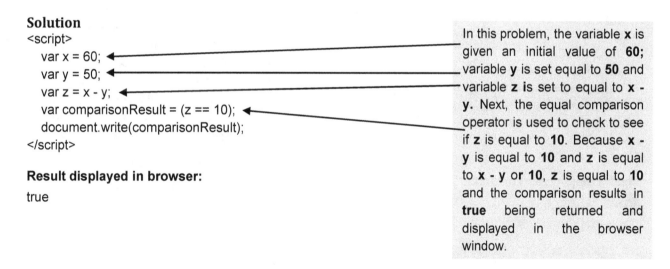

```
<script>
    var x = 60;
    var y = 50;
    var z = x - y;
    var comparisonResult = (z == 10);
    document.write(comparisonResult);
</script>
```

In this problem, the variable **x** is given an initial value of **60**; variable **y** is set equal to **50** and variable **z** is set to equal to **x - y**. Next, the equal comparison operator is used to check to see if **z** is equal to **10**. Because **x - y** is equal to **10** and **z** is equal to **x - y** or **10**, **z** is equal to **10** and the comparison results in **true** being returned and displayed in the browser window.

Result displayed in browser:

true

7.32   Step 1: Declare a string variable called **i** with a value of **97.**

        Step 2: Declare a string variable called **j** with a value of **49.**

        Step 3: Use a comparison operator to see if **i** is not strictly equal to **j** and put the **true/false** Boolean value that's returned by the comparison into a variable called **comparisonResult.**

Step 4: Display the value of **comparisonResult** in the browser window.

Solution

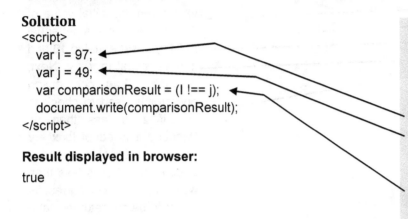

```
<script>
    var i = 97;
    var j = 49;
    var comparisonResult = (I !== j);
    document.write(comparisonResult);
</script>
```

With the strict not equal comparison operator **!==**, you only get a **true** result for the comparison if the operands are not equal in **value** and/or the data **types** are not equal. In this example **i** has a numeric value of **97** while **j** has a numeric value of **49.** So, although both of the variables have the same data type, their values are different, so their comparison with the **strict not equal** comparison operator results in **true** being returned as the result of the comparison. **True** is displayed in the browser window.

Result displayed in browser:

true

7.33 Step 1: Declare a numeric variable called **a** with a value of **250.**

Step 2: Declare a numeric variable called **b** with a value of **a - 50.**

Step 3: Use a comparison operator to see if **b** is less than or equal to **a** and put the **true/false** Boolean value that's returned by the comparison into a variable called **comparisonResult**.

Step 4: Display the value of **comparisonResult** in the browser window.

Solution

```
<script>
    var a = 250;
    var b = a - 50;
    var comparisonResult = (b <= a);
    document.write(comparisonResult);
</script>
```

In this problem, the variable **a** is given the initial value of **250** and **b** is given the initial value of **a - 50**. Next, the **less than or equal to** comparison operator is used to check to see if **b** is less than or equal to **a**. Because **b** equals **a - 50** and **a - 50** is equal to **200,** the comparison (**200<=250**) is **true** and results in **true** being returned and displayed in the browser window.

Result displayed in browser:

true

Chapter 8

JavaScript Operators: Part 4

8.1 JAVASCRIPT LOGICAL OPERATORS

We have already considered JavaScript logical operators briefly in chapter 1 but now we're going to cover them in more depth. Logical operators are used when testing for Boolean (true and false) states. Usually when these operators are used, they are testing Boolean values and return a Boolean result. The following is a list of the major JavaScript arithmetic operators:

- AND
- OR
- NOT

8.1.1 AND (&&)

Returns **true** if all conditions are met. All comparisons must be true for the AND statement to equate to **true**. The logical AND operator (**&&**) returns the boolean value **true** if both operands are **true** and returns **false** otherwise.

Truth Table for AND (&&) Logical Operator (2 comparisons)

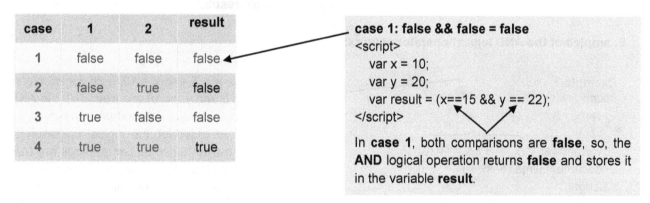

case	1	2	result
1	false	false	false
2	false	true	false
3	true	false	false
4	true	true	true

case 1: false && false = false
```
<script>
    var x = 10;
    var y = 20;
    var result = (x==15 && y == 22);
</script>
```
In **case 1**, both comparisons are **false**, so, the **AND** logical operation returns **false** and stores it in the variable **result**.

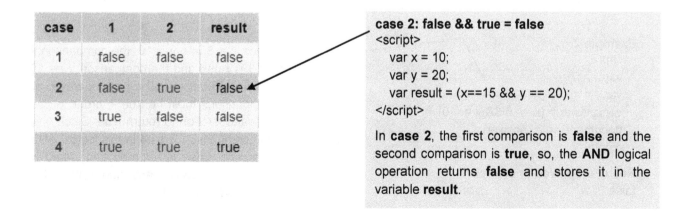

case	1	2	result
1	false	false	false
2	false	true	false
3	true	false	false
4	true	true	true

case 2: false && true = false
```
<script>
    var x = 10;
    var y = 20;
    var result = (x==15 && y == 20);
</script>
```
In **case 2**, the first comparison is **false** and the second comparison is **true**, so, the **AND** logical operation returns **false** and stores it in the variable **result**.

case	1	2	result
1	false	false	false
2	false	true	false
3	true	false	false
4	true	true	true

case 3: true && false = false
```
<script>
   var x = 10;
   var y = 20;
   var result = (x==10 && y == 35);
</script>
```

In **case 3**, the first comparison is **true** and the second comparison is **false**, so, the **AND** logical operation returns **false** and stores it in the variable **result**.

case	1	2	result
1	false	false	false
2	false	true	false
3	true	false	false
4	true	true	true

case 4: true && true = true
```
<script>
   var x = 10;
   var y = 20;
   var result = (x==10 && y == 20);
</script>
```

In **case 4**, the first comparison is **true** and the second comparison is **true**, so, the **AND** logical operation returns **true** and stores it in the variable **result**.

Examples of the AND logical operator at work:

Example 1
```
<script>
   var x = 5;
   var y = 10;
   var answer = (x == 5 && y ==10);
   document.write (answer);
</script>
```

Result displayed in browser:
true

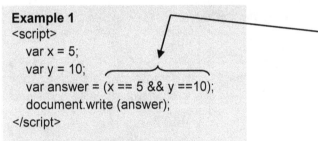

Since **x = 5** and **y = 10**, both comparisons: **x == 5** and **y == 10** are **true**. With the **AND** logical operator, all comparisons must be **true** in order for the logical operation to return **true**. Since all comparisons are **true** in this logical **AND** operation, this results in **true** being returned and stored in the variable **answer** and then displayed in the browser window.

Example 2
```
<script>
   var x = 5;
   var y = 10;
   var answer = (x == 6 && y ==10);
   document.write (answer);
</script>
```

Result displayed in browser:
false

Since **x = 5** and **y = 10**, the comparison **x == 6** is **false** and the comparison **y == 10** is **true**. With the **AND** logical operator, all comparisons must be true in order for the logical operation to return **true**. Since only one comparison is **true** in this logical **AND** operation, **false** is returned and stored in the variable **answer** and then displayed in the browser window.

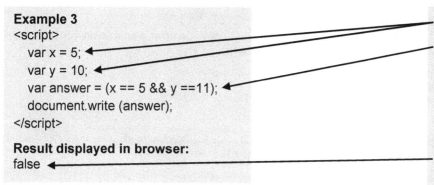

Example 3
```
<script>
    var x = 5;
    var y = 10;
    var answer = (x == 5 && y ==11);
    document.write (answer);
</script>
```
Result displayed in browser:
false

Since **x = 5** and **y = 10**, the comparison **x == 5** is **true** and the comparison **y == 11** is **false**. With the **AND** logical operator, all comparisons must be true in order for the logical operation to return **true**. Since only one comparison is **true** in this logical **AND** operation, **false** is returned and stored in the variable **answer** and then displayed in the browser window.

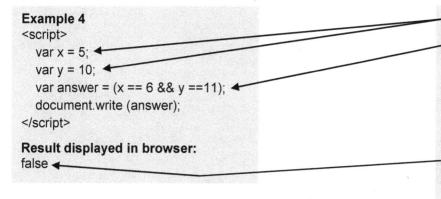

Example 4
```
<script>
    var x = 5;
    var y = 10;
    var answer = (x == 6 && y ==11);
    document.write (answer);
</script>
```
Result displayed in browser:
false

Since **x = 5** and **y = 10**, the comparison **x == 6** is **false** and the comparison **y == 11** is **false**. With the **AND** logical operator, all comparisons must be true in order for the logical operation to return **true**. Since none of the comparisons are **true** in this logical **AND** operation, **false** is returned and stored in the variable **answer** and then displayed in the browser window.

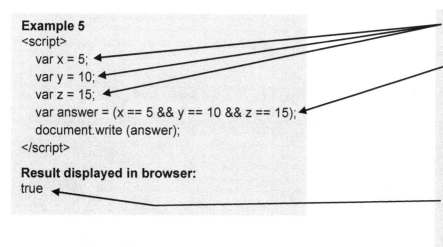

Example 5
```
<script>
    var x = 5;
    var y = 10;
    var z = 15;
    var answer = (x == 5 && y == 10 && z == 15);
    document.write (answer);
</script>
```
Result displayed in browser:
true

Since **x = 5**, **y = 10** and **z = 15**, the comparison **x == 5** is **true**, the comparison **y == 10** is **true** and the comparison **z == 15** is **true**. With the **AND** logical operator, all comparisons must be true in order for the logical operation to return **true**. Since all three of the comparisons are **true** in this logical **AND** operation, **true** is returned and stored in the variable **answer** and then displayed in the browser window.

8.1.2 OR (||)

Returns **true** if one or more conditions are met. One or more of the comparisons must be true for the OR statement to equate to **true**. The logical **OR** operator (||) returns the boolean value **true** if either or both operands is **true** and returns **false** otherwise.

Truth Table for OR (||) Logical Operator (2 comparisons)

case	1	2	result
1	false	false	false
2	false	true	true
3	true	false	true
4	true	true	true

case 1: false || false = false
```
<script>
   var x = 10;
   var y = 20;
   var result = (x==15 || y == 22);
</script>
```

In **case 1**, both comparisons are **false**, so, the **OR** logical operation returns **false** and stores it in the variable **result**.

case	1	2	result
1	false	false	false
2	false	true	true
3	true	false	true
4	true	true	true

case 2: false || true = true
```
<script>
   var x = 10;
   var y = 20;
   var result = (x==15 || y == 20);
</script>
```

In **case 2**, the first comparison is **false** and the second comparison is **true**, so, the **OR** logical operation returns **true** and stores it in the variable **result**.

case	1	2	result
1	false	false	false
2	false	true	true
3	true	false	true
4	true	true	true

case 3: true || false = true
```
<script>
   var x = 10;
   var y = 20;
   var result = (x==10 || y == 35);
</script>
```

In **case 3**, the first comparison is **true** and the second comparison is **false**, so, the **OR** logical operation returns **true** and stores it in the variable **result**.

case	1	2	result
1	false	false	false
2	false	true	false
3	true	false	false
4	true	true	true

case 4: true && true = true
```
<script>
   var x = 10;
   var y = 20;
   var result = (x==10 || y == 20);
</script>
```

In **case 4**, the first comparison is **true** and the second comparison is **true**, so, the **OR** logical operation returns **true** and stores it in the variable **result**.

Examples of the OR logical operator at work:

Example 1
```
<script>
   var x = 5;
   var y = 10;
   answer = (x == 5 || y ==10);
   document.write (answer);
</script>
```

Result displayed in browser:
true

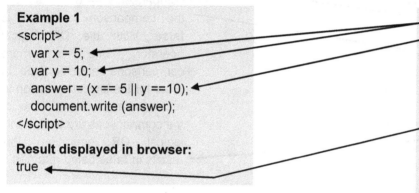

Since **x = 5** and **y = 10**, both comparisons: **x == 5** and **y == 10** are **true**. With the **OR** logical operator, one or more comparisons must be **true** in order for the logical operation to return **true**. Since all comparisons are **true** in this logical **OR** operation, this results in **true** being returned and stored in the variable **answer** and then displayed in the browser window. If only one of the comparisons had been **true** the logical **OR** operation would still have returned a **true**. It doesn't matter how many of the comparisons are **false** as long as at least one is **true** in an **OR** operation.

Example 2
```
<script>
   var x = 5;
   var y = 10;
   var answer = (x == 5 || y ==11);
   document.write (answer);
</script>
```
Result displayed in browser:
true

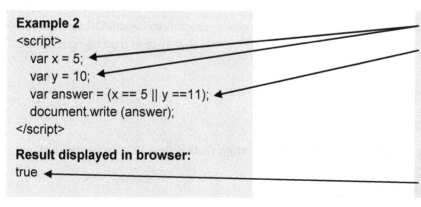

Since **x = 5** and **y = 10**, the comparison **x == 5** is **true** and the comparison **y == 11** is **false**. With the **OR** logical operator, one or more comparisons must be **true** in order for the logical operation to return **true**. Since at least one comparison is **true** in this logical **OR** operation, this results in **true** being returned.

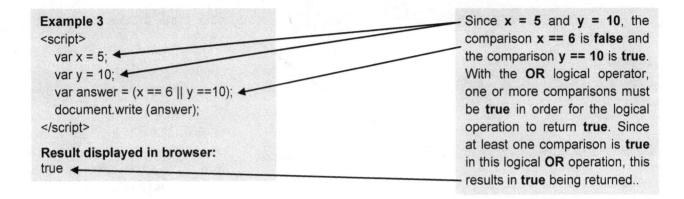

Example 3
```
<script>
    var x = 5;
    var y = 10;
    var answer = (x == 6 || y ==10);
    document.write (answer);
</script>
```

Result displayed in browser:
true

Since **x = 5** and **y = 10**, the comparison **x == 6** is **false** and the comparison **y == 10** is **true**. With the **OR** logical operator, one or more comparisons must be **true** in order for the logical operation to return **true**. Since at least one comparison is **true** in this logical **OR** operation, this results in **true** being returned..

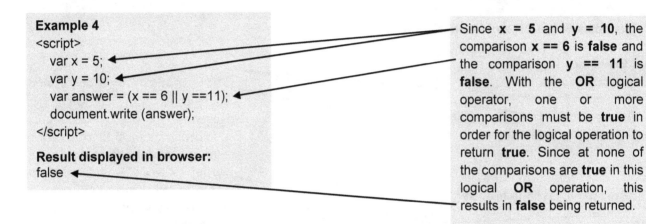

Example 4
```
<script>
    var x = 5;
    var y = 10;
    var answer = (x == 6 || y ==11);
    document.write (answer);
</script>
```

Result displayed in browser:
false

Since **x = 5** and **y = 10**, the comparison **x == 6** is **false** and the comparison **y == 11** is **false**. With the **OR** logical operator, one or more comparisons must be **true** in order for the logical operation to return **true**. Since at none of the comparisons are **true** in this logical **OR** operation, this results in **false** being returned.

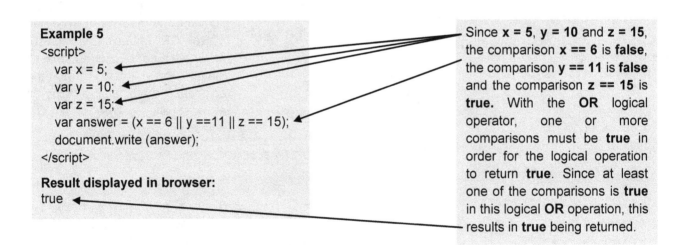

Example 5
```
<script>
    var x = 5;
    var y = 10;
    var z = 15;
    var answer = (x == 6 || y ==11 || z == 15);
    document.write (answer);
</script>
```

Result displayed in browser:
true

Since **x = 5**, **y = 10** and **z = 15**, the comparison **x == 6** is **false**, the comparison **y == 11** is **false** and the comparison **z == 15** is **true**. With the **OR** logical operator, one or more comparisons must be **true** in order for the logical operation to return **true**. Since at least one of the comparisons is **true** in this logical **OR** operation, this results in **true** being returned.

8.1.3 NOT (!)

Reverses the logical state of its operand. If a condition is true, then the Logical NOT operator will make it false.

Examples of the NOT logical operator at work:

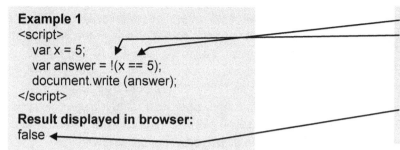

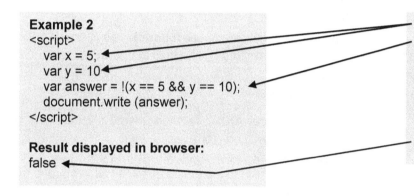

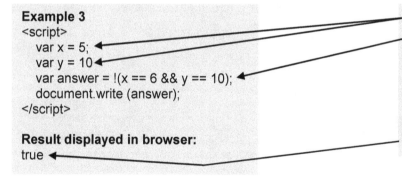

SOLVED PROBLEMS

8.1 Step 1: Create a variable called **a** with a value of **10.**

Step 2: Create a variable called **b** with a value of **20.**

Step 3: Use one logical operator and two comparison operators to see if both **a = 10** is **true** and **b = 20** is **true**. Put the **true/false** value that's returned by the logical operation into a variable called **answer**.

Step 4: Display the value of **answer** in the browser window.

solution

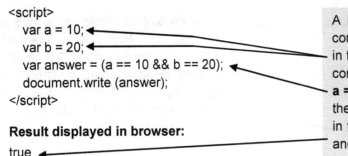

```
<script>
    var a = 10;
    var b = 20;
    var answer = (a == 10 && b == 20);
    document.write (answer);
</script>
```

A logical **AND** operation returns a **true** when all comparisons (one on either side of the **&&** operator in this case) are **true**. Since **a = 10** and **b = 20**, the comparisons **a == 10** and **b == 20** are both **true** and the result of the logical **AND** operation returns **true**. This results in **true** being stored in the variable named **answer** and then displayed in the browser window.

Result displayed in browser:

true

8.2　Step 1: Create a variable called **j** with a value of **30.**

　　　Step 2: Create a variable called **k** with a value of **25.**

　　　Step 3: Use one logical operator and two comparison operators to see if both **j = 30** is **true** and **k = 22** is **true**. Put the **true/false** value that's returned by the logical operation into a variable called **answer.**

　　　Step 4: Display the value of **answer** in the browser window.

Solution

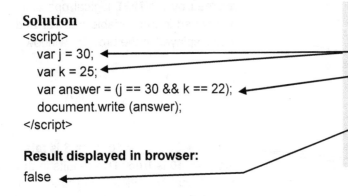

```
<script>
    var j = 30;
    var k = 25;
    var answer = (j == 30 && k == 22);
    document.write (answer);
</script>
```

A logical **AND** operation returns a **true** when all comparisons (one on either side of the **&&** operator in this case) are **true**. Since **j = 30** and **k = 25**, the comparison **j == 30** is **true** but the comparison **k == 22** is **false** so the result of the logical **AND** operation returns **false**. This results in **false** being stored in the variable named **answer** and then displayed in the browser window.

Result displayed in browser:

false

8.3　Step 1: Create a variable called **x** with a value of **45.**

　　　Step 2: Create a variable called **y** with a value of **60.**

　　　Step 3: Use two logical operators and three comparison operators to see if **x = 45** is **true**, **y = 60** is **true** and **y - x = 15** is **true**. Put the **true/false** value that's returned by the logical operation into a variable called **answer.**

　　　Step 4: Display the value of **answer** in the browser window.

Solution

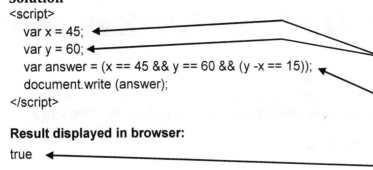

```
<script>
    var x = 45;
    var y = 60;
    var answer = (x == 45 && y == 60 && (y -x == 15));
    document.write (answer);
</script>
```

A logical **AND** operation returns a **true** when all comparisons (three comparisons in this case) are **true**. Since **x = 45** and **y = 60**, the comparison **x == 45** is **true**, the comparison **y == 60** is **true** and the comparison **y - x = 15** is **true** so the result of the logical **AND** operation returns **true**. This results in **true** being stored in the variable named **answer** and then displayed in the browser window.

Result displayed in browser:

true

8.4 Step 1: Create a variable called **a** with a value of **5**.

Step 2: Create a variable called **b** with a value of **6**.

Step 3: Create a variable called **c** with a value of **7**.

Step 4: Use two logical operators and three comparison operators to see if **a = 5** is **true**, **b = 6** is **true** and **c = 7** is **true**. Put the **true/false** value that's returned by the logical operation into a variable called **answer**.

Step 5: Display the value of **answer** in the browser window.

Solution

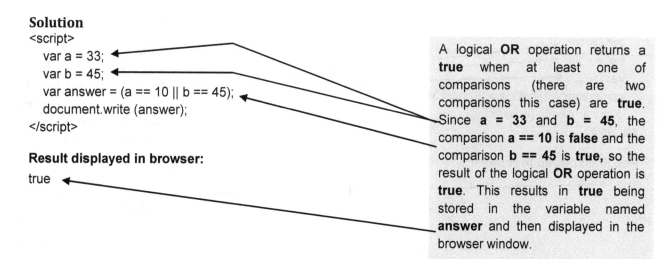

```
<script>
    var a = 5;
    var b = 6;
    var c = 7;
    var answer = (a == 5 && b == 6 && c == 7);
    document.write (answer);
</script>
```

Result displayed in browser:

true

A logical **AND** operation returns a **true** when all comparisons (three comparisons in this case) are **true**. Since **a = 5, b = 6** and **c = 7**, the comparison **a == 5** is **true**, the comparison **b == 6** is **true** and the comparison **c = 7** is **true,** so the result of the logical **AND** operation returns **true**. This results in **true** being stored in the variable named **answer** and then displayed in the browser window.

8.5 Step 1: Create a variable called **a** with a value of **33**.

Step 2: Create a variable called **b** with a value of **45**.

Step 3: Use one logical operator and two comparison operators to see if either **a = 10** or **b = 45** is **true** or if both are **true**. Put the **true/false** value that's returned by the logical operation into a variable called **answer**.

Step 4: Display the value of **answer** in the browser window.

Solution

```
<script>
    var a = 33;
    var b = 45;
    var answer = (a == 10 || b == 45);
    document.write (answer);
</script>
```

Result displayed in browser:

true

A logical **OR** operation returns a **true** when at least one of comparisons (there are two comparisons this case) are **true**. Since **a = 33** and **b = 45**, the comparison **a == 10** is **false** and the comparison **b == 45** is **true,** so the result of the logical **OR** operation is **true**. This results in **true** being stored in the variable named **answer** and then displayed in the browser window.

8.6 Step 1: Create a variable called **x** with a value of **55.**

Step 2: Create a variable called **y** with a value of **70.**

Step 3: Use one logical operator and two comparison operators to see if either **x = 45** or **y = 80** is **true** or if both are **true.** Put the **true/false** value that's returned by the logical operation into a variable called **answer.**

Step 4: Display the value of **answer** in the browser window.

Solution

```
<script>
   var x = 55;
   var y = 70;
   var answer = (x == 45 || y == 80);
   document.write (answer);
</script>
```

Result displayed in browser:

false

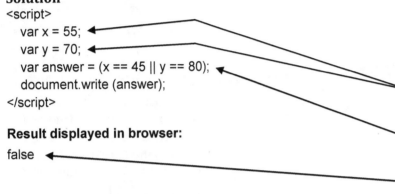

A logical **OR** operation returns a **true** when at least one of comparisons (there are two comparisons this case) are **true.** Since **x = 55** and **y = 70**, the comparison **x == 45** is **false** and the comparison **y == 80** is **false,** so the result of the logical **OR** operation is **false.** This results in **false** being stored in the variable named **answer** and then displayed in the browser window.

8.7 Step 1: Create a variable called **j** with a value of **10.**

Step 2: Create a variable called **k** with a value of **20.**

Step 3: Create a variable called **l** with a value of **30.**

Step 4: Use two logical operators and three comparison operators to see if at least one of the following three comparisons is true: **j < 8, k > 20** or **l < 35.**

Step 5: Put the **true/false** value that's returned by the logical operation into a variable called **answer.**

Step 6: Display the value of **answer** in the browser window.

Solution

```
<script>
   var j = 10;
   var k = 20;
   var l = 30;
   var answer = (j < 8 || k > 20 || l < 35);
   document.write (answer);
</script>
```

Result displayed in browser:

true

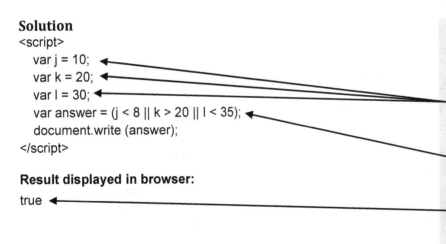

A logical **OR** operation returns a **true** when at least one of comparisons (there are three comparisons this case) are **true.** Since **j = 10, k = 20** and **l = 30,** the comparison **j < 8** is **false,** the comparison **k > 20** is **false** and the comparison **l < 35** is **true.** Since at least one of comparisons in the logical **OR** operations is **true,** the result of the logical **OR** operation is **true.** This results in **true** being stored in the variable named **answer**

8.8   Step 1: Create a variable called **a** with a value of **50.**

Step 2: Create a variable called **b** with a value of **75.**

Step 3: Use one logical operator and two comparison operators to see if either **a > 40** or **b < 70** is **true** or if both are **true**. Put the **true/false** value that's returned by the logical operation into a variable called **answer**.

Step 4: Display the value of **answer** in the browser window.

Solution

```
<script>
    var a = 50;
    var b = 75;
    var answer = (a > 40 || b < 70);
    document.write (answer);
</script>
```

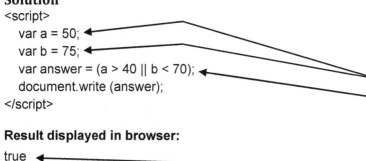

Result displayed in browser:

true

A logical **OR** operation returns a **true** when at least one of comparisons (there are two comparisons this case) are **true**. Since **a = 50** and **b = 75**, the comparison **a > 40** is **true** and the comparison **b < 70** is **false,** so the result of the logical **OR** operation is **true**. This results in **true** being stored in the variable named **answer** and then displayed in the browser window.

8.9   Step 1: Create a variable called **x** with a value of **"Jack".**

Step 2: Create a variable called **y** with a value of **"Joe".**

Step 3: Create a variable called **z** with a value of **"John".**

Step 4: Use two logical operators and three comparison operators to see if at least one of the following three comparisons is true: **x != "Bob", y == "Bill" or z == "Ed".**

Step 5: Put the **true/false** value that's returned by the logical operation into a variable called **answer**.

Step 6: Display the value of **answer** in the browser window.

Solution

```
<script>
    var x = "Jack";
    var y = "Joe";
    var z = "John";
    var answer = (x != "Bob" || y == "Bill" || z == "Ed");
    document.write (answer);
</script>
```

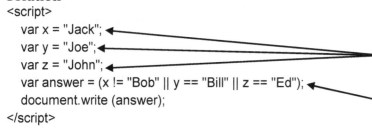

Result displayed in browser:

true

A logical **OR** operation returns a **true** when at least one of comparisons (there are three comparisons this case) are **true**. Since **x = "Jack", y = "Joe"** and **z = "John"**, the comparison **x != "Bob"** is **true**; the comparison **y == "Bill"** is **false** and the comparison **z == "Ed"** is **false**. Since at least one of comparisons in the logical **OR** operations is **true**, the result of the logical **OR** operation is **true**. This results in **true** being stored in the variable named **answer** and then displayed in the browser window.

8.10 Step 1: Create a variable called **x** with a value of 50.

Step 2: Use one logical operator and one comparison operator to see if **x = 50** is **true** and then reverse the Boolean value from **true to false** or from **false to true**.

Step 3: Put the **true/false** value that's returned by the logical **NOT** operation into a variable called **answer**.

Step 4: Display the value of **answer** in the browser window.

Solution

```
<script>
    var x = 50;
    var answer = ( ! (x == 50));
    document.write (answer);
</script>
```

A logical **NOT** operator reverses the logical state of the logical operation that its being used with. Since **x = 50,** the comparison **x == 50** is **true** and the logical NOT operator reverses the true to false.This results in **false** being stored in the variable named **answer** and then displayed in the browser window.

Result displayed in browser:

false

8.11 Step 1: Create a variable called **a** with a value of 17.

Step 2: Create a variable called **b** with a value of 24.

Step 3: Use one logical operator and two comparison operators to see if both **a = 18** and **b = 24** are **true.** Use a **NOT** logical operator to reverse the logical result of the **AND** operation.

Step 4: Put the **true/false** value that's returned by the logical **NOT** **operation into** a variable called **answer**.

Step 5: Display the value of **answer** in the browser window.

Solution

```
<script>
    var a = 17;
    var b = 24;
    var answer = ( ! (a == 18 && b == 24))
    document.write (answer);
</script>
```

A logical **NOT** operator reverses the logical state of the logical operation that its being used with. Since **a = 17** and **b = 24**, the comparison **a == 18** is **false** and the comparison **b == 24** is **true,** so the result of the logical **AND** operation is **false**. The logical **NOT** operator reverses the **false** result from the **AND** operation to **true**. This results in **true** being stored in the variable named **answer** and then displayed in the browser window.

Result displayed in browser:

true

8.12 Step 1: Create **a** variable called **i** with a value of **"red"**.

Step 2: Use one logical operator and one comparison operator to see if **i = "blue"** is **true** and **then reverse** the value returned value from either **true to false** or from **false to true**.

Step 3: Put the **true/false** value that's returned by the logical **NOT** operation into a variable called **answer**.

Step 4: Display the value of **answer** in the browser window.

Solution

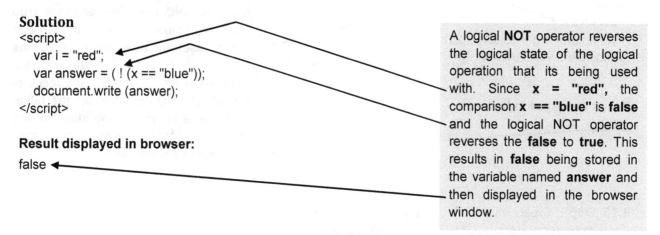

```
<script>
    var i = "red";
    var answer = ( ! (x == "blue"));
    document.write (answer);
</script>
```

A logical **NOT** operator reverses the logical state of the logical operation that its being used with. Since **x = "red"**, the comparison **x == "blue"** is **false** and the logical NOT operator reverses the **false** to **true**. This results in **false** being stored in the variable named **answer** and then displayed in the browser window.

Result displayed in browser:

false

8.13 Step 1: Create a variable called **j** with a value of **15.**

Step 2: Create a variable called **k** with a value of **25.**

Step 3: Create a variable called **l** with a value of **35.**

Step 4: Use two logical operators and three comparison operators to see if **j - 5 = 10** is **true, k + 10 = 6** is **true** and **c = 7** is **true**. Put the **true/false** value that's returned by the logical operation into a variable called **answer**.

Step 5: Display the value of **answer** in the browser window.

Solution

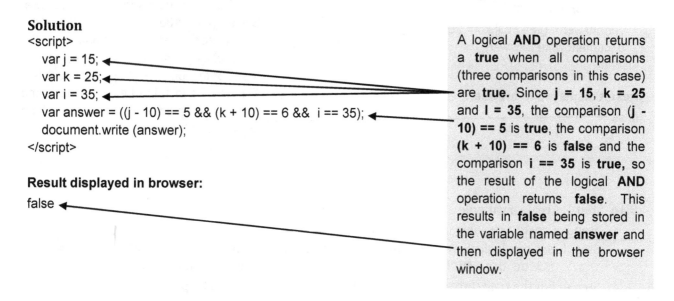

```
<script>
    var j = 15;
    var k = 25;
    var i = 35;
    var answer = ((j - 10) == 5 && (k + 10) == 6 &&  i == 35);
    document.write (answer);
</script>
```

A logical **AND** operation returns a **true** when all comparisons (three comparisons in this case) are **true**. Since **j = 15, k = 25** and **l = 35**, the comparison **(j - 10) == 5** is **true**, the comparison **(k + 10) == 6** is **false** and the comparison **i == 35** is **true,** so the result of the logical **AND** operation returns **false**. This results in **false** being stored in the variable named **answer** and then displayed in the browser window.

Result displayed in browser:

false

8.14 Step 1: Create a variable called **j** with a value of **25.**

Step 2: Use one logical operator and two comparison operators to see if **j > 18** is **true** and **j < 25** is **true**. Put the **true/false** value that's returned by the logical operation into a variable called **answer**.

Step 3: Display the value of **answer** in the browser window.

Solution

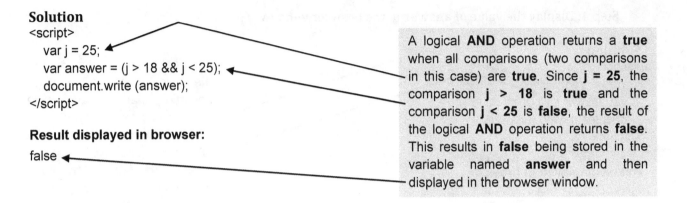

```
<script>
    var j = 25;
    var answer = (j > 18 && j < 25);
    document.write (answer);
</script>
```

Result displayed in browser:

false

> A logical **AND** operation returns a **true** when all comparisons (two comparisons in this case) are **true**. Since **j = 25**, the comparison **j > 18** is **true** and the comparison **j < 25** is **false**, the result of the logical **AND** operation returns **false**. This results in **false** being stored in the variable named **answer** and then displayed in the browser window.

8.15 Step 1: Create a variable called **j** with a value of **100.**

Step 2: Create a variable called **k** with a value of **200.**

Step 3: Use one logical operator and two comparison operators to see if either **j = 50** or **k = 250** is **true** or if both are **true**. Put the **true/false** value that's returned by the logical operation into a variable called **answer.**

Step 4: Display the value of **answer** in the browser window.

Solution

```
<script>
    var j = 100;
    var k = 200;
    var answer = (j == 50 || k == 250);
    document.write (answer);
</script>
```

Result displayed in browser:

false

> A logical **OR** operation returns a **true** when at least one of comparisons (there are two comparisons this case) are **true**. Since **j = 100** and **k = 200**, the comparison **j == 50** is **false** and the comparison **k == 250** is **false,** so the result of the logical **OR** operation is **false**. This results in **false** being stored in the variable named **answer** and then displayed in the browser window.

8.16 Step 1: Create a variable called **j** with a value of **95.**

Step 2: Create a variable called **k** with a value of **45.**

Step 3: Use one logical operator and two comparison operators to see if **j > 80** and/or **k = 30** is **true**. Use a **NOT** logical operator to reverse the logical result of the **OR** operation.

Step 4: Put the **true/false** value that's returned by the logical **NOT** operation into a variable called **answer.**

Step 5: Display the value of **answer** in the browser window.

Solution

```
<script>
    var j = 95;
    var k = 45;
    var answer = ( ! (j > 80 || k == 30))
```
continued on next page

```
document.write (answer);
</script>
```

Result displayed in browser:
false

> A logical **NOT** operator reverses the logical state of the logical operation that its being used with. Since **j = 95** and **k = 45**, the comparison **j > 80** is **true** and the comparison **k == 30** is **false,** so the result of the logical **OR** operation is **true**. The logical **NOT** operator reverses the **true** result from the **OR** operation to **false.** This results in **false** being stored in the variable named **answer** and then displayed in the browser window.

8.17 Step 1: Create a variable called **a** with a value of **"cat".**

Step 2: Create a variable called **b** with a value of **"dog".**

Step 3: Use two logical operators and three comparison operators to see if **a does not equal "fish"** and b equals "dog". Put the **true/false** value that's returned by the logical operation into a variable called **answer.**

Step 4: Display the value of **answer** in the browser window.

Solution
```
<script>
    var a = "cat";
    var b = "dog";
    var answer = (a != "fish" && b == "dog");

    document.write (answer);
</script>
```

> A logical **AND** operation returns a **true** when all comparisons (two comparisons in this case) are **true.** Since **a = "cat"** and **b = "dog"**, the comparison **a != "fish"** is **true** and the comparison **b == "dog"** is **true** so the result of the logical **AND** operation returns **true**. This results in **true** being stored in the variable named **answer** and then displayed in the browser window.

Result displayed in browser:
true

8.18 Step 1: Create a variable called **a** with a value of 2**5.**

Step 2: Create a variable called **b** with a value of **30.**

Step 3: Create a variable called **c** with a value of **40.**

Step 4: Perform an **OR** operation on the two comparisons: **a == 25** and **b == 30.** Use the result of the **OR** operation in an **AND** operation with the comparison **c == 40.**

Step 5: Put the **true/false** value that's returned by the AND operation into a variable called **answer.**

Step 5: Display the value of **answer** in the browser window.

Solution

```
<script>
   var a = 25;
   var b = 30;
   var c = 40;
   var answer = ((a == 25 || b == 30) && c == 40);
   document.write (answer);
</script>
```

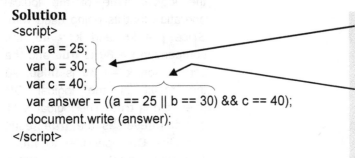

This example uses three variables, three comparisons and two different logical operators (|| and **&&**).The two comparisons in the **OR** operation are grouped together with parentheses, so, we evaluate the **OR** operation first and then use the result in the **AND** operation. **a == 25** is **true** and **b == 30** is **true**, so, the **OR** operation returns **true**. This **true** value is then used in the **AND** operation with the result of the comparison **c== 40**, which is **true**. This means that the **AND** operation also returns a **true** value which is the value that is stored in the variable **answer** and displayed on the browser screen.

Result displayed in browser:

true

8.19 Step 1: Create a variable called **w** with a value of **12**.

Step 2: Create a variable called **x** with a value of **16**.

Step 3: Create a variable called **y** with a value of **20**.

Step 4: Create a variable called **y** with a value of **24**.

Step 5: Perform an **OR** operation on the comparisons: **w == 12** and **x == 10**. Also perform an **OR** operation on the two comparisons: **y == 14** and **z == 24**. Compare the results of the two **OR** operations with an **AND** operator.

Step 6: Put the **true/false** value that's returned by the **AND** operation into a variable called **answer**.

Step 7: Display the value of **answer** in the browser window.

Solution

```
<script>
   var w = 12;
   var x = 16;
   var y = 20;
   var z = 24;
   var answer = ((w == 12 || x == 10) && (y == 14 || z == 24));
   document.write (answer);
</script>
```

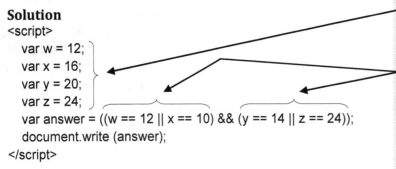

This example uses four variables, three comparisons and two different logical operators (|| and **&&**).The two comparisons in the **OR** operation are grouped together with parentheses, so, we evaluate the **OR** operation first and then use the result in the **AND** operation. **a == 25** is **true** and **b == 30** is **true**, so, the **OR** operation returns **true**. This **true** value is then used in the **AND** operation with the result of the comparison **c== 40**, which is **true**. This means that the **AND** operation also returns a **true** value which is the value that is stored in the variable **answer** and displayed on the browser screen.

Result displayed in browser:

true

8.2 JAVASCRIPT CONDITIONAL (Ternary) OPERATOR

The **conditional (ternary) operator** takes three operands or arguments. It returns one of two expressions depending on the true/false value of the condition. The first argument is a comparison argument, the second is the result upon a true comparison, and the third is the result upon a false comparison. The first argument of the conditional operator is a condition that's evaluated as true or false. The next expression contains the code to be executed if the expression evaluates to true followed by the : character and then the code to be executed if the expression evaluates to false.

Syntax

```
condition ? expression1 : expression2
```

Parameters

condition
> an expression that evaluates to **true** or **false**.

expression1, expression2
> expressions with values of any type.

Description

If condition is true, the operator returns the value of **expr1**; otherwise, it returns the value of **expr2**. The following examples show the ternary operator at work:

Example 1
```
<script>
   var x = true;
   var answer = (x) ? "x = true" : "x = false;
   document.write (answer);
</script>
```

Result displayed in browser:
x = true

We start this example by creating a variable called **x** and setting its valuable to the Boolean value **true**. Next we declare a variable called answer and set it equal to the value returned by the **conditional** (ternary) operation. The **conditional** operation evaluates the condition, which is this case is just the variable **x** (usually the condition is an expression of some kind). Since **x** is **true**, the first expression, **"x = true"** is returned and assigned as the value of the variable **answer** and then this value is displayed in the browser window.

Example 2
```
<script>
   var age = 30;
   var ageToDrive = (age >= 18) ? "legal : "illegal";
   document.write (answer);
</script>
```

Result displayed in browser:
legal

We start this example by creating a variable called **age** and giving it the value 30. Next we declare a variable called **ageToDrive** and set it equal to the value returned by the **conditional** operation. The **conditional** operation evaluates the condition **age >= 18**. Because **age = 30**, the conidtion evaluates to **true**. Since the condition is **true**, the first expression, **"legal"** is returned and assigned as the value of the variable **ageToDrive** and then this value is displayed in the browser window.

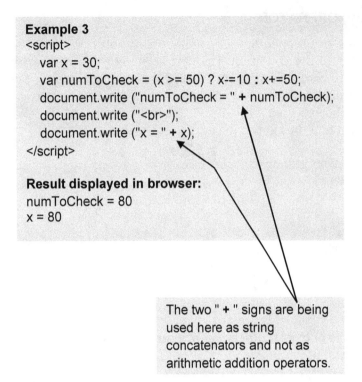

Example 3
```
<script>
   var x = 30;
   var numToCheck = (x >= 50) ? x-=10 : x+=50;
   document.write ("numToCheck = " + numToCheck);
   document.write ("<br>");
   document.write ("x = " + x);
</script>
```

Result displayed in browser:
numToCheck = 80
x = 80

The two " + " signs are being used here as string concatenators and not as arithmetic addition operators.

We start this example by creating a variable called **x** and giving it the value **30**. Next we declare a variable called **numToCheck** and set it equal to the value returned by the **conditional** operation. The **conditional** operation evaluates the condition **x >= 50** to see if it's **true** or **false**. Because **x = 30**, the condition evaluates to **false**. Since the condition is **false**, the second expression (in this case it's not a string to be displayed but code to be executed) which is **x+=10** (+= is a **add and assignment** operator [see chapter 1, page 15] which is equivalent to **x = x + 50**). The three **document.write()** commands result in two lines being displayed. The first line displays the name of the variable **numToCheck** along with its value and the second line displays the name of variable **x** along with its value.

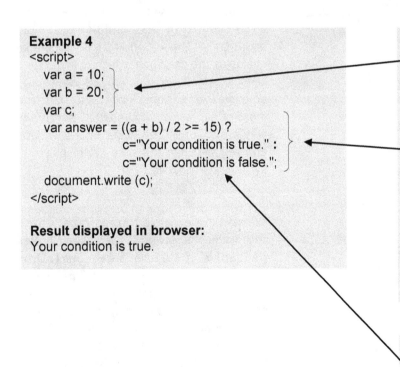

Example 4
```
<script>
   var a = 10;
   var b = 20;
   var c;
   var answer = ((a + b) / 2 >= 15) ?
               c="Your condition is true." :
               c="Your condition is false.";
   document.write (c);
</script>
```

Result displayed in browser:
Your condition is true.

We start this example by creating three variables: **a = 10**, **b = 20** and **c** (**c** is not assigned an initial value. Its value will be assigned as part of the condition operation).Next we declare a variable called **answer** and set it equal to the value returned by the **conditional** operation. The **conditional** operation evaluates the condition **(a+b) / 2 = 15** to see if it's **true** or **false**. Because **a = 10** and **b = 20**, the condition evaluates to **true**. Since the condition is **true**, the first expression which is **c="Your condition is true."**. This value is displayed in the browser window.

A command can be broken up into multiple lines without having any effect on its execution. JavaScript ignores the white space and acts like the command has been written on a single line.

8.20 Step 1: Create a variable called **a** with a value of **11.**

Step 2: Create a variable called **b** with a value of **14.**

Step 3: Use a **conditional operator** to test the condition **(a > b)**. If the comparison is **true,** the first expression, **"a is greater than b"**, will be selected. If the comparison is **false,** the second expression, **"a is not greater than b"**, will be selected. Put the value returned from the **conditional (ternary)** operation into a variable called **result** and then display the value of **result** in the browser window.

Solution

```
<script>
   var a = 11;
   var b = 14;
   var result = (a > b) ? "a is greater than b" :
          "a is not greater than b";
   document.write (result);
</script>
```

Result displayed in browser:

a is not greater than b

We start this problem by creating two variables: **a = 11, b = 14.** Next we declare a variable called **result** and set it equal to the value returned by the **conditional (ternary)** operation. The **conditional** operation evaluates the condition **(a > b)** to see if it's **true** or **false.** Because **a = 11 and b = 14**, the condition evaluates to **false**, so the second expression **"a is not greater than b"** is selected, loaded into the variable **result** and then displayed in the browser window.

8.21 Step 1: Create a variable called **a** with a value of **false.**

Step 2: Use a **conditional operator** to test the condition **(a == false)**. If the comparison is **true,** the first expression, **"a is false"**, will be selected. If the comparison is **false,** the second expression, **"a is true"**, will be selected.

Step 3: Put the value returned from the **conditional (ternary)** operation into a variable called **result** and then display the value of **result** in the browser window.

Solution

```
<script>
   var a = false;
   var result = (a == false) ? "a is false" :
          "a is true";
   document.write (result);
</script>
```

Result displayed in browser:

a is false

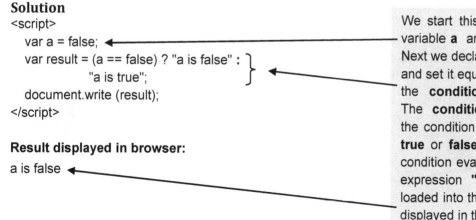

We start this problem by creating the variable **a** and setting it equal to **false.** Next we declare a variable called **result** and set it equal to the value returned by the **conditional (ternary)** operation. The **conditional** operation evaluates the condition **(a == false)** to see if it's **true** or **false.** Because **a = false**, the condition evaluates to **true**, so, the first expression **"a is false"** is selected, loaded into the variable **result** and then displayed in the browser window.

8.22 Step 1: Create a variable called **j** with a value of **100.**

Step 2: Use a **conditional operator** to test the condition **(j < 50)**. If the comparison is **true,** the first expression, ""**j is less than 50**", will be selected. If the comparison is **false,** the second expression, "**j is not less than 50**", will be selected.

Step 3: Put the value returned from the **conditional (ternary)** operation into a variable called **result** and then display the value of **result** in the browser window.

Solution

```
<script>
    var j = 100;
    var result = (j < 50) ? "j is less than 50" :
            "j is not less than 50";
    document.write (result);
</script>
```

We start this problem by creating the variable **j** and setting it equal to **100.** Next we declare a variable called **result** and set it equal to the value returned by the **conditional (ternary)** operation. The **conditional** operation evaluates the condition **(j < 50)** to see if it's **true** or **false.** Because **j = 100**, the condition evaluates to **false,** so, the second expression **"j is not less than 50"** is selected, loaded into the variable **result** and then displayed in the browser window.

Result displayed in browser:

J is not less than 50

8.23 Step 1: Create a variable called **x** with a value of **25.**

Step 2: Create a variable called **y** with a value of **35.**

Step 3: Use a **conditional operator** to test the condition **(x + y == 60)**. If the comparison is **true,** the first expression, "**The sum of x and y is 60**", will be selected. If the comparison is **false,** the second expression, "**The sum of x and y is not 60**", will be selected. Put the value returned from the **conditional (ternary)** operation into a variable called **z** and then display the value of **z** in the browser window.

Solution

```
<script>
    var x = 25;
    var y = 35;
    var z = ((x + y) == 60) ? "The sum of x and y is 60" :
            "The sum of x and y is not 60";
    document.write (z);
</script>
```

We start this problem by creating two variables: **x = 25** and **y = 35.** Next we declare a variable called **z** and set it equal to the value returned by the **conditional (ternary)** operation. The **conditional** operation evaluates the condition **((x + y) == 60)** to see if it's **true** or **false.** Because **x = 25** and **y = 35**, the condition evaluates to **true,** so the first expression **"The sum of x and y is 60"** is selected, loaded into the variable **z** and then displayed in the browser window.

Result displayed in browser:

The sum of x and y is 60

8.24 Step 1: Create a variable called **age** with a value of **18.**

Step 2: Use a **conditional operator** to test the condition **(age >= 21)**. If the comparison is **true,** the first expression, **age + " is old enough to buy beer",** will be selected. If the comparison is **false,** the second expression, **age + " is old not enough to buy beer"**will be selected.

Step 3: Put the value returned from the **conditional (ternary)** operation into a variable called **oldEnough** and then display the value of **oldEnough** in the browser window.

Solution

```
<script>
    var age = 18;
    var oldEnough = ((age >= 21) ?
                age + " is old enough to bey beer" :
                age + " is not old enough to buy beer";
    document.write (oldEnough);
</script>
```

We start this problem by creating the variable **age** and setting it equal to **18.** Next we declare a variable called **oldEnough** and set it equal to the value returned by the **conditional (ternary)** operation. The **conditional** operation evaluates the condition **(age >= 21)** to see if it's **true** or **false**. Because **age**j = **18**, the condition evaluates to **false**, so, the second expression **"18 is not old enough to buy beer"** is selected, loaded into the variable **oldEnough** and then displayed in the browser window.

Result displayed in browser:

18 is not old enough to buy beer

8.25 Step 1: Create a variable called **j** with a value of **true.**

Step 2: Use a **conditional operator** to test the condition **(j == true)**. If the comparison is **true,** the first expression, **"Yes, j is true"**, will be selected. If the comparison is **false,** the second expression, **"No, j is not true"**, will be selected.

Step 3: Display the value returned from the **conditional (ternary)** operation in an **alert box.**

Solution

```
<script>
    var j = true;
    alert ((j == true) ? "Yes, j is true" : "No, j is not true");
</script>
```

We start this problem by creating the variable **j** and setting it equal to **true.** The **conditional** operation evaluates the condition **(j == true)** to see if it's **true** or **false**. Because **j = true**, the condition evaluates to **true**, so, the first expression **"Yes, j is true"** is selected and displayed in the alert box.

Result displayed in alert box:

Yes, j is true

8.26 Step 1: Create a variable called **x** with a value of **"not on sale".**

Step 2: Use a **conditional operator** to test the condition **(x == "on sale")**. If the comparison is **true,** the first expression, **"$10"**, will be selected. If the comparison is **false,** the second expression, **"$15"**, will be selected.

Step 3: Put the value returned from the **conditional (ternary)** operation into a variable called **price** and then display the value of **price** in the browser window preceded by **"The price is "**.

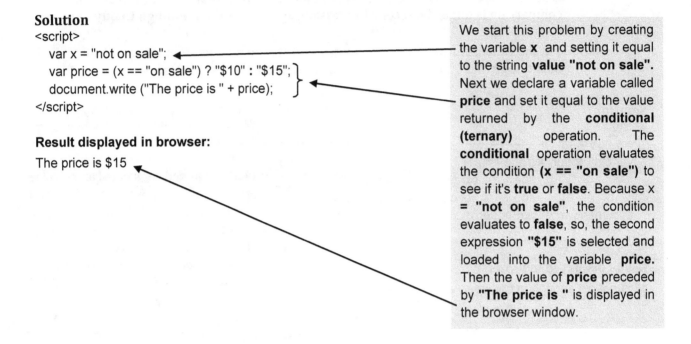

Solution
```
<script>
   var x = "not on sale";
   var price = (x == "on sale") ? "$10" : "$15";
   document.write ("The price is " + price);
</script>
```

Result displayed in browser:

The price is $15

We start this problem by creating the variable **x** and setting it equal to the string **value "not on sale"**. Next we declare a variable called **price** and set it equal to the value returned by the **conditional (ternary)** operation. The **conditional** operation evaluates the condition **(x == "on sale")** to see if it's **true** or **false**. Because x = **"not on sale"**, the condition evaluates to **false**, so, the second expression **"$15"** is selected and loaded into the variable **price.** Then the value of **price** preceded by **"The price is "** is displayed in the browser window.

8.27 Step 1: Create a variable called **a** with a value of **13.**

Step 2: Create a variable called **b** with a value of **17.**

Step 3: Use a **conditional operator** to test the condition **(x + y == 60)**. If the comparison is **true,** the first expression, **"The sum of x and y is 60"**, will be selected. If the comparison is **false,** the second expression, **"The sum of x and y is not 60"**, will be selected. Put the value returned from the **conditional (ternary)** operation into a variable called **z** and then display the value of **z** in the browser window.

Solution
```
<script>
   var a = 13;
   var b = 17;
   var c = ((a +b) == 25) ? "a + b is 25" : "a + b is not 25";
   document.write (c);
</script>
```

Result displayed in browser:

a + b is not 25

We start this problem by creating two variables: **a = 13** and **b = 17.** Next we declare a variable called **c** and set it equal to the value returned by the **conditional (ternary)** operation. The **conditional** operation evaluates the condition **((a + b) == 25)** to see if it's **true** or **false**. Because **a = 13 and b = 17,** the condition evaluates to **false**, so the second expression **"a + b is not 25"** is selected, loaded into the variable **c** and then displayed in the browser window.

8.28 Step 1: Create a variable called **animal** with a value of **"cat"**.

Step 2: Use a **conditional operator** to test the condition **(animal == "dog")**. If the comparison is **true,** the first expression, **"The animal is a dog!"**, will be selected. If the comparison is **false,** the second expression, **"The animal is not a dog!"**, will be selected.

Step 3: Display the value returned from the **conditional (ternary)** operation in an **alert box**.

Solution

```
<script>
    var animal = "cat";
    alert ((animal == "dog") ? "The animal is a dog!" :
                    "The animal is not a dog!");
</script>
```

We start this problem by creating a variable called **animal** and setting it equal to the string value **"cat"**. The **conditional** operation evaluates the condition **(animal == "dog")** to see if it's **true** or **false**. Because **animal = "cat"**, the condition evaluates to **false**, so, the second expression **"The animal is not a dog!"** is selected and displayed in the alert box.

Result displayed in alert box:

The animal is not a dog!

8.29 Step 1: Create a variable called **j** with a value of **"How are "**.

Step 2: Create a variable called **k** with a value of **"you today?"**.

Step 3: Create a variable called **l** with a value of **"combine strings"**.

Step 3: Use a **conditional operator** to test the condition **(l == "combine strings")**. If the comparison is **true,** the first expression, **j + k** will be selected. If the comparison is **false,** the second expression, **"No go!"**, will be selected. Put the value returned from the **conditional (ternary)** operation into a variable called **phrase** and then display the value of **phrase** in the browser window.

Solution

```
<script>
    var j = "How are ";
    var k = "you today?";
    var l = "combine strings";
    var phrase = (l == "combine strings") ?
                phrase = j + k : phrase = "No go!";
    document.write (phrase);
</script>
```

We start this problem by creating three variables: **j = "How are ", k = "you today?"** and **l = "combine strings".** Next we declare a variable called **phrase** and set it equal to the value returned by the **conditional (ternary)** operation. The **conditional** operation evaluates the condition **(l = "combine strings")** to see if it's **true** or **false**. Because **l = "combine srings"**, the condition evaluates to **true**, so the first expression **j + k** (**"How are you today?**) is selected, loaded into the variable **phrase** and then displayed in the browser window.

Result displayed in browser:

How are you today?

Chapter 9

JavaScript Data Types

9.1 WHAT IS A DATA TYPE?

In computer programming, a **data type** is a classification that identifies one of the different types of data, such as integer, string, Boolean and numeric data types. The assigned data type determines the possible values for that the type in question can contain. It also determines the various operations that can be done on values of that particular data type, along with the meaning of the data and the way values of the data type can be stored. Most programming languages contain the concept of data type as one of their key identifying features. Different languages, though, may use different, but similar, terminology.

A data type in most programming languages, such as JavaScript, is a set of data with values that have certain specific predefined characteristics. Usually, a small number of individual data types come built into a programming language. The language usually specifies the range of values for a given data type, how the values are handled and processed by the computer, and how they are stored in computer memory. When computer programs store data in variables, each variable must be assigned a specific data type, either automatically by the computer or manually by the programmer. Some common data types include integers, floating point numbers, Boolean, characters, integer, numeric, strings, and arrays.

Some programming languages require the programmer to define the data type of a variable before assigning it a value. Other languages, such as JavaScript, can automatically assign a variable's data type when the initial data is entered into the variable. For example, if a variable called **num1** is created with the value **15** the variable would be created as an **integer** or **numeric** data type. If the variable is set to **"What's your name?,"** the variable would be assigned a **string** data type.

9.2 JAVASCRIPT DATA TYPES

JavaScript contains several different data types which can hold various types of values. Also, the various data types fall into two separate categories:

- Primitive data type
- Non-primitive (reference) data type

There are five data types in the primitive data type category in JavaScript. They are as follows:

Data Type	Description
String	represents a sequence of characters such **"To be or not to be"**
Number	represents numeric values, such as **150**
Boolean	represents Boolean values, **either true** or **false**
Undefined	represents an **undefined** value
Null	represents a **null** value which is no value at all

JavaScript supports five primitive data types: number, string, Boolean, undefined, and null. These types are referred to as primitive data types because they are the basic data types from which more complex data types can be built. Of the five, only number, string, and Boolean are real data types that actually store data. Undefined and null are types that are only used in special circumstances.

Primitive data types are a basic part of the programming language. They're built into the language, so you don't need to import or include code from a class library to use them. They represent simple values and types such as numbers, strings and Boolean values. The programming language needs the primitive data types in order to perform its most basic functions. Without these primitive data types the language is unusable. The primitive data types sometimes serve as basic building blocks for more complex data types.

JavaScript also contains three non-primitive, or reference, data types which we will cover in detail in later chapters:

Data Type	Description
Object	represents an instance of an object which can have properties and methods
Array	represents an array which can contain one or more items
RegExp	represents a regular expression

JavaScript is a loosely typed or a dynamic language. That means you don't have to declare the type of a variable ahead of time. The type will get determined automatically while the program is being processed. That also means that you can have the same variable as different types:

```
var j;             // j is undefined
var j = 10;        // j is a number
var j = "John"     // j is a string
var j = true       // j is a Boolean value
```

Unlike many other computer programming languages, in JavaScript, the same variable can hold different types of data, at different times, all within the same program. This typing flexibility is called **loose typing** and **dynamic typing**. Both of these terms mean that a JavaScript variable can hold different data types at different times depending on context that the variable is found in.

With a loosely typed or dynamic typed language such as JavaScript, you don't have to declare the data type for a variable ahead of time, that is, whether it will be a string or a number or a Boolean value. Instead the data type is determined by the programming language as the application is being processed. There's no problem if you start out with a string variable and then want to use it as a number or a Boolean value. There's usually no problem with this, as long as the string actually contains a value that resembles a number as opposed to some totally unrelated data type. If you want to replace the number with a string later in the program, this will not cause a problem as JavaScript knows how to deal with this situation.

One thing that you definitely want to keep in mind is that the seeming advantages, simplicity and fewer programming hassles of loose/dynamic typing can really end up causing a lot of problems for the programmer. If you try to add two numbers but JavaScript interprets one of the variables as a string data type, you could end up with a string, instead of the sum of two numbers that you were expecting as the result of the arithmetic operation that you thought you performed. You always have to be aware of the context when you're dealing with the loose/dynamic data typing that's a part of JavaScript.

The following is an expanded explanation of the five primitive data types:

- **Number**—this includes floating point numbers as well as integers, for example 7, 300, 5.386.

- **String**—any number of characters, such as "x", "dog", "I love cats.".

- **Boolean**—this type of value can only have one of two values: true or false.

- **Undefined**—if you attempt to use or access a variable that doesn't exist, the special value **undefined** will be returned. The same undefined value will also be returned if you have declared a variable but forgot to give a value or purposely didn't give it a value. JavaScript will automatically initialize it and give it a value of undefined.

- **Null**—this data type is similar to **undefined** in that it is also a special data type that can have only one value - null. Null means that the variable has no value or nothing. The difference between a null value an undefined value is that if a variable has a null value, it is still defined, but its value is nothing whereas an undefined variable has no defined value.

9.2.1 The JavaScript *number* data type

JavaScript differs from many other programming languages in that it has only one type of number. JavaScript does not define different types of numbers, like integers, floating point short, or long. Also, JavaScript differs from programming languages such as Java in that it doesn't distinguish between integers and floating point numbers.

JavaScript numbers can be written with, or without decimals:

```
var x = 42.00;      // this is a number with 2 decimals
var y = 42;         // this is a number without decimals
var z = 42.00000    // this is a number with 5 decimals
```

Examples showing how JavaScript doesn't unnecessarily display the decimal values if they're all zero:

```
example:
<script>
   var a = 42.0000;
   document.write (a);
</script>

Result displayed in browser:
42
```

```
example:
<script>
   var a = 42.0000;
   var b = a + 5;
   document.write (b);
</script>

Result displayed in browser:
47
```

JavaScript numbers are always stored as double precision floating point numbers, following the international IEEE 754 standard. The double precision floating point format is a **computer number format** which takes up 8 bytes or 64 bits of computer memory and can contain a wide range of values by using a **floating point**. This format stores numbers in 64 bits, where the number is stored in bits 0 to 51, the exponent in bits 52 to 62, and the sign in bit 63. The term **floating point** refers to the fact that a number's decimal point can change its position or "float". This means that it can be placed anywhere in relation to the significant digits of the number (more on floating point numbers in a later chapter).

9.2.1.1 Numeric literals

Literals are used to represent values in JavaScript. These are fixed values, not variables, that the programmer puts into the script. This following are some examples of **numeric literals**:

Integers	Floating Point Numbers	Floating Point Numbers with Exponents	
10	5.625	13e5	(equivalent to 13×10^5, or 1300000)
+2504	33.3333	1.467E4	(equivalent to 1.467×10^4, or 14670)
-127	-7.89	-45.7756e3	(equivalent to -45.7756×10^3, or -45775.6)
1003654	- 2956784	+6.77e-3	(equivalent to 6.77×10^{-3}, or 0.00677

When a number appears directly in a JavaScript program, it's called a **numeric literal**. Note that any numeric literal can be signed, that is, preceded by a minus sign (-) to make the number negative. A numeric literal is a character string selected made up of a combination of digits, the plus sign, the minus sign, and the decimal point. Numeric literals must be formed according to the following rules:

- A literal must contain at least one digit (0-9)
- A literal must contain no more than one sign character (+ or -) and it must be the leftmost character of the string
- A literal must not contain more than one decimal point. The decimal point is treated as an assumed decimal point and may appear anywhere within the literal except as the rightmost character

A floating point number has the following parts.

- A decimal integer which can be signed (preceded by + or -).
- A decimal point ('.').
- A fraction.
- An exponent.

The exponent part is a small "e" or capital "E" followed by an integer, which can be signed as positive (+) or negative (-).

The following are examples of several floating point numbers :

Floating Point Numbers	
6.7934	
-24.85	
15.365e4	(equivalent to 15.365×10^4, or 153650)
1.3787E2	(equivalent to 1.3787×10^2, or 137.87)
5.667e-5	(equivalent to 5.667×10^{-5}, or 153650)
-7.893E-3	(equivalent to $-7.893 \times 10^{-3,}$ or -0.007893)

SOLVED PROBLEMS

9.1 Data types in JavaScript are divided into what two categories?

a) number, string

b) string, null

c) primitive, non-primitive

d) primitive, advanced

Solution

c

9.2 How many JavaScript primitive data types are there?

a) 3

b) 5

c) 6

d) 4

Solution

b

9.3 What are the five JavaScript primitive data types?

a) string, floating point, Boolean, double precision, null

b) string, integer, Boolean, undefined, null

c) string, number, Boolean, undefined, null

d) Boolean, null, string, single precision, double precision

Solution

c

9.4 What is another name for the primitive data type category?

a) integer

b) reference

c) array

d) pseudo-primitive

Answer

b

9.5 Match up the data type description on the right (a - e) with the data type name on the left (1 - 5):

1) string
2) number
3) Boolean
4) undefined
5) null

a) represents values of either true or false
b) represents a variable which has not been assigned a value
c) represents a sequence of characters enclosed by quotes
d) represents values such as 15, 200, 1.75 and -255
e) represents an undefined value

Solution

1) c
2) d
3) a
4) e
5) b

9.6 What are the three non-primitive, or reference, data types?

a) object, array, integer

b) object, array, regular expression

c) floating point, array, regular expression

d) numeric, array, object

Solution

b

9.7 What are is another descriptive name for a loosely typed language?

a) dynamic

b) primitive

c) generalized

d) malleable

Solution

a

9.8 Which one of the following is true about a loosely typed language?

a) You can add additional primitive data types to whenever you need them.

b) You don't have to declare a variable's data type ahead of time.

c) Once a variable's data type has been declared, you can't change it.

d) There are no specific rules regarding data types.

e) The same variable can hold different data types at the same time.

Solution

b

9.9 Match up the variable declaration on the left (1 - 10) with its data type on the right (a - e):

1) var x = 14.25;   a) string
2) var a = "Hello World!";   b) number
3) var j;   c) Boolean
4) var k = null;   d) undefined
5) var m = false;   e) null
6) var b = -33.215
7) var n;
8) var x = true;
9) var c = 1.487e3;
10) var name = "Eddie";

Solution

1) b
2) a
3) d
4) e
5) c
6) b
7) d
8) c
9) b
10) a

9.10 How will the final value of **x** in the following script be displayed in the browser window?

```
<script>
   var x = 17.0000;
   document.write (x);
</script>
```

a) 17.00

b) 17

c) 17.000

d) 17.0000

Solution

b

9.11 How will the final value of **x** in the following script be displayed in the browser window?

```
<script>
    var a = 8.00000;
    var b = 10;
    var x = a + b;
    document.write (x);
</script>
```

a) 18.00000

b) 18.00

c) 18

d) 180

Solution

c

9.12 How will the final value of **x** in the following script be displayed in the browser window?

```
<script>
    var a = 6.0000;
    var b = 2.15;
    var x = a + b;
    document.write (x);
</script>
```

a) 81.5

b) 8.15

c) 8.1500

d) 815.00

Solution

b

9.13 How will the final value of **x** in the following script be displayed in the browser window?

```
<script>
```

```
    var a = 20.00000;
    var b = 5.5;
    var x = a - b;
    document.write (x);
</script>
```

a) 25.5

b) 14.50000

c) 145.0000

d) 14.5

Solution

d

9.14 Which of the following are numeric literals?

a) 10

b) -6.25

c) x

d) 12e4

e) 1.447E10

f) num1

g) 5.85e-6

h) total25

Solution

a, b, d, e, g

9.15 Which of the following are floating point numbers?

a) 2.325

b) -105

c) 3.33E4

d) -15.1

e) 32

f) 6.667E-3

g) 54

h) -8.229e2

Solution

a, c, d, f, h

9.16 What are two equivalent values for each of the following floating point numbers?

a) 1e3

b) 2.35e2

c) 7.6E4

d) -3.15e2

e) 4.768e2

f) 2.82E-3

g) 5E-5

h) -1.555e2

Solution

a) 1×10^3 or 1000

b) 2.35×10^2 or 235

c) 7.6×10^4 or 76000

d) -3.15×10^2 or -315

e) 4.768×10^2 or 476.8

f) 2.82×10^{-3} or 0.00282

g) 5×10^{-5} or 0.00005

h) -1.555×10^2 or -155.5

9.2.2 The JavaScript *string* data type

A Javacode string value is a series of zero or more characters (letters, digits, and punctuation marks). The string data type is used to represent text enclosed within quotation marks in JavaScript. A string (or a text string) is a series of characters like "Robert Louis Stevenson". Strings are always written with quotes. You can use either single quotes or double quotes to enclose a string:

```
Text string examples:
var dogName = "Fido";                                    // text string enclosed within double quotes
var dogName = 'Fido';                                    // text string enclosed within single quotes
var txtString1 = "When in the course of human events";   // text string enclosed within double quotes
var txtString1 = 'When in the course of human events';   // text string enclosed within double quotes
```

Using double quotes or single quotes will have no affect on how the string is displayed:

```
<script>
    var dogName1 = "Fido";                This  string is enclosed in double
    var dogName2 = 'Fido';                quotes.
    document.write (dogName1);
    document.write ("<br>");
    document.write (dogName2);            This  string is enclosed in single
</script>                                quotes.

Result displayed in browser:            The resulting output is identical.
Fido
Fido
```

You can use quotes inside a string that's already surrounded by quotes, as long as they don't match the quotes surrounding the string. This means that double quotation marks can be contained in strings surrounded by single quotation marks, and single quotation marks can be contained in strings surrounded by double quotation marks.

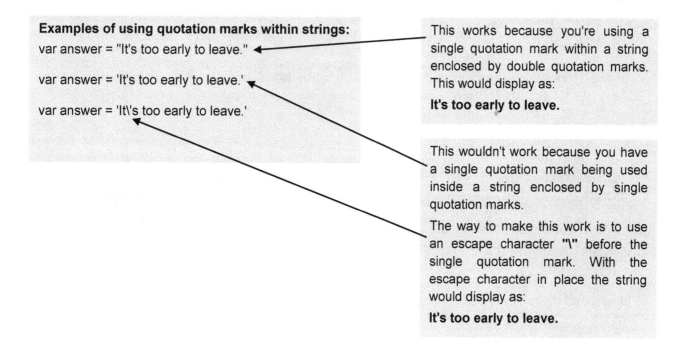

Examples of using quotation marks within strings:

var answer = "It's too early to leave."

var answer = 'It's too early to leave.'

var answer = 'It\'s too early to leave.'

This works because you're using a single quotation mark within a string enclosed by double quotation marks. This would display as:

It's too early to leave.

This wouldn't work because you have a single quotation mark being used inside a string enclosed by single quotation marks.

The way to make this work is to use an escape character "\" before the single quotation mark. With the escape character in place the string would display as:

It's too early to leave.

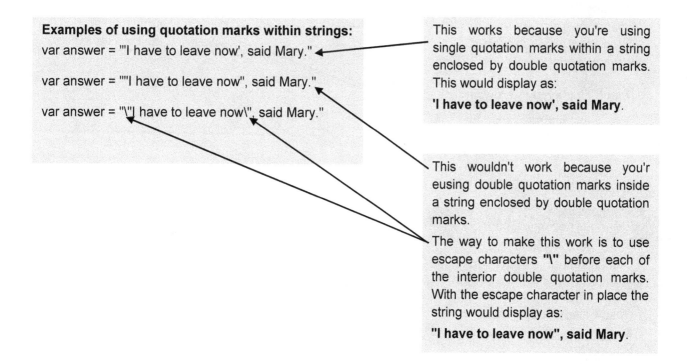

Examples of using quotation marks within strings:

var answer = "'I have to leave now', said Mary."

var answer = ""I have to leave now", said Mary."

var answer = "\"I have to leave now\", said Mary."

This works because you're using single quotation marks within a string enclosed by double quotation marks. This would display as:

'I have to leave now', said Mary.

This wouldn't work because you'reusing double quotation marks inside a string enclosed by double quotation marks.

The way to make this work is to use escape characters "\" before each of the interior double quotation marks. With the escape character in place the string would display as:

"I have to leave now", said Mary.

The **var** keyword is used to declare a variable. If you don't assign the variable a value when you initialize it, then, it is a declared, but uninitialized, variable. If you assign the string variable a value when you declare it, then, it is a declared and initialized variable:

```
var phrase;                    // the variable phrase is declared but not initialized

var phrase = "Hello World!";   // the variable phrase is declared and initialized to the value "Hello World!"
```

If you try to display the value of a declared but uninitialized string variable, a message will be displayed that says **undefined**:

```
<script>
   var answer;
   document.write (answer);
</script>
```

At this point, **answer** has not been given a value, so, its value is **undefined**. When it is initialized and given a value it will then have a defined value.

Result displayed in browser:

undefined

You can declare and initialize a string variable without giving it a value:

```
var phrase = "";
```

"" is called an empty string. Assigning an empty string to a variable changes its value from **undefined** to nothing. If you try to display the value of an string, you won't get an **undefined** message or any blank spaces - you'll get nothing at all.

```
<script>
   var answer = "";
   document.write (answer);
</script>
```

Because the variable **answer** contains an empty string, nothing is displayed in the browser window.

Result displayed in browser:

```
<script>
   var answer = "";
   var frag1 = "How are ";
   var frag2 = "you today?";
   document.write (frag1 + frag2);
</script>
```

If we concatenate **frag1** and **frag2** the displayed result is:
How are you today?

Result displayed in browser:

How are you today?

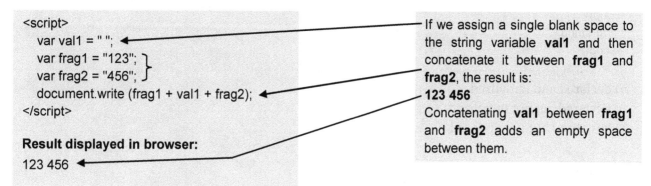

```
<script>
    var answer = "";
    var frag1 = "How are ";
    var frag2 = "you today?";
    document.write (frag1 + answer + frag2);
</script>
```

Result displayed in browser:

How are you today?

If we concatenate **frag1** and **answer** and **frag2,** the displayed result is exactly the same as it was before the empty string variable **answer** was added to the concatenation. Nothing at all is added by an empty string variable - no spaces, no values - nothing.

If we declare and initialize a string variable with the value of a single blank space, then, it now contains a value because a single (or any number of blank spaces) blank space is a value.

```
<script>
    var val1 = " ";
    var frag1 = "123";
    var frag2 = "456";
    document.write (frag1 + val1 + frag2);
</script>
```

Result displayed in browser:

123 456

If we assign a single blank space to the string variable **val1** and then concatenate it between **frag1** and **frag2**, the result is:

123 456

Concatenating **val1** between **frag1** and **frag2** adds an empty space between them.

An empty string has a length of zero. A string that contains one blank space has a length of 1.

```
<script>
    var val1 = "";
    var val2 = " ";
    document.write ("The length of val1 is " + val1.length);
    document.write ("<br>)";
    document.write ("The length of val2 is " + val2.length);
</script>
```

Result displayed in browser:

The length of val1 is 0
The length of val2 is 1

SOLVED PROBLEMS

9.17 Which of the following string variable declarations are valid?

a) var string1 = "My name is 'Shorty'.";

b) var string 1 = "I'm hungry.";

c) var string1 = 'She's coming over later.';

d) var string 1 = 'He\'s going to college now.';

e) var string1 = ""Bill said, "where is my car?"";

f) var string1 = "Mary said, \"Good morning!\"";

g) var string1 = 'Frank said, \"What day is it?"';

Solution
a, b, d, g

9.18 Choose the correct description of the variable **string1**:

```
<script>
   var string1;
</script>
```

a) declared and initialized
b) declared but not initialized
c) initialized but not declared

Solution
b

9.19 Choose the correct description of the variable **carName**:

```
<script>
   var carName = "Ford Bronco";
</script>
```

a) declared and initialized
b) declared but not initialized
c) initialized but not declared

Solution
a

9.20 What is displayed in browser window as the result of the following code:

```
<source>
   var cityState;
   document.write(cityState);
</source>
```

Solution
undefined

9.21 What is displayed in browser window as the result of the following code:

```
<source>
  var cityState = "Atlanta, GA";
  document.write (cityState);
</source>
```

Solution
Atlanta, GA

9.22 What is displayed in browser window as the result of the following code:

```
<source>
  var stateOfBirth = "";
  document.write (stateOfBirth);
</source>
```

Solution
                    - nothing will be displayed in the browser window

9.2.3 The JavaScript *Boolean* data type

The **Boolean** data type in JavaScript is a primitive of type (the most basic class of data type in JavaScript). The Boolean data type has two possible values: **true** and **false**. These values will not be surrounded by quotes. In other words, "true" and "false" are string values whereas **true** and **false** are both Boolean values. If you assign either true or false value to a variable, the type of the variable will be set to Boolean. Boolean variable values are mostly used along with "if", "if else" statements and "while" loops (more on these in a later chapter).

As we've seen, the number and string data types have a very large number of possible values. The Boolean data type, however, has only two. The two legal Boolean values are represented by the literals true and false. A Boolean value represents the truth or falsity of some kind of JavaScript statement. Boolean values are generally the result of comparisons (we covered comparisons and comparison operators in chapter 4) that are made in the course of a JavaScript program. For example:

    x == 50

This comparison tests to see if the value of x is equal to the numeric value of 50. The answer is either true or false. The comparison operator returns either the Boolean value true or false, depending on the outcome of the comparison. If x is equal to 50, the result of the comparison is the Boolean value true. If x is not equal to 50, the result of the comparison is the Boolean value false. Let's look at few examples to see how this works:

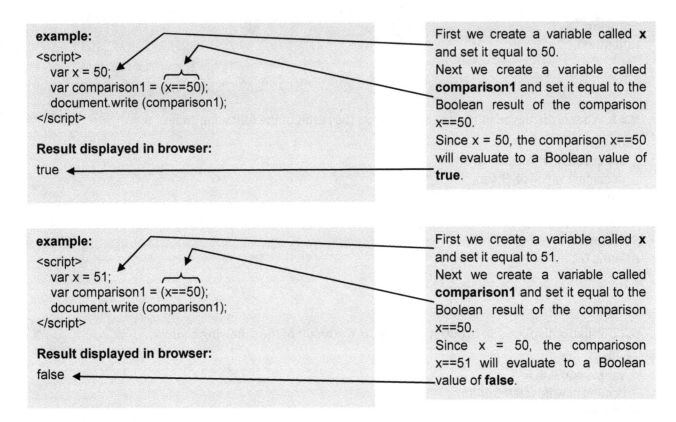

```
example:
<script>
    var x = 50;
    var comparison1 = (x==50);
    document.write (comparison1);
</script>

Result displayed in browser:
true
```

First we create a variable called **x** and set it equal to 50.
Next we create a variable called **comparison1** and set it equal to the Boolean result of the comparison x==50.
Since x = 50, the comparison x==50 will evaluate to a Boolean value of **true**.

```
example:
<script>
    var x = 51;
    var comparison1 = (x==50);
    document.write (comparison1);
</script>

Result displayed in browser:
false
```

First we create a variable called **x** and set it equal to 51.
Next we create a variable called **comparison1** and set it equal to the Boolean result of the comparison x==50.
Since x = 50, the comparioson x==51 will evaluate to a Boolean value of **false**.

Boolean values are often used in JavaScript control structures such as **if** and **if/else** statements and **while** loops (we'll cover these in more depth in a later chapter). For example, the result of an if/else statement in JavaScript usually performs one action if a comparison is true and another action if the value is false. In an if or **if/else** statement you usually combine a comparison (such as ==, !=, > or <) that creates a Boolean value directly along with a statement that uses the Boolean value that's been returned by the comparison. This code checks if **x** equals 50. If the comparison returns a Boolean value of true, it displays "Hello World!" in the browser window; if the comparison returns a Boolean value of false, it displays "Goodbye Cruel World!":

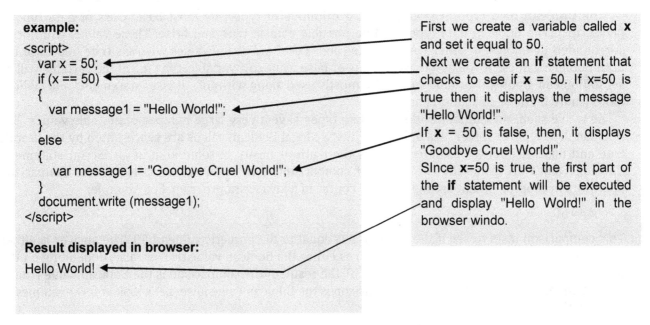

```
example:
<script>
    var x = 50;
    if (x == 50)
    {
        var message1 = "Hello World!";
    }
    else
    {
        var message1 = "Goodbye Cruel World!";
    }
    document.write (message1);
</script>

Result displayed in browser:
Hello World!
```

First we create a variable called **x** and set it equal to 50.
Next we create an **if** statement that checks to see if **x** = 50. If x=50 is true then it displays the message "Hello World!".
If **x** = 50 is false, then, it displays "Goodbye Cruel World!".
SInce **x**=50 is true, the first part of the **if** statement will be executed and display "Hello Wolrd!" in the browser windo.

The **Boolean( )** function is a built-in JavaScript function that is used to convert different data types to a Boolean value. The following table shows how the conversions are made:

Data Type	Result of Conversion to a Boolean Value Using the Boolean() Function
Undefined	always returns **false**
Null	always returns **false**
Boolean	returns the original Boolean value
Number	returns **false** if the number is 0, + 0 or - 0; returns **true** for any other number
String	returns false if the string is empty (""); returns true for any other string value

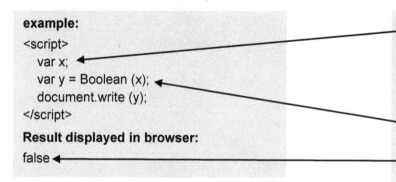

example:
```
<script>
   var x;
   var y = Boolean (x);
   document.write (y);
</script>
```
Result displayed in browser:
false

The variable **x** is not given a value when it's declared so its data type is **undefined**. Using a variable with a data type of **undefined** as the argument in the **Boolean()** function returns **false** (see the above table). Variable **y** is set equal to the **false** value returned by the **Boolean()** function and then displayed on the browser screen.

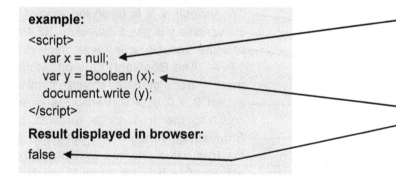

example:
```
<script>
   var x = null;
   var y = Boolean (x);
   document.write (y);
</script>
```
Result displayed in browser:
false

The variable **x** is given a value of **null** when it's declared, so its data type is **null**. Using a variable with a data type of **null** as the argument in the **Boolean()** function returns **false** (see the above table). Variable **y** is set equal to the **false** value returned by the **Boolean()** function and then displayed on the browser screen.

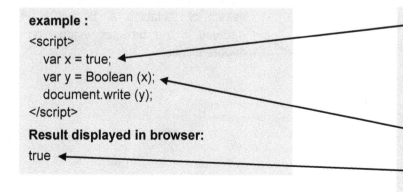

example :
```
<script>
   var x = true;
   var y = Boolean (x);
   document.write (y);
</script>
```
Result displayed in browser:
true

The variable **x** is given a Boolean value of **true** when it's declared, so its data type is **Boolean**. Using a variable with a data type of **Boolean** as the argument in the **Boolean()** function returns the original **Boolean** value of the variable (see the above table). Variable **y** is set equal to the **true** value returned by the **Boolean()** function and then displayed on the browser screen.

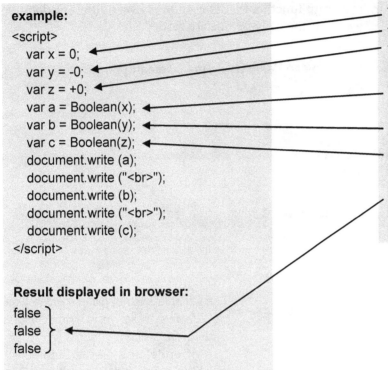

example:

```
<script>
    var x = 0;
    var y = -0;
    var z = +0;
    var a = Boolean(x);
    var b = Boolean(y);
    var c = Boolean(z);
    document.write (a);
    document.write ("<br>");
    document.write (b);
    document.write ("<br>");
    document.write (c);
</script>
```

Result displayed in browser:

false
false
false

The variable **x** is is given the value 0; the variable **y** is given the value - 0 and the variable **z** is given the value + 0. The **Boolean()** function returns **false** if its argument is 0, - 0 or + 0. Variable **a** is set equal to the **false** value returned by **Boolean(x)**. Variable **b** is set equal to the **false** value returned by **Boolean(y)** and variable **c** is set equal to the **false** value returned by **Boolean(z)**. The values of variables **a**, **b** and **c** are displayed in the browser window on 3 separate lines.

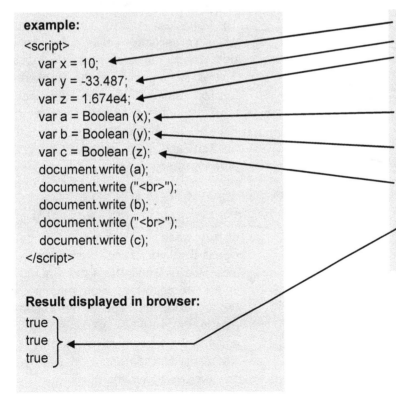

example:

```
<script>
    var x = 10;
    var y = -33.487;
    var z = 1.674e4;
    var a = Boolean (x);
    var b = Boolean (y);
    var c = Boolean (z);
    document.write (a);
    document.write ("<br>");
    document.write (b);
    document.write ("<br>");
    document.write (c);
</script>
```

Result displayed in browser:

true
true
true

The variable **x** is is given the value 10; the variable **y** is given the value - 33.487 and the variable **z** is given the value 1.67e4. The **Boolean()** function returns **true** if its argument is any number except 0, - 0 or + 0. Variable **a** is set equal to the **true** value returned by **Boolean(x)**. Variable **b** is set equal to the **true** value returned by **Boolean(y)** and variable **b** is set equal to the **true** value returned by **Boolean(z)**. The values of variables **a**, **b** and **c** are dislayed in the browser window on 3 separate lines.

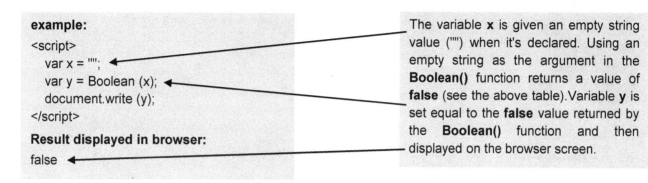

example:

```
<script>
    var x = "";
    var y = Boolean (x);
    document.write (y);
</script>
```

Result displayed in browser:

false

The variable **x** is given an empty string value ("") when it's declared. Using an empty string as the argument in the **Boolean()** function returns a value of **false** (see the above table). Variable **y** is set equal to the **false** value returned by the **Boolean()** function and then displayed on the browser screen.

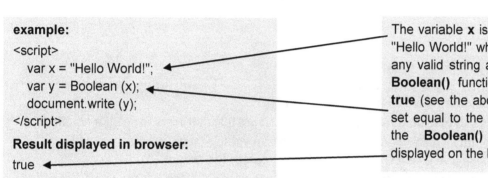

example:

```
<script>
    var x = "Hello World!";
    var y = Boolean (x);
    document.write (y);
</script>
```

Result displayed in browser:

true

The variable **x** is given a string value of "Hello World!" when it's declared. Using any valid string as the argument in the **Boolean()** function returns a value of **true** (see the above table). Variable **y** is set equal to the **true** value returned by the **Boolean()** function and then displayed on the browser screen.

SOLVED PROBLEMS

9.23 What two possible values can a Boolean data type value have?

a) yes, no

b) true, false

c) 0, 1

d) on, off

Solution

b

9.24 If you assign a true or false value to a variable, what data type will the variable be set to?

a) string

b) null

c) Boolean

d) number

Solution

c

9.25 What is the value of variable **y** in the following script and what is its data type?

```
<script>
  var x = 25;
  var y = (x==26);
</script>
```

a) false, Boolean

b) true, Boolean

c) false, number

Solution
a

9.26 Step 1: Declare a variable called **a** with a value of "yes".

Step 2: Create an **if/else** statement (see example on p. 180) that tests to see if **a** equals "yes".

Step 3: If the comparison **a=="yes"** returns a Boolean value of **true**, create a variable called **displayMsg** and give it the value **"I like chocolate ice cream."**

Step 4: If the comparison **a=="yes"** returns a Boolean value of **false**, create a variable called **displayMsg** and give it the value **"I don't like chocolate ice cream."**

Step 5: Display the value of **displayMsg** in the browser window.

Solution
```
<script>
  var a = "yes";
  if ( a == "yes")
  {
     var displayMsg = "I like chocolate ice cream.";
  }
  else
  {
     var displayMsg = "I don't like chocolate ice cream.";
  }
  document.write (displayMsg);
</script>
```

9.27 Step 1: Declare a variable called **firstName** with a value of **"Bob"**.

Step 2: Create an **if/else** statement (see example on p. 180) that tests to see if **firstName** does not equal "Bob".

Step 3: If the comparison **firstName != "Bob"** returns a Boolean value of **true**, create a variable called **displayMsg** and give it the value **"You're not Bob."**

Step 4: If the comparison **firstName != "Bob"** returns a Boolean value of **false**, create a variable called **displayMsg** and give it the value **"Hi, Bob!"**

Step 5: Display the value of **displayMsg** in the browser window.

Solution
```
<script>
  var firstName = "Bob";
  if ( firstName != "Bob")
  {
    var displayMsg = "You're not Bob.";
  }
  else
  {
    var displayMsg = "Hi, Bob!";
  }
  document.write (displayMsg);
</script>
```

9.28 What JavaScript function is used to convert a value that is one of the primitive data types into a Boolean value?

a) boolean( )

b) Boolean( )

c) convert( )

Solution
b

9.29 The **Boolean( )** function always returns either one of what two values?

a) 0, 1

b) true, false

c) yes, no

Solution
b

9.30 If you use an **undefined** value/data type as the argument in a **Boolean( )** function, what Boolean value will be returned?

a) true

b) false

c) negative

d) 0

e) Boolean

Solution

b

9.31 If you use a **null** value/data type as the argument in a Boolean( ) function, what Boolean value will be returned?

a) true

b) false

c) negative

d) 0

Solution

b

9.32 If you use a **Boolean** value/data type as the argument in a **Boolean( )** function, what Boolean value will be returned?

a) true

b) false

c) true or false

d) 0

Solution

c

9.33 If you use a **number** value/data type (with any value but zero) as the argument in a Boolean( ) function, what Boolean value will be returned?

a) true

b) false

c) the Boolean value of the variable

d) 0

Solution

a

9.34 If you use a **number** value/data type with a value of zero as the argument in a **Boolean( )** function, what Boolean value will be returned?

a) true

b) false

c) the numeric value of the variable

Solution

b

9.35 If you use a **number** value/data type with a negative number (any negative number except -0) as the argument in a **Boolean( )** function, what Boolean value will be returned?

a) true

b) false

c) the Boolean value of the variable

d) 0

Solution

a

9.36 Which of the following is an empty string?

a) "empty"

b) " " ◄─────────── these are quote marks with one blank space between them

c) "" ◄─────────── these are quote marks with no spaces between them

Solution

c

9.37 If you use an empty string as the argument in a **Boolean( )** function, what Boolean value will be returned?

a) true

b) false

c) a blank space

Solution

a

9.38 If you use any string value (except an empty string) as the argument in a **Boolean( )** function, what Boolean value will be returned?

a) true

b) false

c) the string value of the variable

Solution

a

9.39 What will the value of variable **k** be that's written to the browser window?

```
<script>
    var j;
    var k = Boolean (j);
    document.write (k);
</script>
```

a) true

b) false

c) undefined

Solution

b

9.40 What will the value of variable **b** be that's written to the browser window?

```
<script>
    var a = null;
    var b = Boolean(a);
    document.write(b);
</script>
```

a) true

b) false

c) undefined

Solution

b

9.41 What will the value of variable **y** be that's written to the browser window?

```
<script>
    var x = false;
    var y = Boolean (x);
    document.write (y);
</script>
```

a) true

b) false

c) undefined

Solution
b

9.42 What will the value of variable **n** be that's written to the browser window?

```
<script>
    var m = 0;
    var n = Boolean (m);
    document.write (n);
</script>
```

a) true

b) false

c) undefined

Solution
b

9.43 What will the value of variable **b** be that's written to the browser window?

```
<script>
    var a = 34.25;
    var b = Boolean (a);
    document.write (b);
</script>
```

a) true

b) false

c) undefined

Solution
a

9.44 What will the value of variable **k** be that's written to the browser window?

```
<script>
   var j = -1.34e4;
   var k = Boolean (j);
   document.write (k);
</script>
```

a) true

b) false

c) undefined

Solution
a

9.45 What will the value of variable **y** be that's written to the browser window?

```
<script>
   var x = "Good morning!";
   var y = Boolean(x);
   document.write (y);
</script>
```

a) true

b) false

c) undefined

Solution
a

9.46 What will the value of variable **b** be that's written to the browser window?

```
<script>
   var a = " ";  ←———————————— quotation marks with one blank space between
   var b = Boolean (a);
   document.write (b);
</script>
```

a) true

b) false

c) undefined

Solution
a

9.47 What will the value of variable **k** be that's written to the browser window?

```
<script>
  var j = "";          ←———————————————— quotation marks with no space between
  var k = Boolean (j);
  document.write (k);
</script>
```

a) true

b) false

c) undefined

Solution

b

9.2.4 The JavaScript *undefined* data type

In JavaScript, a variable without a value, has the value **undefined**. Its data type is also **undefined**. The **undefined** data type in JavaScript is used to indicate that a variable has been declared but hasn't yet been assigned a value. If you write the code:

```
var weeklyPay;          ←————
```
The variable **weeklyPay** is not assigned a value in this statement, so, it's **value** is **undefined** and its **data type** is **undefined**.

the resulting data type for **weeklyPay** will be **undefined** because we didn't assigned it a value. The **undefined** type refers to those variables that haven't been assigned a value.

An empty string is a string that consists of two quotation marks with nothing between them (""). An empty string is said to have an empty value but an empty value is not the same thing as an undefined value. An empty string variable has both a value and a type. The result of the following code is that nothing will be displayed on the browser screen. The value of variable **y** isn't **undefined**. Variable **y** has a definite value and that value is no characters or spaces - it's not even a blank space, it's nothing.

```
<script>
   var y = "";          ←————
   document.write (y);
</script>
```
The variable **y** is assigned the value of an empty string in this statement, so, it's **value** is **""** and its **data type** is **string**. The result displayed in the browser window will be nothing. You will see nothing when you look in the browser window.

```
<script>
   var y;               ←————
   document.write (y);
</script>
```
The variable **y** is not assigned a value in this statement, so, it's **value** is **undefined** and its **data type** is **undefined**. The word "**undefined**" will be displayed in the browser window.

As long as no value is assigned to a variable, its type will be **undefined**. When a value is assigned, it will no longer have the data type **undefined** but instead it will have one of other primitive data types that are supported in JavaScript. The new data type could be either **number**, **string**, **Boolean**, or **null** depending on what value you have assigned to the variable.

What if you wanted a variable that you haven't assigned a value to yet to no longer be assigned as an **undefined** data type, but you don't actually want to assign it a meaningful value. In that case, you could assign it the **null** type.

```
<script>
    var y;
    document.write (y);
    var y = null;
    document.write("<br>");
    document.write (y);
</script>
```

Initially, the variable **y** is not assigned a value so, it's **value** is **undefined** and its **data type** is **undefined**. "undefined" is displayed in the browser window. When **y** is given the value **null**, it still has no value but its data type is no longer **undefined**. Its data type is now **null**.

Result displayed in the browser window:
undefined
null

If you want to, you can explicitly initialize a variable to be **undefined**. This really isn't necessary because any variable that is declared, but not initialized, automatically gets the value of **undefined** whether it's explicitly declared or not. The following two code snippets are identical to one another and produce the same results in the browser window:

```
<script>
    var y = undefined;
    document.write (y);
</script>
```

Variable **y** is explicitly given the value and data type **undefined**, "undefined" is displayed in the browser window.

Result displayed in the browser window:
undefined

```
<script>
    var y;
    document.write (y);
</script>
```

Variable **y** is initialized but not assigned a value. It is automatically given the data type **undefined**, "**undefined**" is displayed in the browser window.

Result displayed in the browser window:
undefined

Although **null** and the **undefined** value and data types are distinct, the == equality operator considers them to be equal to one another because neither a variable with a data type of **null** or a variable with a data type of **undefined** have a value. Consider the following:

```
<script>
    var y = null;
    var x = undefined;
    if (x == y)
    {
        document.write ("x and y are equal");
    }
```

```
    else {
       document.write("x and y are not equal");
    }
   </script>
```

SOLVED PROBLEMS

9.48 In JavaScript, a variable that has been declared but has not been given a value has what data type?

a) number

b) Boolean

c) undefined

d)string

Solution

c

9.49 An empty string consists of what?

a) two quotation marks with one blank space between them

b) two quotation marks with nothing between them

c) a string made up of all zeroes

d)a string that has been assigned the value of null

Solution

b

9.50 What kind of value does an empty string have?

a) empty value

b) null

c) undefined

d)negative

Solution

a

9.51 What data type is an empty string?

a) number

b) Boolean

c) undefined

d)string

e) null

Solution

d

9.52 Does an empty string have an undefined data type?

a) yes

b) no

Solution

b

9.53 After a value is assigned to an empty string variable, what data type will it not be?

a) string

b) null

c) undefined

d) Boolean

Solution

a

9.54 What kind of data type would you assign to a variable that has no value and you don't want it to have a data type of undefined?

a) null

b) Boolean

c) number

d)undefined

Solution

a

9.55 How would you <u>explicitly</u> initialize the variable **firstName** in order to give it an undefined value and data type?

a) var firstName;

b) var firstName = false;

c) var firstName = undefined;

d) var firstName = 0;

Solution

c

9.56 How would you <u>implicitly</u> initialize the variable **firstName** in order to give it an undefined value and data type?

a) var firstName = undefined;

b) var firstName ;

c) var firstName = ""; ◄——————————————— no spaces between the quotation marks

d) var firstName implicit;

Solution

b

9.57 The **== equality** operator compares what?

a) the data type of two variables

b) the value of two variables

c) both the data type and value of two variables

Solution

b

9.58 The **=== identity** operator compares what?

a) the data type of two variables

b) the value of two variables

c) both the data type and value of two variables

Solution

c

9.59 What Boolean value would the following comparison return and put into the variable called result and then display on the browser screen?

```
<script>
    var val1 = null;
    var val2 = undefined;
```

```
    result = (val1 == val2);
    document.write (result);
</script>
```

a) true

b) false

c) null

d) undefined

Solution

a

9.60 What Boolean value would the following comparison return and put into the variable called result and then display on the browser screen?

```
<script>
    var val1 = null;
    var val2 = undefined;
    result = (val1 === val2);
    document.write (result);
</script>
```

a) true

b) false

c) null

d) undefined

Solution

b

9.61 What will be displayed on the browser screen as a result of this script and what is the data type of the variable **j**?

```
<script>
    var j = "";   ◄──────────────── no spaces between the quotation marks
    document.write (j);
</script>
```

Solution
- nothing will be displayed on the browser screen
- the data type of **j** is string

5.62 What will be displayed on the browser screen as a result of this script and what is the data type of the variable **dayOfTheWeek**?

```
<script>
   var dayOfTheWeek;
   document.write (dayOfTheWeek);                    document.write(j);
</script>
```

Solution

- The error message "undefined" will be displayed on the browser screen
- the data type of **dayOfTheWeek** is undefined

9.63 What is the value and data type of the variable **monthOfYear** in line 2 and what is its value and data type in line 3 of the code?

```
<script>
   var monthOfYear;
   var monthOfYear = "February";
</script>
```

Solution

- line 2: undefined, undefined
- line 3: string, "February"

9.64 Which of the two following data types never have a usable value?

a) number

b) null

c) string

d)Boolean

e) undefined

Solution

b, e

9.2.5 The JavaScript *typeof* operator

The **typeof** operator is used to get the data type of its operand. The data type is returned as a string. The operand can be either a literal or a data structure such as a variable, a function, or an object. **typeof** is a unary operator that is placed before its single operand, which can be of any type. Its value is a string indicating the data type of the operand. The **typeof** operator is a unary operator (an operator that only takes one operand) that is placed before its single operand, which can be of any type. Its value is a string indicating the data type of the operand.

The **typeof** operator evaluates to "number", "string", or "Boolean" if its operand is a number, string, or Boolean value. It evaluates to "object" for an operand with a null data and to "undefined" if the operand is undefined.

Syntax

The **typeof** operator is followed by its operand:

```
typeof operand
```

or

```
typeof (operand)  ◄──────────── the parentheses are optional
```

The **typeof** operator is useful when you're troubleshooting code. It identifies the data type of a variable or literal that you're working with, or the data type that an expression evaluates to. Knowing the data type of a variable, a literal or an expression can be helpful because the data type you're working with determines how you can manipulate the data, what actions you can perform on it and what operators you can use with the data.

The **typeof** operator returns type information as a string. There are five (actually seven, but we'll cover the other two returned values in later chapters) possible values that **typeof** returns: "number," "string," "boolean," "object," and "undefined." The **typeof** statement returns "object" for a null value. The parentheses are optional in the **typeof** syntax.

Examples

typeof statement	Value Returned
typeof "Bill"	string
typeof 5.765	number
typeof ("Hello World!")	string
typeof false	Boolean
typeof (true)	Boolean
typeof null	object
typeof (undefined)	undefined
typeof (-5.34e4)	number
typeof (false)	Boolean
typeof true	Boolean
typeof (null)	object
typeof undefined	undefined

The following is a list of the string values that will be returned by the **typeof** operator for a given operand type:

Operand	typeof (operand) evaluates to
Undefined	"undefined"
Null	"object"
Boolean	"Boolean"
Number	"number"
String	"string"

Examples of the **typeof** operator in action:

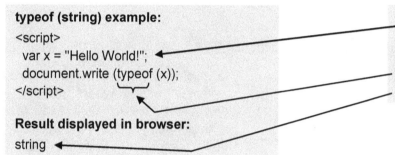

typeof (string) example:
```
<script>
  var x = "Hello World!";
  document.write (typeof (x));
</script>
```

Result displayed in browser:
string

The variable **x** is assigned the value **"Hello World!"** which is a **string** data type so **"string"** is returned by the **typeof** operator and displayed in the browser screen.

typeof (number) example:
```
<script>
  var x = 2.45e5;
  document.write (typeof (x));
</script>
```

Result displayed in browser:
number

The variable **x** is assigned the value 2.45e5 which is a **number** data type so **"number"** is returned by the **typeof** operator and displayed in the browser screen.

typeof (null) example:
```
<script>
  var x = null;
  document.write (typeof (x));
</script>
```

Result displayed in browser:
object

The variable **x** is assigned the value **null** which is a **null** data type, but for some unknown reason, the typeof operator returns "object" when a null value is the operand, so "object" is returned by the **typeof** operator and displayed in the browser screen.

typeof (undefined) example:

```
<script>
  var x;
  document.write (typeof (x));
</script>
```

Result displayed in browser:

undefined

The variable **x** is not assigned a value **"so it's data type is undefined** and **undefined** is returned by the **typeof** operator and displayed in the browser screen.

typeof (Boolean) example:

```
<script>
  var x = true;
  document.write (typeof (x));
</script>
```

Result displayed in browser:

boolean

The variable **x** is assigned the value **true** so it's data type is **Boolean** and **boolean** is returned by the **typeof** operator and displayed in the browser screen.

Here are some other examples of the **typeof** operator in action:

```
<script>
  var x;
  if (typeof x=="undefined")
  {
    document.write ("Variable x is undefined");
  }
  else
  {
    document.write ("Variable x has a defined value");
  }
</script>
```

Result displayed in browser:

Variable x is undefined.

In this example we use an **if/else** statement with a **typeof** operator to determined if the data type of variable **x** is **undefined**. If it is, then we display the message: "**Variable x is undefined**" in the browser window. If the data type of variable **x** isn't **undefined**, then, we display the message: "**Variable x has a defined value**".

Since x is undefined the if statement will display "Variable x is undefined in the browser window.

```
<script>
  var index = 5;
  var result = (typeof (index) == 'number');
  document.write (result);
</script>
```

Result displayed in browser:
true

In this example, variable **x** is set equal to **5** which is a **number** data type. Next we do an **equal** comparison between the result returned from a **typeof** operation with the variable called **index** as the operand and the string '**number**'. Since the value returned by **typeof (index)** is '**number**', the comparison will evaluate to **true**, so, **true** will be loaded into the variable called **result** and then the value of **result** will be displayed in the browser screen.

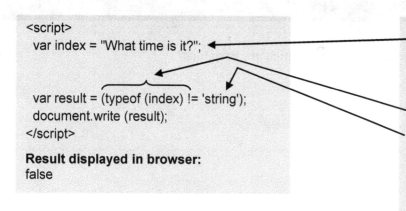

```
<script>
  var index = "What time is it?";

  var result = (typeof (index) != 'string');
  document.write (result);
</script>
```

Result displayed in browser:
false

In this example, variable **x** is set equal to **"What time is it?"** which is a **string** data type. Next we do a **not equal** comparison between the result returned from a **typeof** operation with the variable called **index** as the operand and the string '**string**'. Since the value returned by **typeof (index)** is '**string**', the comparison will evaluate to **false**, so, **false** will be loaded into the variable called **result** and then the value of **result** will be displayed in the browser screen.

Notice the results that this **typeof** examples gives:

```
<script>
  var value1 = 5 + 10;
  var value2 = "5" + "10";
  var value3 = "5" + 10;
  var value4 = 5 + "10";

  var result1 = typeof (value1);
  var result2 = typeof (value2);
  var result3 = typeof (value3);
  var result4 = typeof (value4);

  document.write (result1 + "<br>");
  document.write (result2 + "<br>");
  document.write (result3 + "<br>");
  document.write (result4 + "<br>");

  document.write (value1 + "<br>");
  document.write (value2 + "<br>");
  document.write (value3 + "<br>");
  document.write (value4 + "<br>");
</script>
```

Result displayed in browser:
number
string
string
string
15
510
510
510

In this script we assign various combinations of **number** and **string** values to the variables **value1**, **value2**, **value3** and **value4**. As you can see, the only time a combination results in a **number** data type being loaded into its corresponding result variable is when both **5** & **10** are **numbers** and neither one is a **string**. When either **5** or **10** or both are a **string** then the combination will result in a value with the **string** data type. Also, when a combination results in a **string** data type, the **5** & **10** are concatenated **string** fashion rather than being added arithmetically as can be seen in the results displayed in the browser window.

SOLVED PROBLEMS

9.65 Which of following eight choices are literals and which are variables?

a) "hello"

b) 12.56

c) var1

d) weeklyPay

e) -7.45e6

f) dayOfMonth

g) "What time is it?"

h) msg1

Solution

literals: a, b, e, g
variables: c, d, f, h

9.66 What is the purpose of the **typeof** operator?

a) to assign the data type of a variable or a literal

b) to get the data type of a variable or a literal

c) to change the data type of a variable or a literal

d) to get the value of a variable

Solution

b

9.67 What form is the data type of the operand in a **typeof** operation returned as?

a) undefined

b) null

c) string

d) number

Solution

c

9.68 What of the following is the correct syntax for a **typeof** operation?

a) typeof (operand)

b) TypeOf (operand)

c) typeOf (operand)

d) typeof (variable)

Solution

a

9.69 How many operands does a **typeof** operation have?

a) 1

b) 0

c) 2

d) 3

Solution

a

9.70 What is a **unary** operator?

a) an operator that has no operands

b) an operator that has only one operand

c) an operator that can only use literals and not variables

Solution

b

9.71 What does the **typeof** operator evaluate to if its operand has a null value?

a) "undefined"

b) 0

c) false

d)"object"

Solution

d

9.72 What does the **typeof** operator evaluate to if its operand has an undefined value?

a) "string"

b) "undefined"

c) "number"

d) typeof (variable)

Solution
b

9.73 What does the **typeof** operator evaluate to if its operand has a string value?
a) "string"
b) "undefined"
c) "number"
d) "object"

Solution
a

9.74 What does the **typeof** operator evaluate to if its operand has a Boolean value?
a) "object"
b) "undefined"
c) "number"
d) "Boolean"

Solution
d

9.75 The statement **typeof "hello"** is exactly equivalent to which of the following:
a) typeOf ("hello")
b) typeof ("hello")
c) TypeOf "hello"

Solution
b

9.76 Does it make any difference if you use parentheses around the operand in a **typeof** statement?
a) yes
b) no

Solution
b

9.77 Select the value that's returned by each **typeof** statement (#1-10) on the left from the list of the five possible return values (a-e) on the right:

1) typeof "Goodnight"   a) "string"

2) typeof 3.14156   b) "number"

3) typeof ("How are you?")   c) "Boolean"

4) typeof false   d) "object"

5) typeof null   e) "undefined"

6) typeof (undefined)

7) typeof (true)

8) typeof (-6.85E5)

9) typeof ("Today is Monday")

10) typeof (null)

Solution

1) a

2) b

3) a

4) c

5) d

6) e

7) c

8) b

9) a

10) d

9.78 What will be displayed in the browser screen as a result of the following script?

```
<script>
   var msg1 = "animals";
   document.write (typeof (msg1));
</script>
```

Solution
string

9.79 What will be displayed in the browser screen as a result of the following script?

```
<script>
```

```
    var value = 3.684E3;
    document.write(typeof (value));
</script>
```

Solution
number

9.80 What will be displayed in the browser screen as a result of the following script?

```
<script>
    var j = null;
    document.write (typeof (msg1));
</script>
```

Solution
object

9.81 What will be displayed in the browser screen as a result of the following script?

```
<script>
    var a;
    document.write (typeof (a));
</script>
```

Solution
undefined

9.82 Step 1: Create a string variable called **memorySize** with a value of **"2 Gigabytes"**.
Step 2: Use a **typeof** operator to display the data type of **memorySize** in an alert box.

Solution
```
<script>
    var memorySize = "2 Gigabytes";
    alert (typeof (memorySize));
</script>
```

Result displayed in alert box:
string

9.82 Step 1: Create a numeric variable called **diameter** with a value of **8.234.**

Step 2: Create a variable called **dataType** and use a **typeof** operator to set it equal to the data type of
      diameter.
Step 3: Display the value of **dataType** in the browser

Solution

```
<script>
   var diameter = 8.234;
   var dataType = typeof (diameter);
   prompt (dataType, "This is the data type of the variable 'diameter'." );
</script>
```

Result displayed in browser:

number

Chapter 10

JavaScript Conditional Statements: Part 1

10.1 JAVASCRIPT CONDITIONAL STATEMENTS

In normal JavaScript program execution, the program flow is linear: that is, each statement is processed as it appears from the first statement of the script to the last statement of the script, one statement after another. This linear flow can be interrupted and changed by using a JavaScript conditional statement. You do this by performing some type of conditional test on literals, variables or some combination of the two and then running a block of code if the test evaluates to a preselected Boolean state (true or false). One of the more common approaches to changing the program flow is by using a JavaScript **conditional statement**.

Conditional statements are used to decide the flow of execution (that is, the decision is made by the conditional statement as to which code block will be executed next) based on different conditions. If a condition is true, you can perform one action (all the JavaScript statements necessary to perform the action are set out in an optional block of code) and if the condition is false, you can perform another action (set out in another block of code).

Flowchart of a conditional statement

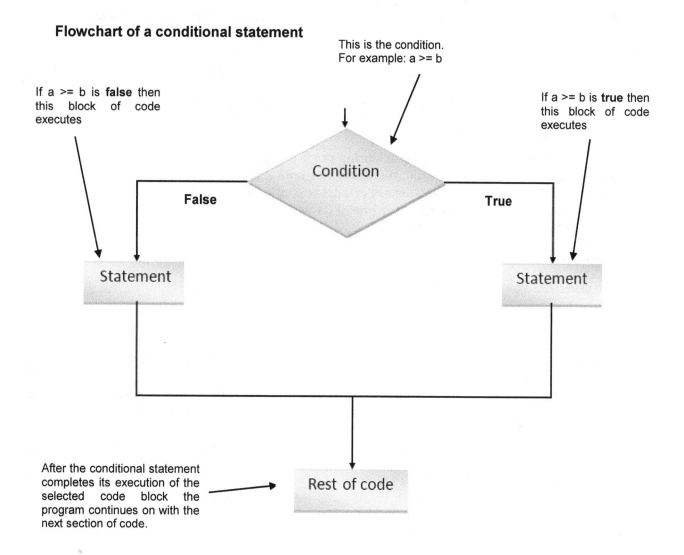

The term **conditional** comes from the fact that a certain logical or comparison condition, or conditions, have to be met or found to be true before the code block associated with the statement is processed. Basically, this means that if some value (the result of an expression, a variable, or possibly a literal) evaluates to true, then execute the code in the following code block; otherwise, jump to the end of the block, and continue code execution at the very next line.

There are five primary types of conditional statements in JavaScript (we'll cover each type of conditional statement in more detail later in the chapter):

- if statement
- if...else statement
- if...else if...if statement
- switch statement
- conditional operator

Conditional Statement	Description
if	use this if you want to execute a set of code when a condition is true
if...else	use this if you want to select one of two sets of code lines to execute
if...else if...if	use this if you want to select one of many sets of lines to execute
switch	use this if you want to select one of many sets of lines to execute
conditional operator	use this if you want to assign a value to a variable based on some condition

There are certain conditions that occur during program execution you may want to check using a conditional statement. For example, did the user enter both a first and last name or a valid zip code? Conditional statements test for the trueness or falseness of conditions like these. The most common conditional check uses the **if** statement (or one of its variations such as the **if...else** statement or the **if...else if...else** statement, as in this example:

```
if (age < 21)
  {
    alert ("The You are too young to buy beer.");
  }
```

The **if** conditional statement in the above example compares the user's age with the number 21 and displays an alert message to the user if the comparison is true. The use of the **if** keyword marks the start of the conditional test which is contained in the parenthetical expression that immediately follows the **if** keyword (in this case, **age < 21**). Programmers use conditional statements like this in most of their JavaScript programs. As we've seen, then, conditional statements are used to decide the flow of execution based on different conditions. If a condition is true, you can perform one action and if the condition is false, you can perform another action.

To summarize what we've covered so far about conditional statements: a conditional statement uses conditional logic (a comparison operator or a logical operator) to determine what block of JavaScript code to execute next. By using some conditional logic to check the stated conditions, we can determine if a certain condition (for example **x == 30**) is true or false. If the condition is true, we transfer execution to a predetermined part of the program. Otherwise, if the condition is false, we transfer execution to some part of the program.

In order to create a condition to be tested in a conditional operation, we need to write a conditional statement with a comparison operator or a logical operator. A comparison operator compares the value of one element with that of another. An expression that uses a comparison operator is referred to as a Boolean expression because it always evaluates to one of the two Boolean values: true or false. either true or false.

We already covered comparison operators and logical operators briefly in chapter 4 but we want to review them briefly so that we can integrate their functionality with the five basic types of comparison operations.

10.1.1 Comparison operators

A comparison operator compares its operands and returns a logical value based on whether the comparison is true. The operands can be numerical, string, logical, or object values. Strings are compared based on standard lexicographical ordering, using Unicode values. In most cases, if the two operands are not of the same type, JavaScript attempts to convert them to an appropriate type for the comparison. This behavior generally results in comparing the operands numerically. The sole exceptions to type conversion within comparisons involve the === and !== operators, which perform strict equality and inequality comparisons. These operators do not attempt to convert the operands to compatible types before checking equality. The following is a list of the major JavaScript arithmetic operators:

- Equal
- Not equal
- Strict equal
- Strict not equal
- Greater than
- Greater than or equal to
- Less than
- Less than or equal to

Equal (==)

Returns true if the operands are equal.

Assume that x = 10 and y = 20 in this example:

Example

```
(x == y) is not true
```

Not (!=)

Returns true if the operands are not equal.

Assume that x = 10 and y = 20 in this example:

Example

```
(x != y) is true
```

Strict Equal (===)

Returns true if the operands are equal and of the same type.

Assume that x = 5 and y =5 in this example and that they are both integer data type:

Examples

(x === y) is true

Assume that x = 10 and is an integer and y = "10" and is a string in this example:

(x === y) is false

Strict Not Equal (!==)

Returns true if the operands are not equal and/or not of the same type.

Assume that x = 5 and is an integer and y =5.0 and is a floating-point number in this example:

Example

(x !== y) is true   integers and floating point values are both **number** types

Greater Than (>)

Returns true if the left operand is greater than the right operand.

Assume that x = 10 and y = 20 in this example:

Example

(x > y) is false

Greater Than Or Equal To (>=)

Returns true if the left operand is greater than or equal to the right operand.

Assume that x = 10 and y = 20 in this example:

Example

(x >= y) is false

Less Than (<)

Returns true if the left operand is less than the right operand.

Assume that x = 10 and y = 20 in this example:

Example

(x > y) is true

Less Than Or Equal To (<=)

Returns true if the left operand is less than or equal to the right operand.

Assume that x = 10 and y = 20 in this example:

Example

(x <= y) is true

Assume that x = 20 and y = 10 in this example:

(x <= y) is false

Table of Comparison operators:

Operator	Name	Description
==	Equal	Checks if the value of two operands are equal or not, if yes, then the condition becomes true.
!=	Not Equal	Checks if the value of two operands are equal or not, if the values are not equal, then the condition becomes true.
===	Strict Equal	Checks if the value and data type of the left operand is the same as the value and data type of the right operand, if yes, then the condition becomes true.
>	Greater Than	Checks if the value of the left operand is greater than the value of the right operand, if yes, then the condition becomes true.
>=	Greater Than or Equal To	Checks if the value of the left operand is greater than or equal to the value of the right operand, if yes, then the condition becomes true.
=	Greater Than or Equal To	Checks if the value of the left operand is greater than or equal to the value of the right operand, if yes, then the condition becomes true.
<	Less Than	Checks if the value of the left operand is less than the value of the right operand, if yes, then the condition becomes true.
<=	Less Than or Equal To	Checks if the value of the left operand is less than or equal to the value of the right operand, if yes, then the condition becomes true.

10.1.2 Logical operators

Logical operators are used when testing for Boolean (true and false) states. Usually when these operators are used, they are testing Boolean values and return a Boolean result. The following is a list of the major JavaScript arithmetic operators:

- AND
- OR
- NOT

AND (&&)

Returns true if two or more conditions are met. All comparisons must be true for the AND statement to equate to TRUE.

Assume that x = 8 and y = 3 in both examples:

Examples

(x < 10 && y > 1)   this statement is true

(x < 6 && y > 1)   this statement is false

(x > 6 && y > 2)   this statement is false

OR (||)

Returns true if one or more conditions are met. One or more of the comparisons must be true for the OR statement to equate to TRUE.

Assume that x = 8 and y = 3 in both examples:

Examples

(x == 5 || y == 7)   this statement is false

(x < 6 || y > 5)   this statement is true

(x < 6 || y < 2)   this statement is true

NOT (!)

Reverses the logical state of its operand. If a condition is true, then the Logical NOT operator will make it false.

Assume that x = 8 and y = 3 in both examples:

Examples

!(x == 5 || y == 7)   this statement is true

!(x < 6 || y > 5)   this statement is false

Table of Logical operators:

Operator	Name	Description
&&	AND	Returns true if all comparisons are true. All comparisons must be true for the AND statement to equate to TRUE.
||	OR	Returns true if at least one of the comparisons are true. One or more of the comparisons must be true for the OR statement to equate to TRUE.
!	NOT	Reverses the logical state of its operand. If a condition is true, then the Logical NOT operator will make it false.

10.2 The if statement

The **if** statement is the fundamental control statement that allows JavaScript to make decisions and execute statements based on the results of some conditional test. Use the **if** statement to specify a block of JavaScript code to be executed if a condition is true. The syntax for a basic if statement is as follows:

```
if (expression) {
    statement(s) to be executed if condition is true
}
```

In the above example a JavaScript comparison or logical expression is evaluated. If the resulting value is true, the statements between the curly braces are executed. If the expression is false, then no statement would be executed and the program will jump to the first statement to appear after the **if** statement. In most cases, you will use comparison operators when making decisions.

There are two main parts to an **if** statement: the conditional statement and the code to be executed. The conditional statement is a statement that will always evaluate to a Boolean value of either true or false. The most common type of conditional statement will check to see if one value equals another value although other comparison operators such as greater than, equal to, etc can also be used.

Another way to think of an **if** statement is as follows: Use the **if** statement if you want to specify a block of JavaScript code to be executed if a condition is true.

```
if (condition) {
    block of code to be executed if the condition is true
}
```

For example:
```
<script>
  var name = "Fred";
  if (name == "Fred") {
     document.write ("Hello Fred.");
  }
  document.write ("What time is it?");
</script>
```

Since the string variable **name** was initialized with the value "**Fred**", the comparison **name == "Fred"** will return **true** and the code between the curly braces will be executed. If the variable name had been initialized with the name "**Joe**" the comparison **name == "Fred"** would have returned **false** and program execution would have skipped over the code between the curly braces and started executing at the first statement after the **if** statement.

IF statement examples:

example:
```
<script>
  var myNum = 23;
  if (myNum = 23) {
     document.write("Your number is 23")
  }
</script>
```

Since the variable **myNum** was initialized with the value **23**, the comparison **myNum == 23** is **true** and the code between the curly braces will execute. This results in "**Your number is 23**" being displayed in the browser window.

Result displayed in browser:
Your number is 23

example:
```
<script>
  var myNum = 45;
  if (myNum = 23) {
    document.write ("Your number is 23")
  }
</script>
```

Result displayed in browser:

Since the variable **myNum** was initialized with the value **45**, the comparison **myNum == 23** is **false** and the code between the curly braces will not execute. This results in nothing being displayed in the browser window.

example:
```
<script>
  var age = 20;
  if (age > 20) {
    document.write ("Your old enough to " +
    "drive.");
  }
</script>
```

Result displayed in browser:

Since the variable **age** was initialized with the value **20**, the comparison **age > 20** is **false** and the code between the curly braces will not execute. This results in nothing being displayed in the browser window. Don't forget to concatenate the string value if it is continued on the next line.

example:
```
<script>
  var moneyAvailable = 250;
  if (moneyAvailable < 300) {
    document.write("You can't afford it!")
  }
</script>
```

Result displayed in browser:
You can't afford it!

Since the variable **moneyAvailable** was initialized with the value **250**, the comparison **moneyAvailable < 300** is **true** and the code between the curly braces will execute. This results in "You can't afford it!" being displayed in the browser window.

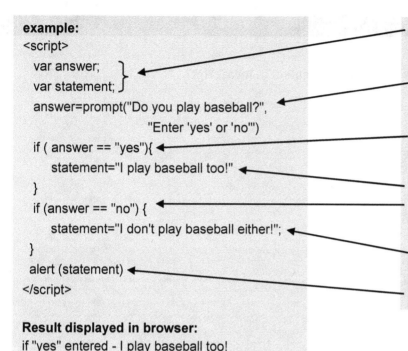

example:
```
<script>
  var answer;
  var statement;
  answer=prompt("Do you play baseball?",
                "Enter 'yes' or 'no'")
  if ( answer == "yes"){
      statement="I play baseball too!"
  }
  if (answer == "no") {
      statement="I don't play baseball either!";
  }
  alert (statement)
</script>
```

First we declare two variables, **answer** and **statement** without initializing them. Then we display a prompt box with **"Do you play baseball?"** in the user prompt section and **"Enter 'yes' or 'no'"** in the user response section. Next we use an **if** statement to check to see if **answer** equals **"yes"**. If it does then we set the value of statement to **"I play baseball too!"** Next, we use another **if** statement to check if answer = **"No"**. If this is **true** than we set statement equal to **"I don't play baseball either!"**. After the second **if** statement we use display the value of **statement** in an alert box.

Result displayed in browser:
if "yes" entered - I play baseball too!
if "no" entered - I don't play baseball either!

---

example:
```
<script>
  var x = 16;
  if (x > 10 && x < 25) {
    alert ("The comparison is true.");
  }
</script>
```

First we declare the variable **x** and initialize it with the value **16**. Since **x** is greater than **10** and less than **25** the comparison in the **if** statement is **true** which causes **"The comparison is true."** to be displayed in an alert box.

Result displayed in browser:
The comparison is true.

---

example:
```
<script>
  var j = 25;
  if (j < 10 || j > 20) {
    alert ("The comparison is true.");
  }
</script>
```

First we declare the variable **j** and initialize it with the value **25**. Since **j** is not less than **10** but it is greater than **20** the comparison in the **if** statement is **true** because only one comparison in an **OR** statement has to be **true** for the **OR** statement to return **true**.. This causes **"The comparison is true."** to be displayed in an alert box.

Result displayed in browser:
The comparison is true.

SOLVED PROBLEMS

10.1 What is the basic form of the **if** conditional statement in JavaScript?

a) if (statement to be executed) {

   condition

   }

b) if (condition) {

   statement to be executed

   }

c) if (condition)

   statement to be executed

   }

Solution

b

10.2 In an **if** statement, what happens if the condition is true?

a) the statement(s) inside the curly braces is/are executed

b) program execution skips to the first statement after the end of the **if** statement

c) true or false are displayed in the browser window

Solution

a

10.3 In an **if** statement, what happens if the condition is false?

a) the statement(s) inside the curly braces is/are executed

b) program execution skips to the first statement after the end of the **if** statement

c) true or false are displayed in the browser window

Solution

b

10.4 The values false, 0 and an empty string all evaluate to what Boolean value in JavaScript??

a) 0

b) true

c) false

Solution

c

10.5 Match the comparison operators on the left (1-8) with their symbols on the left (a-h):

1) greater than   a) <=
2) less than   b) ==
3) greater than or equal to   c) !=
4) less than or equal to   d) >=
5) equal to   e) ===
6) not equal to   f) <
7) identical to   g) !==
8) not identical to   h) >

Solution

1) h

2) f

3) d

4) a

5) b

6) c

7) e

8) g

10.6 What are we comparing when we use the equality (==) operator?

a) the values of two entities

b) the value and data type of the entities

c) the data type and Boolean value of two entities

Solution

a

10.7 What are we comparing when we use the identity (===) operator?

a) the values of two entities

b) the value and data type of two entities

c) the data type and Boolean value of two entities

Solution

b

10.8 true and **false** are what kind of values?

a) identity

b) string

c) Boolean

d) number

Solution

c

10.9 If x = 0, what will the condition **if (x)** evaluate to?

a) true

b) false

c) 0

Solution

b

10.1 Step 1: Create a string variable called **firstName** and set its value to "Mary".

Step 2: Use an **if** statement to see if the value of **firstName** is "Mary". If the value of **firstName** is "Mary", display "Your name is Mary." in the browser window.

Solution

```
<script>
   var firstName = "Mary";
   if (firstName == "Mary") {
      document.write ("Your name is Mary.");
   }
</script>
```

Result displayed in browser:

Your name is Mary.

10.11 Step 1: Create a variable called **selectedNumber** and set its value to 100.

Step 2: Use an **if** statement to see if the value of **selectedNumber** is 100. If the value of

selectedNumber is 100, display "The number you selected is 100." in an alert box.

Solution

```
<script>
  var selectedNumber = 100;
  if (selectedNumber == 100) {
    alert ("The number you selected is 100.");
  }
</script>
```

Result displayed in alert box:

The number you selected is 100.

10.12   Step 1: Create a variable called **age** and set its valueto 68.

       Step 2: Use an **if** statement to see if the value of **age** is greater than or equal to 65. If **age** is greater than or equal to 65, display "You are definitely old enough to retire." in the browser window.

Solution

```
<script>
  var age = 68;
  if (age >= 65) {
    document.write ("You are definitely old enough to retire.");
  }
</script>
```

Result displayed in browser:

You are definitely old enough to retire.

10.13   Step 1: Create a variable called **weeklyPay** and initialize it to a value of 450.

       Step 2: Use an **if** statement to see if the value of **weeklyPay** is less than 500. If it is, display "You make less than $500 a week." in the browser window.

Solution

```
<script>
  var weeklyPay = 450;
  if (weeklyPay < 500) {
    document.write ("You make less than $500 a week.");
  }
</script>
```

Result displayed in browser:

You make less than $500 a week.

10.14 Step 1: Create a variable called **dailyTips** and initialize it to a value of 85.

Step 2: Use an **if** statement to see if the value of **dailyTips** is less than 50. If **dailyTips** is less than 50, display "You make less than $50 a day in tips." on one line in the browser window and then display "To be exact, you make $<value of **dailyTips**> in tips." on the next line in the browser window.

Step 3: Use a second **if** statement to check to see if **dailyTips** is more than 50. If this is true, then, you should display "You make more than $50 a day in tips." on one line in the browser window and then display "To be exact, you make $ <value of **dailyTips**> in tips." on the next line in the browser window.

Solution

```
<script>
   var dailyTips = 85;
   if (dailyTips < 50) {
      document.write ("You make less than $50 a day in tips.");
      document.write ("<br>");
      document.write ("To be exact, you make $" + dailyTips + " in tips.");
   }
   if (dailyTips > 50) {
      document.write ("You make more than $50 a day in tips.");
      document.write ("<br>");
      document.write ("To be exact, you make $" + dailyTips + " in tips.");
   }
</script>
```

Result displayed in browser:

You make more than $50 a day in tips.
To be exact, you make $85 in tips.

10.15 Step 1: Create a variable called **cashInBank** and give it a value of 5000.

Step 2: Create a variable called **priceOfCar** and set it equal to 16000.

Step 2: Use an **if** statement to see if the value of **cashInBank** is less than the value of **priceOfCar**. If this is true, then, display "You can't afford the car." in an alert box.

Solution

```
<script>
   var cashInBank = 5000;
   var priceOfCar = 16000;
   if (cashInBank < priceOfCar) {
      alert ("You can't afford the car.");
   }
</script>
```

Result displayed in browser:

You can't afford the car.

10.16   Step 1: Create a variable called **x** and set its value to 30.

Step 2: Create a variable called **y** and set its value to 60.

Step 3: Use an **if** statement to see if **x** is less than or equal to 40 and if **y** does not equal 50. If both conditions are true then display "The if statement condition is true." in an alert box.

Solution

```
<script>
   var x = 30;
   var y = 60;
   if (x <= 40 && y != 50) {
      alert ("The if statement condition is true.");
   }
</script>
```

The condition in this **if** statement uses the two comparisons (**x <= 40** and **y != 50**) as the operands in a logical **AND** (**&&**) operation. Because this is a logical **AND** operation both comparisons must be **true** in order for the **if** statement to evaluate the condition as **true**. Since **x** is less than or equal to **40** and **y** does not equal **50**, the **if** condition is **true** and the message "The if statement condition is true." is displayed in an alert box.

Result displayed in browser:

The if statement condition is true.

10.17   Step 1: Create a variable called **x** and set its value to 30.

Step 2: Create a variable called **y** and set its value to 60.

Step 2: Use an **if** statement to see if **x** is less than or equal to 40 and if **y** does not equal 50. If both conditions are true then display "The if statement condition is true." in an alert box.

Solution

```
<script>
   var num1 = 50;
   var num2 = 90;
   if (num1 <= 40 && num2 == 90) {
      alert ("The condition is true.");
   }
   if (!(num1 <= 40 && num2 == 90)) {
      alert ("The if statement condition is false.");
   }
</script>
```

This is similar to the previous problem, but if the condition evaluates to **false** we also want to display a message. To accomplish this we add a second **if** statement that tests for the exact opposite condition that's tested for in the first **if** statement. We do this by copying the condition from the first **if** statement and enclosing it inside a **NOT** (!) logical operator which reverses the logical state of its operand. For example, if a condition is **true**, then the logical **NOT** operator will make it **false** and if a condition is **false**, then the logical **NOT** operator will make it **true**. If the condition evaluates to false, the second if statement will cause the message "The if statement condition is false."

Result displayed in browser:

The if statement condition is false.

10.18 Step 1: Create a variable called **answer**.

Step 2: Create a variable called **reply**.

Step 3: Set the value of **answer** to be the value entered into the user response section of a prompt box. The user prompt message should say "Are you male or female?" and the initial message in the user response section before the user enters anything should be "Please enter 'male' or 'female".

Step 4: Use an **if** statement to see if the user entered "male". If the user entered "male" set the value of reply to "Nice to meet you, Sir."

Step 5: Use a second **if** statement to see if the user entered "female". If the user entered "female" set the value of reply to "Hello, Ma'am."

Step 6: Use a third **if** statement to see if the user entered neither "male" nor "female". If this is the case, then, set the value of reply to "Please enter either 'male' or 'female'."

Solution

```
<script>
  var answer;
  var reply;
  answer = prompt("Are you male or female?",
           "Enter 'male' or 'female'");
  if (answer == "male") {
   reply = "Nice to meet you, Sir";
  }
  if (answer == "female") {
   reply = "Hello, Ma'am.";
  }
  if (answer != "male" && answer != "female") {
   reply = "Please enter either 'male' or female'";
  }
  alert (reply);
</script>
```

The first argument in the user prompt statement is the user prompt message. In this case, the message is "Are you male or female?". The second argument in the user prompt statement is the user response default message. The default message is in the user reponse section of the prompt box when the prompt box first appears. The user will enter his response over the default user response message. In this case, the default user reponse message is "Enter 'male' or 'female'." The user will enter his response over this default message.

prompt (*user prompt message, default user response message*)

10.19 Step 1: Create a variable called **correctNumber**.

Step 2: Set the value of **correctNumber** to be the value entered into the user response section of a prompt box. The user prompt message should say "Enter the number 1, 2 or 3.".

Step 3: Use an **if** statement to see if the user entered the number **1**. If the user entered the number 1 display "The number you entered is 1." in an alert box.

Step 4: Use an **if** statement to see if the user entered the number **2**. If the user entered the number 1 display "The number you entered is 2." in an alert box.

Step 5: Use an **if** statement to see if the user entered the number **3**. If the user entered the number 1 display "The number you entered is 3." in an alert box.

Step 5: Use an **if** statement with two AND operators and three NOT EQUAL operators to see if the user didn't enter a 1, 2 or 3. If that's the case, then, display "You were supposed to enter 1, 2 or 3."

Solution

```
<script>
  var correctNumber;
  correctNumber = prompt ("Enter the number 1, 2 or 3.");
  if (correctNumber == 1) {
    alert ("The number you entered is 1.");
  }
  if (correctNumber == 2) {
    alert ("The number you entered is 2.");
  }
  if (correctNumber == 3) {
    alert ("The number you entered is 3.");
  }
  if (correctNumber != 1 && correctNumber != 2 && correctNumber != 3) {
    alert ("You were supposed to enter 1, 2 or 3.");
  }
</script>
```

10.20 When is an identity (===) comparison true?

a) when the two entities being compared have the same data type

b) when the two entities being compared have the same value and the same data type

c) when the two entities being compared have the same value

Solution

b

6.21 What are the three logical operators in JavaScript?

a) XOR, NAND, NOT

b) OR, NOT, AND

c) XOR, NOT, AND

Solution

b

10.22 To what Boolean value will each of the following ten **if** statement conditions evaluate to with the listed variable values ?

	variables	condition	result
1	x = 10, y = 20	if (x != y)	?
2	x = 4, y =11	if (x = y)	?

	variables	condition	result
3	x = 3, y = 7	if (x <= y)	?
4	x = 9, y = 22	if (x >= y)	?
5	w = 5, x = 2, y = 3, z = 4	if ((w + x) === (y + z))	?
6	x = "8", y = 8	if (x === y)	?
7	x = 20, y = 30, z = 15	if (x < (y-z))	?
8	a = 6, b = 2, c = 5	if ((a *b) > (c * a))	?
9	j = 1.5, k = 3, m = 4.5	if ((j * k) == m)	?
10	p = "2.8", q = "2.8"	if (p !== q)	?

Solution

1) true

2) false

3) true

4) false

5) true

6) false

7) false

8) false

9) true

10) false

10.23 Step 1: Create a variable called **y**.

Step 2: Set the value of **y** equal to the value entered into the user response section of a prompt box. The user prompt message should say "Enter the number 1, 2 or 3." and the default user response message should say: "Enter the capital here."

Step 3: Use an **if** statement to see if the user entered "Albany". If the user entered the "Albany" display "You are correct. Albany is the capital of New York." in an alert box.

Step 4: Use an **if** statement to see if the user entered something other than "Albany". If the user entered something other than "Albany" display "Wrong!" in an alert box.

Solution
```
<script>
  var y;
  y = prompt ("What is the capital of NewYork?",
              "Enter the capital here.");
  if (y == "Albany") {
```

```
        alert ("You are correct. Albany is the capital of New York.");
    }
  if (y != "Albany") {
    alert ("Wrong!");
    }
</script>
```

10.24 Step 1: Create a variable called **x** and set it to a value of 10.

Step 2: Create a variable called **y** and set it to a value of 20.

Step 3: Create a variable called **z** and set it to a value of 15.

Step 4: Create a variable called **j** and set it to a value of 15.

Step 5: Create a variable called **k** and don't initialize it.

Step 6: Use an **if** statement to check if **x** does not equal **y**. If this is true then use another **if** statement inside of the first **if** statement to check to see if **z** equals **j**. If this is true then set **k** equal to 50.

Step 7: Close both **if** statements

Step 8: Display the value of **k** in an alert box.

Solution
```
<script>
    var x = 10;
    var y = 20;
    var z = 15;
    var j = 15;
    var k;
    if(x != y) {
        if (z == j) {
            k = 50;
        }
    }
    alert(k);
</script>
```

Result displayed in alert box:
50.

In this problem we have one **if** statement nested inside another **if** statement. The conditions of both **if** statements have to evaluate as **true** before the code inside the second **if** statement will be executed. The nested **if** statement is considered to be part of the interior code of the first **if** statement. After **x != y** evaluates as **true**, we go to the code inside of the first **if** statement which is another **if** statement that checks the condition **z == j**. If this is true, then, **k** is set to a value of 50. After the interior code of the second **if** statement executes, both **if** statements are closed and the value of **k** is displayed in an alert box.

10.25 Step 1: Create a variable called **name1** and initialize it to "Jane";

Step 2: Create a variable called **sex** and initialize it to "female";

Step 3: Use an if statement to check to see if **name1** = "Jane" and **sex** = "female". If the condition is true, display "Jane is a girl." in an alert box.

Solution
```
<script>
```

```
   var name1 ="Jane";
   var sex = "female";
   if (name1 == "Jane" && sex == "female") {
       alert ("Jane is a girl.");
   }
</script>
```

Result displayed in browser:

Jane is a girl.

10.26 To what Boolean value will each of the following twenty logical comparisons evaluate to:

	logical comparison	result
1	true && false	?
2	true || false	?
3	false && true	?
4	false || false	?
5	true || true	?
6	true && true	?
7	(true && false) && true	?
8	(true && true) && false	?
9	(true || false) || false	?
10	(false || true) && true	?
11	(true || false) || false || true)	?
12	(false || true) && (true || false)	?
13	(true && true) || (false || false)	?
14	! (true && false)	?
15	! (false || true)	?
16	(! (true && true)) && (false || false)	?
17	! ((false || true) && (true && false)) || ! ((true || false) && (true && true))	?
18	((false && true) || (false && false)) || (true && true)	?
19	((true && true) && (false || true)(&& (true || false)	?
20	! (! (true || false) && (false || false))	?

Solution

1) false

2) true

3) false

4) false

5) true

6) true

7) false

8) false

9) true

10) true

11) true

12) true

13) true

14) true

15) false

16) false

17) true

18) true

19) true

20) true

10.27 Step 1: Create a variable called **firstName** and initialize it to "Bob";

Step 2: Create a variable called **job** and initialize it to "mechanic";

Step 3: Create an **if** statement that checks to see if the value of the variable **firstName** is equal to "Bob".

Step 4: Create another **if** statement inside the first **if** statement that checks to see if the value of the variable **job** is "mechanic". If this is **true**, display "Bob is a mechanic." in alert box.

Step 5: Close both **if** statements

Solution
```
<script>
  var firstName ="Bob";
  var job = "mechanic";
  if (firstName == "Bob") {
    if (job == "mechanic") {
      alert ("Bob is a mechanic.");
    }
  }
</script>
```

Result displayed in browser:

Bob is a mechanic.

10.28 Step 1: Create a variable called **y** and give it an initial value of 21.

Step 2: Create a variable called **z** and give it an initial value of "21".

Step 3: Use an if statement to determine if y equals z (equality, not identity). If y equals z then display "y has the same value as z." in an alert box.

Step 4: Use an if statement to determine if y does not equal z (equality, not identity). If y equals z, then, display "y does not have the same value as z." in an alert box.

Solution

```
<script>
  var y = 21;
  var z = "21";
  if (y == z) {
    alert ("y has the same value as z.");
  }
  if (y != z) {
    alert ("y does not have the same value as z.");
  }
<script>
```

Result displayed in browser:

y has the same value as z.

10.29 Step 1: Create a variable called **y** and give it an initial value of 21.

Step 2: Create a variable called **z** and give it an initial value of "21".

Step 3: Use an if statement to determine if **y** equals **z** (identity, not equality). If y equals z then display "y has the same value and data type as z." in an alert box.

Step 4: Use an if statement to determine if **y** does not equal **z** (identity, not equality). If **y** equals z then display "y does not have the same value and data type as z." in an alert box.

Solution

```
<script>
  var y = 21;
  var z = "21";
  if (y === z) {
    alert ("y has the same value as z.");
  }
  if (y !== z) {
    alert ("y does not have the same value as z.");
  }
</script>
```

Result displayed in browser:

y does not have the same value as z.

10.30 Step 1: Create a variable called **num1** and assign it a value of 99.
Step 2: Create a variable called **num2** and initialize its value to 55.
Step 3: Create a variable called **num3** and give it a value of 35.
Step 4: Use an **if** statement to determine if the following three comparisons are all true:
  1) **num1** is greater than or equal to 80.
  2) **num2** is less than or equal to 70.
  3) **num3** equals (equality, not identity) 35.
Step 5: If all three comparisons are true display "All 3 comparisons are true." in an alert box.

Solution
```
<script>
   var num1 = 99;
   var num2 = 55;
   var num3 = 35;
   if ((num1 >= 80) && (num2 <= 70) && (num3 == 35)){
      alert ("All 3 comparisons are true.");
   }
</script>
```

Result displayed in browser:

All 3 comparisons are true

10.31 Step 1: Create a variable called **dogName1** and assign it a value of "Rover".
Step 2: Create a variable called **dogName2** and assign it a value of "Fido".
Step 3: Create a variable called **dogName3** and assign it a value of "Spike".
Step 4: Use an if statement to determine if at least one of the following three comparisons are true:
  1) **dogName1** is equal (identity, not equality) to "Rover".
  2) **dogName2** is equal (identity, not equality) to "Duke".
  3) **dogName3** is equal (identity, not equality) to "Jackson".
Step 5: If all three comparisons are true display "All3 comparisons are true." in an alert box.

Solution
```
<script>
   var dogName1 = "Rover";
   var dogName2 = "Fido";
   var dogName3 = "Spike";
```

```
if ((dogName1 === "Rover") || (dogName2 === "Duke") || (dogName3 === "Jackson")) {
    alert ("At least one the comparisons is true.");
}
</script>
```

Result displayed in browser:

At least one of the three comparisons is true.

Note for all problems from 10.32 and on that use a prompt box which asks for a numeric input from the user:

It's important to remember that any value that's returned by a **prompt()** statement and then stored in a variable will always be stored as a a **string** data type. This is no problem if you're dealing with text, but it might present a problem if you plan to receive numeric data through the **prompt()** statement and then manipulate it with one of the arithmetic or logical operators. For example, note the following code:

```
<script>
    var num1;
    var num2;
    num1 = prompt ("Please enter an integer from 1 to 10 inclusive.");
    num2 = prompt ("Please enter an integer from 1 to 10 inclusive.");
    result = num1 + num2;
    alert (result);
</script>
```

This code produces the output "45" (if the user enters a "4" in the first prompt box and a "5" in the second prompt box) in the alert box because **num1** and **num2** are **string data type** variables. This is true because they are inputs from a **prompt()** box and all inputs to a prompt box are stored as **string data type** values.

JavaScript provides two functions to convert **string data type** variables to a **numeric data type**. These are the **parseInt()** and **parseFloat()** functions. The **parseInt()** function converts a **string** to an **integer** value while **parseFloat()** converts a string value to a floating point number. In other words, you would use **parseInt("5")** to convert the string value "5" to an integer and you would use parsFloat(**"5.1463"**) to convert the string value "5.1463" to a floating point number. Remeber that an integer is a whole number without any fractional part while floating-point numbers have a decimal part.

Integer example:

```
    num1 = prompt ("Please enter an integer from 1 to 10 inclusive.");
```

This code will store whatever value was entered into the prompt box as a **string data value** in the variable **num1**. To store **num1** as an **integer** value you must add the following conversion to the code:

```
    num1 = prompt ("Please enter an integer from 1 to 10 inclusive.");
    num1 = parseInt (num1);
```

Floating-point example:

```
num1 = prompt ("Please enter a numeric value with 2 decimal places from 1.00 to 10.00 inclusive.");
```

This code will also store whatever two decimal place value was entered into the prompt box by the user as a **string data value** in the variable **num1**. To store **num1** as a **floating-point** value you must add the following conversion to the code:

```
num1 = prompt ("Please enter a numeric value with 2 decimal places from 1.00 to 10.00 inclusive.");
num1 = parseFloat (num1);
```

We would have to make the following changes to the above code to get it to display the arithmetic sum of the two inputs in the alert box rather than a concatenation of the two values that were entered by the user:

```
<script>
  var num1;
  var num2;
  num1 = prompt ("Please enter an integer from 1 to 10 inclusive.");
  num2 = prompt ("Please enter an integer from 1 to 10 inclusive.");
  num1 = parseInt (num1);
  num2 = parseInt (num2);
  result = num1 + num2;
  alert (result);
</script>
```

One thing to keep in mind is that the confusion about whether an arithmetic addition or a string concatenation is represented by the "+" sign doesn't occur when the arithmetic operation being attempt on values that are assumed to be string values is anything other than the "+" sign. JavaScript is a loosely typed language, which means you don't declare the data types of variables explicitly, so, if the operation that's being attempted between two strings is obviously an arithmetic operation, JavaScript will go ahead and treat the strings as if they were numeric values.

For example, note the following code:

```
<script>
  var num1;
  var num2;
  num1 = prompt ("Please enter an integer from 1 to 10 inclusive.");
  num2 = prompt ("Please enter an integer from 1 to 10 inclusive.");
  result = num1 - num2;
  alert (result);
</script>
```

In this code, there is no confusion about the arithmetic operation being asked for. It's a subtraction operation and can't be anything else, so, the variables are treated as numbers and the subtraction occurs. If the user entered the values "10" and "6", the result in the alert box will be **4**. If we had used the "+" sign in this situation, the result would have been a string concatenation of "10" and "4" which would result in "104" being displayed in the alert box.

10.32 Step 1: Create a variable called **payForWeek.**

Step 2: Create a variable called **hoursWorked** and set its value to the amount entered by the user into the user response section of a prompt box. The user prompt message should say "How many hours did you work this week?."

Step 3: Create a variable called **hourlyRate** and set its value to the amount entered by the user into the user response section of a prompt box. The user prompt message should say "What is your hourly pay rate?."

Step 4: convert **hoursWorked** from a string value to a floating point value

Step 5: convert **hourlyRate** from a string value to a floating point value

Step 6: Use an **if** statement to determine is the value of **hoursWorked** is 40 or less. If this is **true** the user will get straight pay for all his hours. Set payForWeek equal to hours times the hourly rate of pay. Display the total pay for the week in the following format:

"Your pay for the week is $ <value of payForWeek>."

Step 7: Use an **if** statement to determine is the value of **hoursWorked** is greater than. If this is **true** the user will get straight pay for 40 hours and time and a half for the remaining 1.5 hours. So, the user's pay for the week will be 40 times the hourly rate plus the remaining hours timestimes the hourly rate. Figure out how to write the formula. Display the total pay for the week in the following format:

"Your pay for the week is $ <value of payForWeek>."

Step 8: Run the script with the following inputs:

a) hoursWorked = 40, hourlyRate = 10

b) hoursWorked = 60, hourlyRate = 20

Solution

```
<script>
   var payForWeek;
   var hoursWorked = prompt ("How many hours did you work this week?");
   var hourlyRate = prompt ("What is your hourly pay rate?");
   hoursWorked = parseFloat (hoursWorked);
   hourlyRate = parseFloat (hourlyRate);
   if (hoursWorked <= 40) {
     payForWeek = hoursWorked * hourlyRate;
     alert ("Your pay for this week is $" + payForWeek);
   }
   if (hoursWorked > 40) {
     payForWeek = (hourlyRate * 40) + ((hoursWorked - 40) *
                  (hourlyRate * 1.5));
     alert ("Your pay for this week is $" + payForWeek);
   }
</script>
```

Result displayed in browser:

a) Your pay for this week is $400.

b) Your pay for this week is $1400.

10.33 Step 1: Create a variable called **weeklyPay** and set its value to the amount entered by the user into the user response section of a prompt box. The user prompt message should say "Enter your weekly pay in a whole dollar amount."

Step 2: Create a variable called **weeklyBills** and set its value to the amount entered by the user into the user response section of a prompt box. The user prompt message should say "Enter your weekly bills in a whole dollar amount."

Step 3: convert **weeklyPay** from a string value to an integer value

Step 4: convert **hourlyRate** from a string value to an integer value

Step 5: Use an if statement to determine is the value of **weeklyPay** is greater than or equal to **weeklyBills.** If this is true display "You're not in debt." in an alert box.

Step 6: Use another if statement to determine is the value of **weeklyPay** is less than to **weeklyBills.** If this is true display "You're in debt." in an alert box.

Step 7: Run the script with the following inputs:
 a) weeklyPay = 500, weeklyBills = 499
 b) weeklyPay = 300, weeklyBills = 350

Solution
```
<script>
  var weeklyPay = prompt("Enter your weekly pay in a whole dollar amount.");
  var weeklyBills = prompt("Enter your weekly bills in a whole dollar amount.");
  weeklyPay = parseInt(weeklyPay);
  weeklyBills = parseInt(weeklyBills);
  if (weeklyPay >= weeklyBills) {
   alert ("You're not in debt.");
  }
  if (weeklyPay < weeklyBills) {
   alert ("You're in debt.");
  }
</script>
```

Result displayed in browser:

a) You're not in debt.
b) You're in debt.

10.34 Step 1: Create a variable called **a** and give it an initial value of 10.

Step 2: Create a variable called **b** and give it an initial value of 20.

Step 3: Create a variable called **c** and give it an initial value of 35.

Step 4: Use an if statement to determine if the sum of a plus b is greater than the value of c. If this is true display "a + b is greater than c."

Step 5: Use an if statement to determine if the sum of a plus b is not greater than the value of c. If this is true display "a + b is not greater than c."

Solution

```
<script>
   var a = 10;
   var b = 20;
   var c = 35;
   if ((a + b) > c) {
      alert ("a + b is greater than c");
   }
   if (! ((a + b) > c)) {
      alert ("y does not have the same value as z.");
   }
<script>
```

Result displayed in browser:

a + b is not greater than c.

Chapter 11

JavaScript Conditional Statements: Part 2

11.1 The if...else statement

The **if** statement executes a statement if a specified condition is true. If you want to execute some code if a condition is true and another code if the condition is not true, use the **if....else** statement. Use the **else** statement to indicate the block of code that should be executed if the condition is false.

```
if (condition) {
    block of code to be executed if the condition is true
} else {
    block of code to be executed if the condition is false
}
```

Consider the following example:

If the age of the user is less than 21, create a message that says: "You're too young to drink." and assign it to a variable called **message**. If the condition is false, create a message that says: "You're old enough to drink." and assign it to a variable called **message**.

```
if (age < 21) {
    message = "You're too young to drink.";
    document.write (message);
} else {
    message = "Your old enough to drink";
    document.write (message);
}
```

The result dislpayed in the browser will be:

if condition is true: **You're too young to drink.**
if condition is false: **You're old enough to drink.**

Syntax for if...else statement:

```
if (condition)
    statement1
else
    statement2
```

condition
> An expression, usually an arithmetic or Boolean comparison, that evaluates to either true or false.

statement1
statement1 is a block of code that is executed if condition evaluates to **true**. The statement can contain any valid JavaScript code, including more nested **if** statements. If you want to execute

more than one statement, use a block statement with curly braces ({ ... }) to group these statements together as one execution block. If you don't want to execute any statements, use an empty statement.

statement2

statement2 is a block of code that is executed if condition evaluates to **false**. The statement can contain any valid JavaScript code, including more nested **if** statements. If you want to execute more than one statement, use a block statement with curly braces ({ ... }) to group these statements together as one execution block. If you don't want to execute any statements, use an empty statement.

Flowchart of an if...else statement:

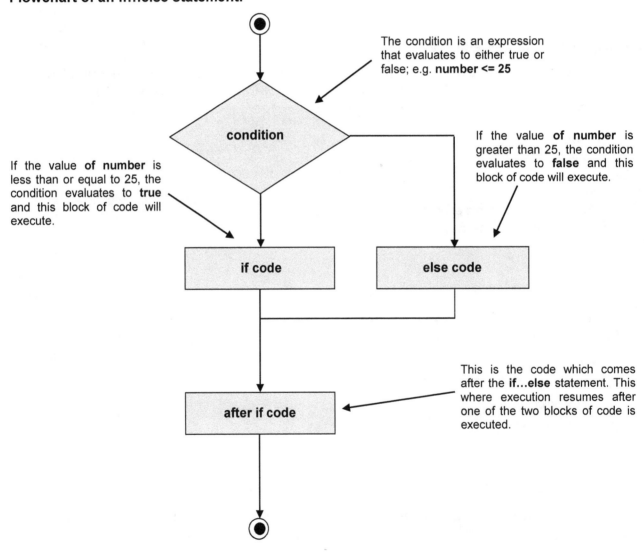

IF...ELSE statement examples:

example:
```
<script>
   var name = "Jack";
   if (name == "Jim") {
      document.write ("Hello Jim.");
   }
   else {
   document.write ("Who are you?");
   }
</script>
```

Result displayed in browser:
Who are you?

Since the string variable **name** was initialized with the value "**Jack**", the comparison **name == "Jim"** will return **false** and the code in the **if** section will be skipped over and the code in the **else** section will be executed. If the variable name had been initialized with the name "**Jim**" the comparison **name == "Jim"** would have returned **true** and the code in the **if** section would have been executed. After the code in the **if** section was executed, the code in the **else** section would be skipped over and execution would start at the first code statement after the **if...else** statement.

example:
```
<script>
   var myNumber = 50;
   if (myNumber >= 75) {
      document.write ("The value of the " +
                  "variable myNumber is " +
                  "greater than or equal " +
                  "to 75.")
   }
   else {
      document.write ("The value of the " +
                  "variable myNumber " +
                  "is less than 75.")
   }
</script>
```

Result displayed in browser:
The value of the variable myNumber is less than 75.

Since the variable **myNumber** was initialized with the value **50**, the comparison **myNumber >= 75** will return **false** and the code in the **if** section will be skipped over and the code in the **else** section will be executed. If the variable **myNumber** had been initialized with some value greater than or equal to 75 the comparison **myNumber >= 75** would have returned **true** and the code in the **if** section would have been executed. After the code in the **if** section was executed, the code in the **else** section would be skipped over and execution would start at the first code statement after the **if...else** statement.

Don't forget to use the string concatenator (+) when you write a string over multiple lines.

example:
```
<script>
  var message;
  var amount1 = 250;
  var amount2 = 150;
  var amount3 = 75
  if ((amount2 + amount3) < amount1) {
    message = "amount2 plus amount3 is " +
              "less than amount1.";
    document.write(message);
  }
  else {
    message = "amount1 is greater than " +
              "both amount2 and amount3 " +
              "combined.";
      document.write(message);
  }
</script>
```

Result displayed in browser:
amount2 plus amount3 is less than amount1

Since the variables **amount1**, **amount2** and **amount3** were initialized with the values **250, 150** and **75**, the comparison **amount2 + amount3 < amount1** will return **true** and the code in the **if** section will be executed and the code in the **else** section will be skipped over. If the comparison had returned false, the code in the **else** section would have been executed and the code in the if section would have been ignored. After the code in the **else** section was processed execution would start at the first code statement after the **if...else** statement.

example:
```
<script>
  var userAnswer;
  var reply;
  var userAnswer=prompt ("Do you eat fish?",
              "Enter 'yes' or 'no'")

  if ( userAswer == "yes"){
      reply="I like fish too!"
  }
  else {
      reply="I don't like fish either!";
  }
  alert (reply)
</script>
```

Result displayed in browser:
if "yes" entered - I like fish too!
if "no" entered - I don't like fish either!

First we declare two variables, **userAnswer** and **reply** without initializing them. Then we display a prompt box with **"Do you eat fish?"** in the user prompt section and **"Enter 'yes' or 'no'"** in the user response section. The variable **userAnswer** is set equal to the value returned by the prompt box. Next we use an **if...else** statement to check to see if **userAnswer** equals "yes". If it does, then we set the value of **reply** to "**I like fish too!**" in the first section of code in the **if** section. If the user entered "no" into the prompt box we will drop down to the **else** section and execute the code found there. This will set the value of **reply** to "**I don't like fish either!**".

SOLVED PROBLEMS

11.1 Step 1: Create a variable called **birthCity** and assign it a value of "New York".

Step 2: Use an **if/else** statement to determine if the value of **birthCity** is "Chicago". If this is **true**, then, display "You were born in Chicago." in an alert box. If **birthCity** does not equal "New York", display "Where were you born?" in an alert box.

Solution

```
<script>
  var birthCity = "New York";
  if (birthCity == "Chicago") {
    alert ("You were born in Chicago.");
  }
  else {
    alert ("Where were you born?");
  }
</script>
```

Result displayed in browser:

Where were you born?

11.2 Step 1: Create a variable called **num1** and assign it a numerical value of 35.

Step 2: Create a variable called **num2** and assign it a numerical value of 15.

Step 3: Use an **if/else** statement to determine if the value of **num1** is less than or equal to the value of **num2**. If **num1** is greater than or equal to **num2**, display "num1 is less than or equal to num2." in the browser window. If the comparison isn't **true**, display "num1 is greater than num2." in the browser window.

Solution

```
<script>
  var num1 = 35;
  var num2 = 15;
  if (num1 <= num2) {
    document.write ("num1 is less that or equal to num2.");
  }
  else {
    document.write ("num1 is greater than num2.");
  }
</script>
```

Result displayed in browser:

num1 is greater than num2.

11.3 Step 1: Create a variable called **age** and assign it a numeric value of 25.

Step 2: Use an **if/else** statement to determine if the value of **age** is greater than or equal to 21. If this is **true**, display "You are old enough to enter this establishment." in an alert box. If this is **false**, display "Come back when you're 21." in alert box.

Solution

```
<script>
  var age = 25;
  if ( age >= 21) {
    alert ("You are old enough to enter this establishment.");
  }
  else {
    alert ("Come back when you're 21.");
  }
</script>
```

Result displayed in browser:

You are old enough to enter this establishment.

11.4 Step 1: Create a variable called **costOfCar** and assign it a numeric value of 10000.

Step 2: Create a variable called **moneySaved** and assign it a numeric value of 8000.

Step 3: Use an **if/else** statement to determine if the value of **costOfCar** is greater than the value of **moneySaved**. If the comparison is **true**, display "You need more money." in the browser window. If the comparison is **false**, display " You have enough money to buy the car."

Solution

```
<script>
  var costOfCar = 10000;
  var moneySaved = 8000;
  if (costOfCar > moneySaved) {
    document.write ("You need more money.");
  }
  else {
    document.write ("You have enough money to buy the car.");
  }
</script>
```

Result displayed in browser:

You need more money..

11.5 Step 1: Create a variable called **userAnswer.**

Step 2: Create a variable called **programReply.**

Step 3: Set the value of **userAnswer** to the value entered by the user into the user response section of a prompt box. The user prompt message should say "Do you like vegetables?" and the default message in the user response area should say "Enter 'yes' or 'no'.".

Step 4: Use an **if/else** statement to determine if the value of **userAnswer** is "yes". If this is true, set the value of **programReply** to "I'm glad to hear you like vegetables." If this is false, set the value of **programReplay** to "That's too bad. Vegetables are good for you."

Step 5: Display the value of **programReply** in an alert box.

Solution

```
<script>
  var userAnswer;
  var programReply;
  userAnswer = prompt("Do you like vegetables?",
                  "Enter 'yes' or 'no'.");
  if ( userAnswer == "yes") {
   programReply = "I'm glad to hear you like vegetables.";
  }
  else {
   programReply = "That's too bad. Vegetables are good for you.";
  }
  alert (programReply);
</script>
```

11.6 Step 1: Create a variable called **x** in one step and then assign it a numeric value of 20 in anther step.

Step 2: Use an **if/else** statement to determine if the value of **x** is less than 30 and greater than **25.** If the comparison is **true**, display "x is between 26 and 29." in the browser window. If the comparison is **false**, display " x is not between 26 and 29."

Solution

```
<script>
  var x;
  var x = 20;
  if ( x < 30 && x > 25) {
   document.write ("x is between 26 and 29.");
  }
  else {
   document.write ("x is not between 26 and 29.");
  }
</script>
```

Result displayed in browser:

x is not between 26 and 29.

11.7 Step 1: Create a variable called **weight** and assign it a numeric value of 250.

Step 2: Use an **if/else** statement to determine if the value of **weight** is less than 150 or greater than 300. If the comparison is **true**, display "You don't fall within the weight range for this job." in an alert box. If the comparison is **false**, display "Congratulations. You're hired!"

Solution

```
<script>
  var weight = 250;
  if (weight < 150 || weight > 300) {
    alert ("You don't fall within the weight range for this job.");
  }
  else {
    alert ("Congratulations. You're hired!.");
  }
</script>
```

Result displayed in browser:

Congratulations. You're hired!

11.8 Step 1: Create a variable called **openingTime** and assign it a numeric value of 7.

Step 2: Create a variable called **closingTime** and assign it a numeric value of 19.

Step 3: Set the value of **arrivalTime** to the value entered by the user into the user response section of a prompt box. The user prompt message should say "What time are you going to arrive?".

Step 4: Use an **if/else** statement to determine if the value of **arrivalTime** is less than 7 or greater than 19. If the comparison is **true**, display "We won't be open when you get here." in an alert box. If the comparison is **false**, display "We'll see you when you get here." in an alert box.

Solution

```
<script>
  var openingTime = 7;
  var closingTime = 19;
  arrivalTime = prompt ("What time are you going to arrive?");
  if (arrivalTime < 7 || arrivalTime > 19) {
    alert ("We won't be open when you get here.");
  }
  else {
    alert ("We'll see you when you get here.");
  }
</script>
```

11.9 Step 1: Create a variable called **a** and assign it a numeric value of 10.

Step 2: Create a variable called **b** and assign it a numeric value of 20.

Step 3: Create a variable called **c** and assign it a numeric value of 45.

Step 4: Create a variable called **d** and assign it a numeric value of 10.

Step 5: Create a variable called **originalNumber** and assign it a numeric value of 10.

Step 6: Create a variable called **change** but don't initialize it yet..

Step 7: Use an **if/else** statement to test whether the value of **c** is greater than the value of **a** plus **b**. If this is **true**, then increment the value in **d** and assign the variable called **change** the string value of "incremented". If the comparison isn't **true**, them, decrement the value in the variable **d** by one and assign the value "decremented" to the string variable **change**.

Step 8: Display two lines in the browser window:
line 1: "The original value of d was <value of **originalNumber**>."
line 2: The value of d now, after it was <value of **change**> , is <value of **d**>.

Solution

```
var a = 10;
var b = 20;
var c = 45;
var d = 10;
var originalNumber = 10;
var change;
if (c > (a + b)) {
  d++;
  change = "incremented"
}
else {
  d--;
  change = "decremented"
}
document.write ("The original value of d was " + originalNumber + ".");
document.write ("<br>");
document.write ("The value of d now, after it was " + change + ", is " + d +".");
</script>
```

> The **increment** and **decrement** operators are discussed in chapter 4, sections 4.2.6 and 4.2.7.

Result displayed in browser:

The original value of d was 10.
The value of d now, after it was incremented, is 11.

11.10 Step 1: Create a variable called **cost** and assign it a numeric value of 300

Step 2: Use an **if/else** statement to check to see if **cost** does not equal 300 (don't use the not equal (!=) operator, instead use the logical NOT (!) operator on the comparison). If the condition returns **true**, display "The variable called cost does not equal 300." in an alert box.). If the condition returns **false**, display "The variable called cost equals 300." in an alert box.

Solution

```
<script>
  var cost = 300;
  if (!(cost == 300)) {
    alert ("The variable called cost does not equal 300.");
  }
  else {
    alert ("The variable called cost equals 300.");
  }
</script>
```

Instead of using the **not equal** operator (**!=**), or **cost != 300,** for the comparison, use the logical **NOT** operator (!) to reverse the result of the comparison: **!(cost = 300)**. Both types of operations produce identical results.

Result displayed in alert box:

The variable called cost equals 300.

11.11 Step 1: Create a variable called **myIQ** but don't assign it a value yet.

Step 2: Set the value of **myIQ** to the value entered by the user into the user response section of a prompt box. The user prompt message should say "Please enter your IQ."

Step 3: Convert **myIQ** to an integer value.

Step 4: Use an **if/else** statement to determine if the value of **myIQ** is greater than 100. If the comparison is **true**, display "You are smarter than average." in the browser window. If the comparison is **false**, display "You're not so smart." in the browser window.

Solution

```
<script>
  var myIQ;
  myIQ =prompt ("Please enter your IQ.");
  myIQ = parseInt(myIQ);
  if (myIQ > 100) {
    document.write ("You are smarter than average.");
  }
  else {
    document.write ("You're not so smart.");
  }
</script>
```

11.12 Step 1: Create a variable called **answer** but don't assign it a value yet.

Step 2: Set the value of **answer** to the value entered by the user into the user response section of a prompt box. The user prompt message should say "Are you an American citizen?." and the default message in the user response area should say "Enter 'yes' or 'no'.".

Step 3: Use an **if/else** statement to determine if the value of **answer** is either 'yes' or 'no'. If the comparison returns **true**, display "Thank you for answering 'yes' or 'no'." in an alert box.

Solution

```
<script>
  var answer;
  answer = prompt("Are you an American citizen?", "Please enter 'yes' or 'no'.");
  if (answer == "yes" || answer == "no") {
    alert ("Thank you for answering 'yes' or 'no'.");
  }
  else {
    alert ("Can't you follow simple instructions?");
  }
</script>
```

11.13 Step 1: Create a variable called **age** but don't assign it a value yet.

Step 2: Set the value of **age** to the value entered by the user into the user response section of a prompt box. The user prompt message should say "Please enter your age in whole years."

Step 3: Convert **age** to an integer value

Step 3: Use an **if/else** statement to determine if the value of **age** is either greater than or equal to 55 or less than or equal to 65. If the comparison returns **true**, display "You're not too old and you're not too young." in an alert box. If the comparison returns **false**, display "You're either old or young. I'm not sure." in an alert box.

Solution

```
<script>
  var age;
  age = prompt ("Please enter your age in whole years.");
  age = parseInt(age);
  if(age >= 55 && age <=65) {
    alert ("You're not too old and not too young.");
  }
  else {
    alert ("You're either old or young. I'm not sure.");
  }
</script>
```

11.14 Step 1: Create a variable called **dailyPay** but don't assign it a value yet.

Step 2: Set the value of **dailyPay** to the value entered by the user into the user response section of a prompt box. The user prompt message should say "How much do you make a day?" and the default message in the user response area should say "Enter a whole dollar amount.".

Step 3: Convert **dailyPay** to an integer value.

Step 4: Use an **if/else** statement to determine if the value of **dailyPay** is greater than 200. If the comparison returns **true**, display "You make more than $200 a day." in the browser window. If the comparison returns **false**, display "You make $200 or less a day." in the browser window.

Solution
```
<script>
  var dailyPay;
  dailyPay = prompt ("How much do you make a day?", "Enter a whole dollar amount.");
  dailyPay = parseInt (dailyPay);
  if (dailyPay > 20dailyPay = parseInt(dailyPay);0) {
    document.write ("You make more than $200 a day.");
  }
  else {
    document.write ("You make $200 or less a day.");
  }
</script>
```

11.15 Step 1: Create a variable called **capitalCity** but don't assign it a value yet.

Step 2: Set the value of **capitalCity** to the value entered by the user into the user response section of a prompt box. The user prompt message should say "What is the capital of Maine?"

Step 3: Use an **if/else** statement to determine if the value of **capitalCIty** is "Augusta". If this is **true**, display "Correct." in an alert box. If this is **false**, display "Sorry. Guess again." in an alert box.

Solution
```
<script>
  var capitalCity;
  capitalCity = prompt ("What is the capital of Maine?");
  if (capitalCity == "Augusta") {
    alert ("Correct.");
  }
  else {
    alert ("Sorry. Guess again.");
  }
</script>
```

11.16 Step 1: Create a variable called **oddOrEven** but don't assign it a value yet.

Step 2: Set the value of **oddOrEven** to the value entered by the user into the user response section of a prompt box. The user prompt message should say "Enter any two-digit number."

Step 4: Convert **oddOrEven** to an integer value.

Step 3: Use an **if/else** statement to determine if the value of **oddOrEven % 2** is equal to **0**. If this is **true**, display "The number you entered is even." in an alert box. If the comparison is **false**, display "The number you entered is odd." in an alert box.

Solution

```
<script>
  var oddOrEven;
  oddOrEven = prompt ("Enter any two-digit integer.");
  oddOrEven = parseInt (oddOrEven);
  if (oddOrEven % 2 == 0) {
    alert ("The number you entered is even.");
  }
  else {
    alert ("The number you entered is odd.");
  }
</script>
```

11.17 Step 1: Create a variable called **integer1** but don't assign it a value yet.

Step 2: Create a variable called **integer2** but don't assign it a value yet.

Step 2: Set the value of **integer1** to the value entered by the user into the user response section of a prompt box. The user prompt message should say "Please enter any two-digit integer."

Step 3: Set the value of **integer2** to the value entered by the user into the user response section of a prompt box. The user prompt message should say "Please enter any one-digit integer."

Step 4: Convert **integer1** to an integer value.

Step 5: Convert **integer2** to an integer value.

Step 6: Create a variable called **remainder** and set it equal to the value returned by the the modulus division of **integer1** by **integer2**.

Step 7: Use an **if/else** statement to determine if the result of the modulus division of **integer1** by **integer2** produces no remainder (modulus division is discussed in depth in chapter 4 section 4.3.6). If the comparison returns **true**, display "integer1 divided by integer2 leaves a remainder of <value of **remainder**>." in the browser window. If the comparison returns false display "integer1 divided by integer2 does not leave a remainder." in the browser window.

Solution

```
<script>
  var integer1;
  var integer2;
  integer1 = prompt ("Please enter any two-digit integer.")
  integer2 = prompt ("Please enter any one-digit integer.")
  integer1 = parseInt (integer1);
  integer2 = parseInt (integer2);
  remainder = integer1 % integer2;
  if (integer1 % integer2 != 0) {
    document.write ("integer1 divided by integer2 leaves a remainder of " + remainder +".");
```

Modulus division (%) is discussed in chapter 4, section 4.3.6.

```
  }
  else{
    document.write ("integer1 divided by integer2 does not leave a remainder.");
  }
</script>
```

11.18 Step 1: Create a variable called **number** but don't assign it a value yet.

Step 2: Set the value of **number** to the value entered by the user into the user response section of a prompt box. The user prompt message should say "Please enter a number between 1 and 10 inclusive."

Step 3: Convert number to an integer value.

Step 4: Use an **if/else** statement to test if the value given by the user was less than 1 or greater than 10. If the test returns **true**, then, display "You were supposed to enter a number between 1 and 10." in an alert box. If the test returned **false**, then, nest another **if/else** statement inside the first **else** section. The nested **if/else** statement will test to see if **number** doesn't equal either 1, 2, 3 or 4. If this test returns **true**, then, display "The number you entered is between 5 and 10." in an alert box. If the test returns **false**, then, display "The number you entered is between 1 and 4 inclusive." in an alert box.

Solution

```
<script>
  var number;
  number = prompt("Please enter an integer between 1 and 10 inclusive.");
  number = parseInt (number);
  if (number < 1 || number > 10) {
    alert ("You were supposed to enter an integer between 1 and 10 inclusive.");
  }
  else {
    if(number !=1 && number != 2 && number != 3 && number !=4) {
      alert ("The number you entered is between 5 and 10.")
    }
    else{
      alert ("The integer you entered is between 1 and 4 inclusive.")
    }
  }
</script>
```

11.19 Step 1: Create a variable called **w** and set it equal to 15.

Step 2: Create a variable called **x** and set it equal to 10.

Step 3: Create a variable called **y** and set it equal to 20.

Step 4: Create a variable called **z** and set it equal to 5.

Step 5: Use an if/else statement to determine if w + x equals y + z. If this is **true**, display "w plus x equals y plus z ." in an alert box. If this is **false**, display "w plus x does not equal y plus z ." in an alert box.

Solution

```
<script>
  var w = 15;
  var x = 10;
  var y = 20;
  var z = 5;
  if ((w + x) == (y + z)){
    alert ("w plus x equals y plus z.");
  }
  else {
    alert ("w plus x does not equal y plus z.");
  }
</script>
```

Result displayed in alert box:

w plus x equals y plus z .

11.20 Step 1: Create a variable called **a** and assign it a numeric value of 10.

Step 2: Create a variable called **b** and assign it a numeric value of 25.

Step 3: Create a variable called **c** and assign it a numeric value of 20.

Step 4: Create a variable called **d** and assign it a numeric value of 15.

Step 5: Use an **if/else** statement to determine if the value of **a + b** is greater than **c** and if **c - d** is less than **a**. If both comparisons are **true**, display "The comparisons are all true." in the browser window. If either, or both, comparisons are **false**, display "At least one of the comparisons is not true." in the browser window.

Solution

```
<script>
  var a = 10;
  var b = 25;
  var c = 20;
  var d = 15;
  if (((a + b) > c) && ((c - d) < a)) {
    document.write ("The comparisons are all true.");
  }
  else {
    document.write ("At least one of the comparisons is not true.")
  }
</script>
```

Result displayed in browser:

The comparisons are all true.

11.21 Step 1: Create a variable called **userName** but don't assign it a value yet.

Step 2: Create a variable called **gender** but don't assign it a value yet.

Step 3: Set the value of **myIQ** to the value entered by the user into the user response section of a prompt box. The user prompt message should say "Please enter your name."

Step 4: Set the value of **userName** to the value entered by the user into the user response section of a prompt box. The user prompt message should say "Please enter your gender." The default message in the user response box should say "Enter 'male' or 'female'.

Step 5: Use an **if/else** statement to determine if the value of **gender** is "male". If this is **true**, display "<username> is a male." in an alert box. If the condition evaluates to **false** , display "<username> is a female." in an alert box.

Solution
```
<script>
  var userName;
  var gender;
  userName = prompt ("Please enter your name.");
  gender = prompt ("Please enter your gender.", "Enter 'male' or 'female'.");
  if(gender == "male") {
   alert (userName + " is a male.");
  }
  else {
   alert (userName + " is a female.");
  }
</script>
```

11.22 Step 1: Create a variable called **payForWeek.**

Step 2: Create a variable called **hoursWorked.**

Step 3: Create a variable called **payRate.**

Step 4: Set the value of **hoursWorked** equal to the amount entered by the user into the user response section of a prompt box. The user prompt message should say "How many hours did you work this week?."

Step 5: Set the value of **payRate** equal to the amount entered by the user into the user response section of a prompt box. The user prompt message should say "How much do you make per hour?."

Step 6: Use an **if/else** statement to determine is the value of **hoursWorked** is 40 or less. If this is **true** the user will get straight pay for all his hours. Set **payForWeek** equal to hours times the hourly rate of pay. Display the total pay for the week in the following format: "You made $ <value of **payForWeek**> this week." Otherwise the user will get straight pay for 40 hours and time and a half for the remaining 1.5 hours. So, the user's pay for the week will be 40 times the hourly rate plus the remaining hours times the hourly rate. Figure out how to write the formula. Display the total pay for the week in the followingformat:

"You made $ <value of **payForWeek**> this week."

Step 7: Run the script with the following inputs:
        a) hoursWorked = 40, hourlyRate = 10
        b) hoursWorked = 60, hourlyRate = 20

Solution

```
<script>
  var payForWeek;
  var hoursWorked;
  var payRate;
  hoursWorked = prompt ("How many hours did you work this week?");
  payRate = prompt ("How much do you make per hour?");
  payRate = parseInt (payRate);
  if (hoursWorked <= 40) {
   payForWeek = hoursWorked * payRate;
   alert ("You made $" + payForWeek + " this week.");
  }
  else {
   payForWeek = (payRate * 40) + ((hoursWorked - 40) * (payRate * 1.5));
   alert ("You made $" + payForWeek + " this week.");
  }
</script>
```

Result displayed in browser:

a) Your pay for this week is $400.
b) Your pay for this week is $1400.

11.23   Step 1: Create a variable called **age** but don't assign it a value yet.
        Step 2: Create a variable called **validDriver** but don't assign it a value yet.
        Step 3: Set the value of **age** to the value entered by the user into the user response
             section of a prompt box. The user prompt message should say "Please enter your age in
             whole years."
        Step 4: Set the value of **validDriver** to the value entered by the user into the user response
             section of a prompt box. The user prompt message should say "Do you have a valid
             driver's license?." and the default message in the user response section should say
             "Please enter 'yes' or 'no'.".
        Step 5: Convert the value of age to an integer value.
        Step 6: Use an **if/else** statement to determine if the result of the condition **age > 20 &&**
             validDriver == "yes" is **true**. If the comparison is **true**, display "You are eligible to be a
             county bus driver." in an alert box. If the comparison is **false** display " You are not
             eligible to be a county bus driver." in an alert box.

Solution

```
<script>
  var age;
  var validDriver
```

```
  age = prompt ("Please enter your age in whole years.");
  age = parseInt (age);
  validDriver = prompt ("Do you a valid driver's license?", "Please enter 'yes' or 'no'");
  if (age > 20 && validDriver == "yes") {
    alert ("You are eleigible to be a county bus driver.");
  }
  else {
    alert ("You are not eleigible to be a county bus driver.");
  }
</script>
```

11.24 Step 1: Create a variable called **citizen** but don't assign it a value yet.

Step 2: Create a variable called **moneyInBank** but don't assign it a value yet.

Step 3: Create a variable called **gender** but don't assign it a value yet.

Step 4: Create a variable called **IQ** but don't assign it a value yet.

Step 5: Set the value of **citizen** to the value entered by the user into the user response section of a prompt box. The user prompt message should say "Are you a citizen of the United States?." and the default message in the user response section should say "Please enter 'yes' or 'no'.".

Step 6: Set the value of **moneyInBank** to the value entered by the user into the user response section of a prompt box. The user prompt message should say "Do you have at least one million dollars in the bank?" and the default message in the user response section should say "Please enter 'yes' or 'no'.".

Step 7: Set the value of **gender** to the value entered by the user into the user response section of a prompt box. The user prompt message should say "What is your gender?" and the default message in the user response section should say "Please enter 'male' or 'female'".

Step 8: Set the value of **IQ** to the value entered by the user into the user response section of a prompt box. The user prompt message should say "What is your IQ?" .

Step 9: Convert the value of **IQ** to an integer value;

Step 10: Use an **if/else** statement to determine if the condition **citizen == "yes" && moneyInBank == "yes" && gender == "male" && IQ > 140** is **true**. If the comparison is **true**, display the "Welcome to the club!." in the browser window. If the comparison is **false** display "Sorry, Charlie." in browser window.

Solution
```
<script>
  var citizen;
  var moneyInBank;
  var gender;
  var IQ;
  citizen = prompt ("Are you a citizen of the United States?", "Please enter 'yes' or 'no'.");
  moneyInBank = prompt ("Do you have at least one million dollars in the bank?", "Please enter 'yes'or 'no'.");
  gender = prompt ("What is your gender?", "Please enter 'male' or 'female'.");
  IQ = prompt ("What is your IQ?");
  IQ = parseInt (IQ);
```

```
  if (citizen == "yes" && moneyInBank == "yes" && gender == "male" && IQ > 140) {
    document.write ("Welcome to the club!");
  }
  else {
    document.write ("Sorry, Charlie");
  }
</script>
```

11.25 Step 1: Create a variable called **gradePointAverage** but don't assign it a value yet.

Step 2: Create a variable called **weight** but don't assign it a value yet.

Step 3: Create a variable called **favoriteSport** but don't assign it a value yet.

Step 4: Set the value of **gradePointAverage** to the value entered by the user into the user response section of a prompt box. The user prompt message should say "Please enter your grade point average (include 2 decimal places)."

Step 5: Set the value of **weight** to the value entered by the user into the user response section section of a prompt box. The user prompt message should say "Please enter your weight in whole pounds".

Step 6: Set the value of **favoriteSport** to the value entered by the user into the user response section of a prompt box. The user prompt message should say "What is your favorite sport?" and the default message in the user response section should say "Please enter 'football', 'baseball' or 'rugby'.".

Step 7: Convert **gradePointAverage** to a floating point value.

Step 8 Convert **weight** to an integer value.

Step 9: Use an **if/else** statement to determine if the condition **gradePointAverage > 3.5 &&weight >= 220 && favoriteSport == "rugby"** is **true**. If the comparison is **true**, display the "Welcome to the rugby team." in the browser window. If the comparison is **false** display "We don't need you right now." in browser window.

Solution

```
<script>
  var gradePointAverage;
  var weight;
  var favoriteSport;
  gradePointAverage = prompt ("Please enter your grade point average (include 2 decimal places).");
  weight = prompt ("Please enter your weight in whole pounds.");
  favoriteSport = prompt ("Please enter your favorite sport.", "Enter 'football', 'baseball' or 'rugby'.");
  gradePointAverage = parseFloat(gradePointAverage);
  weight = parseInt (weight);
  if (gradePointAverage > 3.5 && weight >= 220 && favoriteSport == "rugby") {
    document.write("Welcome to the rugby team.");
  }
  else {
    document.write ("We don't need you right now.");
  }
</script>
```

11.26 Step 1: Create a variable called **x** and assign it a numeric value of 10.

Step 2: Create a variable called **y** and assign it a numeric value of 5.

Step 3: Create a variable called **a** and assign it a numeric value of 2.

Step 4: Create a variable called **b** and assign it a numeric value of 20.

Step 5: Create a variable called **c** and assign it a numeric value of 25.

Step 6: Use an **if/else** statement to determine if the value **of (((x == y) || c == 25) && (x / y) == 2)** is true. If the condition evaluates to true **true**, display "The result of the condition testing is TRUE." in the browser window. If the result of the condition testing is false **false**, display "The result of the condition testing is FALSE." in the browser window.

Solution

```
<script>
  var x = 10;
  var y = 5;
  var a = 2;
  var b = 20;
  var c = 25;
  if (((x == y) || c == 25) && (x / y) == 2) {
    document.write ("The result of the condition testing is TRUE.")
  }
  else {
    document.write ("The result of the condition testing is FALSE.")
  }
</script>
```

Result displayed in browser:

The result of the condition testing is TRUE.

Chapter 12

JavaScript Conditional Statements: Part 3

12.1 The if...else if...else statement

As we've already seen, the **if** statement executes a statement if a specified condition is true. If you want to execute some code if a condition is true and another code if the condition is not true, use the **if....else** statement. Use the **else** statement to indicate the block of code that should be executed if the condition is false. A further addition to this is the **if...else if...else** statement. Use this statement if you want to test multiple conditions in sequence. You must have a normal **if** statement before you can use the **else if** statement since the **else if** statement is an add-on to the **if** statement and can't exist by itself. It has to be used in association with an **if** statement. The **else if** statement is considered only if the test in the **if** section (or another preceding **else if** statement) evaluates to **false** and you want to test for another condition. As you recall, the **else** statement doesn't test for anything. It's code block executes automatically if the test in the **if** section (or a previous **else if** statement) fails. The **if...if else...else** statement has the following structure:

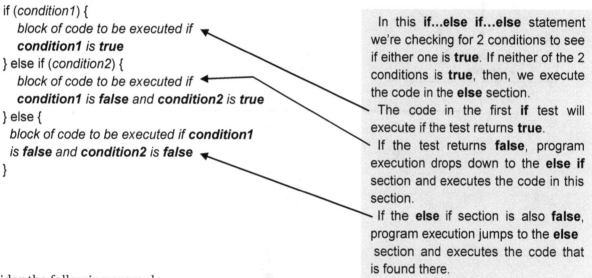

```
if (condition1) {
    block of code to be executed if
    condition1 is true
} else if (condition2) {
    block of code to be executed if
    condition1 is false and condition2 is true
} else {
    block of code to be executed if condition1
    is false and condition2 is false
}
```

In this **if...else if...else** statement we're checking for 2 conditions to see if either one is **true**. If neither of the 2 conditions is **true**, then, we execute the code in the **else** section.

The code in the first **if** test will execute if the test returns **true**.

If the test returns **false**, program execution drops down to the **else if** section and executes the code in this section.

If the **else** if section is also **false**, program execution jumps to the **else** section and executes the code that is found there.

Consider the following example:

If the current **time** is less than 12 p.m., display the message "How are you this morning?" in an alert box. If this test returns **false**, then, use an **if else** statement to see if the **time** is less than 6 p.m. If this is true, then, display the message "Good afternoon.". If this test returns **false**, then, use a second **if else** statement to see if the **time** is less than 9 p.m. If this is **true**, then, display the message "Good evening.". If this test returns **false**, then, drop down to the **else** statement which will automatically execute and display the message "Good night.".

```
if (time < 12) {
    alert ("How are you this morning?");
} else if (time < 18) {
    alert ("Good afternoon.");
} else if (time < 21) {
    alert ("Good evening");
} else {
    alert ("Good night.");
}
```

Flowchart of an if...else if...else statement:

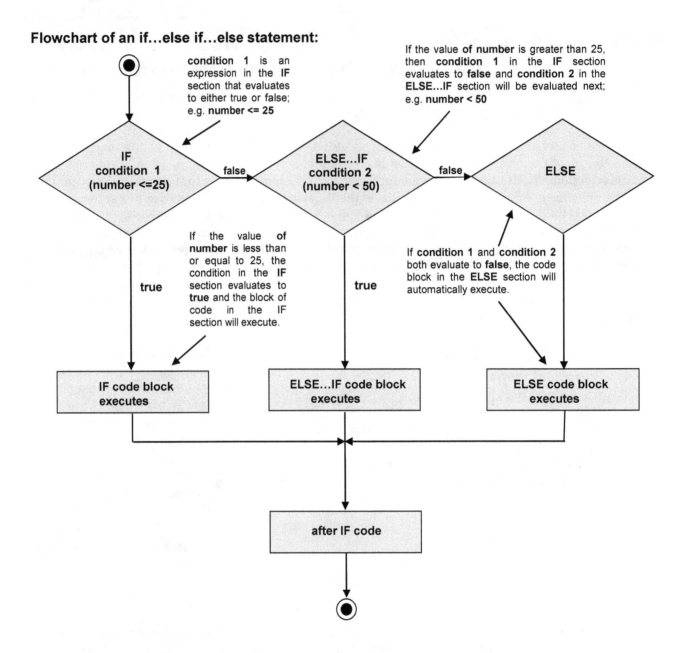

condition 1 is an expression in the IF section that evaluates to either true or false; e.g. **number <= 25**

If the value **of number** is greater than 25, then **condition 1** in the **IF** section evaluates to **false** and **condition 2** in the **ELSE...IF** section will be evaluated next; e.g. **number < 50**

If the value of **number** is less than or equal to 25, the condition in the **IF** section evaluates to **true** and the block of code in the IF section will execute.

If **condition 1** and **condition 2** both evaluate to **false**, the code block in the **ELSE** section will automatically execute.

Syntax for if...else if...else statement:

```
if (condition1) {
    statement 1: block of code to be executed if condition1 is true
}
else if (condition2) {
    statement 2: block of code to be executed if the condition1 is false and condition2 is true
}
else {
    statement 3: block of code to be executed if the condition1 is false and condition2 is false
}
```

condition1

An expression, usually an arithmetic or Boolean comparison, that evaluates to either true or false

statement1

Statement1 is a block of code that is executed if the condition in the **if** section evaluates to **true**. The statement can contain any valid JavaScript code, including more nested **if** statements. If you want to execute more than one statement, use a block statement with curly braces ({ ... }) to group these statements together as one execution block. If you don't want to execute any statements, use an empty statement.

condition2

An expression, usually an arithmetic or Boolean comparison, that evaluates to either true or false.

statement2

Statement2 is a block of code that is executed if the condition in the **if** section evaluates to **false** and the condition in the **else...if** section evaluates to **true**. The statement can contain any valid JavaScript code, including more nested **if** statements. If you want to execute more than one statement, use a block statement with curly braces ({ ... }) to group these statements together as one execution block. If you don't want to execute any statements, use an empty statement.

statement3

Statement2 is a block of code that automatically executes if the condition in the **if** and the **else...if** sections both evaluate to **false**. The statement can contain any valid JavaScript code, including more nested **if** statements. If you want to execute more than one statement, use a block statement with curly braces ({ ... }) to group these statements together as one execution block. If you don't want to execute any statements, use an empty statement.

IF...ELSE IF...ELSE statement examples:

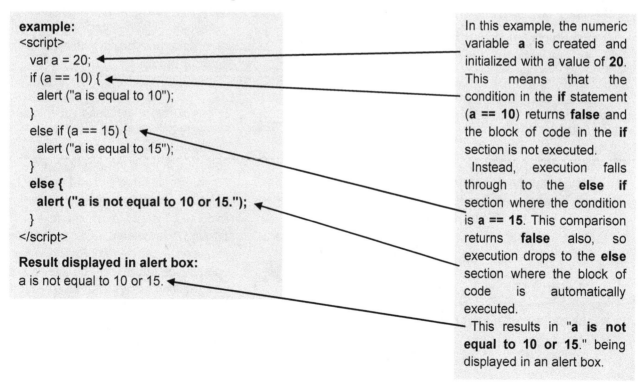

example:
```
<script>
  var a = 20;
  if (a == 10) {
    alert ("a is equal to 10");
  }
  else if (a == 15) {
    alert ("a is equal to 15");
  }
  else {
    alert ("a is not equal to 10 or 15.");
  }
</script>
```

Result displayed in alert box:
a is not equal to 10 or 15.

In this example, the numeric variable **a** is created and initialized with a value of **20**. This means that the condition in the **if** statement (**a == 10**) returns **false** and the block of code in the **if** section is not executed.

Instead, execution falls through to the **else if** section where the condition is **a == 15**. This comparison returns **false** also, so execution drops to the **else** section where the block of code is automatically executed.

This results in "**a is not equal to 10 or 15.**" being displayed in an alert box.

example:
```
<script>
  var car = "Corvette";
  if (car == "Corvette") {
    document.write ("That's a nice car!");
  } else if (car == "VW Beetle"){
    document.write ("That's a nice car, too.");
  } else {
    document.write ("What kind of a car is that?");
  }
</script>
```

Result displayed in alert box:
That's a nice car!

In this example, the string variable **car** is created and initialized with a value of **"Corvette"**. This means that the condition in the **if** statement (**car == "Corvette**) is **true** and the block of code in the **if** section is executed. This results in "**That's a nice car!**." being displayed in the browser window..

example:
```
<script>
  var car = "VW Beetle";
  if (car == "Corvette") {
    document.write ("That's a nice car!");
  } else if (car == "VW Beetle") {
    document.write ("That's a nice car, too.");
  } else {
    document.write ("What kind of a car is that?");
  }
</script>
```

Result displayed in alert box:
That's a nice car, too.

In this example, the string variable **car** is created and initialized with a value of **"VW Beetle"**. This means that the condition in the **if** statement (**car == "Corvette**) is **false** and and the block of code in the **if** section is not executed. Instead, execution falls through to the **else if** section where the condition is **car == "VW Beetle"**. This comparison returns **true** so the block of code in the **if...else** section is executed. This results in "**That's the nice car, too.**" being displayed in the browser window.

example:
```
<script>
  var car = "Lincoln";
  if (car == "Corvette") {
    document.write ("That's a nice car!");
  } else if(car == "VW Beetle") {
    document.write ("That's a nice car, too.");
  } else {
    document.write ("What kind of a car is that?");
  }
</script>
```

Result displayed in alert box:
What kind of car is that?

In this example, the string variable **car** is created and initialized with a value of **"Lincoln"**. This means that the condition in the **if** statement (**car == "Corvette**) is **false** and and the block of code in the **if** section is not executed. Instead, execution falls through to the **else if** section where the condition is **car == "VW Beetle"**. This comparison returns returns **false** also, so execution drops to the **else** section where the block of code is automatically executed. This results in "**What kind of car is that?**"" being displayed in the browser window.

example:
```
<script>
  var n = prompt("Enter a number up to 200");
  var message = "You entered a number ";
  n =  parseInt (n);
  if (n >= 1 && n < 10) {
    alert (message + "greater than 0 and " +
        "less than 10");
  }
  else if (n >= 10 && n < 20) {
    alert (message + "greater than or equal " +
        "to 10 and less than 20");
  }
  else if (n >= 20 && n < 30) {
    alert (message + "greater than or equal " +
        "to 20 and less than 30");
  }
  else if (n >= 30 && n < 40) {
    alert (message + "greater than or equal " +
        "to 30 and less than 40");
  }
  else if (n >= 40 && n <= 100) {
    alert (message + "greater than or equal to " +
        "40 and less than or equal to 100");
  }
  else if (n < 1 || n > 100)
    {alert (message + "less than 1 " +
        "or greater than 100");
  }
  else
    {alert ("You did not enter a number!")}
</script>
```

In this example, we create an **if..else if..else** statement with 5 **else if** sections. This is useful when we have more than two conditions that we want to test for. We test for six conditions in this example. As each condition returns **false** execution drops down to the next **if else** statement until we come to one that is **true**. When that happens, the code block in that **if else** section is executed and program execution skips to the first code statement below the **if..else if...else** statement. If the **if** condition and none of the **else if** conditions return **true**, then, the code block in the **else** section is automatically executed.

The results for entering 10 different individual numbers are given in the results box below.

Results displayed in alert box:

Number entered:	Message displayed:
5	"You entered a number greater than 0 and less than 10"
12	"You entered a number greater than or equal to 10 and less than 20"
25	"You entered a number greater than or equal to 20 and less than 30"
39	"You entered a number greater than or equal to 30 and less than 40"
45	"You entered a number greater than or equal to 40 and less than 100"
0	"You entered a number less than 1 or greater than 100"
150	"You entered a number less than 1 or greater than 100"
18	"You entered a number greater than or equal to 10 and less than 20"
41	"You entered a number greater than or equal to 40 and less than 100"
67	"You entered a number greater than or equal to 40 and less than 100"

SOLVED PROBLEMS

12.1 When should you use an **if else** statement?

a) if you want to test for just 1 condition

b) if you want to test for multiple conditions

c) if you don't want to test for any conditions

Solution

b

12.2 What 2 sections can precede an **if else** section?

a) if, else if

b) else, if

c) else if, else

Solution

a

12.3 What 2 sections can follow an **if else** section?

a) if, else if

b) else, if

c) else if, else

Solution

c

12.4 Is a condition ever associated with the **else** section?

a) yes

b) no

Solution

b

12.5 How many else **if** sections can there be in **if...else if..else** statement?

a) 1

b) 3

c) as many as you need

Solution

c

12.6 What happens if the condition in an **if...else** section is true?

a) the code block in the **else if** section executes and then the code block in the **else** section executes

b) program execution jumps to the first line of code after the **if...else if...else** statement

c) the code block in the else section executes, then, the program jumps to the first line of code that comes after the **if...else if...else** statement

Solution

c

12.7 What happens if the conditions in the **if** and **else if** sections both return **false**?

a) program execution jumps to the first line of code after the **if...else if...else** statement

b) the code block in the **else** section executes

c) the program stops

Solution

b

12.8 Step 1: Create a variable called **age** and assign it a numeric value of 39.

Step 2: Create an **if...else if...else** statement to solve this problem. In the **if** section, test to see if **age** is less than 13. If this is **true**, display "Hello, pre-teen!" in an alert box. If this is **false**, check to see if **age** is less than 20. If this is **true**, display "Hello, teenager!" in an alert box. If this is **false**, display "Hello, old-timer!" in an alert box.

Solution

```
<script>
  var age = 39;
  if (age < 13) {
    alert ("Hello pre-teen!");
  }
  else if (age < 20) {
    alert ("Hello teenager!");
  }
  else {
    alert ("Hello old-timer!");
  }
</script>
```

Result displayed in browser:
Hello, old-timer!

12.9 Step 1: Create a variable called **x** and assign it a numeric value of 25.

Step 2: Create an **if/else if/else** statement to solve this problem. In the **if** section, test to see if **x** is equal to 10. If this is **true**, display "x is equal to 10" in an alert box. If this is **false**, check to see if **x** is equal to 20. If this is **true**, display "x is equal to 20" in an alert box. If this is **false**, display "x is not equal to 10 or 20" in an alert box.

Solution

```
<script>
 var x = 25;
 if (x == 10) {
   alert ("x is equal to 10.");
 }
 else if (x == 20) {
   alert ("x is equal to 20.");
 }
 else {
   alert ("x is not equal to 10 or 20.");
 }
</script>
```

Result displayed in browser:
x is not equal to 10 or 20.

12.10 Step 1: Create a string variable called **favoriteColor** and assign it the value "red".

Step 2: Create an **if/else if/else** statement to solve this problem. In the **if** section, test to see if **favoriteColor** is equal to "red". If this is **true**, display "I like red, too!"" in an alert box. If this is **false**, check to see if **favoriteColor** equals "blue". If this is **true**, display "Blue is nice," in an alert box. If it is **false**, display "What is your favorite color?" in an alert box.

Solution

```
<script>
 var favoriteColor = "red";
 if (favoriteColor == "red") {
   alert ("I like red, too!");
 }
 else if (favoriteColor == "blue") {
   alert("Blue is nice.");
 }
 else {
   alert ("What is your favorite color?");
```

```
    }
</script>
```

Result displayed in browser:

I like red, too!

12.11 Step 1: Create a string variable called **food** and assign it a value of "steak".

Step 2: Create an **if/else if/else** statement to solve this problem. In the **if** section, test to see if **food** is equal to "fish". If this is **true**, display "Fish is good with white wine!"" in the browser window.. If this is **false**, check to see if **food** is equal to "steak". If this is **true**, display "Steak is good with red wine!" in the browser window. If this is **false**, display "Everything is good with beer!" in the browser window.

Solution

```
<script>
 var food = "steak";
 if (food == "fish") {
   document.write ("Fish is good with white wine!");
 }
 else if(food == "steak") {
   document.write ("Steak is good with red wine!");
 }
 else {
   document.write ("Everything is good with beer!");
 }
</script>
```

Result displayed in browser:

Steak is good with red wine!

12.12 Step 1: Create a variable called **num** but don't assign it a value yet.

Step 2: Set the value of **num** to the value entered by the user into the user response section of a prompt box. The user prompt message should say "Enter an integer from 1 to 30.

Step 3: Convert **num** to an integer value.

Step 4: Create an **if/else if/else** statement to solve this problem. In the **if** section, test to see if **num** is greater than or equal to 1 and less than or equal to 20. If this is **true**, display " You entered a number between 1 and 10 inclusive. " in an alert box. If it is **false**, check to see if **num** is greater than 10 and less than or equal to 20. If this is **true**, display " You entered a number between 11 and 20 inclusive. " in an alert box. If this is **false**, check to see if **num** is greater than 20 and less than or equal to 30. If this is **true**, display " You entered a number between 21 and 30 inclusive. " in an alert box. If this is **false**, display " You were supposed to enter a number between 1 and 30 inclusive. " in an alert box.

Solution

```
<script>
 var num;
 num = prompt ("Enter an integer from 1 to 30.");
 num = parseInt (num);
 if (num >= 1 && num <= 10) {
   alert ("You entered a number between 1 and 10 inclusive.");
 }
 else if (num > 10 && num <= 20) {
   alert ("You entered a number between 11 and 20 inclusive.");
 }
 else if (num > 20 && num <= 30){
   alert ("You entered a number between 21 and 30 inclusive.");
 }
 else {
   alert ("You were supposed to enter a number between 1 and 30 inclusive.");
 }
</script>
```

12.13 Step 1: Create a string variable called **friend** and assign it a value of "Ed'.

Step 2: Create an **if/else if/else** statement to solve this problem. In the **if** section, test to see if **friend** equals "Bob". If this is **true**, display "Hello, Bob." in an alert box. If this is **false**, check to see if **friend** is equal to "Ed". If this is **true**, display "Hello, Ed" in an alert box. If this is **false**, display "Who are you?" in an alert box.

Solution

```
<script>
 var friend = "Ed";
 if (friend == "Bob") {
   alert ("Hello, Bob.");
 }
 else if (friend == "Ed"){
   alert ("Hello, Ed.");
 }
 else {
   alert ("Who are you?");
 }
</script>
```

Result displayed in browser:

Hello, Ed.

12.14 Step 1: Create a variable called **time** but don't assign it a value yet.

Step 2: Set the value of **time** to the value entered by the user into the user response section

Step 3: Convert **time** to an integer value.

of a prompt box. The user prompt message should say "Enter a military time value.". The default message in the user response section should say "Enter a value from 0 to 23."

Step 4: Create an **if/else if/else** statement to solve this problem. In the **if** section, test to see if **time** is less than 12. If this is **true**, display "It's not noon yet. " in the browser window. If this is **false**, check tosee if **time** is less than 15. If this is **true**, display " It's early afternoon." in the browser window. If this is **false**, check to see if **time** is less than 18. If this is **true**, display " It's late afternoon. " in the browser window. If this is **false**, display " You were supposed to enter a value between 1 and 23. " in the browser window.

Solution

```
<script>
 var time;
 time = prompt ("Enter a military time value.", "Enter a value from 0 to 23");
 time = parseInt (time);
 if(time < 12) {
   document.write ("It's not noon yet.");
 }
 else if (time < 15) {
   document.write ("It's early afternoon.");
 }
 else if(time < 18) {
   document.write ("It's late afternoon.");
 }
 else if (time <= 23) {
   document.write ("It's evening.");
 }
 else {
   document.write ("You were supposed to enter a vaue between 1 and 23.");
 }
</script>
```

12.15 Step 1: Create a variable called **myAge** and assign it a numeric value of 35.

Step 2: Create a variable called **yourAge** and assign it a numeric value of 45.

Step 3: Create an **if/else if/else** statement to solve this problem. In the **if** section, test to see if **myAge** is greater than **yourAge**. If this is **true**, display "I'm older than you are." in an alert box. If this is **false**, check to see if **myAge** is less than **yourAge**. If this is **true**, display "I'm younger than you are." in an alert box. If this is **false**, display "We're both the same age." in an alert box.

Solution

```
<script>
 var myAge = 35;
 var yourAge = 45;
 if(myAge > yourAge) {
   alert("I'm older than you are.");
 }
```

```
else if (myAge < yourAge) {
   alert ("I'm younger than you are.");
 }
 else {
  alert ("We're the same age.");
 }
</script>
```

Result displayed in browser:

I'm younger than you are.

12.16 Step 1: Create a variable called **testScore** but don't assign it a value yet.

Step 2: Set the value of **testScore** to the value entered by the user into the user response section of a prompt box. The user prompt message should say "Please enter your test score.". The default message in the user response section should say "Please enter a value from 1 to 100."

Step 3: Convert **testScore** to an integer value.

Step 4: Create an **if/else if/else** statement to solve this problem. In the **if** section, test to see if **testScore** is greater than or equal to 90. If this is **true**, display "You got an 'A'." in the browser window. If this is **false**, check to see if **testScore** is greater than or equal to 80. If this is **true**, display "You got a 'B'." in the browser window. If this is **false**, check to see if **testScore** is greater than or equal to 70. If this is **true**, display "You got an 'C'." in the browser window. If this is **false**, check to see if **testScore** is greater than or equal to 60. If this is **true**, display "You got an 'D'." in the browser window. If this is **false**, display "You got an 'F' in the browser window.

Solution

```
<script>
 var testScore;
 testScore = prompt ("Please enter your test score.", "Enter a value from 1 to 100.");
 testScore = parseInt (testScore);
 if (testScore >= 90) {
   document.write ("You got an 'A'.");
 }
 else if (testScore >= 80) {
   document.write ("You got an 'B'.");
 }
 else if (testScore >= 70) {
   document.write ("You got an 'C'.");
 }
 else if (testScore >= 60) {
   document.write ("You got an 'D'.");
 }
 else {
```

```
document.write ("You got an 'F'.");
 }
</script>
```

12.17 Step 1: Create a variable called **testScore** but don't assign it a value yet.

Step 2: Create a variable called **grade** but don't assign it a value yet.

Step 3: Set the value of **testScore** to the value entered by the user into the user response section of a prompt box. The user prompt message should say "Please enter your test score.". The default message in the user response section should say "Please enter a value from 1 to 100."

Step 4: Convert **testScore** to an integer value.

Step 5: Create an **if/else if/else** statement to solve this problem. In the **if** section, test to see if **testScore** is greater than or equal to 90. If this is **true**, assign the value "A" to **grade**. If this is **false**, check to see if **testScore** is greater than or equal to 80. If this is **true**, assign the value "B" to **grade**. If this is **false**, check to see if **testScore** is greater than or equal to 70. If this is **true**, assign the value "C" to **grade**. If this is **false**, check to see if **testScore** is greater than or equal to 60. If this is **true**, assign the value "D" to **grade**. If this is **false**, assign the value "F" to **grade**

Step 5: display the value of **grade** in an alert box.

Solution

```
<script>
 var testScore;
 var grade;
 testScore = prompt ("Please enter your test score.", "Enter a value from 0 to 100.");
 testScore = parseInt (testScore);
 if (testScore >= 90) {
   grade = "A";
 }
 else if (testScore >= 80) {
   grade = "B";
 }
 else if (testScore >= 70) {
   grade = "C";
 }
 else if (testScore >= 60) {
   grade = "D";
 }
 else {
   grade = "F";
 }
 alert("Grade = " + grade);
</script>
```

12.18 Step 1: Create a variable called **stateSalesTaxRate** but don't assign it a value yet. The value will
be assigned later.

Step 2: Create a variable called **stateCode** but don't assign it a value yet.

Step 3: Create a variable called **message** but don't assign it a value yet.

Step 4: Set the value of **stateCode** to the value entered by the user in the user response section
of a prompt box. The user prompt message should say "Please enter the 2-letter code for
Florida, New York or Georgia.". The default message in the user response section should
say: "Please enter 'FL', 'NY' or 'GA'."

Step 3: Create an **if/else if/else** statement to solve this problem. In the **if** section, test to see if
stateCode is equal to "FL". If this is **true**, set **stateSalesTaxRate** to 2.5 and set **message**
equal to " The state sales tax rate for Florida is <**stateSalesTaxRate**>%.". If this is **false**,
test to see if **stateCode** is equal to "NY". If this is **true**, set **stateSalesTaxRate** to 4.0 and
set **message** equal to " The state sales tax rate for New York is <**stateSalesTaxRate**>%.".
If this is f**alse**, test to see if **stateCode** is equal to "GA". If this is **true**, set
stateSalesTaxRate to 2.0 and set **message** equal to " The state sales tax rate for Georgia
is <**stateSalesTaxRate**>%.". If this is **false**, set message equal to "You didn't follow
directions.".

Solution

```
<script>
 var stateSalesTaxRate;
 var stateCode;
 var message;
 stateCode = prompt ("Please enter the 2-letter code for Florida, New York or Georgia.",
             "Please enter 'FL', 'NY' or 'GA'");
 if (stateCode == "FL") {
   stateSalesTaxRate = 2.5
   message = "The state sales tax rate for Florida is " + stateSalesTaxRate +"%.";
 }
 else if (stateCode == "NY") {
   stateSalesTaxRate = 4.0
   message = "The state sales tax rate for New York is " + stateSalesTaxRate +"%.";
 }
 else if (stateCode == "GA" ) {
   stateSalesTaxRate = 2.0
   message = "The state sales tax rate for Georgia is " + stateSalesTaxRate +"%.";
 }
 else {
   message = "You didn't follow directions.";
 }
 alert (message)
</script>
```

12.19 Step 1: Create a variable called **result**.

Step 2: Create a variable called **amount1** and set it equal to 300.

Step 3: Create a variable called **amount2** and set it equal to 200.

Step 4: Create a variable called **amount3** and set it equal to 75..

Step 5: Create an **if/else if/else** statement to solve this problem. In the **if** section, test to see if **amount1** minus **amount2** is less than **amount3**. If this is **true**, display "amount1 minus amount2 is less than amount3." in the browser window. If this is **false**, test to see if **amount1** minus **amount2** is greater than **amount3**. If this is **true**, display "amount1 minus amount2 is greater than amount3." in the browser window. If this is **false** display "amount1 minus amount2 is equal to amount3." in the browser window.

Solution

```
<script>
 var result;
 var amount1 = 300;
 var amount2 = 200;
 var amount3 = 75;
 if ((amount1 - amount2) < amount3) {
   document.write ("amount1 minus amount2 is less than amount3.");
 }
 else if ((amount1 - amount2) > amount3) {
   document.write ("amount1 minus amount2 is greater than amount3.");
 }
 else {
   document.write ("amount1 minus amount2 is equal to amount3.");
 }
</script>
```

Result displayed in browser:

amount1 minus amount2 is greater than amount3.

12.20 Step 1: Create a variable called **j** and assign it a value of 100.

Step 2: Create a variable called **message** but don't initialize it.

Step 3: Create an **if/else if/else** statement to solve this problem. In the **if** section, test to see if **j** is greater than 0 and less than 30. If this is **true**, then, assign the value " j is between 1 and 29 inclusive" to the variable **message**. If this is **false**, test to see if **j** is greater than or equal to 30 and less than 70. If this is **true**, then, assign the value "j is between 30 and 69 inclusive" to the variable **message**. If this is **false**, then, assign the value "j is greater than 100" to the variable **message**.

Step 4: display the value of **message** in an alert box.

Solution

```
<script>
 var j = 100;
 var message;
```

```
if (j > 0 && j < 30) {
  message = "j is between 1 and 29 inclusive";
}
else if (j >= 30 && j < 70) {
  message = "j is between 30 and 69 inclusive";
}
else if (j >= 70 && j <= 100) {
  message = "j is between 70 and 100 inclusive";

}
else {
  message = "j is greater than 100";
}
alert (message);
</script>
```

Result displayed in browser:

j is between 70 and 100 inclusive

12.21 Step 1: Create a variable called **weight** but don't assign it a value yet.

Step 2: Create a variable called **height** but don't assign it a value yet.

Step 3: Create a variable called **message** but don't assign it a value yet.

Step 4: Set the value of **height** to the value entered by the user into the user response section of a prompt box. The user prompt message should say "Please enter your height in inches.".

Step 5: Set the value of **weight** to the value entered by the user into the user response section of a prompt box. The user prompt message should say "Please enter your weight in pounds.".

Step 6: Convert **weight** to an integer value.

Step 7: Convert **height** to an integer value.

Step 8: Create an **if/else if/else** statement to solve this problem. In the **if** section, test to see if **height** is greater than or equal to 60 and less than or equal to 69. If this is **true**, use a nested **if/else** statement to test to see if **weight** is greater than or equal to 125 and less than 200. If this is **true**, assign the value "Your height and weight are within acceptable bounds for this job." to the variable **message**. If this is **false** assign the value "Your height and weight are not within acceptable bounds for this job." to the variable **message**. If the enclosing **if** statement is **false**, test to see if **height** is greater than or equal to 70 and less than or equal to 74. If this is **true**, use a nested **if/else** statement to test if **weight** is greater than or equal to 200 and less than 300. If this is **true**, assign the value "Your height and weight are within acceptable bounds for this job." to the variable **message**. If this is **false** assign the value "Your height and weight are not within acceptable bounds for this job." to the variable **message**. If the enclosing **else if** statement is **false**, assign the value "You're too tall for this job." to the variable **message**.

Step 9: display the value of **message** in the browser window.

Solution

```
<script>
  var weight;
  var height;
  var message;
  height = prompt ("Please enter your height in inches.");
  weight = prompt ("Please enter your weight in pounds.");
  height = parseInt (height);
  weight = parseInt (weight);
  if (height >= 60 && height <= 69) {
   if (weight >= 125 && weight < 200) {
    message = "Your height and weight are within acceptable bounds for this job.";
   }
   else {
    message = "Your height and weight are not within accepatable bounds for this job.";
   }
  }
  else if (height >= 70 && height <= 74) {
   if (weight >= 200 && weight <= 300) {
    message = "Your height and weight are within acceptable bounds for this job.";
   }
   else {
    message = "Your height and weight are not within acceptable bounds for this job.";
   }
  }
  else if (height >= 75 && height <= 80) {
   if (weight >= 300 && weight <= 400) {
    message = "Your height and weight are within acceptable bounds for this job.";
   }
   else {
    message = "Your height and weight are not within acceptable bounds for this job.";
   }
  }
  else {
   message = "Your too tall for this job.";
  }
  document.write (message);
</script>
```

12.22 Step 1: Create a variable called **a** but don't assign it a value yet.

Step 2: Create a variable called **b** but don't assign it a value yet.

Step 3: Create a variable called **c** but don't assign it a value yet.

Step 4: Create a variable called **answer** but don't assign it a value yet.

Step 5: Set the value of **a** to the value entered by the user into the user response section of a prompt box. The user prompt message should say ("Please enter a one-digit integer between 1 and 10 for variable a.".

Step 6: Set the value of **b** to the value entered by the user into the user response section of a prompt box. The user prompt message should say "Please enter a one-digit integer between 1 and 10 for variable b.".

Step 7: Set the value of **c** to the value entered by the user into the user response section of a prompt box. The user prompt message should say "Please enter a one-digit integer between 1 and 10 for variable c.".

Step 8: Convert **a** to an integer value.

Step 9: Convert **b** to an integer value.

Step 10: Convert **c** to an integer value.

Step 11: Create an **if/ else** statement to solve this problem. In the **if** section, test to see if **a** is equal to **b**. If this is **true**, use a nested **if/else** statement to test to see if **a** is equal to **c**. If this is **true**, assign the value "all are equal." to the variable **answer**. If this is **false**, assign the value "a and b are equal." to the variable **answer**. If the enclosing **if** statement is **false**, use a nested **if/else** statement in the **else** section of the enclosing **if/else** statement to test to see if **a** is equal to **c**. If this is **true**, assign the value "a and c are equal." to the variable **answer**. If this is **false**, assign the value "b and c are equal." to the variable **answer**. If the enclosing **if else** statement is **false**, assign the value "all are different." to the variable **answer**.

Step 12: display the value of **answer** in an alert box.

Solution

```
<script>
  var a;
  var b;
  var c;
  var answer;
  a = prompt ("Please enter a one-digit integer between 1 and 10 for variable a.");
  b = prompt ("Please enter a one-digit integer between 1 and 10 for variable b.");
  c = prompt ("Please enter a one-digit integer between 1 and 10 for variable c.");
  a = parseInt (a):
  b = parseInt (b):
  c = parseInt (c):
  if (a == b) {
   if (a == c) {
   answer = "all are equal";
    }
    else {
        answer = "a and b are equal";
    }
  }
  else {
   if (a == c)
   {
   answer = "a and c are equal";
```

```
    }
    else {
     if (b == c) {
         answer = "b and c are equal";
     }
     else {
         answer = "all are different";
     }
    }
   }
  alert (answer);
</script>
```

Chapter 13

JavaScript Conditional Statements: Part 4

13.1 The switch statement

The **switch** statement in JavaScript is used in a manner similar to of a series of **if/else if** statements. The **switch** statement evaluates a series of conditions and if a match is found, the program executes the block of code in that particular section. A **switch** statement usually has three or more sections, each with a condition to be evaluated, although, there is no limit to the number of conditional sections that a switch statement can accommodate. The **switch** statement is a conditional statement like an **if** statement. The **switch** statement is useful when you want to execute one of several code blocks that are based on the return value of a single, specified expression.

The syntax of a **switch** statement is as follows:

```
switch (expression) {
  case value1:
    //block of code that will be executed when the result of expression matches value1
    [break;]
  case value2:
    // block of code that will be executed when the result of expression matches value2
    [break;]
    ...
  case valueN:
    // block of code that will be executed when the result of expression matches valueN
    [break;]
  default:
    // block of code that will be executed when none of the values match the value of the expression
    [break;]
}
```

Explanation of syntax terms:

expression

An expression (or a literal) that is tested against each case value.

case value1 (also called the **case label**)

This is the first value that is tested against the switch expression (or literal) for a match. If value1 matches the switch expression, the block of code in this case will execute. When the program looks for a case value comparison match with the switch expression, it uses strict comparison, === (both the value and the data type must match). When all statements in the code block have been executed, the **break** keyword is encountered which causes the program to jump out of the switch statement and begin execution at the first code statement after the end of the switch statement.

case value2 (also called the **case label**)

This is the first value that is tested against the switch expression (or literal) for a match. If value1 matches the switch expression, the block of code in this case will execute. When the program looks for a case value comparison match with the switch expression, it uses strict comparison, === (both the value and the data type must match). When all statements in the code block have been executed, the **break** keyword is encountered which causes the program to jump out of the switch statement and begin execution at the first code statement after the end of the switch statement.

case valueN (also called the **case label**)

This is the first value that is tested against the switch expression (or literal) for a match. If value1 matches the switch expression, the block of code in this case will execute. When the program looks for a case value comparison match with the switch expression, it uses strict comparison, === (both the value and the data type must match). When all statements in the code block have been executed, the **break** keyword is encountered which causes the program to jump out of the switch statement and begin execution at the first code statement after the end of the switch statement.

default

This is the block of code that will be executed when there are no matches between any of the previous
case values and the switch expression (or literal).

switch statement examples:

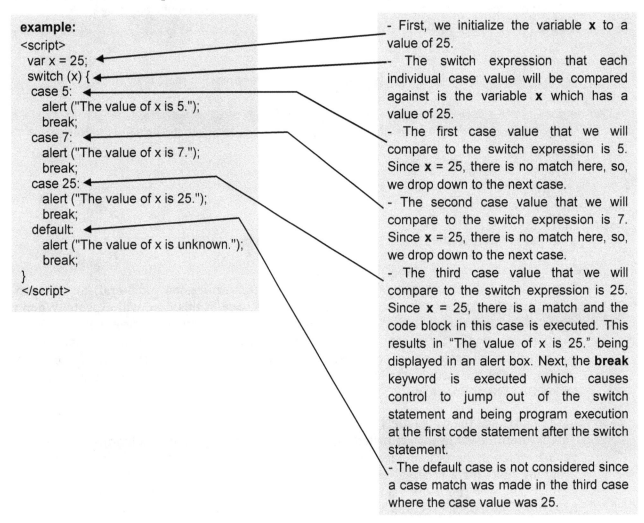

example:
```
<script>
  var x = 25;
  switch (x) {
    case 5:
      alert ("The value of x is 5.");
      break;
    case 7:
      alert ("The value of x is 7.");
      break;
    case 25:
      alert ("The value of x is 25.");
      break;
    default:
      alert ("The value of x is unknown.");
      break;
  }
</script>
```

- First, we initialize the variable **x** to a value of 25.
- The switch expression that each individual case value will be compared against is the variable **x** which has a value of 25.
- The first case value that we will compare to the switch expression is 5. Since **x** = 25, there is no match here, so, we drop down to the next case.
- The second case value that we will compare to the switch expression is 7. Since **x** = 25, there is no match here, so, we drop down to the next case.
- The third case value that we will compare to the switch expression is 25. Since **x** = 25, there is a match and the code block in this case is executed. This results in "The value of x is 25." being displayed in an alert box. Next, the **break** keyword is executed which causes control to jump out of the switch statement and being program execution at the first code statement after the switch statement.
- The default case is not considered since a case match was made in the third case where the case value was 25.

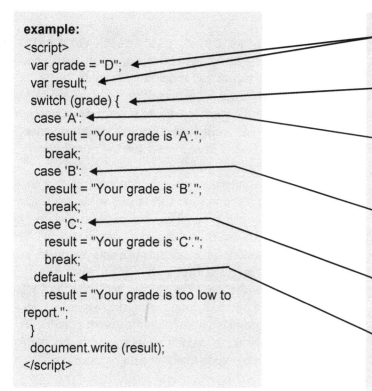

example:
```
<script>
  var grade = "D";
  var result;
  switch (grade) {
   case 'A':
     result = "Your grade is 'A'.";
     break;
   case 'B':
     result = "Your grade is 'B'.";
     break;
   case 'C':
     result = "Your grade is 'C'.";
     break;
   default:
     result = "Your grade is too low to
report.";
   }
  document.write (result);
</script>
```

First, we initialize the value of variable **grade** to "D" and create the variable **result** with no value.

The switch expression that each individual case value will be compared against is the variable **grade** which has a value of "D".

The first case value that we will compare to the switch expression is "A". Since **grade** = "D", there is no match here so we drop down to the next case.

The second case value that we will compare to the switch expression is "B". Since **grade** = "D", there is no match here, so, we drop down to the next case.

The third case value that we will compare to the switch expression is "C". Since **grade** = "D", there is no match here, so, we drop down to the **default** case and automatically execute the code block. This results in the message "Your grade is too low to report." Being displayed in the browser window.

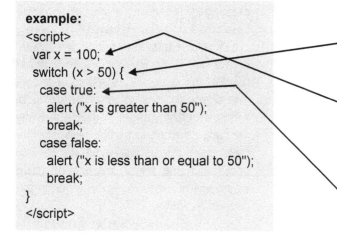

example:
```
<script>
  var x = 100;
  switch (x > 50) {
   case true:
     alert ("x is greater than 50");
     break;
   case false:
     alert ("x is less than or equal to 50");
     break;
}
</script>
```

The switch condition can also be a comparison as in this example: **x > 50**. When the switch condition is a comparison, only two cases are used without a default case and the case values are **true** and **false**.

First, we create a variable called **x** and initialize its value to 100.

The switch expression / comparison will evaluate to either **true** or **false** depending on the value of **x** (in this case, it evaluates to **true** since **x = 100**).

The first case value that we will compare to the value returned by the switch expression / comparison is **true**. Since **x** = 100, the comparison **x > 50** will return **true** making this a match. The code block in this first case will then execute resulting in "x is greater than 50" being displayed in an alert box.

There is no default case since the comparison has to evaluate to either **true** or **false**.

```
example:
<script>
 var num1 = 50;
 var num2 = 25;
 switch ((num1 - num2) == num2) {
   case true:
     result="The comparison is true.";
     break;
   case false:
     result = "The comparison is false.";
     break;
}
alert (result);
</script>
```

First, we create a variable called **num1** and initialize its value to 50. Next, we create a variable called **num2** and initialize its value to 25.

The switch expression / comparison will evaluate to either **true** or **false** depending on the value of **num1** and **num2** (in this case, it evaluates to **true** since **num1 – num2** equals 25 and **num2** equals 25.

The first case value is **true**. Since the switch comparison returns **true**, this first case is a match making this a match so, the code block in this first case will then execute resulting in "The comparison is true." being displayed in an alert box. Next, the **break** keyword is executed which causes control to jump out of the switch statement and being program execution at the first code statement after the switch statement.

There is no default case since the comparison has to evaluate to either **true** or **false**.

```
example
<script>
var grade = prompt ("Please enter a " +
    "number between 1 and 100 inclusive");
grade = parseInt(grade);
switch (true) {
  case (grade >= 95 && grade <= 100 ):
   if (grade >= 95 && grade <= 100){
    result = "Your grade is 'A+'.";
   }
   else if (grade >= 90 && grade < 95) {
    result = "Your grade is 'A-'.";
   }
   break;
  case (grade >= 80 && grade < 90):
   if (grade >=85 && grade < 90) {
    result = "Your grade is 'B+'.";
   }
   else if (grade >=80 && grade < 85){
    result = "Your grade is 'B-'.";
   }
   break;
```

(continued on next page)

First, we create a variable called **grade** and set it equal to the value entered into a prompt box with the user prompt message "Please enter a number between 1 and 100 inclusive."

In this **switch** statement, the switch expression is the Boolean value **true** and each of the case values are comparisons that check for the value of **grade** to be within a certain range. If **grade** is within the range described by the case label the case comparison will evaluate to **true** and match the switch expression (**true**) which will result in the code block in that case to execute.

The first case checks for **grade** to be greater than or equal to 95 and less than or equal to 100. If this is true, then, an **if/else** statement is used with further comparisons to determine if the final grade is an A+ or an A-. As usual, the case ends with a break statement, so, no more of the switch statement is executed.

(continued on next page)

```
case (grade >=70 && grade <= 80):
  if (grade >=75 && grade < 80) {
    result = "Your grade is 'C+'.";
  }
  else if (grade >=70 && grade < 75) {
    result = "Your grade is 'C-'.";
  }
  break;
case (grade >=60 && grade < 70):
  if (grade >=65 && grade < 70) {
    result = "Your grade is 'D+'.";
  }
  else if(grade >=60 && grade < 65){
    result="Your grade is 'D-'.";
  }
  break;
default:
    result=" Your grade is 'F'.";
    break;
}
alert (result);
</script>
```

There are three more cases that follow the first case and operate in the same way as the first case, but they're checking for the variable **grade** to be in ranges that result in a final grade of B (B+ or B-), C (C+ or C-) or D (D+ or D-).

The default section automatically displays the message "Your grade is 'F'." without any comparisons having to be made.

SOLVED PROBLEMS

13.1 The **switch** statement is similar to which of the following:

a) a series of alert boxes

b) a series of comparisons

c) a series of **if/else if** statements

Solution

c

13.2 When is a **switch** statement most useful?

a) when you can't use an **if** statement

b) when you want to execute one of several code blocks based on the return value of a single expression

c) when you're dealing with Boolean logic

Solution

b

13.3 What is the **default** block of code used for?

a) the **default** block of code is executed when no matches are found between any of the previous **case** values and the **switch** expression

b) the **default** block of code is executed when there is no match with the first two **case** values

c) the **default** block of code is executed when the break keyword is encountered by the program

Solution

a

13.4 Which is more efficient:

a) repeated **if** statements

b) repeated **if/else** statements

c) repeated **if/else if/else** statements

d) a single **switch** statement

Solution

d

13.5 The **case** keyword is followed by what?

a) a value and a colon

b) a value and a semi-colon

c) a comparison and a value

Solution

a

13.6 What is the first thing a switch statement does when it executes?

a) it skips the first **case** code block and goes to the second **case**

b) it computes the value of the **switch expression** and then looks for a **case** label that matches that value

c) it jumps to the default section and executes the code block found there

Solution

b

13.7 What if no match is found between any of the **case labels** and the **switch expression**?

a) the code in the **break** section is executed

b) program control jumps to the first code statement after the **switch** statement

c) the code block in the **default** section is executed

Solution

c

13.8 Do you have to have a **default** section in a **switch** statement?

a) yes

b) no

Solution

b

13.9 What does the **break** statement do?

a) it causes program execution to jump to the end of the switch statement

b) it stops the program from executing any more code

c) it causes program control to jump to the beginning of the **switch** statement

Solution

a

6.92 Which version of the switch keyword is correct?

a) Switch

b) SWITCH

c) switch

Solution

c

13.10 Where is the switch expression found?

a) in parentheses immediately following the switch keyword

b) after the break keyword

c) after each case keyword

Solution

a

13.11 What three types of data can be used in the **switch expression**?

a) variable, Boolean, number

b) variable, number, string

c) number, Boolean, variable

Solution

b

13.12 A switch statement and an if statement are both what ype of statement??

a) conditional

b) comparison

c) Boolean

Solution

b

13.13 Step 1: Create a variable called **a**.

Step 2: Add a switch statement with 2 cases and a default section. The switch will use the variable **a** as its test expression. The first case should test to see if **a** equals 10. If this is **true**, display "The value of a is 10" in an alert box and then break out of the switch statement. If this is **false**, go to the next case which will test to see if **a** equals 20. If this is **true**, display "The value of a is 20" in an alert box and then break out of the switch statement. If this is **false**, display "The value of a is unknown" in an alert box.

Solution

```
<script>
 var a = 20;
 switch (a) {
   case 10:
     alert ("The value of a is 10");
     break;
   case 20:
     alert ("The value of a is 20");
     break;
   default:
```

```
        alert ("The value of a is unknown");
    }
</script>
```

Result displayed in browser:

The value of a is 20

13.14 Step 1: Create a variable called **car** and give it the value "Mazda".

Step 2: Add a switch statement with 2 cases and a default section. The switch will use the variable **car** as its test expression. The first case should test to see if **car** equals "Ford". If this is true, display "The car is a Ford" in an alert box and then break out of the switch statement. If this is false, go to the next case which should test to see if **car** equals "Toyota". If this is true, display "The car is a Toyota" in an alert box and then break out of the switch statement. If this is false, display "The make of the car is unknown" in an alert box.

Solution

```
<script>
  var car = "Mazda";
  switch (car) {
    case "Ford":
      document.write ("The car is a Ford.");
      break;
    case "Toyota":
      document.write ("The car is a Toyota.");
      break;
    default:
      document.write ("The make of the car is unknown.");
  }
</script
```

Result displayed in browser:

The make of the car is unknown.

13.15 Step 1: Create a variable called **letterGrade** and initialize its value to "C".

Step 2: Create a variable called **message.**

Step 3: Create a switch statement with 3 cases and a default section. The switch will use the variable **letterGrade** as its test expression. The first case should test to see if **letterGrade** equals "A". If this is **true**, set the value of **message** to "You made an 'A'." in an alert box and then break out of the switch statement. If this is **false**, go to the next case which should test to see if **letterGrade** equals "B". If this is **true**, set the value of **message** to "You made a 'B'." in an alert box and then break out of the switch statement. If this is **false**, go to the next case which should test to see if **letterGrade** equals "C". If this is

true, set the value of **message** to " You made a 'C'." in an alert box and then break out of the switch statement. If this is **false** then set the value of the variable **message** to "You didn't do too well."

Step 4: Display the value of **message** in an alert box.

Solution

```
<script>
  var letterGrade = "C";
  var message;
  switch (letterGrade) {
    case "A":
     message = "You made an 'A'.";
     break;
    case "B":
     message = "You made a 'B'.";
     break;
    case "C":
     message = "You made a 'C'.";
     break;
   default:
     message = "You didn't do too well.";
  }
  alert (message);
</script>
```

Result displayed in browser:

You made a 'C'.

13.16 Step 1: Create a variable called **j** and initialize its value to 75.

Step 2: Add a switch statement with two cases and no default section. The switch will use the comparison **j > 40** as its test expression. This will evaluate to either **true** or **false**, so, there are only two cases (**true** and **false**) and no **default** section. The first case should test to see if **j > 40** is true. If this is **true**, display "j is greater than 40 ." in an alert box. If this is **false**, go to the next case which will test to see if **j > 40** is false (since it failed the **true** case, it has to be false, so, you could have just used a default here instead of another case). If **j > 40** is **false** (which means that the case is true) display "j is not greater than 40." in an alert box.

Solution

```
<script>
  var j = 75;
  switch (j > 40) {
    case true:
     alert ("j is greater than 40.");
     break;
    case false:
```

```
  alert ("j is not greater than 40.");
  break;
  }
</script>
```

Result displayed in browser:

j is greater than 40.

13.17 Rewrite problem 13.16 using one **case** and a **default** section. Also initialize the variable **j** to a value of 35 instead of 75 as in problem 13.16.

Solution
```
<script>
  var j = 35;
  switch (j > 40) {
    case true:
      alert ("j is greater than 40.");
      break;
    default:
      alert ("j is not greater than 40.");
      break;
  }
</script>
```

Result displayed in browser:

j is not greater than 40.

13.18 Step 1: Create a variable called **x** and initialize its value to 30.

Step 2: Create a variable called **y** and initialize its value to 15.

Step 3: Create a variable called **result** but don't initialize it.

Step 4: Add a switch statement with two cases and no default section. The switch will use the comparison **(x - y) == y** as its expression. Since the expression is a comparison, it will evaluate to either **true** or **false.** The first case (with a case value of **true**) will be a match if **(x - y) == y** is true. If this is **true**, set the string variable **result** equal to "x minus y equals y.". If this is **false**, go to the next case (with a case value of **false**) which will be a match if **(x - y) == y** is false. If this is the case, then, set the string variable **result** equal to the string value "x minus y does not equal y.".

Step 5: Display the value of the variable **result** in the browser window.

Solution
```
<script>
  var x = 30;
  var y = 15;
```

```
var result;
switch ((x - y) == y) {
   case true:
     result = "x minus y equals y.";
     break;
   case false:
     result = "x minus y does not equal y.";
     break;
  }
  document.write (result);
</script>
```

Result displayed in browser:

j is greater than 40.

13.19 Step 1: Create a variable called **n** but don't initialize it.

Step 2: Create a variable called **msg** but don't initialize it.

Step 3: Assign the value entered by the user in the user response section of a prompt box to the variable **n**. The user prompt section message should say "Enter an integer" between 1 and 50 inclusive."

Step 4: Convert **n** to an integer value.

Step 4: Create a switch statement with 3 cases and a default section. The switch statement will use the Boolean value **true** as its expression. Each case value will be a comparison that tests to see if the variable **n** is within a certain range. If **n** is within the range specified by the case value (which in this case is a comparison) then the case value will be a match with the switch expression and the code block in that case will execute.

The first case value will be **n >= 1 && n <= 10.** If this is **true**, set the string variable **msg** to the value "You entered an integer between 1 and 10 inclusive." and follow that with a **break** keyword.

The second case value will be **n >= 11 && n <= 25.** If this is **true**, set the string variable **msg** to the value "You entered an integer between 11 and 25 inclusive." and follow that with a **break** keyword.

The third case value will be **n >= 26 && n <= 50.** If this is **true**, set the string variable **msg** to the value"You entered an integer between 26 and 50 inclusive." and follow that with a **break** keyword. If none of the cases are true set the string variable **msg** to the value "You didn't enter an integer between 1 and 50 inclusive."

Step 4: Display the value of **msg** in an alert box.

Solution

```
<script>
  var n;
  var msg;
  n = prompt ("Enter an integer between 1 and 50 inclusive.");
  n = parseInt (n);
  switch (true) {
```

```
    case (n >= 1 && n <= 10):
      msg = "You entered an integer between 1 and 10 inclusive.";
      break;
    case (n >= 11 && n <= 25):
      msg = "You entered an integer between 11 and 25 inclusive.";
      break;
    case (n >= 26 && n <= 50):
      msg = "You entered an integer between 26 and 50 inclusive.";
      break;
    default:
      msg = "You didn't enter an integer between 1 and 50.";
      break;
  }
  alert (msg);
</script>
```

13.20 Step 1: Create a variable called **yearsOld** but don't give it a value .

Step 2: Assign the value entered by the user in the user response section of a prompt box to the variable **yearsOld**. The user prompt section message should say "Please enter your age in years."

Step 3: Convert **yearsOld** to an integer value.

Step 4: Add a switch statement with three cases and no default section. The switch expression should be the Boolean value **true**. In other words, the case values will be checked to see if they have the value **true**. The case that has a value of true will have its code block executed.

The first case value will test to see if **yearsOld** is less than 13. If this is **true**, display the message "You're still pretty young." in an alert box. Follow that with a break command.

The second case value will test to see if **yearsOld** is less than 21 (if this is **true**, then, we know that **yearsOld** is between 13 and 20 inclusive). If this is **true**, display the message "You're almost an adult." in an alert box. Follow that with a break command.

The third case value will test to see if **yearsOld** is less than 50 (if this is **true**, then, we know that **yearsOld** is between 21 and 29 inclusive). If this is **true**, display the message "You're middle-aged." in an alert box. Follow that with a break command.

The default case value will automatically display the message "Hello, old-timer." in an alert box (only if there was no match with the first three cases).

Solution

```
<script>
  var yearsOld;
  yearsOld = prompt ("Please enter your age in years.");
  yearsOld = parseInt (yearsOld);
  switch (true) {
   case (yearsOld < 13):
     alert ("You're still pretty young.");
     break;
```

```
      case (yearsOld < 21):
        alert ("You're almost an adult.");
        break;
      case (yearsOld < 50):
        alert ("You're middle-aged.");
        break;
      default:
        alert ("Hello, old-timer.");
        break;
    }
</script>
```

13.21 Step 1: Create a variable called **numberEntered**.

Step 2: Create a variable called **x.**

Step 3: Assign the value entered by the user in the user response section of a prompt box to the variable **numberEntered**. The user prompt section message should say "Please enter one of the following numbers: 10, 20 or 30.".

Step 4: Convert **numberEntered** to an integer value.

Step 4: Add a switch statement with three cases and a default that tests the variable **numberEntered** for a value of 10, 20 or 30.

- if the first case value of "10" is a match to the variable **numberEntered**, set **x** equal to "You entered 10." and include a **break** keyword.

- if the second case value of "20" is a match to the variable **numberEntered**, set **x** equal to "You entered 20." and include a **break** keyword.

- if the third case value of "30" is a match to the variable **numberEntered**, set **x** equal to "You entered 30." and include a **break** keyword.

- if none of the cases are a match display "You didn't enter 10, 20 or 30."

Step 5: Display the value of **x** in an alert box.

Solution

```
<script>
  var numberEntered;
  var x;
  numberEntered = prompt ("Please enter one of the following numbers: 10, 20 or 30.");
  numberEntered = parseInt (numberEntered);
  switch (numberEntered) {
    case("10"):
      x = "You entered 10.";
      break;
    case ("20"):
      x = "You entered 20.";
      break;
    case ("30"):
      x = "You entered 30.";
      break;
```

```
    default:
        x = "You didn't enter 10, 20 or 30.";
        break;
  }
  alert (x);
</script>
```

13.22 Step 1: Create a variable called **favoriteColor**.

Step 2: Create a variable called **response.**

Step 3: Assign the value entered by the user in the user response section of a prompt box to the variable **favorite color**. The user prompt section message should say "Please enter one of the following color names: "'red', 'blue', or 'green'."

Step 4: Add a switch statement with three cases and a default that tests the variable **favoriteColor** for a value of 'red', "blue' or 'green'.".
- if the first case value of "red" is a match to the variable **favorite color**, set **response** equal to "Red is a fiery color." and include a **break** keyword.
- if the first case value of "blue" is a match to the variable **favorite color**, set **response** equal to "Blue is the color of the sky." and include a **break** keyword.
- if the first case value of "green" is a match to the variable **favorite color**, set **response** equal to "Green is the color of nature." and include a **break** keyword.
- if none of the cases are a match display "Apparently, you made and incorrect entry."

Step 5: Display the value of **response** in an alert box.

Solution

```
<script>
  var favoriteColor;
  var response;
  favoriteColor = prompt ("Please enter one of the following color names: 'red', 'blue', or 'green'.");
  switch (favoriteColor) {
    case ("red"):
      response = "Red is a fiery color.";
      break;
    case ("blue"):
      response = "Blue is the color of the sky.";
      break;
    case ("green"):
      response = "Green is the color of nature.";
      break;
    default:
response = "Apparently, you made an incorrect entry.";
      break;
  }
  alert (response);
</script>
```

13.23 Step 1: Create a variable called **itemPurchased.**

Step 2: Create a variable called **quantity.**

Step 3: Create a variable called **price.**

Step 4: Create a variable called **taxRate.**

Step 5: Assign the value entered by the user in the user response section of a prompt box to the variable **itemPurchased**. The user prompt section message should say "Please enter one of the following items: 'comb', 'pen', 'lighter', or 'hammer'.");

Step 6: Assign the value entered by the user in the user response section of a prompt box to the variable **quantity**. The user prompt section message should say "How many do you want.");

Step 7:

Step 8: Add a switch statement with four cases and a default that tests the variable **itemPurchased** for a value of "comb", "pen", "lighter", or "hammer".

- if the first case value of "comb" is a match to the variable **itemPurchased**, set **price** equal to the number 1.39, **taxRate** to the number 0.05 and include a **break** keyword.
- if the first case value of "pen" is a match to the variable **itemPurchased**, set **price** equal to the number 0.69, **taxRate** to the number 0.06 and include a **break** keyword.
- if the first case value of "lighter" is a match to the variable **itemPurchased**, set **price** equal to the number 2.89, **taxRate** to the number 0.03 and include a **break** keyword.
- if the first case value of "hammer" is a match to the variable **itemPurchased**, set **price** equal to the number 5.00, **taxRate** to the number 0.06 and include a **break** keyword.
- if none of the cases are a match display "I didn't recognize that entry."

Step 9: Set the value of **totalPrice** to **quantity * (price + (price * taxRate)).**

Step 10: display in the browser window: "The total amount of your purchase is $ <**totalPrice** rounded to two decimal places> ". JavaScript doesn't have a direct way to round a number with a decimal value, so, you have to do it in the roundabout way shown here.

Step 11: Check the results for the following inputs:

a) itemPurchased = "comb" / quantity = 6

b) itemPurchased = "pen" / quantity = 27

c) itemPurchased = "lighter" / quantity = 9

d) itemPurchased = "hammer" / quantity = 5

Solution

```
<script>
 var itemPurchased;
 var quantity;
 var price;
 var taxRate;
 itemPurchased = prompt ("Please enter the name of the item purchased.",
             "Please enter one of the following items: 'comb', " +
             "'pen', 'lighter', or 'hammer'.");
 quantity = prompt ("How many do you want?");
 quantity = parseInt (quantity);
```

```
switch(itemPurchased){
  case ("comb"):
   price = 1.39;
   taxRate = .05;
   break;
  case ("pen"):
   price = 0.69;
   taxRate = .05;
   break;
  case ("lighter"):
   price = 2.89;
   taxRate = .05;
   break;
  case ("hammer"):
   price = 5.49;
   taxRate = .06;
   break;
  default:
   alert ("I didn't recognize that entry.");
   break
 }
 totalPrice = quantity * (price + (price * taxRate));
 document.write ("The total amount of your purchase is $" + (Math.round(totalPrice * 100)/100));
</script>
```

Result displayed in browser window:
a) The total amount of your purchase is $8.76
b) The total amount of your purchase is $19.56
c) The total amount of your purchase is $27.31

13.24 Step 1: Create a variable called **militaryTime.**

Step 2: Assign the value entered by the user in the user response section of a prompt box to the variable **militaryTime**. The user prompt section message should say "Enter the hour in military time." and the default message in the user response section should say "Enter an integer from 0 to 23.".

Step 3: Convert militaryTime to an integer value.

Step 4: Add a switch statement with four cases and a default that tests the four case comparison values for a Boolean value of **true**.

- The first case will check to see if the comparison **militaryTime < 12** is a match for the switch condition which is the Boolean value **true**. If there is a match, display "It's either very late at night or it's morning." in an alert box and follow this with the . **break** keyword

- The second case will check to see if the comparison **militaryTime < 15** is a match for the switch condition which is the Boolean value **true**. If there is a match, display "It's between noon and 3pm." in an alert box and follow this with the **break** keyword.

- The third case will check to see if the comparison **militaryTime < 18** is a match for the switch condition which is the Boolean value **true**. If there is a match, display "It's between 3pm and 6pm." in an alert box and follow this with the **break** keyword to conclude the switch statement comparisons.
- The fourth case will check to see if the comparison **militaryTime < 23** is a match for the switch condition which is the Boolean value **true**. If there is a match, display "It's night." in an alert box and follow this with the **break** keyword.
- if none of the cases are a match display "You didn't enter what you were supposed to enter.".

Solution

```
<script>
 var militaryTime;
 militaryTime = prompt ("Enter the hour in military time.",
             "Enter an integer from 0 to 23.");
 militaryTime = parseInt (militaryTime);
 switch(true) {
  case (militaryTime < 12):
    alert ("It's either very late at night or it's morning.");
    break;
  case (militaryTime < 15):
    alert ("It's between noon and 3pm.");
    break;
  case (militaryTime < 18):
    alert ("It's between 3pm and 6pm.");
    break;
  case (militaryTime <= 23):
    alert ("It's night.");
    break;
  default:
    alert ("You didn't enter what you were supposed to enter.");
    break;
 }
</script>
```

13.25 Step 1: Create a variable called **testScore.**

Step 2: Assign the value entered by the user in the user response section of a prompt box to the variable **testScore**. The user prompt section message should say "Please enter your final test score." and the default message in the user response section should say "Enter an integer from 1 to 100.".

Step 3: Convert testScore to an integer value.

Step 4: Add a switch statement with five cases and a default that tests the five case comparison values against the switch expression for a Boolean value of **true**.

- The first case will check to see if the comparison **testScore >= 90** is a match for the switch condition **true**. If there is a match, display "Your final grade is an 'A'." in the browser window and follow this with the **break** keyword.

   - The second case will check to see if the comparison **testScore >= 80** is a match for the switch condition **true**. If there is a match, display "Your final grade is an 'B'." in the browser window and follow this with the **break** keyword.

   - The third case will check to see if the comparison **testScore >= 70** is a match for the switch condition **true**. If there is a match, display "Your final grade is an 'C'." in the browser window and follow this with the **break** keyword.

   - The fourth case will check to see if the comparison **testScore >= 60** is a match for the switch condition **true**. If there is a match, display "Your final grade is an 'D'." in the browser window and follow this with the **break** keyword.

   - The fifth case will check to see if the comparison **testScore < 60** is a match for the switch condition **true**. If there is a match, display "Your final grade is an 'F'." in the browser window and follow this with the **break** keyword.

   - if none of the cases are a match display "You didn't enter an integer between 1` and 100 inclusive."

Solution

```
script>
 var testScore;
 testScore = prompt ("Please enter your final test socre.",
           "Enter an integer from 1 to 100.");
 testScore = parseInt (testScore);
 switch(true) {
  case (testScore >= 90):
    document.write("Your final grade is an 'A'.");
    break;
  case (testScore >= 80):
    document.write ("Your final grade is an 'B'.");
    break;
  case (testScore >= 70):
    document.write ("Your final grade is an 'C'.");
    break;
  case (testScore >= 60):
    document.write ("Your final grade is an 'D'.");
    break;
  case (testScore < 60):
    document.write ("Your final grade is an 'F'.");
    break;
  default:
    document.write ("You didn't enter an integer between 1` and 100 inclusive.");
    break;
 }
</script>
```

13.26 Step 1: Create a variable called **result**.

Step 2: Create a variable called **integer1.**

Step 3: Create a variable called **integer2.**

Step 4: Create a variable called **integer3.**

Step 5: Assign the value entered by the user in the user response section of a prompt box to the variable **integer1**. The user prompt section message should say " Please enter an integer between 1 and 100 inclusive.".

Step 6: Assign the value entered by the user in the user response section of a prompt box to the variable **integer2**. The user prompt section message should say " Please enter an integer between 1 and 100 inclusive.".

Step 7: Assign the value entered by the user in the user response section of a prompt box to the variable **integer1**. The user prompt section message should say " Please enter an integer between 1 and 100 inclusive.".

Step 8: Convert **integer1** to an integer value.

Step 9: Convert **integer2** to an integer value.

Step 10: Convert **integer7** to an integer value.

Step 11: Create a switch statement with 3 cases and no default section. The switch statement will use the Boolean value **true** as its expression.

The first case value will be **(integer1 + integer2) < integer3.** If this is **true**, set the string variable **result** to the value ""(integer1 plus integer2) is less than integer3)" and follow that with a **break** keyword.

The second case value will be **(integer1 + integer2) > integer3.** If this is **true**, set the string variable **result** to the value ""(integer1 plus integer2) is greater than integer3)" and follow that with a **break** keyword.

The third case value will be **(integer1 + integer2) == integer3.** If this is **true**, set the string variable **result** to the value ""(integer1 plus integer2) is equal to integer3)" and follow that with a **break** keyword.

Step 12: Display the value of **result** in an alert box.

Solution

```
<script>
    var result;
    var integer1;
    var integer2;
    var integer3;
    integer1 = prompt("Please enter an integer between 1 and 100 inclusive.");
    integer2 = prompt("Please enter an integer between 1 and 100 inclusive.");
    integer3 = prompt("Please enter an integer between 1 and 100 inclusive.");
    integer1 = parseInt(integer1);
    integer2 = parseInt(integer2);
    integer3 = parseInt(integer3);
    switch (true) {
        case((integer1 + integer2) < integer3):
            result = "(integer1 plus integer2) is less than integer3)";
            break;
```

```
    case((integer1 + integer2) > integer3):
       result = "(integer1 plus integer2) is greater than integer3)";
       break;
    case((integer1 + integer2) == integer3):
       result = "(integer1 plus integer2) is equal to integer3)";
       break;
  }
  document.write(result);
</script>
```

13.27 Step 1: Create a variable called **weight**.

Step 2: Create a variable called **height.**

Step 3: Create a variable called **message.**

Step 4: Assign the value entered by the user in the user response section of a prompt box to the variable **height**. The user prompt section message should say " Please enter your heigh in inches.".

Step 5: Assign the value entered by the user in the user response section of a prompt box to the variable **weight**. The user prompt section message should say " Please enter your weight in pounds.".

Step 6: Convert **weight** to an integer value.

Step 7: Convert **height** to an integer value.

Step 8: Create a switch statement with 3 cases and a default section. The switch statement will use the Boolean value **true** as its expression.

The first case value will be **height >= 60 && height <= 69.** If this is **true**, add an **if/else** statement that checks to see if **weight >=125 && weight < 200** is **true**. If this is **true**, then, set the value of the string variable **message** to "Your height and weight are within acceptable bounds for this job." If the if condition is false, set the value of the string variable **message** to "Your height and weight are not within acceptable bounds for this job.".

The second case value will be **height >= 70 && height <= 74.** If this is **true**, add an **if/else** statement that checks to see if **weight >=200 && weight < 300** is **true**. If this is **true**, then, set the value of the string variable **message** to "Your height and weight are within acceptable bounds for this job.". If the if condition is false, then, set the value of the string variable **message** to "Your height and weight are not within acceptable bounds for this job.".

The third case value will be **height>=75 && height <= 80.** If this is **true**, add an **if/else** statement that checks to see if **weight >=300 && weight < 400** is **true**. If this is **true**, then, set the value of the string variable **message** to "Your height and weight are within acceptable bounds for this job.". If the **if** condition is false, set the value of the string variable **message** to "Your height and weight are not within acceptable bounds for this job.".

If none of the cases are a match, set the value of the string variable **message** to "Your height and weight are not within acceptable bounds for this job."

Step 9: Display the value of **message** in the browser window.

Solution

```
<script>
  var weight;
  var height;
  var message;
  height = prompt("Please enter your height in inches.");
  weight = prompt("Please enter your weight in pounds.");
  height = parseInt(height);
  weight = parseInt(weight);
  switch(true) {
    case(height >= 60 && height <= 69):
      if(weight >=125 && weight < 200) {
        message = "Your height and weight are within acceptable bounds for this job.";
      }
      else {
        message = "Your height and weight are not within acceptable bounds for this job.";
      }
      break;
    case(height >= 70 && height <= 74):
      if(weight >=200 && weight < 300) {
        message = "Your height and weight are within acceptable bounds for this job.";
      }
      else {
        message = "Your height and weight are not within acceptable bounds for this job.";
      }
      break;
    case(height >= 75 && height <= 80):
      if(weight >=300 && weight <= 400) {
        message = "Your height and weight are within acceptable bounds for this job.";
      }
      else {
        message = "Your height and weight are not within acceptable bounds for this job.";
      }
      break;
    default:
      message = "You're to tall for this job.";
      break;
  }
  document.write(message);
</script>
```

Chapter 14

JavaScript Loops

14.1 JAVASCRIPT LOOPS

Loops consist of a set of instructions that are used to repeat the same block of code over and over again until a specified condition returns **true** or **false** depending on what you need in the particular situation. In order to control how many times the loop repeats and executes its code block, a counter variable is used that increments or decrements with each repetition of the loop. One of the main advantages of a loop is that it can execute a block of code as many times as necessary. Loops are especially useful if you want to run the same code over and over again, but use a changing value each time.

There are several different kinds of loops but they all perform the same basic operation which is to repeat the instructions that are set out in a block of code within the loop. This will occur a number of times (or zero times) until a predetermined condition is met, such as a counter reaching a certain value. The different loop types give the programmer a variety of ways to determine the starting and ending specifications for the loop. There are a number of situations where one type of loop is more effective and efficient than one of the other types.

JavaScript supports several different kinds of loops:

- **for** - loops through a block of code a number of times
- **for/in** - loops through the properties of an object (we won't be considering this type of loop until a later chapter)
- **while** - loops through a block of code while a specified condition is true
- **do/while** - also loops through a block of code while a specified condition is true

The **for** statements are best used when you want to perform a loop a specific number of times. The **while** statements are best used to perform a loop an undetermined number of times. The **for** loop is used when you know in advance how many times the script should perform. For example you should use a **for** loop if you wanted it to create exactly 25 lines or display the numbers 1 through 25. The **while** loop is used when you want the loop to continue until a certain condition becomes **true**.

14.2 THE FOR LOOP

The **for** loop is the most frequently used loop in JavaScript. The **for** loop is a JavaScript method that allows a certain action (contained in an internal block of code) to be performed over and over again until a certain tes condition that has previously evaluated to **true** now evaluates to **false**. In other words, the **for** loop continues to iterate through its code block until a specified condition returns **false**.

The for loop statement consists of four distinct parts:

```
for (initialize statement; condition statement; increment statement) {
    code block statements

}
```

The 4 statements in the **for** loop execute in the following order:

- The **Initialize Statement** is executed before the loop starts.

- The **Condition Statement** defines the condition for running the loop and executes before every loop iteration. If the condition evaluates to **true**, then, the **Code Block** will execute again.

- The **Code Block** executes every time that the condition statement evaluates to **true**.

- The **Increment Statement** is executed each time after the loop (the code block) has been executed.
- The **Condition Statement** runs again after the Increment Statement has been executed and if the condition evaluates to **true,** the **Code Block** statements will run again. This loop continues until the **Increment Statement execution** causes the **Condition Statement** to evaluate to **false.** When this occurs, program execution jumps to the first statement after the **for** loop.

The syntax for the **for** loop can also be thought of in the following way:

```
for (loop initialization; test condition; iteration) {
    code block
}
```

loop initialization statement
This statement initializes your counter to a starting value. The loop initialization statement is executed before the loop begins. This is typically used to initialize a counter variable.

test condition statement
This statement tests to see if a given condition is true or false. The test/condition statement is an expression that is evaluated before each loop iteration. If the condition is true, then the code given inside the loop (the statement/code block section) will be executed. If the condition evaluates to false, control will come out of the loop and begin executing the first statement after the loop.

iteration statement
This statement is where you increment or decrement your counter variable (usually increment). This statement consists of an expression to be evaluated at the end of each loop iteration. This occurs before the next evaluation of the test/condition statement.

statement/code block
This is the internal block of code that is executed as long as the test/condition statement evaluates to true. If you want to execute multiple statements within the loop, use a block statement ({ ... }) to group the multiple statements.

The following is an example of a **for** loop:

```
<script>
    var text = "";



    for (i = 0; i < 5; i++) {
        text += "The number is " + i + "<br>";



    }
    document.write (text);
</script>
```

i = 0 is the **loop initialization** section of the **for** loop. This sets the counter variable (in this case **i**) to its initial value of 0 (although we're starting with **i = 0** in this example, the counter can be initialized at any value).

i < 5 is the **test condition**. As long as the value of **i** is less than 5, the code block in the interior of the **for** loop will execute another time.

i++ is the **iteration statement**. Without this statement the value of **i** would never change and the loop would repeat forever. In this case, the value of **i** is incremented by one after each iteration of the loop. After the code block executes, the value of i is incremented and then tested to see if it is still less than 5. If **i** is still less than 5, the code block is executed again. If the value of i is equal to or greater than 5 after the iteration statement executes, program execution will jump out of the **for** loop and begin at the first statement after the **for** loop. Remember that: **text += "The number is " + i + "<br>";** means the same thing as **text = text + "The number is " + i + "<br>";**

This **for** loop will result in the following output being displayed in the browser window:

The number is 0
The number is 1
The number is 2
The number is 3
The number is 4

Flowchart of a *for* loop

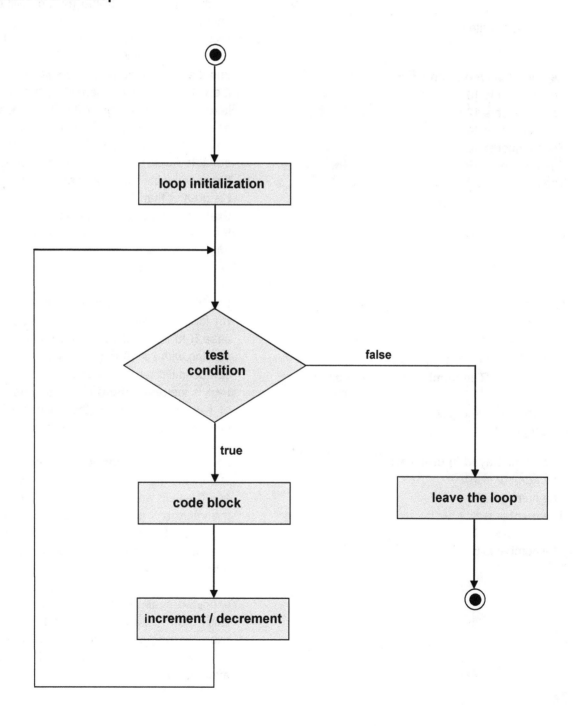

More *for* loop examples:

example:
```
<script>
  var text = "";



  for (i = 10; i <= 20; i = i + 2) {
    text += "The number is " + i + "<br>";
  }
  document.write (text);
</script>
```

Result displayed in browser:
The number is 10
The number is 12
The number is 14
The number is 16
The number is 18
The number is 20

i = 10 is the **loop initialization** section of the **for** loop. This sets the counter variable (in this case **i**) to its initial value of 10 (although we're starting with **i = 10** in this example, the counter can be initialized at any value).

i <= 20 is the **test condition**. As long as the value of **i** is less than or equal to 20, the code block in the interior of the **for** loop will execute another time.

I = i + 2 is the **iteration statement**. Without this statement the value of **i** would never change and the loop would repeat forever. In this case, the value of **i** is incremented by two after each iteration of the loop. After the code block executes, the value of i is incremented by 2 and then tested to see if it is still less than or equal to 20. If **i** is still less than or equal to 20, the code block is executed again. If the value of i is greater than 20 after the iteration statement executes, program execution will jump out of the **for** loop and begin at the first statement after the **for** loop.

example:
```
<script>
  var text = "";
  for (i = 10; i > 5; i--) {
    text += "The number is " + i + "<br>";
  }
  document.write (text);
</script>
```

Result displayed in browser:
The number is 10
The number is 9
The number is 8
The number is 7
The number is 6

i = 10 is the **loop initialization** section of the **for** loop. This sets the counter variable (in this case **i**) to its initial value of 10 (although we're starting with **i = 10** in this example, the counter can be initialized at any value).

i > 5 is the **test condition**. As long as the value of **i** is greater than 5, the code block in the interior of the **for** loop will execute another time.

I = i -- is the **iteration statement**. Without this statement the value of **i** would never change and the loop would repeat forever. In this case, the value of **i** is decremented by 1 after each iteration of the loop. After the code block executes, the value of **i** is decremented by 1 and then tested to see if it is still greater than 5. If **i** is still greater than 5, the code block is executed again. If the value of **i** is equal to or less than 5 after the iteration statement executes, program execution will jump out of the **for** loop and begin at the first statement after the **for** loop.

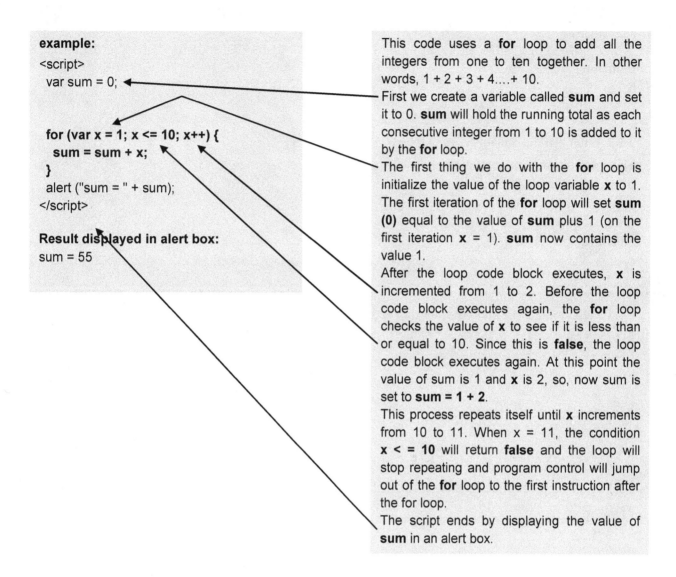

example:
```
<script>
  var sum = 0;

  for (var x = 1; x <= 10; x++) {
    sum = sum + x;
  }
  alert ("sum = " + sum);
</script>
```

Result displayed in alert box:
sum = 55

This code uses a **for** loop to add all the integers from one to ten together. In other words, 1 + 2 + 3 + 4....+ 10.

First we create a variable called **sum** and set it to 0. **sum** will hold the running total as each consecutive integer from 1 to 10 is added to it by the **for** loop.

The first thing we do with the **for** loop is initialize the value of the loop variable **x** to 1. The first iteration of the **for** loop will set **sum (0)** equal to the value of **sum** plus 1 (on the first iteration **x** = 1). **sum** now contains the value 1.

After the loop code block executes, **x** is incremented from 1 to 2. Before the loop code block executes again, the **for** loop checks the value of **x** to see if it is less than or equal to 10. Since this is **false**, the loop code block executes again. At this point the value of sum is 1 and **x** is 2, so, now sum is set to **sum = 1 + 2**.

This process repeats itself until **x** increments from 10 to 11. When x = 11, the condition **x < = 10** will return **false** and the loop will stop repeating and program control will jump out of the **for** loop to the first instruction after the for loop.

The script ends by displaying the value of **sum** in an alert box.

SOLVED PROBLEMS

14.1 What is the purpose of a loop?

a) to repeat a block of code 5 or more times

b) to repeat a block of code over and over again until a certain condition is met

c) to repeatedly display the value of the loop variable until the counter counts down to zero

Solution

b

14.2 Does the loop variable keep the same value on each iteration of the loop or does its value vary?

a) it stays the same

b) it varies

Solution

b

14.3 What are the 3 main types of loops?

a) for, conditional, incremental
b) while, when, decremental
c) for, while, do while

Solution

c

14.4 What loop is the most frequently used JavaScript loop?

a) for
b) while
c) do while

Solution

a

14.5 A for loop continues to iterate through its code block until the condition evaluates to what ?

a) true
b) false
c) zero

Solution

b

14.6 What 4 statements does a for loop consist of?

a) initialize statement, finalize statement, reset statement, code block statements
b) condition statement, for statement, loop statement, ciode block statements
c) initialize statement, condition statement, increment/decrement statement, code block statements

Solution

c

14.7 Which statement is executed before the loop starts?

a) code block statements
b) initialize statement

c) increment/decrement statement

Solution

c

14.8 The condition statement must evaluate to what value in order for the loop to execute again?

a) false

b) true

c) zero

Solution

b

14.9 What 2 statements execute on every iteration after the code block executes?

a) condition statement, initialize statement

b) initialize statement, loop variable statement

c) increment/decrement statement, condition statement

Solution

c

14.10 What must happen before the code block executes?

a) the counter decrements to zero

b) the condition statement evaluates to true

c) the counter increments to the value of the loop variable

Solution

b

14.11 Step 1: Create a **for** loop that uses **j** as the loop variable.

       Step 2: Set the initial value of **j** to 0.

       Step 3: The loop should continue to repeat itself as long as j is less than 6.

       Step 4: Increment **j** by 1 (use the increment operator) after each iteration.

       Step 5: The code block should display each successive value of j on separate lines.

Solution

```
<script>
   for (j = 0; j < 6; j++) {
     document.write (j + "<br>");
   }
</script>
```

Result displayed in browser:

0
1
2
3
4
5

14.12 Step 1: Create a **for** loop that uses **k** as the loop variable.

Step 2: Set the initial value of **k** to 5.

Step 3: The loop should continue to repeat itself as long as **k** is less than 11.

Step 4: Increment **k** by 1 (use the increment operator) after each iteration.

Step 5: The code block should display each successive value of **k** from 5 to 10 on separate lines.

Solution

```
<script>
   for (k = 5; k < 11; k++) {
      document.write (k + "<br>");
   }
</script>
```

Result displayed in browser:

5
6
7
8
9
10

14.13 Step 1: Create a **for** loop that uses **x** as the loop variable.

Step 2: Set the initial value of **x** to 25.

Step 3: The loop should continue to repeat itself as long as **x** is greater than 20.

Step 4: Decrement **x** by 1 (use the increment operator) after each iteration.

Step 5: The code block should display each successive value of **x** from 25 backwards to 20 on separate lines.

Solution

```
<script>
   for (x = 25; x > 20; x--) {
      document.write (x + "<br>");
   }
</script>
```

Result displayed in browser:

25
24
23
22
21

14.14 Step 1: Create a string variable called **display** and set its initial value to "" (empty string).

Step 2: Create a **for** loop that uses **x** as the loop variable.

Step 3: Set the initial value of **x** to 25.

Step 4: The loop should continue to repeat itself as long as **x** is greater than 20.

Step 5: Decrement **x** by 1 (don't use the decrement operator) after each iteration.

Step 6: The code block should concatenate the current value of **x** to the string variable **display** and put each new value of **x** on a new line.

Step 7: After the **for** loop completes, show the value of **display** in the browser window.

Solution

```
<script>
   var display = "";
   for(x = 25; x > 20; x = x - 1) {
      display = display + x + "<br>";;
   }
   document.write (display);
</script>
```

Result displayed in browser:

25
24
23
22
21

*** The next four problems will be similar to the previous four but they will be described in a different way to increase your ability to analyze and solve programming problems

14.15 Step 1: Create a **for** loop that uses **count** as the loop variable.

Step 2: The **for** loop should cause the integers 1 through 5 to be displayed on separate lines in the browser window.

Step 3: Don't use the increment operator

Solution

```
<script>
```

```
   for (count = 1; count <= 5; count = count + 1) {
      document.write (count + "<br>");
   }
</script>
```

Result displayed in browser:

1
2
3
4
5

14.16 Step 1: Create a **for** loop that uses the variable **counter** as the loop variable.

Step 2: The **for** loop should cause the integers 100 through 105 to be displayed on separate lines in the browser window.

Step 3: Don't use the increment operator

Solution

```
<script>
   for(counter = 100; counter <= 105; counter = counter + 1) {
      document.write (counter + "<br>");
   }
</script>
```

Result displayed in browser:

100
101
102
103
104
105

14.17 Step 1: Create a **for** loop that uses **y** as the loop variable.

Step 2: The **for** loop should display the descending integers 5, 4, 3, 2, 1 and 0 on separate lines in the browser window.

Step 3: Use the decrement operator

Solution

```
<script>
   for(y = 5; y >= 0; y--) {
      document.write(y + "<br>");
   }
</script>
```

Result displayed in browser:

5
4
3
2
1
0

14.18 Step 1: Create a **for** loop that uses **ctr** as the loop variable.

Step 2: The **for** loop should count down from 75 to 70 and display each integer on separate lines in the browser window.

Step 3: Don't use the decrement operator

Solution

```
<script>
   for (ctr = 75; ctr >= 70; ctr = ctr - 1) {
      document.write (ctr + "<br>");
   }
</script>
```

Result displayed in browser:

75
74
73
72
71
70

14.19 Step 1: Create a **for** loop that uses **x** as the loop variable.

Step 2: The **for** loop should start at 1 and count up to 5 in increments of 1 (1, 2, 3, 4, 5). On each iteration, the loop should use an **if/else** statement to check if x is less than or equal to 3. If this is **true**, display "The value of x is less than or equal to 3." in an alert box. If this is **false**, display "The value of x is greater than 3." in an alert box.

Solution

```
<script>
   for (x = 1; x <= 5; x++) {
     if (x <= 3) {
       alert ("The value of x is less than or equal to 3.");
     }
     else {
       alert ("The value of x is greater than 3.");
     }
   }
</script>
```

Result displayed in alert box:

The value of x is less than or equal to 3.
The value of x is less than or equal to 3.
The value of x is less than or equal to 3.
The value of x is greater than 3.
The value of x is greater than 3.

14.20 Step 1: Create a **for** loop that uses **x** as the loop variable.

Step 2: The **for** loop should display all even integers between 2 and 10 inclusive on separate lines in the browser window.

Step 3: Don't use the increment operator (you can't use it since **x** must be incremented by 2 on each iteration).

Solution

```
<script>
   for (x = 2; x <= 10; x = x + 2) {
   document.write (x + "<br>");
   }
</script>
```

Result displayed in browser:

2
4
6
8
10

14.21 Step 1: Create a **for** loop that uses **x** as the loop variable.

Step 2: The loop should start at 0 and count up to 6 in increments of 1. On each iteration use an **if/else** statement to determine if the value of **x** is even or odd (use modulo division to accomplish this). If **x** is even, display "<value of x> is an even number." in the browser window. If **x** is odd, display "<value of x> is an odd number.". Put each sentence on a separate line.

Solution

```
<script>
   for (x = 0; x <= 6; x++) {
   if (x % 2 == 0) {
      document.write (x + " is an even number.<br>");
   }
   else {
      document.write (x + " is an odd number.<br>");
   }
```

```
   }
</script>
```

Result displayed in browser:

0 is an even number
1 is an odd number.
2 is an even number
3 is an odd number.
4 is an even number
5 is an odd number.
6 is an even number

14.22 Step 1: Create a **for** loop that uses **k** as the loop variable.

Step 2: The loop should start at 20 and count down to 1 on each iteration. The loop should use an if statement to see if k is divisible by 6 (with no remainder). If k is divisible by 6, display "<value of k> is divisible by 6." in the browser window. If k is not divisible by 6, display "<value of k> is not divisible by 6." in the browser window.

Step 3: Put each sentence on a separate line.

Solution

```
<script>
   for (k = 20; k >= 1; k--) {
     if (k % 6==0) {
       document.write (k + " is divisible by 6.<br>");
     }
   }
</script>
```

Result displayed in browser:

18 is divisible by 6.
12 is divisible by 6.
 6 is divisible by 6.

14.23 Step 1: Create a **for** loop that uses **y** as the loop variable.

Step 2: The loop should start at 0 and count up to 3 in increments of 1. The loop should use a switch statement with 4 cases that test the value of y for the values: 0, 1, 2, 3.
If y = 0, display "The value of y is 0." in the browser window.
If y = 0, display "The value of y is 1." in the browser window.
If y = 0, display "The value of y is 2." in the browser window.
If y = 0, display "The value of y is 3." in the browser window.

Step 3: Put each sentence on a separate line.

Solution

```
<script>
```

```
    for (y = 0; y <= 3; y++) {
      switch(y) {
        case 0:
          document.write ("The value of y is 0.<br>");
          break;
        case 1:
          document.write ("The value of y is 1.<br>");
          break;
        case 2:
          document.write ("The value of y is 2.<br>");
          break;
        case 3:
          document.write ("The value of y is 3.<br>");
          break;
      }
    }
</script>
```

Result displayed in browser:

The value of y is 0.
The value of y is 1.
The value of y is 2.
The value of y is 3.

14.24 Step 1: Create a **for** loop that uses **z** as the loop variable.

Step 2: The loop should start at 0 and count up to 0.6 in increments of 0.1. On each iteration of loop, display the value of **z** in the browser window.

Use the **toFixed()** method on each value of **z** so only 1 decimal place will be visible.

Step 3: Put each sentence on a separate line.

Solution

```
<script>
    for (z = 0; z <= 0.5; z = z + 0.1) {
      document.write (z.toFixed (1) + "<br>");
    }
</script>
```

Result displayed in browser:

0.0
0.1
0.2
0.3
0.4
0.5

14.25 Step 1: Create a **for** loop that uses **x** as the loop variable.

Step 2: The loop should be set up to start at 1 and count up to 10 in increments of 1. Use an **if** statement to check if x equals 5. If this is **true**, then, change the value of **x** from 5 to 7. Also display the following message in the browser window: "The value of x will now change from 5 to 8 so that 5 will not be displayed. 8 will be displayed in its place.");

Step 3: After the **if** statement on each iteration display the value of **x** in the browser window. Each value of **x** should be displayed on its own line.

Solution

```
<script>
   for (x = 1; x <= 10; x++) {
    if (x == 5) {
      x = 7;
      document.write ("The value of x will now change from 5 to 8. 5 will not be displayed. 8 will be " +
                  "displayed in its place.");
    }
    document.write (x + "<br>");
   }
</script>
```

Result displayed in browser:

1
2
3
4
The value of x will now change from 5 to 8 so that 5 will not be displayed. 8 will be displayed in its place.
8
9
10

14.3 THE WHILE LOOP

The **while** statement creates a loop that executes a code block that's contained within the **while** statement. The code block will execute as long as the test condition evaluates to **true**. The test condition evaluating to **true** is what causes the loop to iterate. The condition is evaluated before executing the code block. In other words, the purpose of a **while** loop is to execute a statement or code block repeatedly as long as an **expression** is true. Once the expression becomes **false,** the loop terminates. The **while** loop is a programming technique that allows you to repeat a specific block of code over and over again while a conditional statement is **true.**

while loop syntax:

```
while (condition) {
  code block (statement(s) to be executed if condition is true)
}
```

condition

The condition is an expression that's evaluated before each iteration of the loop. If the condition evaluates to **true**, the code block will be executed. When the condition evaluates to **false**, the program control will jump to the first statement after the **while** loop. The condition will be an expression that can evaluate to **true** or **false**. While the Boolean expression is **true**, the JavaScript code in the code block is executed.

code block

This is the code block (set of JavaScript instructions) that is executed as long as the condition evaluates to **true**. If you want to execute more than one statement within the code block, you should use a block statement ({ ... }) to group the multiple statements.

From this, we can see that there are two key parts to a JavaScript **while** loop:

1) The conditional statement that has to be **true** in order for the code in the code block to be executed.
2) The code in the code block that is contained in curly braces "{ ...}" which will be executed if the condition is **true.**

When a **while** loop starts to execute, the JavaScript interpreter evaluate the condition in order to see if it is **true**. If the condition is **true**, the code between the curly braces will be executed. At the end of the code block, the **while** loop will go back to the condition statement and evaluate it again to see if it is still **true**. If it's **true**, the code block will be executed again. This process will repeat itself until the condition evaluates to **false**. At that point, program execution will jump out of the **while** loop and begin execution at the first code statement after the **while** loop.

A **while** loop is similar to a **for** loop but its basic parts are laid out differently. The following for loop displays the value of **x** in an alert box on each of its 3 iterations:

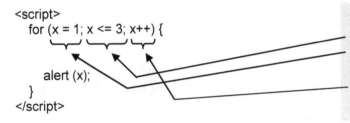

```
<script>
   for (x = 1; x <= 3; x++) {


       alert (x);
   }
</script>
```

In the **for** loop, the middle term inside the parentheses **(x <= 3)** tells the loop how long to keep going. Also, the initial value of **x** (x=1) is defined in the first term inside the parentheses. The amount by which **x** is changed is also defined in the third term inside the parentheses.

The following **while** loop does the same thing as the above **for** loop:

```
<script>
   var x = 1;
   while (x <= 3) {


       alert (x);
       x++;
   }
</script>
```

As you can see, the **while** loop accomplishes the same results as the **for** loop but it's organized differently. In the **while** loop, only the middle term that tells the loop how long to keep going is inside the parentheses. The counter variable (in this case, **x**) has to be defined and given an initial value outside of the **while** loop and previous to its execution. Unlike the **for** loop the counter variable in a while is not automatically updated by the amount set out within the parentheses. Instead, the amount by which the counter variable (**x**, in this case) changes is set out in the code block (in our **while** loop example, the counter **x** is incremented by 1 each time).

Flowchart of a *while* loop

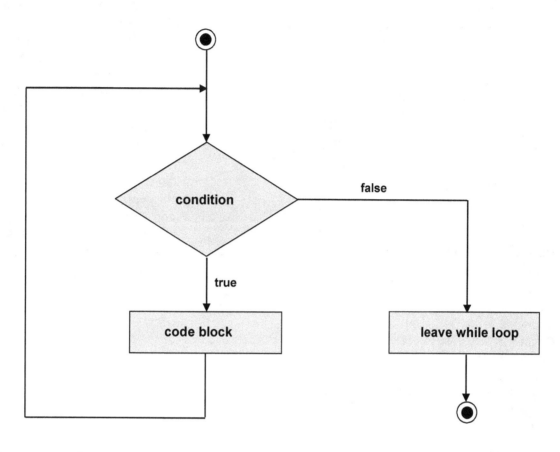

while **loop examples:**

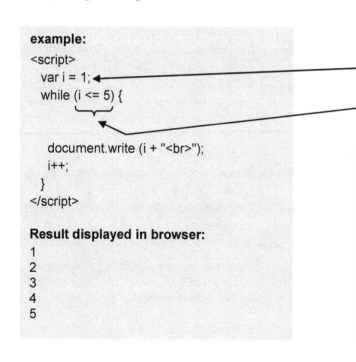

example:
```
<script>
  var i = 1;
  while (i <= 5) {


  document.write (i + "<br>");
  i++;
  }
</script>
```

Result displayed in browser:
```
1
2
3
4
5
```

The first step is to declare the variable that will be used in the condition. In this case, we'll use the variable **i** and initialize its value to 1. The **while** loop starts by checking to see if **i** is less than or equal to 5. Since **i** = 1 at this point, the code block will be executed. The last statement in the code block increments **i** by 1 which changes the value of **i** from 1 to 2. When the code block has been completely executed, the condition of the **while** loop is checked again to see if the value of **i** is still less than or equal to 5. At this point, **i** = 2, so, the code block in the while loop executes again. This process continues until **i** = 6. When **i** is no longer less than or equal to 5, execution jumps out of the **while** loop and starts at the first statement after the **while** loop.

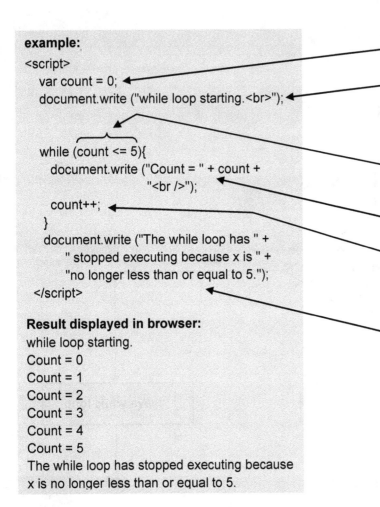

example:
```
<script>
    var count = 0;
    document.write ("while loop starting.<br>");


    while (count <= 5){
        document.write ("Count = " + count +
                "<br />");
        count++;
    }
    document.write ("The while loop has " +
        " stopped executing because x is " +
        "no longer less than or equal to 5.");
</script>
```

Result displayed in browser:
while loop starting.
Count = 0
Count = 1
Count = 2
Count = 3
Count = 4
Count = 5
The while loop has stopped executing because
x is no longer less than or equal to 5.

The variable **count** is declared and set to 0. **count** will act as the condition variable for the **while** loop. Before the **while** loop starts to execute, we display "while loop starting" on the first line of the browser window. When the **while** loop starts to execute, the first thing done is to check the condition (**count** <= 5). Since **count** = 0, the condition returns **true** and the code block executes. On each iteration, "Count = <value of count>." is displayed on the next line in the browser window. Then **count** is incremented. This process continues until **count** is increment to 6. When this happens, the condition will return **false** and the **while** loop stops executing. The last step is to display "The while loop has stopped executing because x is no longer less than or equal to 5." on the next line in the browser window.

example:
```
<script>
    var x = 10;
    while (x <= 20) {


    if (x == 15) {
        break;
    }
    document.write (x + "<br>");
    x++;
    }
</script>
```

Result displayed in browser:
10
11
12
13
14

This example is similar to the previous two examples except that it tests to see if the value of the **while** loop condition variable (in this case, **x**) is equal to 15. When **x** == 15 becomes true, the **break*** command is executed which causes program execution to jump out of the **while** loop and resume execution at the first statement after the **while** loop. Because of the **break** command, the value of **x** never increments past 15. Also the **document.write** command is not executed when **x** = 15, so, the output consists of the integers from 10 to 14.

*A **break** statement that's found anywhere within a **while** loop will cause the **while** loop to terminate even if the **break** statement is found within an **if** statement that's contained in the **while** loop.

example:
```
<script>
  var k = 1;
  while (k < 10) {
    document.write (k + "<br>");
    k= k + 2;
  }
</script>
```
Result displayed in browser:
```
1
3
5
7
9
```

This **while** loop prints out the odd numbers from 1 to 9. The loop variable **k** starts with a value of 1 and is incremented by 2 on each iteration until **k** is equal to 10. At that point the condition is **false** and the loop stops repeating.

example:
```
<script>
  var x = 3;
  while (x<= 10000) {
    document.write (x + "<br>");
    x = x * x;
  }
</script>
```
Result displayed in browser:
```
3
9
81
6561
```

This **while** loop squares **x** on each iteration and prints out the value of on separate lines. The loop will continue to iterate as long as **x** is less than or equal to 10000.

example:
```
<script>
  var x = 0;
  while(x < 5) {
    x++;
    if (x == 3){
       continue;
    }
    document.write (x + "<br />");
  }
</script>
```

Result displayed in browser:
```
1
2
4
5
```

The **continue statement** breaks an iteration (in the loop) if a specified condition occurs, and continues with the next iteration in the loop. In this example, when **x** increments from 2 to 3, the current iteration will stop executing when it reaches the **continue** statement (because **x==3** on this iteration) and the next iteration will start without executing any of the code after the continue statement (this only happens on the iteration in which **x = 3**).

*A **continue** statement that's found anywhere within a **while** loop will cause the **while** loop to break out of the current iteration even if the **continue** statement is found within an **if** statement that's contained in the **while** loop.

SOLVED PROBLEMS

14.26 The code block in a **while** loop will continue to execute as long as:

a) the test condition evaluates to false

b) the test condition evaluates to true

c) the test condition evaluates to 0

Solution

b

14.27 When is the condition evaluated?

a) before executing the code block

b) after executing the code block

c) while the code block is being executed

Solution

a

14.28 What is the purpose of a **while** loop?

a) to execute a single statement or a code block until the statement or code block is completed

b) to take the place of a for loop with long code blocks

c) to execute a single statement or a code block as long as the condition is true

Solution

c

14.29 When does a **while** loop stop repeating (iterating)?

a) when the code block is completed

b) when the condition evaluates to false

c) when the condition evaluates to 0

d) when the condition evaluates to true

Solution

b

14.30 What is the syntactical structure of a **while** loop?

a) while (*code block*) {

    condition

  }

b) while (*condition*) {

    code block

  }

c) while (*condition*) {

    code block

    condition test

  }

Solution

b

14.31 What is the condition in a **while** loop?

a) an expression that is evaluated before each iteration of the loop

b) an expression that is evaluated after each iteration of the loop

c) a block of code that's executed on each iteration of the loop

Solution

a

14.32 What happens if the condition in a **while** loop evaluates to true?

a) the code block will be updated according to instructions contained in the condition expression

b) the code block will not be executed until the nbext iteration

c) the code block will be executed

Solution

c

14.33 What happens if the condition in a while loop evaluates to false?

a) program control will jump to the first statement after the while loop

b) the code block will be executed one last time and then program control will jump to the first statement after the while loop

c) the while loop starts over again and keeps repeating until the condition expression evaluates to true

Solution

a

14.34 What is the code block in a **while** loop?

a) a set of JavaScript instructions that is executed as long as the condition is true

b) a set of JavaScript instructions that determines how many times the loop will repeat itself

c) a true or false value that changes on each loop iteration

Solution

a

14.35 What symbols should you enclose the code block with if there are multiple statements in the code block?

a) ( )

b) { }

c) [ ]

Solution

b

14.36 What are the two key parts to a **while** loop?

a) condition, code block

b) condition, Boolean statement

c) if statement, code block

Solution

a

14.37 What happens when the code block is completed?

a) the while loop ends and the first statement after the while loop is executed

b) the code block repeats itself until the user presses the escape key

c) the while loop will go back to the condition statement and evaluate it to see if the code block should repeated again

Solution

c

14.38 How many expressions does a **for** loop have within its parentheses?

a) 2

b) 3

c) 1

Solution

b

14.39 How many expressions does a **while** loop have within its parentheses?

a) 1

b) 2

c) 3

Solution

a

14.40 Write the code for a **for** loop that does the following 4 things:

1) uses a loop variable called **k**
2) keeps iterating as long as **k** is less than or equal to 5
3) increments by 1 after each iteration
4) on each iteration it should display the value of **k** in an alert box

Solution
```
<script>
   for (k = 1; k <= 5; k++) {
     alert (k);
   }
</script>
```

14.41 Accomplish the same thing as problem 7.40 but use a **while** loop.

Solution
```
<script>
   var k = 1;
   while (k <= 5) {
     alert (k);
     k++;
   }
</script>
```

14.42 Step 1: Create a **while** loop that uses a loop variable called **k** with an initial value of 1
Step 2: The loop should continue to repeat as long as **k** is less than or equal to 4.
Step 3: **k** should increment by 1 on each iteration.
Step 4: The value of **k** should be displayed in the browser window (each value of k should be displayed on a separate line) each time the code block repeats.

Solution

```
<script>
  var k = 1;
  while (k <= 4) {
   document.write (k + "<br>");
   k++;
  }
</script>
```

Result displayed in browser:

1
2
3
4

14.43 Step 1: Create a **while** loop that uses a loop variable called **m** with an initial value of 5.
Step 2: The loop should continue to repeat as long as **m** is greater than or equal to 1.
Step 3: **m** should decrement by 1 on each iteration.
Step 4: The value of **m** should be displayed in the browser window (each value of **m** should be displayed on a separate line) each time the code block repeats

Solution

```
<script>
  var m = 5;
  while (m >= 1) {
   document.write (m + "<br>");
   m--;
  }
</script>
```

Result displayed in browser:

5
4
3
2
1

14.44 Step 1: Create a **while** loop that uses a loop variable called **counter** with an initial value of 10.

Step 2: The loop should continue to repeat as long as **counter** is less than or equal to 15.

Step 3: **m** should increment by 1 on each iteration.

Step 4: On each iteration, display the loop number (on separate lines for each iteration) in the following way:

"loop number = <value of counter>"

Step 5: After the while loop has completed, display the following message on 2 separate lines in browser window:

"The while loop has just completed its last iteration."

" It stopped because counter is no longer less than or equal to 15."

Solution
```
<script>
   var counter = 10;
   while (counter<=15) {
    document.write ("loop number = " + counter + "<br>");
    counter++;
   }
   document.write ("The while loop has just completed its last iteration.<br>" +
             "It stopped because counter is no longer less than or equal to 15.");
</script>
```

Result displayed in browser:

loop number = 10
loop number = 11
loop number = 12
loop number = 13
loop number = 14
loop number = 15
The while loop has just completed its last iteration.
It stopped because counter is no longer less than or equal to 15.

14.45 Step 1: Create a **while** loop that uses a loop variable called **a** with an initial value of 21. The purpose of the while loop is to display all odd integers between 21 and 29 inclusive.

Step 2: The loop should continue to repeat as long as **a** is less than 30.

Step 3: **a** should increment by 2 on each iteration.

Step 4: The value of a should displayed on its own line for each iteration of the loop.

Solution
```
<script>
   var a = 21;
   while (a < 30) {
    document.write (a + "<br>");
    a = a + 2;
```

```
 }
</script>
```

Result displayed in browser:

21
23
25
27
29

14.46 Step 1: Create a **while** loop that uses a loop variable called **y** with an initial value of 4. The purpose of the while loop is to square **y** on each iteration and display the value of **y** on separate lines as long as the value of **y** is less than 100000.
Step 2: The loop should continue to repeat as long as **y** is less than 100000.
Step 3: the value of **y** should be squared on each iteration.
Step 4: On each iteration, display the value of **y** on a separate line.

Solution

```
<script>
 var y = 4;
 while (y < 100000) {
  document.write (y + "<br>");
  y = y * y;
  }
</script>
```

Result displayed in browser:

4
16
256
65536

14.47 Step 1: Create a **while** loop that uses a loop variable called **z** with an initial value of 100. The purpose of the **while** loop is to display the first value of **z** (100) on its own line and then increment **z** by 20 on each iteration and display its value on separate lines. On the iteration where **z** equals 120, the loop should skip that iteration jump to the next iteration, but before it jumps out of the current iteration it should increment **z** by 20.
Step 2: The loop should continue to repeat as long as **z** is less than or equal to 200.
Step 3: The value of **z** should be incremented by 20 on each iteration. If **z** = 120, increment z by 20 and jump out of the current iteration to the next iteration (don't display the value of **z**) . Use the **continue** statement to jump out of the current iteration and start a new

one.

Step 4: On each iteration, display the value of **z** on a separate line (the value of z will not be displayed on the iteration where z = 120).

Solution

```
script>
 var z = 100;
 while (z <= 200) {
  if (z == 120) {
    z = z + 20;
    continue;
  }
  document.write (z + "<br>");
  z = z + 20;
 }
</script>
```

Result displayed in browser:

100
140
160
180
200

14.48 Convert the following **for** loop into a **while** loop:

```
<script>
 for (j = 10; j <= 14; j++) {
    document.write (j + "<br>");
 }
</script>
```

Solution

```
<script>
 var j = 10;
 while (j <= 14) {
  document.write (j + "<br>");
  j++;
 }
</script>
```

Result displayed in browser:

10
11
12
13
14

14.49 Convert the following **for** loop into a **while** loop:

```
<script>
  for (k = 105; k > 100; k--) {
    document.write (k + "<br>");
  }
</script>
```

Solution

```
<script>
  var k = 105;
  while (k > 100) {
    document.write (k + "<br>");
    k--;
  }
</script>
```

Result displayed in browser:

105
104
103
102
101

14.50 Convert the following **for** loop into a **while** loop:

```
<script>
  for (x = 21; x <= 25; x = x + 1) {
    if (x <= 23) {
      document.write ("The value of x is less than or equal to 23.<br>");
    }
    else {
      document.write ("The value of x is greater than 23.<br>");
    }
  }
</script>
```

Solution

```
<script>
  var x = 21;
  while(x <= 25) {
    if(x <= 23) {
      document.write ("The value of x is less than or equal to 23.<br>");
      x = x + 1;
    }
    else {
      document.write ("The value of x is greater than 23.<br>");
      x = x + 1;
    }
  }
</script>
```

Result displayed in browser:

The value of x is less than or equal to 23.
The value of x is less than or equal to 23.
The value of x is less than or equal to 23.
The value of x is greater than 23.
The value of x is greater than 23.

14.51 Convert the following **for** loop into a **while** loop:

```
<script>
  for (j = 1; j <= 6; j = j + 1) {
    if (j % 2 == 0) {
    document.write (j + " is an even number.<br>");
    }
    else {
      document.write (j + " is an odd number.<br>");
    }
  }
</script>
```

Solution

```
<script>
  var j = 1;
  while (j <= 6) {
    if (j % 2 == 0) {
    document.write (j + " is an even number.<br>");
    }
    else {
      document.write (j + " is an odd number.<br>");
    }
    j = j + 1;
  }
</script>
```

Result displayed in browser:

1 is an odd number.
2 is an even number.
3 is an odd number.
4 is an even number.
5 is an odd number.
6 is an even number.

14.4 THE DO... WHILE LOOP

The **do...while** statement creates a loop that executes a JavaScript statement or a block of multiple JavaScript statements once, before it checks to see if the condition is **true**, If the condition is **true** the loop will repeat itself as long as the condition remains **true**. The **do...while** statement is used when you want to run a loop at least one time, no matter what. Unlike the **while** statement which will not loop at all if the condition isn't met on the first iteration, a **do...while** loop is executed one time before the conditional expression is evaluated, so, the code block will always execute at least one time. As with the **while** loop, on any line in a **do...while** block, you can use the **break** statement to cause program flow to jump out of the loop, or you can use the **continue** statement to go directly to the next iteration. As you can see, the **do...while** loop is similar to the **while** loop except that the condition check happens at the end of the loop. This means that the loop will always be executed at least once, even if the condition is **false**.

do/while loop syntax

do
  code block (statement(s) to be executed if condition is true)
while (*condition*);

statement

    The statement is a single JavaScript statement or a block of multiple JavaScript statements that is executed at least once and will be re-executed each time the condition evaluates to **true**. If the code block contains multiple statements within the loop, you should use a block statement { ... } to group those statements.

condition

    The condition is an expression that is evaluated after each iteration through the loop. If the conditional expression evaluates to **true**, the code block will be re-executed. When the condition evaluates to **false**, program execution passes to the first statement that follows the **do...while** loop.

Flowchart of a *do/while* loop

As you can see, the **do...while loop** is a little different than the **while** loop. The main thing to remember is that, unlike the **while** loop, in the **do...while** loop the condition is checked at the end of the loop. So even if the conditional expression is initially **false**, the code statements within the code block will be executed at least once. This is the basic difference between the **while** loop and the **do/while** loop.

The following is an example of a typical **do...while** loop:

```
<script>
   var i = 0;
   do {
     document.write ("The number is " + i + "<br>");
     i++;
   }
   while (i < 10);
</script>
```

You can see how the **do...while** loop is created in the same way as the **while** loop except that the condition comes at the end of the loop rather than at the beginning. The condition (**i < 10**) isn't checked until after the code block executes for the first time instead of before the code block executes as it does in a **while** loop.

Result displayed in browser:

The number is 0
The number is 1
The number is 2
The number is 3
The number is 4
The number is 5
The number is 6
The number is 7
The number is 8
The number is 9

do...while loop examples:

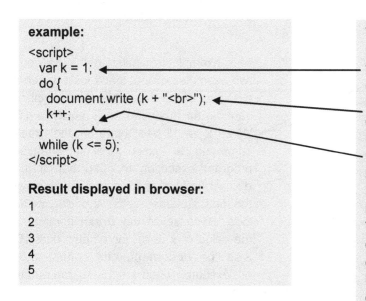

example:
```
<script>
   var k = 1;
   do {
     document.write (k + "<br>");
     k++;
   }
   while (k <= 5);
</script>
```

Result displayed in browser:

1
2
3
4
5

The first step is to declare the variable that will be used in the condition. In this case, we'll use the variable **k** and initialize its value to 1. The **do...while** loop starts by executing the code block which writes the current value of **k** on its own line in the browser window. After the code block executes, **k** is tested to see if its value is less than or equal to 5. Since the conditional statement isn't tested until after the code block is executed, the code block in a **do...while** loop will always execute on the first iteration. The loop will continue to repeat until the value of **k** is no longer less than or equal to 5. The current value of k will be displayed on its own line in the browser window during each iteration of the loop.

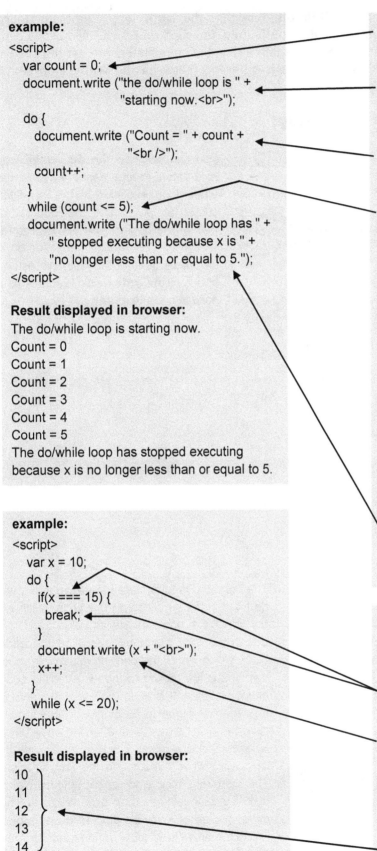

example:

```
<script>
  var count = 0;
  document.write ("the do/while loop is " +
                 "starting now.<br>");
  do {
    document.write ("Count = " + count +
                   "<br />");
    count++;
  }
  while (count <= 5);
  document.write ("The do/while loop has " +
      " stopped executing because x is " +
      "no longer less than or equal to 5.");
</script>
```

Result displayed in browser:

The do/while loop is starting now.
Count = 0
Count = 1
Count = 2
Count = 3
Count = 4
Count = 5
The do/while loop has stopped executing
because x is no longer less than or equal to 5.

The variable **count** is declared and set to 0. **count** will act as the condition variable for the **do/while** loop. Before the **do/while** loop starts to execute, we display "The do/while loop is starting now." on the first line of the browser window. The **do...while** loop starts by executing the code block which writes "Count = <current value of **count**>"on its own line in the browser window. After the code block executes, **count** is tested to see if its value is less than or equal to 5. Since the conditional statement isn't tested until after the code block is executed, the code block in a **do...while** loop will always execute on the first iteration. The loop will continue to repeat until the value of **count** is no longer less than or equal to 5. The current value of **count** will be displayed on its own line in the browser window during each iteration of the loop. The value of counter will be displayed as follows: "Counter = <current value of counter>".

This process continues until **count** is increment to 6. When this happens, the condition will return **false** and the **do...while** loop stops executing. The last step is to display "The do/while loop has stopped executing because x is no longer less than or equal to 5." on the next line in the browser window.

example:

```
<script>
  var x = 10;
  do {
    if(x === 15) {
      break;
    }
    document.write (x + "<br>");
    x++;
  }
  while (x <= 20);
</script>
```

Result displayed in browser:

10
11
12
13
14

This example is similar to the previous two examples except that it tests to see if the value of the **do...while** loop condition variable (in this case, **x**) is equal to 15. When **x** == 15 becomes true, the **break** command is executed which causes program execution to jump out of the **do...while** loop and resume execution at the first statement after the **do...while** loop. Because of the **break** command, the value of **x** never increments past 15. Also the **document.write** command is not executed when **x** = 15, so, the output consists of the integers from 10 to 14.

example:
```
<script>
  var y = 3;
  do {
    document.write (y + "<br>");
    y= y + 2;
  }
  while (y < 10);
</script>
```

Result displayed in browser:
```
3
5
7
9
```

This **do...while** loop prints out the odd numbers from 3 to 9. The loop variable **y** starts with a value of 3 and is incremented by 2 on each iteration at the end of the code block until **y** is equal to 11. At that point the condition **(y<10)** is **false** and the loop stops repeating.

example:
```
<script>
  var z = 4;
  do {
    document.write (z + "<br>");
    z = z * z;
  }
  while (z<= 10000);
</script>
```

Result displayed in browser:
```
4
16
256
```

This **do...while** loop squares **z** (which is give the initial value of 4) on each iteration and prints out the value of on separate lines. The loop will continue to iterate as long as **z** is less than or equal to 10000. On the 4th iteration, z squared is equal to 65536. Since 65536 is greater than 10000, the loop ends.

example:
```
<script>
  var x = 1;
  do{
    if (x == 3){
      x++;
      continue;
    }
    document.write (x + "<br />");
    x++;
  }
  while(x < 5);
</script>
```

Result displayed in browser:
```
1
2
4
```

The **continue statement** breaks one iteration of the loop) if a specified condition occurs (in this case, if **x==3**), and continues with the next iteration in the loop. In other words, when **x** increments from 2 to 3, the current iteration will stop executing when it reaches the **continue** statement and the next iteration will start without executing any of the code after the **continue** statement (this only happens on the iteration in which **x** = 3). The next iteration will start only if the conditional expression still evaluates to **true**. The conditional variable must be incremented before the continue statement is executed or the value of **x** will never change and the loop will never stop.

SOLVED PROBLEMS

14.52 On the first iteration of a **do...while** loop, is the condition checked before or after the code block is executed

a) before

b) after

Solution

b

14.53 When is the condition check done on each loop iteration after the initial iteration?

a) after the iteration

b) before the iteration

Solution

a

14.54 The **do...while** loop will continue to repeat itself as long as the condition evaluates to what?

a) true

b) false

Solution

a

14.55 The **do...while** loop will run for a minimum of how many times?

a) 0

b) 1

c) 2

Solution

b

14.56 Is the condition checked before or after the code block in a **while** loop?

a) before

b) after

Solution

a

14.57 Is the condition checked before or after the code block in a **do...while** loop?

a) before

b) after

Solution

b

14.58 What does the break statement do when it's found in a **do...while** loop?

a) it causes the do/while loop to start all over again

b) it causes program execution to jump out of the do/while loop and go to the first code statement after the loop

c) it brings the entire program to an end

Solution

b

14.59 What does the continue statement do when it's found in a **do...while** loop?

a) it causes program execution to jump out of the current loop iteration and go directly to the next iteration

b) it causes the code block to execute over and over again until the condition evaluates to false

c) it causes the program to jump out of the loop to the first code statement after the do/while loop

Solution

a

14.60 The **do...while** loop is similar to the while loop except for what?

a) The code block will always execute at least 2 times in a do/while loop

b) The loop will repeat if the condition evaluates to false

c) The condition check occurs at the end of a do/while loop instead of at the beginning as it happens in a while loop

Solution

c

14.61 How many JavaScript statements can you put in **do...while** loop's code block section?

a) 3

b) as many as you want

c) 1

Solution

b

14.62 If the code block in a **do...while** loop contains more than 1 code statement, which of the following enclosures should you put around them:

a) [ ]

b) ( )

c) { }

Solution

c

14.63 When the condition in a **do...while** loop evaluates to false, what happens to program execution?

a) it jumps to the first code statement that follows the do/while loop

b) the loop will repeat the current iteration

c) the loop will start all over again from the beginning

Solution

a

14.64 Create **do...while** loop that does the following 4 things:

1) uses **x** as the loop variable with an initial value of 1

2) displays the value of **x** on its own line in the browser window on each iteration as follows:

    "The value of x is <value of x>."

3) increments **x** by 1 on each iteration

4) continues to loop as long as **x** is less than 5

Solution

```
<script>
   var x = 1;
   do {
     document.write ("The value of x is " + x + "<br>");
     x++;
   }
```

```
    while (x < 5);
</script>
```

Result displayed in browser:

The value of x is 1
The value of x is 2
The value of x is 3
The value of x is 4

14.65 Create a **do.while** loop that does the following 6 things:

1) uses **k** as the loop variable with an initial value of 20

2) before the loop starts display: "The do/while loop will begin now." on a separate line in the browser window

3) displays the value of **k** on its own line in the browser window on each iteration as follows:
   "The present value of k is <value of k>."

4) increments **k** by 1 on each iteration

5) continues to loop as long as **k** is less than or equal to 23

6) after the loop has completed, display: "The do/while loop has stopped executing because k is no longer less than or equal to 23.

Solution
```
<script>
   var k = 20;
   document.write ("The do/while loop will begin now.<br>");
   do {
    document.write ("The present value of k is " + k + "<br>");
    k++;
   }
   while (k <= 23);
   document.write ("The do/while loop has stopped executing " +
                   "because k is no longer less than 23.<br>");
</script>
```

Result displayed in browser:

The do/while loop will begin now.
The present value of k is 20
The present value of k is 21
The present value of k is 22
The present value of k is 23
The do/while loop has stopped executing because k is no longer less than 23.

14.66 Write the code to accomplish the following:

1) Create a **do...while** loop that uses a variable called **number** as the loop variable. Give the **number** an initial value of 50.

2) On each iteration of the loop print out the value of **number** on its own line in the browser window and then increment **number** by 1.

3) The loop should continue to repeat itself as long as **number** is less than or equal to 60.

4) When **number** is incremented to 55, jump out of the loop and go to the first code statement after the loop

Solution

```
<script>
  var number = 50;
  do {
    if (number == 55) {
      break;
    }
    document.write (number + "<br>");
    number++;
  }
  while (number <= 60);
</script>
```

Result displayed in browser:

50
51
52
53
54

14.67 Write the code to accomplish the following:

1) Create a **do...while** loop that uses a variable called **oddNumbers** as the loop variable. Give the variable **oddNumbers** an initial value of 11.

2) The loop will print out the odd numbers from 11 to 19 on separate lines in the browser window.

3) Increment the loop by 2 on each iteration.

4) The loop should repeat itself as long as **oddNumbers** is less than or equal to 19.

Solution

```
<script>
  var oddNumbers = 11;
  do {
    document.write(oddNumbers + "<br>");
    oddNumbers = oddNumbers + 2;
  }
  while (oddNumbers <= 19);
</script>
```

Result displayed in browser:

11

13
15
17
19

14.68 Write the code to accomplish the following:

1) Create a **do...while** loop that uses a variable called **y** as the loop variable. Give the variable **y** an initial value of 35.
2) The loop should display the value of **y** in the browser window on a separate line for each iteration..
3) The loop variable **y** should increment by 1 on each iteration.
4) The loop should continue to repeat itself as long as **y** is less than or equal to 40.
5) When **y** = 38, increment y by 1, jump out of the current iteration, and start the next iteration.

Solution
```
<script>
  var y = 35;
  do{
    if (y == 38) {
      y++;
      continue;
    }
    document.write (y + "<br>");
    y++;
  }
  while (y <= 40);
</script>
```

Result displayed in browser:
35
36
37
39
40

14.69 Convert the following **while** loop into a **do/while** loop:
```
<script>
  var num = 5;
  while (num < 10) {
    alert (num);
    num++;
  }
</script>
```

Solution

```
<script>
  var num = 5;
  do {
    alert (num);
    num++;
  }
  while (num<10);
</script>
```

Result displayed in browser:

5
6
7
8
9

14.70 Convert the following **while** loop into a **do...while** loop:

```
<script>
  var n = 15;
  while (n >= 11) {
    document.write (n + "<br>");
    n--;
  }
</script>
```

Solution

```
<script>
  var n = 15;
  do {
    document.write (n + "<br>");
    n--;
  }
  while (n >= 11);
</script>
```

Result displayed in browser:

15
14
13
12
11

14.71 Convert the following **while** loop into a **do/while** loop:

```
<script>
```

```
var counter = 100;
  while (counter <= 105) {
    document.write ("loop number = " + counter + "<br>");
    counter++;
  }
  document.write ("The loop is now completed<br>" +
          "It stopped because the counter is<br>" +
          "no longer less that or equal to 105.");
</script>
```

Solution

```
<script>
  var counter = 100;
  do {
    document.write ("loop number = " + counter + "<br>");
    counter++;
  }
  while (counter <= 105);
  document.write ("The loop is now completed<br>" +
          "It stopped because the counter is<br>" +
          "no longer less that or equal to 105.");
</script>
```

Result displayed in browser:

loop number = 100
loop number = 101
loop number = 102
loop number = 103
loop number = 104
loop number = 105
The loop is now completed
It stopped because the counter is
no longer less that or equal to 105.

14.72 Write the code to accomplish the following:

1) Create a **do...while** loop that uses a variable called **a** as the loop variable. Give the variable **a** an initial value of 21.
2) The loop should display the value of **a** in the browser window on a separate line for each iteration..
3) The loop variable **a** should increment by 2 on each iteration.
4) The loop should continue to repeat itself as long as **a** is less than 30.
5) The loop will display all of the odd integers from 21 to 29..

Solution

```
<script>
  var a = 21;
  do {
```

```
      document.write (a + "<br>");
      a = a + 2;
    }
  while (a < 30);
</script>
```

Result displayed in browser:

21
23
25
27
29

14.73 Same as 7.72, but display all of the even integers from 50 through 58

Solution
```
<script>
  var a = 50;
  do {
    document.write (a + "<br>");
    a = a + 2;
  }
  while (a < 59);
</script>
```

Result displayed in browser:

50
52
54
56
58

14.74 Write the code to accomplish the following:

1) Create a **do...while** loop that uses a variable called **x** as the loop variable. Give the variable **a** an initial value of 5.
2) The loop should display the initial value of **x** in the browser window on the first iteration and then on each subsequent iteration the value of **x** squared will be displayed on its own line in the browser window.
3) Instead of incrementing **x**, **x** should be squared on each repeat of the loop.
4) The loop should continue to repeat itself as long as the value of **x** is less than 1000000.

Solution
```
<script>
    var x = 5;
```

```
  do {
     document.write (x + "<br>");
     x = x * x;
  }
  while (x < 1000000);
</script>
```

Result displayed in browser:
```
5
25
625
390625
```

14.75 Write the code to accomplish the following:

1) Create a **do...while** loop that uses a variable called **var1** as the loop variable. Give the variable **var1** an initial value of 200.
2) The loop should display the value of **var1** on its own line in the browser window on each repeat of the loop and increment var1 by 20 after it's displayed.
3) When var1 is equal to 220, jump out of the current loop iteration and start the next iteration (don't forget to increment **var1** by 20).
4) The loop should continue to repeat itself as long as the value of **var1** is less than or equal to 300.

Solution
```
<script>
  var var1 = 200;
  do {
    if (var1 == 220) {
      var1 = var1 + 20;
      continue;
    }
    document.write (var1 + "<br>");
    var1 = var1 + 20;
  }
  while (var1 <= 340);
</script>
```

Result displayed in browser:
```
200
240
260
280
300

320
340
```

14.76 Convert the following **for** loop into a **do...while** loop:

```
<script>
 for (m=20; m <= 24; m++) {
   document.write (m + "<br>");
 }
</script>
```

Solution

```
<script>
  var m = 20;
  do{
   document.write (m + "<br>");
   m++;
 }
  while(m <= 24);
</script>
```

Result displayed in browser:

20
21
22
23
24

14.77 Convert the following **for** loop into a **do...while** loop:

```
<script>
  for(k = 55; k > 50; k--) {
    document.write (k + "<br>");
  }
</script>
```

Solution

```
<script>
  for(k = 55; k > 50; k--) {
    document.write (k + "<br>");
  }
</script>
```

Result displayed in browser:

20
21
22
23
24

14.78 Convert the following **for** loop into a **do...while** loop:

```
<script>
 for (x = 101; x <= 110; x = x + 2) {
   if ( x <= 105) {
     document.write ("The value of x is less than or equal to 105.<br>");
   }
   else {
     document.write ("The value of x is greater than 105.<br>");
   }
 }
</script>
```

Solution

```
<script>
 var x = 101;
 do{
   if ( x <= 105) {
     document.write ("The value of x is less than or equal to 105.<br>");
     x = x + 2;
   }
   else {
     document.write ("The value of x is greater than 105.<br>");
     x = x + 2;
   }
 }
 while (x <= 110);
</script>
```

Result displayed in browser:

The value of x is less than or equal to 105.
The value of x is less than or equal to 105.
The value of x is less than or equal to 105.
The value of x is greater than 105.
The value of x is greater than 105.

14.79 Write the code to accomplish the following:

1) Create a **do...while** loop that uses a variable called **s** as the loop variable. Give the variable **s** an initial value of 10.

2) The loop should increment by 1 on each iteration and should continue to loop as long as **s** is less than or equal to 16.

3) On each iteration the loop should perform modulus division to determine if the value of **s** is odd or even.

4) If the value of **s** is even, display the following message on its own line in the browser window:
      "<value of s> is an even number."

5) If the value of **s** is odd, display the following message on its own line in the browser window:
      "<value of s> is an odd number."

Solution

```
<script>
 var s = 10;
 do{
  if( s % 2 == 0) {
    document.write(s + " is an even number.<br>");
  }
  else {
    document.write(s + " is an odd number.<br>");
  }
  s++;
 }
 while(s <= 15);
</script>
```

Result displayed in browser:

10 is an even number.
11 is an odd number.
12 is an even number.
13 is an odd number.
14 is an even number.
15 is an odd number.

Chapter 15

JavaScript Strings: Part 1

15.1 THE JAVASCRIPT STRING DATA TYPE

We briefly discussed the JavaScript string data type in section 9.2.2 but we're going to cover the subject more deeply in this section. A JavaScript string value is a series of zero or more characters (letters, digits, and punctuation marks). JavaScript strings are used for storing and manipulating text. The **string data type** is used to represent text enclosed within quotation marks (either single or double quotation marks) in JavaScript. A string (also called a text string) is a series of characters like "It is a beautiful day". Strings are always written with quotes. You can use either single quotes or double quotes to enclose a string:

Text string examples:

var girlName = "Donna";	// text string enclosed within **double** quotes
var girlName = 'Donna';	// text string enclosed within **single** quotes
var txtString1 = "To be or not to be.";	// text string enclosed within **double** quotes
var txtString1 = 'To be or not to be.';	// text string enclosed within **single** quotes

Using double quotes or single quotes will have no effect on how the string is displayed:

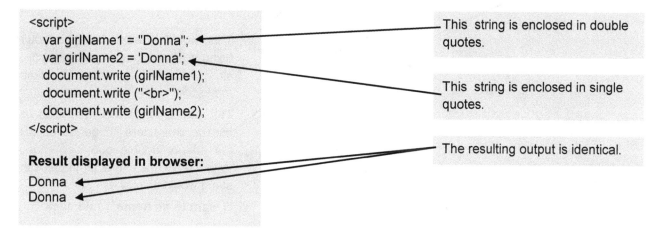

```
<script>
    var girlName1 = "Donna";
    var girlName2 = 'Donna';
    document.write (girlName1);
    document.write ("<br>");
    document.write (girlName2);
</script>
```

This string is enclosed in double quotes.

This string is enclosed in single quotes.

The resulting output is identical.

Result displayed in browser:
Donna
Donna

You can use quotes inside a string that's already surrounded by quotes, as long as they don't match the quotes surrounding the string. This means that double quotation marks can be contained in strings surrounded by single quotation marks, and single quotation marks can be contained in strings surrounded by double quotation marks.

Examples of using quotation marks within strings:
var answer = "It's too early to leave."

This works because you're using a single quotation mark within a string (in the word *it's*) that's enclosed by double quotation marks. This will display as:

It's too early to leave.

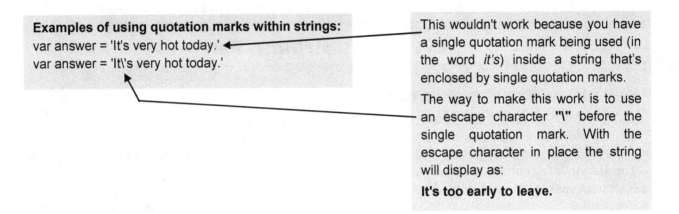

Examples of using quotation marks within strings:

var answer = 'It's very hot today.'

var answer = 'It\'s very hot today.'

This wouldn't work because you have a single quotation mark being used (in the word *it's*) inside a string that's enclosed by single quotation marks.

The way to make this work is to use an escape character **"\"** before the single quotation mark. With the escape character in place the string will display as:

It's too early to leave.

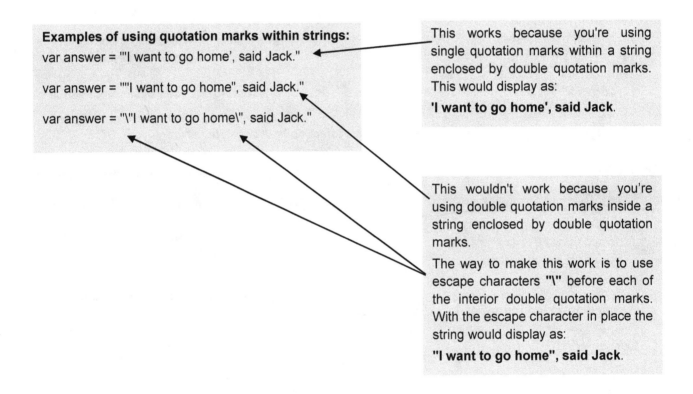

Examples of using quotation marks within strings:

var answer = "'I want to go home', said Jack."

var answer = ""I want to go home", said Jack."

var answer = "\"I want to go home\", said Jack."

This works because you're using single quotation marks within a string enclosed by double quotation marks. This would display as:

'I want to go home', said Jack.

This wouldn't work because you're using double quotation marks inside a string enclosed by double quotation marks.

The way to make this work is to use escape characters **"\"** before each of the interior double quotation marks. With the escape character in place the string would display as:

"I want to go home", said Jack.

As we've seen, the **var** keyword is used to declare a variable. If you don't assign the variable a value when you initialize it, then, it is a declared, but uninitialized , variable. If you assign the string variable a value when you declare it, then, it is a declared and initialized variable:

var greeting;   // the variable **greeting** is declared but not initialized

var greeting = "Hello there.";   // the variable **greeting** is declared and initialized to "Hello there."

If **you try** to display the value of a declared but uninitialized string variable, a message will be displayed that says **undefined**:

```
<script>
  var reply;
  document.write (reply);
</script>
```

At this point, **reply** has not been given a value, so, its value is **undefined**. When it is initialized and given a value it will then have a defined value.

Result displayed in browser:
undefined

You can declare and initialize a string variable without giving it a value:

```
var sentence = "";
```

"" is called an **empty string**. Assigning an empty string to a variable changes its value from **undefined** to nothing. If you try to display the value of an empty string, you won't get an **undefined** message or any blank spaces - you'll get nothing at all.

```
<script>
  var reply = ""
  document.write (reply);
</script>
```

Because the variable **reply** contains an empty string, nothing is displayed in the browser window.

Result displayed in browser:

```
<script>
  var reply = "";
  var part1 = "How are ";
  var part2 = "you feeling?";
  document.write (part1 + part2);
</script>
```

If we use the "+" sign to concatenate **part1** and **part2,** the displayed result is:
How are you feeling?

Result displayed in browser:
How are you feeling?

```
<script>
  var x = "";
  var partg1 = "How are ";
  var part2 = "you feeling?";
  document.write (part1 + reply + part2);
</script>
```

If we concatenate **part1** and **x,** (this is an empty string) and **part2,** the displayed result is exactly the same as it was before the empty string variable **x** was added to the concatenation. Nothing at all is added by an empty string variable - no spaces, no values - nothing.

Result displayed in browser:
How are you feeling?

If we declare and initialize a string variable with the value of a single blank space, then, it now contains a value because a single (or any number of blank spaces) blank space is a value.

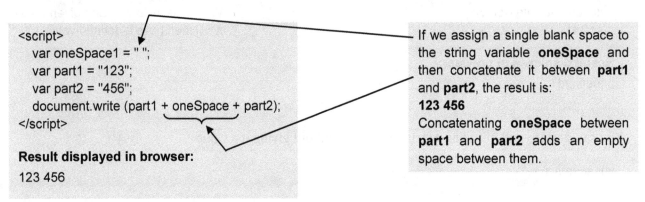

```
<script>
   var oneSpace1 = " ";
   var part1 = "123";
   var part2 = "456";
   document.write (part1 + oneSpace + part2);
</script>
```

Result displayed in browser:
123 456

If we assign a single blank space to the string variable **oneSpace** and then concatenate it between **part1** and **part2**, the result is:
123 456
Concatenating **oneSpace** between **part1** and **part2** adds an empty space between them.

An empty string has a length of zero. A string that contains one blank space has a length of 1.

```
<script>
   var noSpace = "";
   var oneSpace = " ";
   document.write ("The length of the variable called noSpace is " +
                   noSpace.length);
   document.write ("<br>)";
   document.write ("The length of the variable called oneSpace is " +
                   oneSpace.length);
</script>
```

Result displayed in browser:

The length of the variable called noSpace is 0
The length of the variable called oneSpace is 1

The length of a string (the total number of characters in the string) can be found by using the string property called **length.** We'll get into string properties and methods more deeply later in the chapter.

15.1.1 Long Strings

Sometimes, the code you write will include strings that may be very long and cover a large part of the code line width or even take up multiple code lines. Instead of having strings that go on and on, or wrap around to the next line, you'll probably want to break the string into multiple lines in the source code (but not in the display) without affecting the actual string contents. There are basically two ways you can accomplish this. The first way is to use the "+" (concatenation) operator to combine multiple strings together that are coded on separate lines but should display on a single line. For example:

```
var longString = "This is string is unusually long and needs " +
                 "to be divided up into multiple lines " +
                 "so that the line of code doesn't take " +
                 "up the whole coding line.";
```

The long string that appears above on 4 coding lines will be displayed in the browser window on just one line (unless it's too long to fit on just 1 line in the browser window; in that case it will wrap around to the next line).

Another way to accomplish the same thing is to use the backslash character ("\") at the end of each line (instead of quotation marks and the concatenation ("+") sign) to indicate that the coding for the string will continue on the next line. Make sure that you don't add a space or any other character after the backslash or this method will not work. The coding should look like this:

```
var longString = "This is string is unusually long and needs \
                 to be divided up into multiple lines \
                 so that the line of code doesn't take \
                 up the whole coding line.";
```

SOLVED PROBLEMS

15.1 Which of the following string variable declarations are valid? If they're not valid, why not?

a) var string1 = "My name is 'Shorty'.";

b) var string 1 = "I'm hungry.";

c) var string1 = 'She's coming over later.';

d) var string 1 = 'He\'s going to college now.';

e) var string1 = ""Bill said, "where is my car?"";

f) var string1 = "Mary said, \"Good morning!\"";

g) var string1 = 'Frank said, \"What day is it?\"';

Solution

a) valid

b) valid

c) invalid; the apostrophe (single quotation) in *She's* is found in a string that's enclosed in the same single quotation marks

d) valid; without the escape character, the string would be invalid because the apostrophe in *He's* is found in a string that enclosed with the same single quotation marks, but the escape character before the apostrophe (single quotation mark) causes this potential problem to be ignored

e) invalid; You can't use double quotation marks within a string that's enclosed by double quotations

f) valid; same as above but the escape character fixes the problem

g) valid; this string would be valid without the escape characters, but the presence of the escape characters doesn't affect it's validity

15.2 Choose the correct description of the variable **myString**:

```
<script>
  var myString;
</script>
```

a) the variable myString is declared but not initialized

b) the variable myString is declared and initialized
c) the variable myString is initialized but not declared

Solution
a

15.3 Choose the correct description of the variable **mansName**:

```
<script>
   var mansName = "Ed Smith";
</script>
```

a) the variable **myString** is declared and initialized
b) the variable **myString** is declared but not initialized
c) the variable **myString** is initialized but not declared

Solution
a

15.4 What will appear in browser window as the result of the following code:

```
<source>
   var firstName;
   document.write(firstName);
</source>
```

Solution
undefined (until you give a string variable a value, even if it's only "" or " ", it's undefined)

15.5 What is displayed in browser window as the result of the following code:

```
<source>
   var firstname = "George";
   document.write (firstName);
</source>
```

Solution
George

15.6 What is displayed in browser window as the result of the following code:
```
<source>
```

```
    var dateOfBirth = "";
    document.write (dateOfBirth);
</source>
```

Solution

nothing will be displayed in the browser window

15.7 Display the following string on a single line in the browser window but break it up into 3 separate lines in the code using the "+" operator:
      "That which we call a rose by any other name would smell as sweet."
     Divide the string (in the code) after "rose" and after "name."

Solution
```
<script>
   document.write ("That which we call a rose " +
                   "by any other name " +
                   "would smell as sweet.");
</script>
```

15.8 Same as problem 8.7 but use a backslash instead of the "+" operator.

Solution
```
<script>
   document.write ("That which we call a rose \
                   by any other name \
                   would smell as sweet.");
</script>
```

15.9 Display the following string on a single line in the browser window but break it up into 3 separate lines in the code using the "+" operator:
      'Will all great Neptune's ocean wash this blood clean from my hand?'
    Divide the string after "Neptune's" and after "blood." Notice that single quotes are used to enclose the string and that there is an apostrophe in "Neptune's". The string will cause an error in this form. Leave the single quotation marks in place but make the necessary correction to the apostrophe so the string will display without an error.

Solution
```
<script>
 document.write ('Will all great Neptune\'s ' +
         'ocean wash this blood ' +
         'clean from my hand?');
</script>
```

15.10 Same as problem 8.9 but use backward slashes.

Solution
```
<script>
   document.write ('Will all great Neptune\'s \
                   ocean wash this blood \
                   clean from my hand?');
</script>
```

15.2 JAVASCRIPT STRING PROPERTIES

Strings have 3 properties: length, constructor and prototype. They are listed in the following table:

Property	Description
length	returns the length of a string
constructor	returns the string's constructor function
prototype	allows you to add properties and methods to an object

The only string property we will discuss in this book is the **length** property. The **length** property returns the total number of characters (including spaces) in the string under consideration.

examples of string length property:

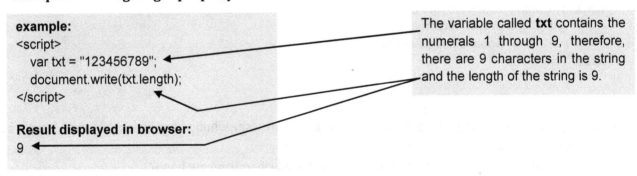

```
example:
<script>
   var txt = "123456789";
   document.write(txt.length);
</script>

Result displayed in browser:
9
```

The variable called **txt** contains the numerals 1 through 9, therefore, there are 9 characters in the string and the length of the string is 9.

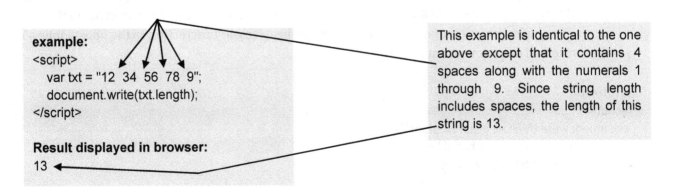

```
example:
<script>
   var txt = "12  34  56  78  9";
   document.write(txt.length);
</script>

Result displayed in browser:
13
```

This example is identical to the one above except that it contains 4 spaces along with the numerals 1 through 9. Since string length includes spaces, the length of this string is 13.

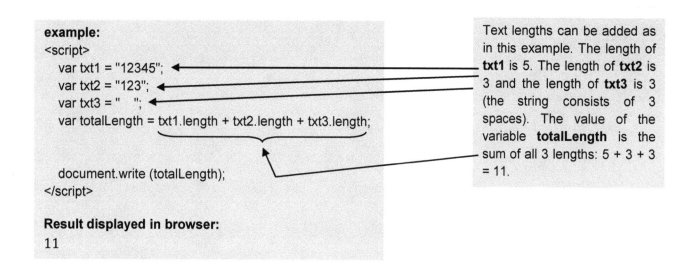

example:
```
<script>
  var txt1 = "12345";
  var txt2 = "123";
  var txt3 = "   ";
  var totalLength = txt1.length + txt2.length + txt3.length;

  document.write (totalLength);
</script>
```

Text lengths can be added as in this example. The length of **txt1** is 5. The length of **txt2** is 3 and the length of **txt3** is 3 (the string consists of 3 spaces). The value of the variable **totalLength** is the sum of all 3 lengths: 5 + 3 + 3 = 11.

Result displayed in browser:
11

Chapter 16

JavaScript Strings: Part 2

16.1 JAVASCRIPT STRING METHODS

JavaScript methods are the actions that can be performed on objects. In this case, the object is a string and string methods are actions that we can perform on strings such as changing all the letters in a string to upper or lower case or extracting a smaller substring (sub-section of a string) from a string. The following is a table which describes 17 0f the 21 JavaScriptstring methods:

Method	Description
charAt()	returns the character at the specified index (position)
charCodeAt()	returns the Unicode of the character at the specified index
concat()	joins two or more strings, and returns a copy of the joined strings
fromCharCode()	converts Unicode values to characters
indexOf()	returns the position of the first found occurrence of a specified value in a string
lastIndexOf()	returns the position of the last found occurrence of a specified value in a string
match()	searches a string for a match against a regular expression, and returns the matches
replace()	searches a string for a value and returns a new string with the value replaced
search()	searches a string for a value and returns the position of the match
slice()	extracts a part of a string and returns a new string
split()	splits a string into an array of substrings
substr()	extracts a part of a string from a start position through a number of characters
substring()	extracts a part of a string between two specified positions
toLowerCase()	converts a string to lowercase letters
toString()	returns the value of a String object
toUpperCase()	converts a string to uppercase letters
trim()	removes whitespace from both ends of a string

16.1.1 charAt ()

The **charAt()** method returns the character at the specified index in a string. The index of the first character is 0, the second character is 1, and so on.

Syntax

```
string.charAt(index)
```

Parameter Values

Parameter	Description
index	Required. An integer representing the index of the character you want to return

examples of the charAt() method:

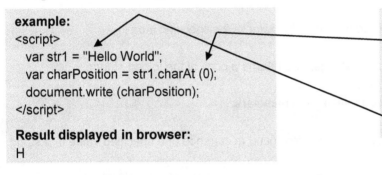

```
example:
<script>
  var str1 = "Hello World";
  var charPosition = str1.charAt (0);
  document.write (charPosition);
</script>

Result displayed in browser:
H
```

The index value for the **charAt()** method in this example is 0. This means that the method will look at the 0 position (the 1st character position) of the string and return the value at this position. In this case the character at the 0 position is "H"

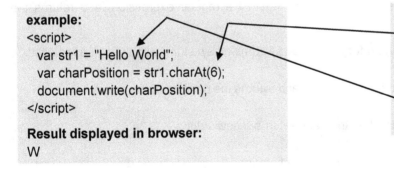

```
example:
<script>
  var str1 = "Hello World";
  var charPosition = str1.charAt(6);
  document.write(charPosition);
</script>

Result displayed in browser:
W
```

The index value for the **charAt()** method in this example is 6. This means that the method will look at the 6 position (the 7th character position) of the string and return the value at this position. In this case the character at the 6 position is "W"

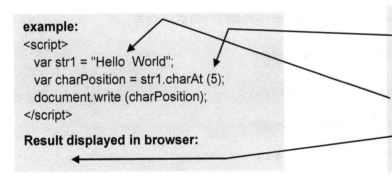

```
example:
<script>
  var str1 = "Hello  World";
  var charPosition = str1.charAt (5);
  document.write (charPosition);
</script>

Result displayed in browser:
```

The index value for the **charAt()** method in this example is 5. This means that the method will look at the 5 position (the 6th character position) of the string and return the value at this position. In this case the character at the 5 position is a space or " ". An empty space will be displayed as the result in the browser window.

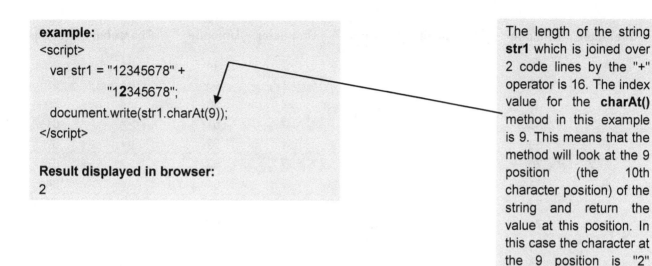

example:
```
<script>
  var str1 = "12345678" +
           "12345678";
  document.write(str1.charAt(9));
</script>
```

Result displayed in browser:
2

The length of the string **str1** which is joined over 2 code lines by the "+" operator is 16. The index value for the **charAt()** method in this example is 9. This means that the method will look at the 9 position (the 10th character position) of the string and return the value at this position. In this case the character at the 9 position is "2" (There is also a "2" at the 1 position).

16.1.2 charCodeAt ()

The **charCodeAt()** method returns the numeric Unicode value of the character at the specified index in a string. The index of the first character is 0, the second character 1, and so on. Unicode code values range from 0 to 1,114,111. The first 128 Unicode code values are a direct match of the ASCII character set. **charCodeAt()** always returns a value that is less than 65,536.

You can use the **charCodeAt()** method together with the length property to return the Unicode value of the last character in a string. The index of the last character is -1, the next to the last character is -2, and so on.

Syntax

```
string.charCodeAt(index)
```

Parameter Values

Parameter	Description
index	An integer greater than or equal to 0 and less than the length of the string

Unicode

Unicode is international encoding standard that was designed to be used with different languages and character sets. In the Unicode standard each letter, digit, or symbol is assigned a unique numeric value that applies across different platforms and programs. Unicode provides a unique number for every character, no matter what the platform, program, or language. Unicode is a computing industry standard for the consistent encoding, representation, and handling of text expressed in the majority of the world's writing systems. It was developed in conjunction with the Universal Character Set standard and is officially referred to as *The Unicode Standard*. The latest version of Unicode contains a collection of more than 120,000 characters that make up over 125 old and modern scripts, along with numerous other symbol sets. The following chart lists the decimal Unicode values for a variety of English letters, numbers and symbols:

Character	Unicode	Character	Unicode	Character	Unicode	Character	Unicode
A	65	a	97	0	48	:	58
B	66	b	98	1	49	;	59
C	67	c	99	2	50	<	60
D	68	d	100	3	51	=	61
E	69	e	101	4	52	>	62
F	70	f	102	5	53	?	63
G	71	g	103	6	54	@	64
H	72	h	104	7	55	[	91
I	73	i	105	8	56	\	92
J	74	j	106	9	57	]	93
K	75	k	107	(blank)	32	^	94
L	76	l	108	!	33	_	95
M	77	m	109	"	34	`	96
N	78	n	110	#	35	{	123
O	79	o	111	$	36	|	124
P	80	p	112	%	37	}	125
Q	81	q	113	&	38	~	126
R	82	r	114	'	39		
S	83	s	115	(	40		
T	84	t	116	)	41		
U	85	u	117	*	42		
V	86	v	118	+	43		
W	87	w	119	,	44		
X	88	x	120	-	45		
Y	89	y	121	.	46		
Z	90	z	122	/	47		

examples of the charCodeAt() method:

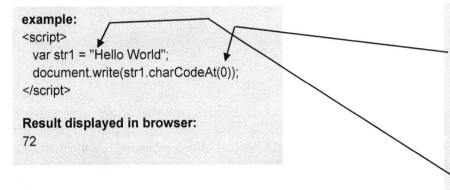

example:
```
<script>
  var str1 = "Hello World";
  document.write(str1.charCodeAt(0));
</script>
```

Result displayed in browser:
72

The index value for the **charCodeAt()** method in this example is 0. This means that the method will look at the 0 position (the 1st character position) of the string and return the Unicode value for the character at this position. In this case the character at the 0 position is "H" which, according the chart above, has a Unicode decimal value of 72

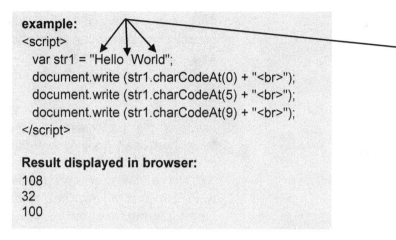

example:
```
<script>
  var str1 = "Hello World";
  document.write (str1.charCodeAt(0) + "<br>");
  document.write (str1.charCodeAt(5) + "<br>");
  document.write (str1.charCodeAt(9) + "<br>");
</script>
```

Result displayed in browser:
108
32
100

In this example, the index values in the **charCodeAt()** methods point to the 1st, 6th and 10th characters in the string. This corresponds to the characters "H", blank, and "d" in the string. The chart tells us that the Unicode values of these characters are 108, 32, and 100.

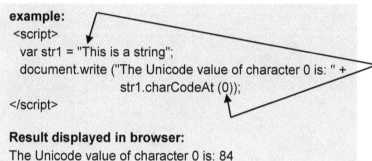

example:
```
<script>
  var str1 = "This is a string";
  document.write ("The Unicode value of character 0 is: " +
                  str1.charCodeAt (0));
</script>
```

Result displayed in browser:
The Unicode value of character 0 is: 84

In this example, we display the Unicode value of the character at position 0. The character at this position is "T", so, 84 is displayed in the display message.

16.1.3 fromCharCode ()

The **fromCharCode()** method converts Unicode values into characters (letters, numbers or symbols.

Syntax

```
String.fromCharCode(n1, n2, …, nX)
```

Parameter Values

Parameter	Description
n1, n2, … nX	returns the characters represented by 1 or more Unicode values

examples of the fromCharCode() method:

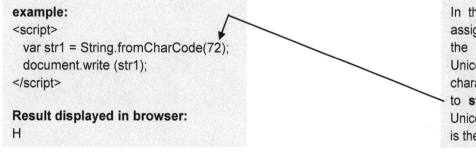

example:
```
<script>
  var str1 = String.fromCharCode(72);
  document.write (str1);
</script>
```

Result displayed in browser:
H

In this example we want to assign just one character to the string called **str1**. The Unicode value for the character we want to assign to **str1** is 72. If go to the Unicode chart we find that 72 is the Unicode value for "H".

example:
```
<script>
  var str1 = String.fromCharCode(72, 69, 76, 76, 79);
  document.write(str1);
</script>
```

Result displayed in browser:
HELLO

This example is similar to the previous one except that we want to assign 5 characters to the variable **str1**. If we check the characters that correspond to the 5 Unicode values (72, 69, 76, 76,79) that are being used as the parameters for the **fromCharCode()** method we find that they are: "H", "E", "L", "L", and "O". Notice that you always use the word "String" at the beginning of the method: **String.fromCharCode()**

example:
```
<script>
  var str1 = String.fromCharCode(65, 32, 66, 32, 67);
  document.write(str1);
</script>
```

Result displayed in browser:
A B C

This example is similar to the previous one except that we want to assign 3 characters to **str1** and we want to put a space (ASCII=60) between each character. If we check the characters that correspond to the 5 Unicode values that are being used as the parameters for the **fromCharCode()** method we find that they are: "A B C". Remember that Unicode character 32 is a blank space.

16.1.4 concat ()
The **concat()** method joins two or more strings, and returns a copy of the joined strings.

Syntax

```
string.concat(string1, string2, ..., stringX)
```

Parameter Values

Parameter	Description
string1, string2, ..., stringX	Required. The strings to be joined.

examples of the concat() method:

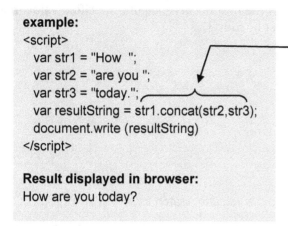

example:
```
<script>
  var str1 = "How  ";
  var str2 = "are you ";
  var str3 = "today.";
  var resultString = str1.concat(str2,str3);
  document.write (resultString)
</script>
```

Result displayed in browser:
How are you today?

This example uses the **concat()** method to concatenate **str2** ("are you ") and **str3** ("today? ") to **str1** ("How "). The result displayed in the browser window is "How are you?"

example:
```
<script>
  var str1 = "How<br>";
  var str2 = "are you<br>";
  var str3 = "today?";
  var resultString = str1.concat(str2,str3);
  document.write (resultString);
</script>
```

Result displayed in browser:
How
are you
today?

This example is identical to the first example except that we added 2 line breaks to the strings in order to print the complete string on 3 browser lines.

example:
```
<script>
  var str1 = "How  ";
  var resultString = str1.concat("are you ","today?");
  document.write(resultString)
</script>
```

Result displayed in browser:
How are you today?

This example is identical to the first example except that instead of appending the values of string variables (**str2** and **str3**) to **str1**, we append string literals ("are you " and "today?") to it.

8.3.5 indexOf () method

The **indexOf()** method returns the character position of the first occurrence of a specified value in a string. This method returns -1 if the value to search for can't be found.

Syntax

```
string.indexOf(searchvalue,start)
```

Parameter Values

Parameter	Description
searchvalue	Required. A string representing the value to search for.
start	Optional. The location within the calling string to start the search from. It can be any integer between 0 and the length of the string. The default value is 0.

examples of the indexOf() method:

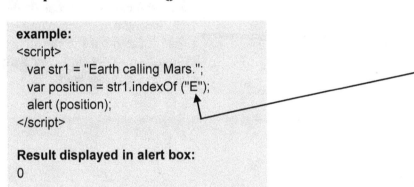

example:
```
<script>
  var str1 = "Earth calling Mars.";
  var position = str1.indexOf ("E");
  alert (position);
</script>
```

Result displayed in alert box:
0

In this example, the **indexOf()** method is used to search for the first occurrence of "E" starting with position 0. Since no starting position (position where the search begins from) was listed, the default starting position is 0.

example:
```
<script>
  var str1 = "Earth calling Mars.";
  var position = str1.indexOf("E", 1);
  alert(position);
</script>
```

Result displayed in alert box:
-1

In this example, the **indexOf()** method is used to search for the first occurrence of "E" starting with position 1. Since the only occurrence of "E" is at position 0, the **indexOf()** method finds no occurrence of "E". When the searched for character isn't found, the method returns -1.

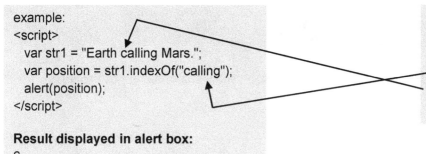

example:
```
<script>
  var str1 = "Earth calling Mars.";
  var position = str1.indexOf("calling");
  alert(position);
</script>
```

Result displayed in alert box:
6

In this example, the **indexOf()** method is used to search for the first occurrence of the string "calling". This string begins at position 6, so, 6 is displayed in the alert box.

example:
```
<script>
  var str1 = "Earth calling Mars.";
  var position1 = str1.indexOf("a");
  var position2 = str1.indexOf("a", position1 + 1);
  alert(position1 + "  " + position2);
</script>
```

Result displayed in alert box:
1 7

In this example, the **indexOf()** method is used to search for the first 2 occurrences of "a". The position of the first occurrence of "a" is assigned to the variable position1. We want to start our search for the second occurrence of "a" at the first position following the first occurrence of "a". Since this position is equivalent to position1 + 1, we use this value as the starting point from which we search for the 2nd occurrence of "a".

SOLVED PROBLEMS

16.1 Is **length** a string property or a string method?

a) method

b) property

Solution
b

16.2 What is returned by the **length** property?

a) the total number of characters (not including spaces) in the string

b) the total number of characters (including spaces) in the string

c) the number of centimeters that the string will take up in the browser window

Solution

b

16.3 If you have a string called **firstName**, how would you get the value of its length property?

a) length.firstName
b) string.firstName.length
c) firstName.length

Solution

c

16.4 What would the length property be for the following strings?

a) "Hello World."
b) "x--?mn.."
c) "How are you?"

Solution

a) 12
b) 8
c) 12

16.5 Write the code to accomplish the following:

1) Create a string variable called **fullName** and and give it an initial value of "John Adams".
2) Use the **length** property to display the total number of characters that **fullName** contains in the browser window.

Solution
```
<script>
  var fullName = "John Adams";
  document.write (fullName.length);
</script>
```

Result displayed in browser:
10

16.6 Write the code to accomplish the following:

1) Create a string variable called **phoneNumber** and and set its initial value to "1-800-765-3400"

2) Use the **length** property to display the total number of characters that **phoneNumber** contains in the browser window.

Solution
```
<script>
  var phoneNumber = "1-800-765-3400";
  document.write (phoneNumber.length);
</script>
```

Result displayed in browser:

14

16.7 Write the code to accomplish the following:

1) Create 3 string variables with the names **name1**, **name2** and **name3** and give them the initial values "Mary", "Francine" and "Edith".
2) Create a variable called **totalLength** and set it equal to the sum of the value of the lengths of the 3 variables.
3) Display the length of the 3 string variables on 3 separate lines in the browser window as follows:
    "The length of <variable name> = <variable length>."
4) Display the value of **totalLength** on its own line in the browser window as follows:
    "The total length of all 3 strings = <value of **totalLength**>."

Solution
```
<script>
  var name1 = "Mary";
  var name2 = "Francine";
  var name3 = "Edith";
  var totalLength = name1.length + name2.length + name3.length;
  document.write ("The length of name1 = " + name1.length + "<br>");
  document.write ("The length of name2 = " + name2.length + "<br>");
  document.write ("The length of name3 = " + name3.length + "<br>");
  document.write ("The total length of all 3 strings = " + totalLength);
</script>
```

Result displayed in browser:

The length of name1 = 4
The length of name2 = 8
The length of name3 = 5
The total length of all 3 strings = 17

16.8 Write the code to accomplish the following:

1) Create a variable called **vegetable** that gets its value from a prompt box with the prompt: Enter the

name of a vegetable."

2) Create a variable called **inputLength** and assign it the value of the length of the value entered by the user in the prompt box.

3) Display 2 lines in the browser window:

"The vegetable that you entered is <value of **vegetable**>."

"The word <value of **vegetable**> contains <value of **inputLength**> characters."

Solution

```
<script>
   var vegetable = prompt("Enter the name of a vegetable.");
   var inputLength = vegetable.length;
   document.write("The vegetable name that you entered is " + vegetable + ".<br>");
   document.write("The word " + vegetable + " contains " + inputLength + " characters.");
</script>
```

Result displayed in browser:

example: if the user enters "potato" the result in the browser window will be:

The vegetable name that you entered is potato.
The word potato contains 6 characters.

16.9 What is the correct syntax for the **characterAt( )** method?

a) *index.string*(charAt())
b) *index*.charAt(*string*)
c) *string*.charAt(*index*)

Solution

c

8.10 What does the value on the left side of the dot (".") in the **charAt( )** method indicate?

a) the character value that you're searching for
b) the name of the string that you're searching in
c) the position in the string of the character that you're looking for

Solution

b

8.21 What does the index value in the **charAt( )** method indicate?

a) the number of times that the character you're searching for should appear before you find its position

b) the position of the character in the string that you want to identify

c) the number of characters in the string you're searching

Solution
b

8.22 What does the **charAt()** method return?

a) the character at the position in the string indicated by the index value

b) the total number of characters in the string

c) the number of times a certain character appears in the string

Solution
a

16.13 Write the code to accomplish the following:

1) Create a string variable called **sentence1** and assign it the value "Are you on vacation?"

2) Create a variable called **char** and use the **charAt()** method to assign it the value of the character at position 4 in the string

Solution
```
<script>
  var sentence1 = "Are you on vacation?";
  var char = sentence1.charAt(4);
  document.write(char);
</script>
```

Result displayed in browser:

y

16.14 Write the code to accomplish the following:

1) Create a string variable called **phrase** and assign it the value "Hello everyone!"

2) Create a variable called **charValue** and use the **charAt()** method to assign it the value of the character at position 9 in the string

Solution
```
<script>
  var phrase = "Hello everyone!";
  var charValue = phrase.charAt(9);
  document.write(charValue);
</script>
```

Result displayed in browser:

r

16.15 Write the code to accomplish the following:
1) Create a string variable called **number** and assign it the value "3.14159265".
2) Create a numeric variable called **charPosition** and assign it the value of 6.
3) Create a variable called **charValue** and use the **charAt()** method to assign it the value of the character in the variable **number** at the position represented by the variable **charPosition**.

Solution
```
<script>
  var number = "3.14159265";
  var charPosition = 6;
  var charValue = number.charAt(charPosition);
  document.write(charValue);
</script>
```

Result displayed in browser:

9

16.16 Write the code to accomplish the following:
1) Create a string variable called **greeting** and assign it the value "HELLO".
2) Create a variable called **char0** and use the **charAt( )** method to assign it the value of the character at position 0 in the variable **greeting**.
3) Create a variable called **char1** and use the **charAt( )** method to assign it the value of the character at position 1 in the variable **greeting**.
4) Create a variable called **char2** and use the **charAt( )** method to assign it the value of the character at position 2 in the variable **greeting**.
5) Create a variable called **char3** and use the **charAt( )** method to assign it the value of the character at position 3 in the variable **greeting**.
6) Create a variable called **char5** and use the **charAt( )** method to assign it the value of the character at position 5 in the variable **greeting**.
7) Concatenate all 5 of the variables (char0 - char4) and display the resulting value in the browser window.

Solution
```
<script>
  var greeting = "HELLO";
  var char0 = greeting.charAt(0);
  var char1 = greeting.charAt(1);
  var char2 = greeting.charAt(2);
```

```
    var char3 = greeting.charAt(3);
    var char4 = greeting.charAt(4);
    document.write (char0 + char1 + char2 + char3 + char4);
</script>
```

Result displayed in browser:
HELLO

16.17 Write the code to accomplish the following:

1) Create a string variable called **name** and assign it the value "Fred".
2) Create a numeric variable called **length** and set its value equal to the length of the variable **name**.
3) Create a string variable called **copy** and assign it the value of an empty string ("").
4) Create a **for** loop with a loop variable called **x** and set its initial value to 0. **x** should increment by 1 on each repeat of the loop. The loop should continue to repeat as long as **x** is less than the value of the variable called **length**.
5) On each repeat of the loop concatenate the character at the position in the variable **name** that's represented by **x** to the variable **copy**. In other words, **copy** starts out as an empty string and on each repeat of the loop the next character in **name** is appended to it. When the loop is through, each character in **name** should have been copied to **copy**.
6) After the loop has completed, display the value of **copy** in the browser window. The **for** loop should cause the characters at position 0, 1, 2, 3 and 4 in **name** to be concatenated together and displayed in the browser window.

Note: for loops were covered on pages 293 - 297.

Solution
```
<script>
    var name = "Fred";
    var length = name.length;
    var copy = "";
    for (x = 0;x < length; x++) {
        copy = copy + name.charAt (x);
    }
    document.write (copy);
</script>
```

Result displayed in browser:
Fred

16.18 Write the code to accomplish the following:

1) Create a string variable called **food** and assign it the value "spaghetti".
2) Create a numeric variable called **length** and set its value equal to the length of the variable **food**.

3) Create a string variable called **copy** and assign it the value of an empty string ("").

4) Create a variable called **x** and set its value to 0.

5) Create a **while** loop that continues to loop as long as **x** is less than the value of variable **length**.

6) On each repeat of the loop concatenate the character at the position in the variable **food** that's represented by **x** to the variable **copy**. In other words, **copy** starts out as an empty string and on each repeat of the loop the next character in **food** is appended to it. When the loop is through, each character in **food** should have been copied to **copy**.

7) Increment **x** by 1.

8) After the loop has completed, display the value of **copy** in the browser window. The **while** loop should cause the characters at position 0, 1, 2, 3, 4, 5, 6, 7 and 8 in **food** to be concatenated together and displayed in the browser window.

Note: **while** loops were covered on pages 307 - 311.

Solution
```
<script>
   var food = "spaghetti";
   var length = food.length;
   var copy ="";
   var x = 0;
   while (x < length) {
      copy = copy + food.charAt (x);
      x = x + 1;
   }
   document.write (copy);
</script>
```

Result displayed in browser:

spaghetti

16.19 Write the code to accomplish the following:

1) Create a string variable called **pi** and assign it the value "3.14159265".

2) Create a numeric variable called **length** and set its value equal to the length of the variable **pi**.

3) Create a string variable called **copy** and assign it the value of an empty string ("").

4) Create a variable called **x** and set its value to 0.

5) Create a **do/while** loop that continues to loop while **x** is less than the value of variable **length**.

6) On each repeat of the loop concatenate the character at the position in the variable **pi** that's represented by **x** to the variable **copy**. In other words, **copy** starts out as an empty string and on each repeat of the loop the next character in **pi** is appended to it. When the loop is through, each character in **pi** should have been copied to **copy**.

7) Increment **x** by 1.

8) After the loop has completed, display the value of **copy** in the browser window. The **while** loop should cause the characters at position 0, 1, 2, 3, 4, 5, 6, 7,8 and 9 in **pi** to be concatenated together

and displayed in the browser window.

Note: **while** loops were covered on pages 307 - 311.

Solution
```
<script>
  var pi = "3.14159265";
  var length = pi.length;
  var copy = "";
  var x = 0;
  do{
   copy = copy + pi.charAt(x);
   x = x + 1;
  }
  while (x < length);
  document.write (copy);
</script>
```

Result displayed in browser:

3.14159265

8.20 What is proper syntax for the **charCodeAt()** method?

a) *index.string*.charCodeAt()

b) *index*.charCodeAt(*string*)

c) *string*.charCodeAt(*index*)

Solution

c

8.21 What does the **charCodeAt()** return?

a) the character at the position in the string that's indicated by the index value

b) the numeric Unicode value of the character at the given index

c) the nmber of characters in the string

Solution

b

16.22 What is the Unicode standard?

a) the international encoding standard that was designed to be used with different languages and character sets

b) the international encoding standard that was designed to be used with the 20 major languages and character sets of the world

c) the international encoding standard that was designed to be used with hex, binary, octal and decimal number representations

Solution

a

8.23 How many characters can be represented by Unicode?

a) over 12,000
b) over 1,000,000
c) over 120,000

Solution

c

16.24 What are the Unicode values for the following characters (see the chart on p. 350):

a) ?
b) G
c) y
d) (blank)
e) 8
f) A
g) a
h) @
i) +
j) <

Solution

a) 63
b) 71
c) 121
d) 32
e) 56
f) 65
g) 97
h) 64
i) 43
j) 60

16.25 Write the code to accomplish the following:

1) Create a string variable called **string2** and assign it the value "What's up?".
2) Display the Unicode value of the character at position 9 in the variable **string2.**

Solution
```
<script>
  var string2 = "What's up?";
  document.write(string2.charCodeAt(9));
</script>
```

Result displayed in browser:
63

16.26 Write the code to accomplish the following:

1) Create a string variable called **x** and assign it the value "Take it easy".
2) Display the Unicode value of the character at position 7 in the variable **x.**

Solution
```
<script>
  var x = "Take it easy";
  document.write(x.charCodeAt(7));
</script>
```

Result displayed in browser:
32

16.27 If you have a string called **phrase**, how would you find the Unicode value of its 8th character (not
position 8 but the 8th character, which is in position 7).

a) charCodeAt(8).phrase
b) phrase.charCodeAt(7)
c) phrase.charCodeAt(8)

Solution
b

8.28 Write the code to accomplish the following:

1) Create a string variable **sentence** and set its value equal to "What time is it?".
2) Display the following on the browser page:

　　"sentence = <string value of **sentence**>."

　Go to a new line. Go to the next line after that. In other words, leave a blank line between this
　section and the next).

3) Display the following on the browser page:

   "Character at position 0 = <character at position 0 in **sentence**>"

   Go to a new line.

4) Display the following on the browser page:

   "Unicode value = <Unicode value of character at position 0 in **sentence**>"

   Go to a new line. Go to the next line after that. In other words, leave a blank line between this section and the next).

5) Display the following on the browser page:

   "Character at position 5 = <character at position 5 in **sentence**>"

   Go to a new line.

6) Display the following on the browser page:

   "Unicode value = <Unicode value of character at position 5 in **sentence**>"

   Go to a new line. Go to the next line after that. In other words, leave a blank line between this section and the next).

7) Display the following on the browser page:

   "Character at position 10 = <character at position 10 in **sentence**>"

   Go to a new line.

8) Display the following on the browser page:

   "Unicode value = <Unicode value of character at position 10 in **sentence**>"

Solution

```
<script>
    var sentence = "What time is it?";
    document.write ("Sentence = " + sentence + "<br><br>");
    document.write ("Character at position 0 = " + sentence.charAt(0) + "<br>");
    document.write ("Unicode value = " + sentence.charCodeAt(0) + "<br><br>");
    document.write ("Character at position 5 = " + sentence.charAt(5) + "<br>");
    document.write ("Unicode value = " + sentence.charCodeAt(5) + "<br><br>");
    document.write ("Character at position 10 = " + sentence.charAt(10) + "<br>");
    document.write ("Unicode value = " + sentence.charCodeAt(10) );
</script>
```

Result displayed in browser:

Sentence = What time is it?

Character at position 0 = W
Unicode value = 87

Character at position 5 = t
Unicode value = 116

Character at position 10 = i
Unicode value = 105

16.29 Write the code to accomplish the following:

1) Create a string variable **w** and set its value equal to "What's your name?".

2) Create a string variable **x** and set its value equal to the length value of the string variable **w**.

3) Create a string variable **y** and set it equal to the character at position 3 of the string variable **w**.

4) Create a string variable **z** and set it equal to the Unicode value of the character at position 3 of the string variable **w**.

2) Display the following on the browser page:

"The value of the string is: "<value of **w**>"."   - Use backslash escape characters (see section 5.2.2) to enclose the string value of **w** in double quotation marks.

Go to a new line.

3) Display the following on the browser page:

"The length of the string is: <length of **w**>"

Go to a new line.

4) Display the following on the browser page:

"The character at position 3: <the character at position 3 of **w**>"   - Use backslash escape characters (see p. 175) to enclose the string value of **w** in double quotation marks.

Go to a new line.

5) Display the following on the browser page:

"The Unicode value of the character at position 3: <the Unicode value of the character at position 3 of **w**>"

Solution

```
<script>
  var w = "What's your name?";
  var x = w.length;
  var y = w.charAt(3);
  var z = w.charCodeAt(3);
  document.write ("The value of the string is: \"" + w + "\"<br>");
  document.write ("The length of the string is: " + x + "<br>");
  document.write ("The character at position 3: \"" + y + "\"<br>");
  document.write ("The Unicode value of the character at position 3 is " + z);
</script>
```

Result displayed in browser:

The value of the string is: "What's your name?"
The length of the string is: 17
The character at position 3: "t"
The Unicode value of the character at position 3 is 116

16.30 Write the code to accomplish the following:

1) Create a string variable called **fruit** and assign it the value "apple".

2) Create a numeric variable called **length** and set its value equal to the length of the variable **fruit**.

3) Create a string variable called **unicodeValues** and assign it the value of an empty string ("").

4) Create a **for** loop with a loop variable called **j** and set its initial value to 0. **j** should increment by 1 on each repeat of the loop. The loop should continue to repeat as long as **j** is less than the value of the variable called **length**.

5) On each repeat of the loop concatenate the character at the position in the variable **fruit** that's represented by **j** to the variable **unicodeValues**. In other words, **unicodeValues** starts out as an empty string and on each repeat of the loop the Unicode value for the each character in **fruit** is appended to it one at a time. When the loop is through, the Unicode value for each character in **fruit** should have been copied to **unicodeValues**.

6) After the loop has completed, display the value of **unicodeValues** in the browser window. The **for** loop should cause the Unicode values for the characters at position 0, 1, 2, 3 and 4 in **fruit** to be concatenated together and displayed in the browser window. Each Unicode value should display on a separate line.

Note: **for** loops were covered on pages 293 - 297.

Solution
```
<script>
  var fruit = "apple";
  var length = fruit.length;
  var unicodeValues = "";
  for (j = 0; j < length; j++ ) {
    unicodeValues = unicodeValues + fruit.charCodeAt(j) + "<br>";
  }
  document.write (unicodeValues);
</script>
```

Result displayed in browser:

97
112
112
108
101

16.31 Write the code to accomplish the following:

1) Create a string variable called **vegetable** and assign it the value "potato".

2) Create a numeric variable called **length** and set its value equal to the length of the variable **vegetable**.

3) Create a string variable called **unicodeValues** and assign it the value of an empty string ("").

4) Create a variable called **k** and assign it the value 0.

5) Create a **while** loop should continue to repeat as long as **k** is less than the value of **length**.

6) On each repeat of the loop concatenate the character at the position in the variable **vegetable** that's represented by **k** to the variable **unicodeValues**. In other words, **unicodeValues** starts out as an empty string and on each repeat of the loop the Unicode value of each successive character in **fruit** is appended to it. When the loop is through, the Unicode value for each character in **vegetable** should

have been copied to **unicodeValues**. Increment **k** by 1 on each repeat of the loop.

7) After the loop has completed, display the value of **unicodeValues** in the browser window. The **for** loop should cause the Unicode values for the characters at position 0, 1, 2, 3, 4 and 5 in **vegetable** to be concatenated together and displayed in the browser window. Each Unicode value should display on a separate line.

Note: **for** loops were covered on pages 307 - 311.

Solution

```
<script>
  var vegetable = "potato";
  var length = vegetable.length;
  var unicodeValues = "";
  var k = 0;
  while(k < length) {
    unicodeValues = unicodeValues + vegetable.charCodeAt(k) + "<br>";
    k = k + 1;
  }
  document.write(unicodeValues);
</script>
```

Result displayed in browser:

112
111
116
97
116
111

16.32 Write the code to accomplish the following:

1) Create a string variable called **num1** and assign it the value "50.334".

2) Create a numeric variable called **num1Length** and set its value equal to the length of the variable **num1**.

3) Create a string variable called **unicodeValues** and assign it the value of an empty string ("").

4) Create a variable called **counter** and assign it the value 0.

5) Create a **do/while** loop that should continue to repeat as long as **counter** is less than the value of **num1Length**. Use the variable **counter** as the loop variable.

6) On each repeat of the loop concatenate the character at the position in the variable **num1** that's represented by **counter** to the variable **unicodeValues**. In other words, **unicodeValues** starts out as an empty string and on each repeat of the loop the Unicode value of each successive character in **num1** is appended to it. When the loop is through, the Unicode value for each character in **num1** should have been copied to **unicodeValues**. Increment **counter** by 1 on each repeat of the loop.

7) After the loop has completed, display the value of **unicodeValues** in the browser window. The **do/while** loop should cause the Unicode values for the characters at position 0, 1, 2, 3, 4 and 5 in **num1** to be concatenated together and displayed in the browser window. Each Unicode value

should display on a separate line.

Note: for loops were covered on pages 321 - 325.

Solution

```
<script>
  var num1 = "50.334";
  var num1Length = num1.length;
  var unicodeValues = "";
  var counter = 0;
  do{
    unicodeValues = unicodeValues + num1.charCodeAt(counter) + "<br>";
    counter++;
  }
  while(counter < num1Length);
  document.write(unicodeValues);
</script>
```

Result displayed in browser:

53
48
46
51
51
52

16.33 What does the **fromCharCode()** method do?

a) it converts characters into their equivalent Unicode values

b) it converts Unicode values into characters (numbers, letters, symbols)

c) it converts an entire strng (regardless of how many characters it contains) into its equivalent Unicode values

Solution

b

8.34 What is the correct syntax for the **fromCharacterCode( )** method?

a) String.fromCharacterCode (*n1, n2, ..., nX*)

b) fromCharacterCode.String(*n1, n2, ..., nX*)

c) (*n1, n2, ..., nX*).fromCharacter Code.String

Solution

a

16.35 What comes first in the **fromCharCode( )** method?

a) fromCharCode

b) (n1, n2, ..., nX)

c) the literal word "String"

Solution

c

16.36 Was the literal word "String" used in the **charAt( )** or the **charCodeAt( )** methods as it is in the **fromCharCode()** method?

a) yes

b) no

Solution

b

16.37 What is used in the **charAt( )** method and the **charCodeAt( )** method instead of the literal word "String"?

a) the name of the string variable that's being operated on by the **fromCharCode()** method

b) the contents of the string variable that's being operated on by the **fromCharCode()** method

c) the Unicode value of the first character of the string that's being operated on by the **fromCharCode()** method

Solution

a

16.48 How many Unicode values can you convert in a fromCharCode() method?

a) 1

b) 10 maximum

c) unlimited

Solution

a

8.39 The following **fromCharCode()** methods will return what characters? (Use chart on p. 350)

a) String.fromCharCode(64)

b) String.fromCharCode(72, 101, 108, 108, 11))
c) String.fromCharCode(51, 46, 49, 52, 49, 54)
d) String.fromCharCode(101, 100, 64, 121, 97, 104, 111, 111, 46, 99, 111, 109)
e) String.fromCharCode(36, 49, 48, 56, 46, 51, 50)
f) String.fromCharCode(105, 102, 32, 120, 61, 56)

Solution
a) @
b) Hello
c) 3.1416
d) ed@yahoo.com
e) $108.32
f) if x = 8

16.40 What do the "n" s in the **fromCharCode()** method stand for?
a) the positions of the characters to be converted
b) the characters in the string that's being operated on by the **fromCharCode()** method
c) the UNicode values to be converted to characters

Solution
c

16.41 Is the literal word "String" always used at the beginning of the **fromCharCode()** method?
a) yes
b) no

Solution
a

16.42 Write the code to accomplish the following:

1) Create a string variable called **greeting** and use **the fromCharCode()** method to assign it the characters represented by the Unicode values 72, 105 and 33.
2) Display the value of **greeting** in the browser window

Solution
```
<script>
  var greeting = String.fromCharCode(72, 105, 33);
  document.write (greeting);
</script>
```

Result displayed in browser:

Hi!

16.43 Write the code to accomplish the following:

1) Create a string variable called **mathProblem** and use **the fromCharCode()** method to assign it the characters represented by the Unicode values 51, 32, 43, 32, 52, 32, 61, 32 and 55.

2) Display the value of **mathProblem** in the browser window

Solution
```
<script>
  var mathProblem = String.fromCharCode(51, 32, 43, 32, 52, 32, 61, 32, 55);
  document.write (mathProblem);
</script>
```

Result displayed in browser:

3 + 4 = 7

16.44 Write the code to accomplish the following:

1) Create a string variable called **x** and assign it the value entered by the user in a prompt box with the user prompt message "Please enter a 2-digit number".

2) If the user entered a number greater than or equal to 10 and also less than 100 create a variable called **msg** and assign it the character value of the Unicode values 79 and 75. Display the value of **msg** in the browser window.

3) If the user didn't enter a number greater than or equal to 10 and also less than 100, then display the following message in the browser window: "You were supposed to enter a 2-digit number!".

Solution
```
<script>
  var x = prompt("Please enter a 2-digit number");
  if (x >= 10 && x < 100) {
    var msg = String.fromCharCode(79, 75);
    document.write(msg);
  }
  else {
    document.write ("You were supposed to enter a 2-digit number!");
  }
</script>
```

16.45 Write the code to accomplish the following:

1) Create a string variable called **ucValue1** and give it the value 99 (the Unicode value for "c").

2) Create a string variable called **ucValue2** and give it the value 99 (the Unicode value for "a").

3) Create a string variable called **ucValue3** and give it the value 99 (the Unicode value for "t").

4) Create a string variable called **word1** and use the **fromCharCode()** method to assign it the characters represented by the variables **ucValue1**, **ucValue2** and **ucValue3**.

Solution

```
<script>
  var ucValue1 = 99;
  var ucValue2 = 97;
  var ucValue3 = 116;
  var word1 = String.fromCharCode(ucValue1, ucValue2, ucValue3);
  document.write(word1);
</script>
```

Result displayed in browser:

cat

16.46 Write the code to accomplish the following:

1) Create a string variable called **animal** and set it equal to the characters represented by the Unicode values 104, 111, 114, 115 and 101.

2) Create numeric variable called **length** and set it equal to the length of the string variable **animal**.

3) Create a string variable called **unicodeValues** as an empty string.

4) Display the value of the string variable **animal** in the browser window.

5) Create a **for** loop that uses **x** as the loop variable. **x** should start out at 0 and increment by 1 on each repetition of the loop.

6) The loop should continue to repeat as long as **x** is less than the value of **length**. Remember that since the variable horse has 5 characters, its first character position position is position 0 and the last position is position 4. If the length of the variable is 5, then, we never want x to be greater than length - 1.

Solution

```
<script>
  var animal = String.fromCharCode(104, 111, 114, 115, 101);
  var length = animal.length;
  var unicodeValues = "";
  document.write ("animal = " + animal + "<br><br>");
  for(x = 0; x < length; x++) {
    unicodeValues = unicodeValues + animal.charCodeAt(x) + "<br>";
  }
  document.write ("The Unicode values for " + animal + " are: <br>");
  document.write (unicodeValues);
</script>
```

Result displayed in browser:

animal = horse

The Unicode values for horse are:
104
111
114
115
101

16.47 Same as 8-56 but use a **while** loop

Solution
```
<script>
   var animal = String.fromCharCode(104, 111, 114, 115, 101);
   var length = animal.length;
   var unicodeValues = "";
   var x = 0;
   document.write("animal = " + animal + "<br><br>");
   while(x < length) {
     unicodeValues = unicodeValues + animal.charCodeAt(x) + "<br>";
     x++;
   }
   document.write("The Unicode values for " + animal + " are: <br>");
   document.write(unicodeValues);
</script>
```

Result displayed in browser:
animal = horse

The Unicode values for horse are:
104
111
114
115
101

16.48 Same as 8-56 but use a **do/while** loop

Solution
```
<script>
   var animal = String.fromCharCode(104, 111, 114, 115, 101);
   var length = animal.length;
   var unicodeValues = "";
   var x = 0;
   document.write("animal = " + animal + "<br><br>");
```

```
  do {
     unicodeValues = unicodeValues + animal.charCodeAt(x) + "<br>";
     x++;
  }
  while(x < length);
  document.write("The Unicode values for " + animal + " are: <br>");
  document.write(unicodeValues);
</script>     unicodeValues = unicodeValues + animal.charCodeAt(x) + "<br>";
```

Result displayed in browser:

animal = horse

The Unicode values for horse are:
104
111
114
115
101

16.48 What does the **concat()** method do?

a) it joins 2 or more strings and returns the Unicode values for all the characters in the strings
b) it joins two or more strings, and returns a copy of the joined strings
c) it separates a long string into several designated shorter strings

Solution

b

16.49 What is the correct syntax for the **concat( )** method?

a) concat (*string1, string2, ..., stringX*)
b) string. (*string1, string2, ..., stringX*).concat
c) *string*.concat (*string1, string2, ..., stringX*)

Solution

c

16.50 What is represented by *string* at the beginning of the **concat( )** method in the syntax model?

a) the name of the first string that the other strings are joined to
b) its only purpose is to fill space
c) thelast string to be connected

Solution

a

16.51 What is represented by (*string1, string2, ..., sringX*) in the **concat( )** syntax model?

a) the Unicode values of the characters in the strings to be connected
b) the only purpose is to fill space in the syntax model
c) the strings to be joined to the string represented by *string* in the **concat( )** syntax model

Solution

c

16.52 Write the code to accomplish the following:

1) Create a string variable called **letter1** and assign it the value of "d".
2) Create a string variable called **letter2** and assign it the value of "o".
3) Create a string variable called **letter3** and assign it the value of "g".
4) Create a string variable called **animalType** and use the **concat( )** method to give it the value of all 3 strings concatenated together.
5) Display the value of **animalType** in the browser window.

Solution
```
<script>
    var letter1 = "d";
    var letter2 = "o";
    var letter3 = "g";
    var animalType = letter1.concat(letter2, letter3);
    document.write(animalType);
</script>
```

Result displayed in browser:

dog

8.53 Write the code to accomplish the following:

1) Create a string variable called **str1** and assign it the value of "Now ".
2) Create a string variable called **str2** and assign it the value of "is the ".
3) Create a string variable called **str3** and assign it the value of "time!".
4) Create a string variable called **newString** and use the **concat( )** method to give it the value of all 3 strings concatenated together.
5) Display the value of **newString** in the browser window.

Solution

```
<script>
  var str1 = "Now ";
  var str2 = "is the ";
  var str3 = "time!";
  var newString = str1.concat(str2, str3);
  document.write(newString);
</script>
```

Result displayed in browser:

Now is the time!

16.54 Write the code to accomplish the following:

1) Create a string variable called **sentenceFrag1** and assign it the value "My name is ".
2) Create a string variable called **fullSentence** and use the **concat( )** method to give it the value of **sentenceFrag1** concatenated with the string literals "Dave. " and "What's yours?".
3) Display the value of **fullSentence** in the browser window.

Solution

```
<script>
  var sentenceFrag1 = "My name is ";
  var fullSentence = sentenceFrag1.concat("Dave. ", "What's yours?");
  document.write(fullSentence);
</script>
```

Result displayed in browser:

My name is Dave. What's yours?

16.55 Write the code to accomplish the following:

1) Create a string variable called **str1** and assign it the value "It's a".
2) Create a string variable called **str2** and assign it the value "beautiful".
3) Create a string variable called **str3** and assign it the value "day".
4) Create a string variable called **str4** and assign it the value "today".
5) When the above 4 strings are concatenated together, the contents of each string should appear on its own line.
6) Create a string variable called **y** and use the **concat ()** method to give it the value of **str1** concatenated with the strings **str2**, **str3** and **str4**.
7) Display the value of **y** in the browser window.

Solution

```
<script>
```

```
    var str1 = "It's a<br>";
    var str2 = "beautiful<br>";
    var str3 = "day<br>";
    var str4 = "today!";
    var y = str1.concat(str2, str3, str4);
    document.write(y);
</script>
```

Result displayed in browser:

It's a
beautiful
day
today!

16.56 Write the code to accomplish the following:

1) Create a string variable called **y** and use the **concat( )** method to give it the value of the string literal "What's " concatenated with the string literals "your " and "name?".

2) Display the value of **y** in the browser window.

Solution
```
<script>
    var y = "What's".concat("your ", "name?");
    document.write(y);
</script>
```

Result displayed in browser:

What's your name?

16.57 What does the **indexOf( )** method do?

a) it returns the character position of the first occurrence of a specified value in a string

b) it returns the character position of the first occurrence of a specified Unicode value in a string

c) it inserts a character into the specified position of a string

Solution

a

16.58 Which of the following is the correct syntax model for the **indexOf( )** method?

a) indexOf(*string*)

b) indexOf(*searchvalue, start*)

c) *string*.indexOf(*searchvalue, start*)

Solution

c

16.59 What does the term *string* refer to in the **indexOf( )** method syntax model?

a) the character that is being searched for
b) the name of the string that's being searched through
c) The string that will be compiled from the characters that are searched for and found

Solution

b

16.60 What does the term *searchvalue* refer to in the **indexOf( )** method syntax model?

a) a string representing the value to be searched for
b) the name of the string that's being searched through
c) the Unicode value of the characters that are being searched for

Solution

a

16.61 What does the term *start* refer to in the **indexOf( )** method syntax model?

a) the first character to be searched for
b) the name of the string to be searched
c) the character position to start the search at

Solution

c

16.62 What part(s) of the syntax model for the **indexOf( )** method are optional?

a) *searchvalue*
b) *string*
c) *start*

Solution

c

16.63 What happens if you don't add a value for *startvalue* when you use the **indexOf( )** method?

a) the search starts at character position 0

b) the method won't work properly

c) the search automatically starts at the last character in the search string and works its way backwards

Solution

a

8.64 What does the **indexOf( )** return if you search for a value that doesn't exist in the string that's being searched?

a) the **indexOf()** method will return 0

b) the **indexOf()** method will return -1

c) an error message will be generated

Solution

b

16.65 What if you're using the **indexOf( )** method to search for an "a" in a string and the string contains 3 occurrences of the letter "a": one at position 3, one at position 6 and 1 at position 8? Which position will be returned by the **indexOf( )** method?

a) 3

b) 6

c) 8

Solution

a

16.66 What if you set the start value in **problem 8.75** to 4? Which position will be returned?

a) 3

b) 6

c) 8

Solution

b

16.67 What if you set the start value in **problem 8.75** to 9? Which position will be returned?

a) 3

b) 6

c) 8

d) -1; remember that if the search character can't be found in the search string, the **indexOf( )** method returns -1

Solution

d (remember that if the search character can't be found in the search string, the **indexOf( )** method returns -1)

16.68 Is the **indexOf( )** method case sensitive with regard to the character being searched for?

a) yes

b) no

Solution

a

16.69 Is anything changed in the way an **indexOf( )** method example works if you add a start value of 0 to it?

a) yes

b) no

Solution

b (remember that if you don't add a *start* value, the **indexOf( )** method begins its search at character 0 anyway)

16.70 Write the code to accomplish the following:

1) Create a string variable called **x** and initialize it with the value "Hello there!".

2) Create a variable called **charPos** and use the **indexOf ()** method to assign it the value of the character position of the first occurrence of "e" in the variable **x**.

3) Display the value of **charPosition** in the browser window.

Solution

```
<script>
  var x = "Hello there!";
  var charPosition = x.indexOf("e");
```

```
  document.write (charPosition);
</script>
```

Result displayed in browser:

1

16.71 Write the code to accomplish the following:

1) Create a string variable called **x** and initialize it with the value "Hello there!".

2) Create a variable called **charPos** and use the **indexOf( )** method to assign it the value of the character position of the second occurrence of "e" in the variable **x**. Use a literal (an actual number, not a variable) start value to begin the search at the next character position after the first occurrence of "e".

3) Display the value of **charPosition** in the browser window.

Solution
```
<script>
  var x = "Hello there!";
  var charPosition = x.indexOf("e", 2);
  document.write (charPosition);
</script>
```

Result displayed in browser:

8

16.72 Write the code to accomplish the following:

1) Create a string variable called **x** and initialize it with the value "Hello there!".

2) Create a variable called **charPos1** and use the **indexOf( )** method to assign it the value of the character position of the first occurrence of "e" in the variable **x**.

3) Create a variable called **charPos2** and use the **indexOf( )** method to assign it the value of the character position of the second occurrence of "e" in the variable **x**. Start the search for "e" at the next position after the character position where the first occurrence of "e" was found.

4) Display the value of charPos1 in the browser window in the following manner:
   "First occurrence of 'e' = position <value of charPos1>"

4) Display the value of charPos2 in the browser window on a new line in the following manner:
   "Second occurrence of 'e' = position <value of charPos2>"

Solution
```
<script>
  var x = "Hello there!";
  var charPos1 = x.indexOf("e");
  var charPos2 = x.indexOf("e", charPos1 + 1);
```

```
document.write ("First occurrence of 'e' = position " + charPos1 + "<br>");
document.write ("Second occurrence of 'e' = position " + charPos2);
</script>
```

Result displayed in browser:

First occurrence of 'e' = position 1

Second occurrence of 'e' = position 8

16.73 Write the code to accomplish the following:

1) Create a string variable called **greeting** and initialize it with the value "Goodbye".
2) Create a variable called **charPos** and use the **indexOf()** method to assign it the value of the character position of the first occurrence of the letter "z" (the letter "z" does not occur in the search string).
3) Display the value of **charPosition** in the browser window.

Solution
```
<script>
  var greeting = "Goodbye";
  var charPos = greeting.indexOf("z");
  document.write(charPos);
</script>
```

Result displayed in browser:

-1 ————————▶ if the search character is not found, the **indexOf()** method returns -1

16.74 Write the code to accomplish the following:

1) Create a string variable called **greeting** and initialize it with the value "Goodbye".
2) Create a string variable called **char** and give it the initial value "z";
3) Create a variable called **charPos** and use the **indexOf()** method to assign it the value of the character position of the first occurrence of the letter represented by the variable **char** (the value of char is "z" but use the variable **char** in the **indexOf()** method).
4) If the character represented by the variable **char** is not found, then, display the following message in an alert box:
    "<value of char> could not be found in the string."
  If the character represented by the variable **char** is found, then, display the following message in an alert box:
    "<value of char> was found at position <value of charPos>."

Solution
```
<script>
```

```
  var greeting = "Goodbye";
  var char = "z";
  var charPos = greeting.indexOf(char)
  if(charPos == -1) {
    alert (char + " could not be found in the string.");
  }
  else {
    alert (char + " was found at position " + charPos);
  }
</script>
```

Result displayed in alert box:

z could not be found in the string.

16.75 Same code as **problem 8.84** but substitute "b" for the value of char

Solution
```
<script>
  var greeting = "Goodbye";
  var char = "b";
  var charPos = greeting.indexOf(char)
  if(charPos == -1) {
    alert (char + " could not be found in the string.");
  }
  else {
    alert (char + " was found at position " + charPos);
  }
</script>
```

Result displayed in alert box:

b was found at position 4

16.76 Write the code to accomplish the following:

1) Create a string variable called **str1** and initialize it with the value "How are you?".
2) Create a variable called **startPos** and use the **indexOf()** method to assign it the value of the character position of the first occurrence of the multi-character string "are" in the variable **str1**.
3) Display the value of **charPosition** in the browser window.

Solution
```
<script>
  var str1 = "How are you?";
  var startPos = str1.indexOf("are");
  document.write(startPos);
```

```
</script>
```

Result displayed in browser:

4

16.77 Same code as **problem 8.86** but search for "add" instead of "are.

Solution

```
<script>
  var str1 = "How are you?";
  var startPos = str1.indexOf("add");
  document.write(startPos);
</script>
```

Result displayed in browser:

-1

16.78 Same code as **problem 8.86** but create a string variable called **searchFor** and set it equal to "are". Use the **indexOf( )** method to search for the string "are" but use the string variable as the search value instead of the string literal "are".

Solution

```
<script>
  var str1 = "How are you?";
  var searchFor = "are";
  var startPos = str1.indexOf(searchFor);
  documen.write(startPos);
</script>
```

Result displayed in browser:

4

Chapter 17

JavaScript Strings: Part 3

17.1 MORE JAVASCRIPT STRING METHODS

17.1.1 lastIndexOf()

The **lastIndexOf( )** method returns the position of the last occurrence of a specified value in the string that's being searched. The string is searched from the end to the beginning, but the index returned is in reference to the beginning of the string just as with the **indexOf( )** method. In other words, the first character in the string being searched is referred to as position 0 regardless of which method you're using. The **lastIndexOf( )** method returns -1 if the value to search for can't be found in the search string. Like the **indexOf( ) method,** the **lastIndexOf( )** method is also case sensitive. The **fromIndex** parameter is optional and it indicates the index at which to start searching backwards in the string. It can be any integer. The default value is the length of the string - 1, so the whole string will be searched. If the **fromIndex** parameter is greater than the length of the string - 1, the whole string will be searched.

Syntax

```
string.lastIndexOf(searchvalue,[, fromIndex])
```

Parameter Values

Parameter	Description
searchvalue	Required. A string (multi or single character) representing the value to search for.
fromIndex	Optional. The position where to start the search (searching backwards). If omitted, the default value is the string length -1

examples of the lastIndexOf() method:

example:
```
<script>
   var str1 = "monologue";
   var charPosition = str1.lastIndexOf("o");
   document.write(charPosition);
</script>
```

Result displayed in alert box:
5

In this example, the **lastIndexOf()** method is used to search for the last occurrence of the letter "o" starting at the end of the string and working backwards. Since the optional **fromIndex** parameter was omitted, the search automatically starts at the end of the string. In this string, there are 3 occurrences of the letter "o" at positions 1, 3 and 5. Since the **lastIndexOf()** method looks for the occurrence of the search value ("o") starting at the end of the string (or starting from the position indicated by the **fromIndex** parameter if it is used) and working backwards through the string to the left, the first occurrence of the letter "o" using this method is at position 5.

example:
```
<script>
   var str1 = "monologue";
   var charPosition = str1.lastIndexOf("o", 4));
   document.write(charPosition);
</script>
```

Result displayed in alert box:
3

In this example, the **lastIndexOf()** method is used to search for the last occurrence of the letter "o" starting at position 4 in the string ("l" is at position 4) and working backwards. In this string, there are 3 occurrences of the letter "o" at positions 1, 3 and 5. Since, In this case , the **fromIndex** parameter is set to 4, the **lastIndexOf()** method will look for the occurrence of the search value ("o") starting at position 4 and work its way backwards through the string to the left. Using this method, the first occurrence of the letter "o" to the left of the **fromIndex** value, which is position 4, is position 3.

example:
```
<script>
   var str1 = "monologue";
   var charPosition = str1.lastIndexOf("o", 2));
   document.write(charPosition);
</script>
```

Result displayed in alert box:
1

In this example, the **lastIndexOf()** method is used to search for the last occurrence of the letter "o" starting at position 2 in the string ("n" is at position 2) and working backwards. In this string, there are 3 occurrences of the letter "o" at positions 1, 3 and 5. Since, In this case , the **fromIndex** parameter is set to 2, the **lastIndexOf()** method will look for the occurrence of the search value ("o") starting at position 2 and work its way backwards through the string to the left. Using this method, the first occurrence of the letter "o" to the left of the **fromIndex** value, which is position 2, is position 1.

example:
```
<script>
   var str1 = "catcatcat";
   var charPosition = str1.lastIndexOf("cat");
   document.write(charPosition);
</script>
```

Result displayed in alert box:
6

In this example, the **lastIndexOf()** method is used to search for the last occurrence of the string "cat" starting at the end of the string and working backwards. Since the optional *fromIndex* parameter was omitted, the search automatically starts at the end of the string. In this string, there are 3 occurrences of the string "cat" at positions 0, 3 and 6. Since the **lastIndexOf()** method looks for the occurrence of the search value ("cat") starting at the end of the string (or starting from the position indicated by the *fromIndex* parameter if it is used) and working backwards through the string to the left, the beginning of the first occurrence of the string "cat" using this method is at position 6.

example:
```
<script>
  var str1 = "catcatcat";
  var charPosition = str1.lastIndexOf("cat", 5));
  document.write(charPosition);
</script>
```

Result displayed in alert box:
3

In this example, the **lastIndexOf()** method is used to search for the last occurrence of the string "cat" starting at position 5 in the string ("t" is at position 5) and working backwards. In this string, there are 3 occurrences of the string "cat" at positions 0, 3 and 6. Since, In this case , the **fromIndex** parameter is set to 5, the **lastIndexOf()** method will look for the occurrence of the search value ("cat") starting at position 5 and work its way backwards through the string to the left until it finds the beginning character ("c") of the string. Using this method, the first occurrence of the string "cat" to the left of the **fromIndex** value, which is position 5, is position 3.

example:
```
<script>
  var str1 = "catcatcat";
  var charPosition = str1.lastIndexOf("cat", 1));
  document.write(charPosition);
</script>
```

Result displayed in alert box:
0

In this example, the **lastIndexOf()** method is used to search for the last occurrence of the string "cat" starting at position 1 in the string ("a" is at position 1) and working backwards. In this string, there are 3 occurrences of the string "cat" at positions 0, 3 and 6. Since, In this case , the **fromIndex** parameter is set to 1, the **lastIndexOf()** method will look for the occurrence of the search value ("cat") starting at position 1 and work its way backwards through the string to the left until it finds the beginning character ("c") of the string. Using this method, the first occurrence of the string "cat" to the left of the **fromIndex** value, which is position 1, is position 0.

17.1.2 replace ()

The **replace()** method searches a string for a specified value (*searchvalue*) and replaces the specified value with a new string (*newvalue*). This method makes no changes to the original string. By default the **replace()** method only replaces the first occurrence of the string to be replaced or the search string.

Syntax

```
string.replace(searchvalue,newvalue)
```

Parameter Values

Parameter	Description
searchvalue	Required. The old string value that will be replaced by the new string value
newvalue	Required. The value to replace the *searchvalue* with

examples of the replace() method:

example:
```
<script>
    var sentence1 = "I love cats.";
    var sentence2 = sentence1.replace("cat", "dog");
    document.write(sentence1 + "<br>");
    document.write(sentence2);
</script>
```

Result displayed in alert box:
I love cats.
I love dogs.

In this example, the **replace()** method is used to search for the first occurrence of "cats" in the string variable **sentence1** and replace it with "dogs". The resulting altered string is assigned to the variable **sentence2** while the string variable **sentence1** is left unchanged. Remember that this method only replaces the first occurrence of the search value ("cat") with the new value ("dog").

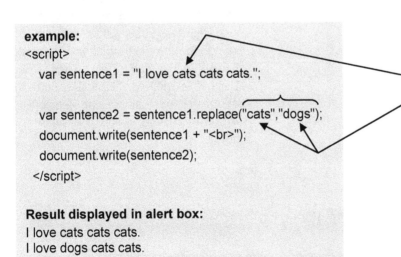

example:
```
<script>
    var sentence1 = "I love cats cats cats.";

    var sentence2 = sentence1.replace("cats","dogs");
    document.write(sentence1 + "<br>");
    document.write(sentence2);
</script>
```

Result displayed in alert box:
I love cats cats cats.
I love dogs cats cats.

In this example, the **replace()** method is used to search for the first occurrence of "cats" in the string variable **sentence1** and replace it with "dogs". The resulting altered string is assigned to the variable **sentence2** while the string variable **sentence1** is left unchanged. As we said above, the **replace()** method, in the way that we've been using it so far, only replaces the first occurrence of the search value. In the next example we see how to replace all occurrences of the search value with the new value.

example:
```
<script>
   var sentence1 = "I love cats cats cats.";
   var sentence2 = sentence1.replace(/cats/gi,"dogs");
   document.write(sentence1 + "<br>");
   document.write(sentence2);
  </script>
```

Result displayed in alert box:
I love cats cats cats.
I love dogs cats cats.

In this example, the **replace()** method is used to search for multiple occurrence of "cats" in the string variable **sentence1** and replace each one of its occurrences with "dogs". The resulting altered string is assigned to the variable **sentence2** while the string variable **sentence1** is left unchanged. In order to replace all occurrences of the search value ("cats") we had to use something called **a regular expression** (we'll deal with regular expressions in depth in a later chapter). Notice that the search value "cats" is enclosed by forward slashes instead of quotation marks and that the letters "g" and "i" follow it. The forward slashes denote the beginning and of a regular expression. The letter "g" indicates to search for all occurrences of the expression and the "i" indicates that the search is case insensitive. If we wanted an exact search match (case included) then, we would have left the "i" out. We only covered this now because there is no other way to use the **replace()** method to replace multiple occurrences of the search value.

example:
```
<script>
   var sentence1 = "I love cats.";
   var sentence2 = sentence1.replace("birds","dogs");
   document.write(sentence1 + "<br>");
   document.write(sentence2);
  </script>
```

Result displayed in alert box:
I love cats.
I love cats.

In this example, the **replace()** method is used to search for the first occurrence of "birds" in the string variable **sentence1** and replace it with "dogs". Because the search value "birds" isn't contained in the string that's being searched, nothing is changed. The **replace()** method returns the original value of sentence1 ("I love cats.") and assigns it to sentence2.

17.1.3 search ()

The **search()** method searches a string for a specified string value, and returns the position of the match. The **search()** method is very similar to the **indexOf()** method. The main difference is that, in addition to the search value in a **search()** method being a string, it can also be a regular expression (we will cover regular expressions in depth in a later chapter). Another difference between the **search()** method and the **indexOf()** method is that you can't use an optional start position with the **search()** method. The search will always begin at position 0 with the **search()** method even if you add a start position value (it will be ignored). The value returned by the **search()** method is a number that represents the position of the first occurrence of the specified *searchvalue*, or -1 if no match is found.

Syntax

string.search(*searchvalue*)

Parameter Values

Parameter	Description
searchvalue	Required. A string or regular expression.

examples of the search() method:

example:
```
<script>
  var phrase = "Round 'bout midnight.";
  var charPos = phrase.search("b");
  alert(charPos);
</script>
```

Result displayed in alert box:
7

In this example, the **search()** method is used to search for the first occurrence of "b" starting with position 0. The **search()** method never uses an optional **start** value. The search always starts at the beginning of the string.

example:
```
<script>
  var phrase = "Round 'bout midnight.";
  var charPos = phrase.search("b", 10);
  alert(charPos);
</script>
```

Result displayed in alert box:
7

In this example, the **search()** method is again used to search for the first occurrence of "b" starting with position 10. In this example, we added a value of 10 for the start position but since the **search()** method ignores the start position value the search starts at the beginning of the string and gives us the same result as the previous example.

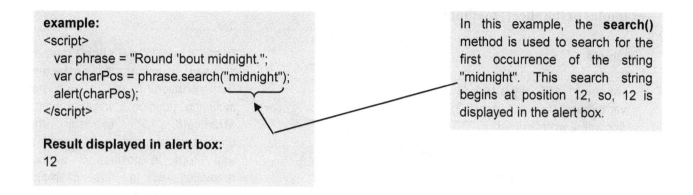

example:
```
<script>
  var phrase = "Round 'bout midnight.";
  var charPos = phrase.search("midnight");
  alert(charPos);
</script>
```

Result displayed in alert box:
12

In this example, the **search()** method is used to search for the first occurrence of the string "midnight". This search string begins at position 12, so, 12 is displayed in the alert box.

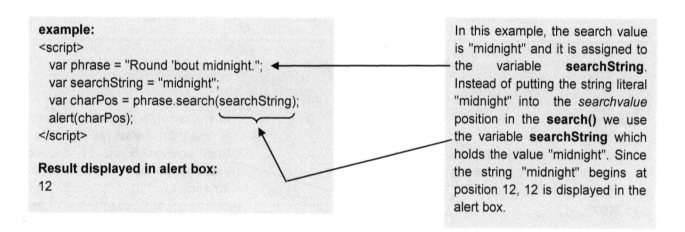

example:
```
<script>
  var phrase = "Round 'bout midnight.";
  var searchString = "midnight";
  var charPos = phrase.search(searchString);
  alert(charPos);
</script>
```

Result displayed in alert box:
12

In this example, the search value is "midnight" and it is assigned to the variable **searchString**. Instead of putting the string literal "midnight" into the *searchvalue* position in the **search()** we use the variable **searchString** which holds the value "midnight". Since the string "midnight" begins at position 12, 12 is displayed in the alert box.

17.1.4 slice ()

The **slice()** method extracts parts of a string and returns the extracted parts in a new string. Use the **start** and **end** parameters to specify the part of the string you want to extract. The first character has the position 0, the second has position 1, and so on. Use a negative number to select from the end of the string.

Syntax

```
string.slice(start,end)
```

Parameter Values

Parameter	Description
start	Required. The position where to begin the extraction. First character is at position 0
end	Optional. The position (up to, but not including) where to end the extraction. If omitted, slice() selects all characters from the start-position to the end of the string

examples of the slice() method:

example:
```
<script>
  var string1 = "Today is Monday.";
  var extract1 = string1.slice(0,3);
  document.write(extract1);
</script>
```

Result displayed in alert box:
Tod

In this example, the **slice()** method is used to extract all characters from position 0 up to, but not including, position 3. In other words **str.slice(0, 3)** extracts the characters at position 0, 1 and 2 and stops at position 3 without extracting it. In this example, positions 0, 1 and 2 equate to the string "Tod".

example:
```
<script>
  var string1 = "Today is Monday.";
  var extract1 = string1.slice(6,8);
  document.write(extract1);
</script>
```

Result displayed in alert box:
is

In this example, the **slice()** method is used to extract all characters from position 6 up to, but not including, position 7. In other words **str.slice(6, 8)** extracts the characters at position 6 and 7 and stops at position 8 without extracting it. In this example, positions 6 and 7 equate to the string "is".

example:
```
<script>
  var string1 = "Today is Monday.";
  var extract1 = string1.slice(0);
  document.write(extract1);
</script>
```

Result displayed in alert box:
Today is Monday.

In this example, the **slice()** method is used to extract all the characters in the string starting at position 0. If you don't add an *end* value, the **slice()** method will extract everything after the *start* value. In other words **str.slice(0)** extracts all characters from position 0 to the end of the string. In this example, positions 0 and all positions after equate to the string "Today is Monday".

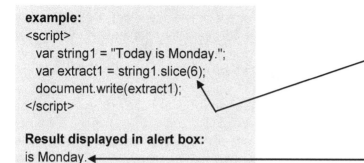

example:
```
<script>
  var string1 = "Today is Monday.";
  var extract1 = string1.slice(6);
  document.write(extract1);
</script>
```

Result displayed in alert box:
is Monday.

In this example, the **slice()** method is used to extract all the characters in the string starting at position 6. If you don't add an *end* value, the **slice()** method will extract everything after the *start* value. In other words **str.slice(6)** extracts all characters from position 6 to the end of the string. In this example, positions 6 and all positions after equate to the string "is Monday".

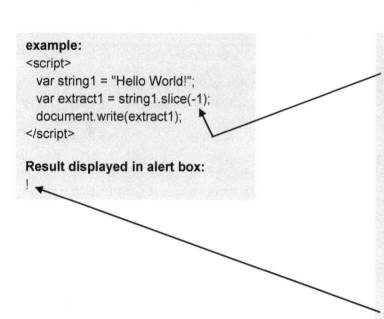

example:
```
<script>
  var string1 = "Hello World!";
  var extract1 = string1.slice(-1);
  document.write(extract1);
</script>
```

Result displayed in alert box:
!

In this example, the **slice()** method is used to extract characters starting at the end of the string. When a negative number (in this case -1) is used as the start value in the **slice()** method, it means that your using the end of the string as a starting reference point. The *start* value -1 refers to the last character in the string. If you use -0 as the start value, it's the same as using 0 as the *start* value. In other words, **str.slice(-0)** is equivalent to **str.slice(0)** and it will extract and return the entire string. In this example, we have -1 as the *start* value and no *end* value. This means that the extraction starts at the end of the string and extracts the last character ("!")..

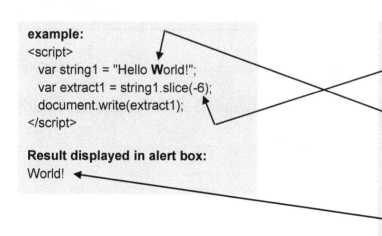

example:
```
<script>
  var string1 = "Hello World!";
  var extract1 = string1.slice(-6);
  document.write(extract1);
</script>
```

Result displayed in alert box:
World!

In this example, the **slice()** method starts at the 6th character from the end of the string, which is "W" and is designated by -6 as the *start* value.("!" is designated by position -1, "d" is -2, "l" is -3, "r" is -4, "o" is -5 and "W" is -6). Because no end value is given, the slice() method will start the extraction at position -6 and extract all characters following position -6 to the end of the string. In this case, the characters from position -6 to the end of the string are "W", "o", "r", "l" , "d" and "!".

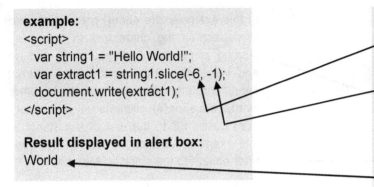

example:
```
<script>
  var string1 = "Hello World!";
  var extract1 = string1.slice(-6, -1);
  document.write(extract1);
</script>
```

Result displayed in alert box:
World

In this example, the **slice()** method starts at the 6th character from the end of the string, which is "W" and is designated by -6 as the *start* value. The **end** value in this example is -1 which means that the extraction starts at position -6 ("W") and proceeds up to, but not including, position -1. So, the extraction starts at "W" and extracts all characters up to, but not including, "!". The resulting extraction is "World".

example:
```
<script>
  var string1 = "Hello World!";
  var extract1 = string1.slice(-12, -7);
  document.write(extract1);
</script>
```

Result displayed in alert box:
Hello

In this example, the **slice()** method starts at the 12th character from the end of the string, which is "H" and is designated by -12 as the *start* value. The **end** value in this example is -7 which means that the extraction starts at position -12 ("H") and proceeds up to, but not including, position -7 So, the extraction starts at "H" and extracts all characters up to, but not including, the blank space between "o" and "W".. The resulting string extraction consists of the characters "Hello".

SOLVED PROBLEMS

17.1 What value does the **lastIndexOf()** method return?

a) the position in the search string of the second occurrence of the character specified in the **lastIndexOf()** method

b) the position in the search string of the last occurrence of the character specified in the **lastIndexOf()** method

c) the position in the search string of the first occurrence of the character specified in the **lastIndexOf()** method

Solution
b

17.2 Where in the string being searched does the **lastIndexOf()** method begin its search?

a) after the first occurrence of the value that's being searched for

b) at the beginning of the string being searched

c) at the end of the string being searched

Solution

c

17.3 The index value (the position of the character being searched for) returned by the **lastIndexOf()** method is in reference to:

a) the beginning of the string that is being searched through for the value specified by the **lastIndexOf()** method

b) the end of the string that is being searched through for the value specified by the **lastIndexOf()** method

Solution

a

17.4 If the value "a" is being searched for by the **indexOf()** method and it appears three times in the search string at positions 3, 7 and 9, what index would the **lastIndexOf()** method return?

a) 9

b) 3

c) 7

Solution

a

17.5 What does the **lastIndexOf()** method return when the search value (the character being searched for)

isn't found in the search string (the string being searched through)?

a) 0

b) 1

c) -1

Solution

c

17.6 Is the lastIndexOf() method case sensitive?

a) yes
b) no
c) only in special cases

Solution

a

17.7 How many parameters does the lastIndexOf() method have?

a) 1
b) 2
c) 3

Solution

b

17.8 What are the 2 parameters of the lastIndexOf() method?

a) *searchvalue, startPosition*
b) *searchvalue. stringLength*
c) *searchvalue, fromIndex*

Solution

c

17.9 Which one of the lastIndexOf() method's 2 parameters are optional?

a) *searchvale*
b) *fromIndex*

Solution

b

17.10 What does the optional *fromIndex* parameter in the lastIndexOf() method indicate?

a) the index (character position) at which to stop the backwards search from the end of the string
b) the index at which to start the backwards search in the string
c) the index at which to start the forwards search in the string

Solution

b

17.11 If a string contains 10 characters, what is the index value of its last character?

a) 9

b) 10

c) 11

Solution

a

17.12 If the string that is being searched through has 6 characters and you don't supply a value for the optional **fromIndex** value in the **lastIndexOf()** method, what default value is added by the method?

a) 6

b) 5

c) 7

Solution

b

17.13 What happens if the string to be searched has 5 characters and you supply a value of 5 or greater for the **fromIndex** parameter in the **lastIndexOf()** method?

a) an error message will be generated

b) no search will occur

c) the entire string will be searched

Solution

c

17.14 The **searchvalue** parameter in the **lastIndexOf()** method can contain what kind of value?

a) any single or multi-character value

b) any single character value

c) any single or multi-character alphabetic value

Solution

a

17.15 Which one of the following examples is the correct syntax model for the **lastIndexOf()** method?

a) lastIndexOf.*searchvalue.fromIndex.string*

b) *string*.lastIndexOf(*searchvalue, fromIndex*)

c) *string.searchvalue*(lastIndexOf, *fromIndex*)

Solution

b

17.16 Which parameter is required in the **lastIndexOf()** method and which one is optional?

a) Optional: *searchvalue*
   Required: *fromIndex*

b) Optional: *fromIndex*
   Required: *serchvalue*

Solution

b

17.17 Write the code to accomplish the following:

1) Create a string variable called **word1** and initialize it with the value "anagram".

2) Create a variable called **index1** and use the **lastIndexOf()** method to assign it the value of the last occurrence of the letter "a" in the string variable **word1**.

3) Display the value of **index1** in the browser window.

Solution
```
<script>
  var word1 = "anagram";
  var index1 = word1.lastIndexOf("a");
  document.write(index1);
</script>
```

Result displayed in browser:

5

17.18 Write the code to accomplish the following:

Same as problem 17.17 but start the backwards search at index (character position) 4.

Solution
```
<script>
  var word1 = "anagram";
  var index1 = word1.lastIndexOf("a", 4);
```

```
  document.write(index1);
</script>
```

Result displayed in browser:

2

17.19 Write the code to accomplish the following:

Same as problem 17.17 but start the backwards search at index (character position) 0.

Solution
```
<script>
  var word1 = "anagram";
  var index1 = word1.lastIndexOf("a", 4);
  document.write(index1);
</script>
```

Result displayed in browser:

0

17.20 Write the code to accomplish the following:

1) Create a string variable called **str3** and initialize it with the value "oneonetwotwo".
2) Create a variable called **charPos1** and use the **lastIndexOf()** method to assign it the value of the last occurrence of the string value "two" in the string variable **str3**.
3) Display the value of **charPos1** in the browser window.

Solution
```
<script>
  var str3 = "oneonetwotwo";
  var charPos1 = str3.lastIndexOf("two");
  document.write(charPos1);
</script>
```

Result displayed in browser:

9

17.21 Write the code to accomplish the following:

Same as problem 17.20 but start a backwards search for "tw" starting at position 8

Solution

```
<script>
  var str3 = "oneonetwotwo";
  var charPos1 = str3.lastIndexOf("tw", 8);
  document.write(charPos1);
</script>
```

Result displayed in browser:

6

17.22 Write the code to accomplish the following:

1) Create a string variable called **x** and initialize it with the value "dogdogdog".
2) Create a variable called **y** and use the **lastIndexOf()** method to assign it the value of the
   last occurrence of the string value "dogd" in the string variable **x**.
3) Display the value of **y** in the browser window.

Solution
```
<script>
  var x = "dogdogdog";
  var y = x.lastIndexOf("dogd");
  document.write(y);
</script>
```

Result displayed in browser:

3

17.23 Write the code to accomplish the following:

Same as problem 17.122 but start the search at position 4

Solution
```
<script>
  var x = "dogdogdog";
  var y = x.lastIndexOf("dogd", 4);
  document.write(y);
</script>
```

Result displayed in browser:

3

17.24 Write the code to accomplish the following:

1) Create a string variable called **phrase** and initialize it with the value "Where are you?".

2) Create a string variable called **searchFor** and initialize it with the value "are".

3) Create a variable called **charPos1** and use the **lastIndexOf()** method to assign it the value of the last occurrence of the string value "are" in the string variable **phrase**.

4) Display the value of **y** in the browser window.

Solution
```
<script>
  var phrase = "Where are you?";
  var searchFor = "are";
  var charPos1 = phrase.lastIndexOf(searchFor);
  document.write(charPos1);
</script>
```

Result displayed in browser:

6

17.25 What does the **replace()** method do?

a) it replaces all occurrences of a specified character with another character

b) it replaces the entire original string with a new string and discards the original string

c) it searches through a string for a specified substring value and replaces it with a new string value

Solution

c

17.26 Are any changes made to the original string by the **replace()** method?

a) yes

b) no

Solution

b

17.27 How many parameters does the replace() method have?

a) 1

b) 2

c) 3

Solution

b

17.28 What are the 2 parameters of the **replace()** method?

a) *searchvalue, newvalue*

b) *searchstring, replacevalue*

c) *stringvalue, newvalue*

Solution

a

17.29 Which replace() method parameters are required?

a) *searchvalue*

b) *newvalue*

c) both

Solution

c

17.30 What is the purpose of the **searchvalue** parameter in the **replace()** method?

a) *searchvalue* represents the new string value that will replace the old string value

b) *searchvalue* represents the original string that will not be changed

c) *searchvalue* represents the old string value that will be replaced the new string value

Solution

c

17.31 What is the purpose of the *newvalue* parameter in the **replace()** method?

a) *newvalue* represents the value that is being searched for in the original string

b) *newvalue* represents the new string value that will replace the string value represented by the **searchvalue** parameter

c) *newvalue* represents the entire new altered string that the **replace()** method creates

Solution

b

17.32 If the value of **string1** is "My name is Fred" and the *searchvalue* parameter is "Fred" and the **newvalue** parameter is "John", what will be the value of string1 after the **replace()** method executes?

a) My name is Fred

b) My name is John

Solution
a

17.33 If the result returned by the **replace()** method in problem 8-120 is put into a string variable called **string2**, what will be the value of **string2** after the **replace()** method has executed?

a) My name is Fred
b) My name is John

Solution
b

17.34 What will be the final values of the string variables **sentence1** and **sentence2** as the result of the following code:

```
<script>
  var sentence1 = "He likes football";
  var sentence2 = sentence1.replace("football", "baseball");
</script> '
```

a) sentence1: He likes football
   sentence2: He likes baseball
b) sentence1: He likes baseball
   sentence2: He likes baseball
c) sentence1: He likes baseball
   sentence2: He likes football

Solution
a

17.35 If the string value represented by the **searchvalue** parameter occurs 3 times in the string that's being searched through, how many occurrences of **searchvalue** are replaced by the **newvalue** parameter with the **replace()** method?

a) all 3 occurrences of the *searchvalue* will be replace
b) only the last occurrence of *searchvalue* will be replace
c) by default, only the first occurrence of the *searchvalue* parameter is replaced by the **replace()** method

Solution
c

17.36 What will be the final values of the string variables **sentence1** and **sentence2** as the result of the following code:

```
<script>
  var sentence1 = "Their names are Mary, Mary and Mary";
  var sentence2 = sentence1.replace("Mary", "Doris");
</script>
```

a) sentence1: Their names are Mary, Mary and Mary
    sentence2: Their names are Doris, Doris and Doris
b) sentence1: Their names are Mary, Mary and Mary
    sentence2: Their names are Doris, Mary and Mary
c) sentence1: Their names are Doris, Mary and Mary
    sentence2: Their names are Doris, Mary and Mary

Solution
b

17.37 Write the code to accomplish the following:

1) Create a string variable called **str1** and initialize it with the value "The field contains corn, corn and more corn"
2) Create a variable called **str2** and use the **replace()** method to replace the first occurrence of "corn" with "wheat" in **str2**.
3) Display the value of **str1** and **str2** on their own lines in the browser window as follows:
      "str1 = <value of str1>"
      "str2 = <value of str2>"

Solution
```
<script>
  var str1 = "The field contains corn, corn and more corn";
  var str2 = str1.replace("corn", "wheat");
  document.write("str1 = " + str1 + "<br>");
  document.write("str2 = " + str2);
</script>
```

Result displayed in browser:
str1 = The field contains corn, corn and more corn
str2 = The field contains wheat, corn and more corn

17.38 Write the code to accomplish the following:

1) Create a string variable called **phrase1** and initialize it with the value "Today is Monday"
2) Create a variable called **phrase2** and use the **replace()** method to replace the first occurrence (and only occurrence in this example) of "Monday" with "Tuesday"
3) Display the value of **phrase1** and **phrase2** on their own lines in the browser window as follows:

"phrase1 = <value of phrase1>"
"phrase2 = <value of phrase2>"

Solution
```
<script>
  var phrase1 = "Today is Monday";
  var phrase2 = phrase1.replace("Monday", "Tuesday");
  document.write("phrase1 = " + phrase1 + "<br>");
  document.write("phrase2 = " + phrase2 + "<br>");
</script>
```

Result displayed in browser:

phrase1 = Today is Monday
phrase2 = Today is Tuesday

17.39 Write the code to accomplish the following:

1) Create a string variable called **x** and initialize it with the value "I was born in Ohio"
2) Create a string variable called **y** and initialize it with the value " Ohio"
3) Create a string variable called **z** and initialize it with the value "Florida"
4) Create a variable called **x** and use the **replace()** method to replace the first occurrence of the value represented by the string variable **y** with the value represented by the string variable **z**.
5) Display the value of **x** and **w** on their own lines in the browser window as follows:

"original sentence = <value of x>"
"new sentence = <value of w>"

Solution
```
<script>
  var x = "I was born in Ohio";
  var y = "Ohio";
  var z = "Florida";
  var w = x.replace(y, z);
  document.write("original sentence = " + x + "<br>");
  document.write("new sentence = " + w + "<br>");
</script>
```

Result displayed in browser:

original sentence = I was born in Ohio
new sentence = I was born in Florida

17.40 Write the code to accomplish the following:

Same as problem 8-125 except use "Corn" for the *searchvalue* parameter instead of "corn"

Solution
```
<script>
  var str1 = "The field contains corn, corn and more corn";
  var str2 = str1.replace("Corn", "wheat");
  document.write("str1 = " + str1 + "<br>");
  document.write("str2 = " + str2);
</script>
```

Result displayed in browser:

str1 = The field contains corn, corn and more corn
str2 = The field contains corn, corn and more corn

17.41 Write the code to accomplish the following:

Same as problem 8-125 except use a regular expression so that all occurrences of "corn" are replaced by "wheat"

Solution
```
<script>
  var str1 = "The field contains corn, corn and more corn";
  var str2 = str1.replace(/corn/g, "wheat");
  document.write("str1 = " + str1 + "<br>");
  document.write("str2 = " + str2);
</script>
```

Result displayed in browser:

str1 = The field contains corn, corn and more corn
str2 = The field contains wheat, wheat and more wheat

17.42 Write the code to accomplish the following:

1) Create a string variable called **str1** and initialize it with the value "I love ice cream"
2) Create a variable called **str2** and use the **replace()** method to replace the first occurrence of "ice milk" (it's not in the original string) with "caket" in **str2**.
3) Display the value of **str1** and **str2** on their own lines in the browser window as follows:

      "str1 = <value of str1>"
      "str2 = <value of str2>"

Solution
```
<script>
  var str1 ="I love ice cream";
  var str2 = str1.replace("ice milk", "cake");
  document.write("str1 = " + str1 + "<br>");
  document.write("str2 = " + str2);
</script>
```

Result displayed in browser:

str1 = I love ice cream
str2 = I love ice cream

17.43 What does the **search()** method do?

a) it searches a string for a specified substring value and returns the position of the matched string if it's found
b) it searches a string at a specified position and returns the character value at that position
c) it searches a string for a specified substring value and replaces that value with another string

Solution
a

17.44 The **search()** method is very similar to what other string method?

a) replace()
b) charAt()
c) indexOf()

Solution
c

17.45 What is the main difference between the **search()** method and the **indexOf()** method?

a) there is no difference
b) in addition to the search value being a string as is the case with both the **search()** method and the **indexOf()** method, the search value can also be a regular expression with the **search()** method
c) the search() method can search for multiple characters but the **indexOf()** method can only search for single characters

Solution
b

17.46 Where does the search always begin with the **search()** method?

a) the search begins at the last character position and works backwards through the string
b the search will begin at the starting position indicated in the search() method parameters
c) the search will always begin at position 0

Solution

c

17.47 What if you add a start position to the **search()** method?

a) the **search()** method will ignore the added start position and start at position 0

b) it will begin its search at the supplied start value

c) an error message will be displayed

Solution

a

17.48 What value does the **search()** method return if the character being searched for can't be found in the string?

a) 1

b) 0

c) -1

Solution

c

17.49 Which of the following is the correct syntax model for the **search()** method?

a) *string*.search(*searchvalue, start*)

b) *string*.searchvalue(*string*)

c) *string*.search(*searchvalue*)

Solution

c

17.50 The **searchvalue** parameter for the **search()** method must be in what form?

a) a string or a regular expression

b) a string only

c) a number only

Solution

a

17.51 The **searchvalue** parameter for the **indexOf()** method must be in what form?

a) a string or a regular expression

b)a string only

c)a number only

Solution

b

17.52 What value will be displayed in an alert box as the result of this code?

```
<script>
  var str1 = "What time is it?";
  var charPosition = str1.search("m");
  alert(charPosition);
</script>
```

Solution

7

17.53 What value will be displayed in an alert box as the result of this code?

```
<script>
  var str1 = "How old are you?";
  var charPosition = str1.search("o", 3);
  alert(charPosition);
</script>
```

Solution

1

17.54 Is the **indexOf()** method case sensitive?

a) yes

b) no

Solution

a

17.55 Is the **search()** method case sensitive?

a) yes

b) no

Solution

a

17.56 What value will be displayed in an alert box as the result of this code?

```
<script>
  var str1 = "Four score and seven";
  var charPosition = str1.search("R", 2);
  alert(charPosition);
</script>
```

Solution

-1

17.57 What value will be displayed in an alert box as the result of this code?

```
<script>
  var str1 = "It's raining out";
  var charPosition = str1.search(/rain/);
  alert(charPosition);
</script>
```

Solution

5

17.58 What value will be displayed in an alert box as the result of this code?

```
<script>
  var str1 = "It's raining out";
  var charPosition = str1.search(/Rain/);
  alert(charPosition);
</script>
```

Solution

-1

17.159 What value will be displayed in an alert box as the result of this code?

```
<script>
  var str1 = "It's raining out";
  var charPosition = str1.search(/Rain/i);
  alert(charPosition);
</script>
```

Solution

5

17.60 Write the code to accomplish the following:

1) Create a string variable called **str1** and initialize it with the value "What month is this?"
2) Create a variable called **charPosition** and use the **search()** method to find the starting position of the first (and only) occurrence of "month" in **str1**.
3) Display the value of **charPosition** in an alert box.

Solution
```
<script>
  var str1 = "What month is this?";
  var charPosition = str1.search("month");
  alert(charPosition);
</script>
```

Result displayed in browser:
5

17.61 Write the code to accomplish the following:

1) Create a string variable called **str1** and initialize it with the value "My name is BOB".
2) Create a variable called **charPosition** and use the **search()** method to find the starting position of the first (and only) occurrence of "BOB" in **str1**.
3) Display the value of **charPosition** in an alert box.

Solution
```
<script>
  var str1 = "My name is BOB";
  var charPosition = str1.search("BOB");
  alert(charPosition);
</script>
```

Result displayed in browser:
11

17.62 Write the code to accomplish the following:

1) Create a string variable called **x** and initialize it with the value "It is now 8:15".
2) Create a string variable called **y** and initialize it with the value "now".
3) Create a variable called **z** and use the **search()** method to find the starting position of the first (and only) occurrence of "now" in the string variable **x**. Use the string variable **y** as the **searchvalue** parameter.
3) Display the value of **z** in an alert box.

Solution
```
<script>
```

```
var x = "It is now 8:15";
  var y = "now";
  var z = x.search(y);
  alert(z);
</script>
```

Result displayed in browser:
11

17.63 Write the code to accomplish the following:

1) Create a string variable called **phrase** and initialize it with the value "Today is the day".
2) Create a variable called **position** and use the **search()** method to find the starting position of the first (and only) occurrence of "the" in **phrase**. Use a regular expression as for the *searchvalue* parameter.
3) Display the value of **position** in an alert box.

Solution
```
<script>
  var phrase = "Today is the day";
  var position = phrase.search(/the/);
  alert(position);
</script>
```

Result displayed in browser:
9

17.64 Write the code to accomplish the following:

1) Create a string variable called **x** and initialize it with the value "Today is the day".
2) Create a variable called **y** and use the **search()** method to find the starting position of the first occurrence of "BUT" in the string variable **x**. Use a regular expression as for the *searchvalue* parameter.
3) Display the value of **position** in an alert box.

Solution
```
<script>
  var x = "Life is but a dream";
  var y = x.search(/BUT/);
  alert(y);
</script>
```

Result displayed in browser:
-1

17.65 Write the code to accomplish the following:

Same as problem 8-151 but make the search case insensitive

Solution
```
<script>
  var x = "Life is but a dream";
  var y = x.search(/BUT/i);
  alert(y);
</script>
```

Result displayed in browser:

8

17.66 What does the **slice()** method do?

a) it slices a string in half and returns the halves as 2 new strings

b) it extracts parts of a string and returns the extracted parts as a new string

c) it slices out part of a string and discards it

Solution

b

17.67 How many parameters does the **slice()** method have?

a) 0

b) 1

c) 2

Solution

c

17.68 What are the **slice()** methods 2 parameters?

a) *start, end*

b) *start, searchvalue*

c) *slice, end*

Solution

a

17.69 Is the **slice()** method's *start* parameter required or optional?

a) required
b) optional

Solution
a

17.70 Is the **slice()** method's *end* parameter required or optional?

a) required
b) optional

Solution
b

17.71 What does the **slice()** method's *start* parameter represent?

a) how many characters to extract
b) the position where the substring extraction ends
c) the position where the substring extraction begins

Solution
c

17.72 What does the **slice()** method's *end* parameter represent?

a) the position (up to but including) where the extraction ends
b) the position (up to but including) where the extraction begins
c) the last position in the string that's being searched

Solution
a

17.73 What happens if you don't supply an *end* parameter for the **slice()** method?

a) an error message will be displayed
b) the entire string will be selected
c) all characters will be selected from the start position to the end of the string

Solution
c

17.74 Which of the following is the correct syntax model for the **slice()** method?

a) *string*.slice(*start, end*)

b) slice.*string*(*end, start*)

c) slice.*string*(*start, end*)

Solution

a

17.75 What characters will be sliced out from **str1** and returned by the **slice()** method in the following examples:

a) var str1 = "It's hot outside";
   var str2 = str1.slice(0);

b) var str1 = "It's hot outside";
   var str2 = str1.slice(8);

c) var str1 = "It's hot outside";
   var str2 = str1.slice(0, 6);

d) var str1 = "It's hot outside";
   var str2 = str1.slice(5);

e) var str1 = "It's hot outside";
   var str2 = str1.slice(5, 8);

f) var str1 = "It's hot outside";
   var str2 = str1.slice(9, 20);

Solution

a) It's hot outside

b) outside

c) It's h

d) hot outside

e) hot

f) outside

17.76 What would you use if you wanted to start the search for the characters to be selected by the **slice()** method from the end of the string being searched through?

a) you can't do it

b) a negative number, starting with -1

c) a positive number

Solution

a

17.77 What characters will be sliced out from **str1** and returned as **str2** by the **slice()** method in the following examples:

a) var str1 = "Who's that girl?";
   var str2 = str1.slice(-1);

b) var str1 = "Who's that girl?";
   var str2 = str1.slice(-5);

c) var str1 = "Who's that girl?";
   var str2 = str1.slice(-10, -7);

d) var str1 = "Who's that girl?";
   var str2 = str1.slice(-16);

e) var str1 = "Who's that girl?";
   var str2 = str1.slice(-10, -2);

f) var str1 = "Who's that girl?";
   var str2 = str1.slice(-30);

g) var str1 = "Who's that girl?";
   var str2 = str1.slice(-50, -11);

Solution

a) ?
b) girl?
c) tha
d) Who's that girl?
e) that gir
f) Who's that girl?
g) Who's

17.78 Write the code to accomplish the following:

1) Create a string variable called **str1** and initialize it with the value "My name is Jackson".

2) Create a variable called **str2** and use the **slice()** method to select all characters from position 11 to the end of **str1**. Assign the value of the result to **str2**. Don't use an *end* parameter.

3) Display the value of **str2** in an alert box.

Solution

```
<script>
  var str1 = "My name is Jackson";
  var str2 = str1.slice(11);
  alert(str2);
</script>
```

Result displayed in browser:

Jackson

17.79 Write the code to accomplish the following:

Same as problem 8-166 but use a start and end parameter to achieve the same result

Solution
```
<script>
  var str1 = "My name is Jackson";
  var str2 = str1.slice(11, 18);
  alert(str2);
</script>
```

Result displayed in browser:
Jackson

17.80 Write the code to accomplish the following:

Same as problem 8-166 but start the search from the end of the string and only use a **start** parameter

Solution
```
<script>
  var str1 = "My name is Jackson";
  var str2 = str1.slice(-7);
  alert(str2);
</script>
```

Result displayed in browser:
Jackson

17.81 Write the code to accomplish the following:

1) Create a string variable called **str1** and initialize it with the value "I'm 50 years old today".
2) Create a variable called **str2** and use the **slice()** method to slice out the string "I'm". Assign the value
   returned by the **slice()** method to **str2**. Use both the *start* and *end* parameters.
3) Display the value of **str2** in an alert box.

Solution
```
<script>
  var str1 = "I'm 50 years old today";
  var str2 = str1.slice(0, 3);
  alert(str2);
</script>
```

Result displayed in browser:
I'm

17.82 Write the code to accomplish the following:

1) Create a string variable called **str1** and initialize it with the value "What planet is this?".
2) Create a variable called **str2** and use the **slice()** method to slice out the entire string using only a start parameter. Assign the value returned by the **slice()** method to **str2**.
3) Display the value of **str2** in an alert box.

Solution
```
<script>
  var str1 = "What planet is this?";
  var str2 = str1.slice(0);
  alert(str2);
</script>
```

Result displayed in browser:
What planet is this?

17.83 Write the code to accomplish the following:

Same as problem 17-82 but use both a *start* and an *end* parameter.

Solution
```
<script>
  var str1 = "My name is Jackson";
  var str2 = str1.slice(0, 20);
  alert(str2);
</script>
```

Result displayed in browser:
Jackson

17.84 Write the code to accomplish the following:

Same as problem 17-82 but use a negative **start** parameter and no **end** parameter.

Solution
```
<script>
  var str1 = "My name is Jackson";
  var str2 = str1.slice(-20);
  alert(str2);
</script>
```

Result displayed in browser:
Jackson

17.85 Write the code to accomplish the following:

1) Create a string variable called **str1** and initialize it with the value "Today is Sunday".
2) Create a variable called **str2** and use the **slice()** method to slice out the string "Sun". Use negative start and end parameters.
3) Display the value of **str2** in an alert box.

Solution

```
<script>
  var str1 = "Today is Sunday"
  var str2 = str1.slice(-6, -3);
  alert(str2);
</script>
```

Result displayed in browser:

Sun

Chapter 18

JavaScript Strings: Part 4

18.1 MORE JAVASCRIPT STRING METHODS

18.1.1 split ()

The **split()** method is used to split a string into an **array** of substrings, and returns the new array. If an empty string ("") is used as the separator, the string is split between each character. The **split()** method does not change the original string.

Syntax

```
string.split(separator, limit)
```

Parameter Values

Parameter	Description
separator	Optional. Specifies the character, or the regular expression, to use for splitting the string. If omitted, the entire string will be returned.
limit	Optional. An integer that specifies the number of splits, items after the split limit will not be included.

The result of the **split** method is an array of strings split at each point where *separator* occurs in the string. The *separator* is not returned as part of any array element.

An **array** is a variable that can be used to store multiple values. This is its main difference from a regular variable that can only hold one value. Each individual value in an array is referred to as an element. The elements are contained in individual compartments that are referenced by index numbers starting with 0. In other words, the first value entered into an array will be stored at index 0 and the fifth element entered into an array will be stored at index 4. In the following examples, we will create arrays and then access the values contained in them both one at a time and collectively (arrays will be covered in much more detail in a later chapter):

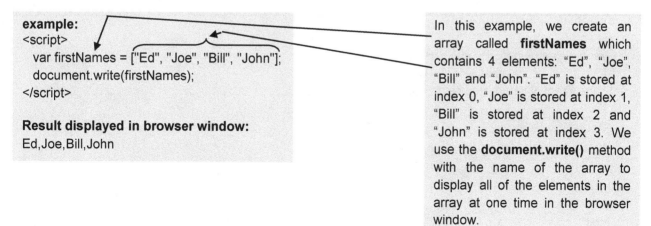

example:
```
<script>
  var firstNames = ["Ed", "Joe", "Bill", "John"];
  document.write(firstNames);
</script>
```

Result displayed in browser window:
Ed,Joe,Bill,John

In this example, we create an array called **firstNames** which contains 4 elements: "Ed", "Joe", "Bill" and "John". "Ed" is stored at index 0, "Joe" is stored at index 1, "Bill" is stored at index 2 and "John" is stored at index 3. We use the **document.write()** method with the name of the array to display all of the elements in the array at one time in the browser window.

The following is a pictorial representation of the **firstNames** array:

firstNames array

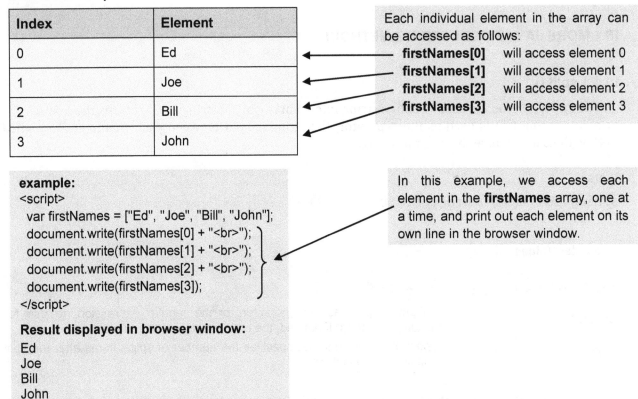

Index	Element
0	Ed
1	Joe
2	Bill
3	John

Each individual element in the array can be accessed as follows:

firstNames[0]   will access element 0
firstNames[1]   will access element 1
firstNames[2]   will access element 2
firstNames[3]   will access element 3

example:
```
<script>
  var firstNames = ["Ed", "Joe", "Bill", "John"];
  document.write(firstNames[0] + "<br>");
  document.write(firstNames[1] + "<br>");
  document.write(firstNames[2] + "<br>");
  document.write(firstNames[3]);
</script>
```

In this example, we access each element in the **firstNames** array, one at a time, and print out each element on its own line in the browser window.

Result displayed in browser window:
Ed
Joe
Bill
John

The number of elements in an array can be determined by accessing its **length** property. For example, **firstNames.length** in the example below would return 4 since there are 4 elements in the array. As we've seen, the index values in a 4-element array run from 0 to 3. This allows us to use a **for** loop to loop through the array using the variable **i** (or any other variable) as both the counter and as the index value and to continue looping as long as **i** is less than the length of the array. The highest index in the **firstnames** array is 3 and the length of the array is 4. So, when the **for** loop reaches 4 (the array length value) the loop should stop because there are no more elements after index 3. This can be seen in the following example:

example:
```
<script>
  var firstNames = ["Ed", "Joe", "Bill", "John"];
  for(i = 0; i < firstNames.length; i++) {
    document.write(firstNames[i] + "<br>");
  }
</script>
```

Result displayed in browser window:
Ed
Joe
Bill
John

We'll be considering arrays in much more depth in a later chapter but this brief introduction will help us to understand what's going on with the **split()** method's use of arrays.

examples of the split() method:

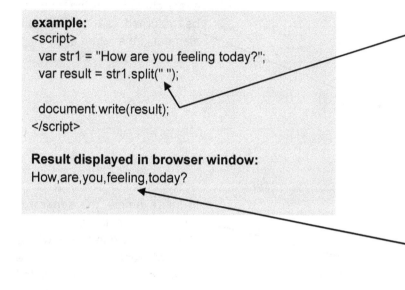

example:
```
<script>
 var str1 = "How are you feeling today?";
 var result = str1.split(" ");

 document.write(result);
</script>
```

Result displayed in browser window:
How,are,you,feeling,today?

In this example, the **separator** parameter is a single blank space, so, each blank space in the string is used to demarcate where each element in the returned array ends. Also the rest of the characters after the last separator are returned as an individual array element. Since no **limit** parameter is included after the **separator** parameter, the entire string will be split into array elements. As you can see, each element array is returned with all individual elements separated by commas. Since there are 4 blank spaces, the result will be an array containing 5 elements.

example:
```
<script>
 var str1 = "How are you feeling today?";
 var result = str1.split(" ", 3);
 document.write(result);
</script>
```

Result displayed in alert box:
How,are,you

This example is almost identical to the above example except that a *limit* parameter value of 3 is included. This means that none of the string after the third separator is returned as part of the return array. Since the third blank space appears after "you", only "How", "are" and "you" are included in the return array.

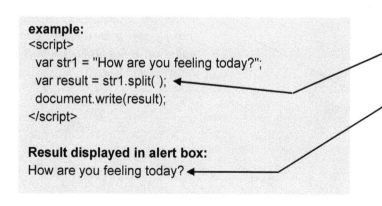

example:
```
<script>
 var str1 = "How are you feeling today?";
 var result = str1.split( );
 document.write(result);
</script>
```

Result displayed in alert box:
How are you feeling today?

In this example, the **separator** parameter has been omitted so the entire string is returned in an array with only 1 element – "How are you feeling today?"

example:
```
<script>
  var str1= "How are you feeling today?";
  var result = str1.split("");

  document.write(result);
</script>
```

Result displayed in alert box:
H,o,w, ,a,r,e, ,y,o,u, ,d,o,i,n,g, ,t,o,d,a,y,?

In this example, the **separator** parameter consists of 2 quotation marks with nothing between them. This causes every character in the string to be returned as a separate element in the return array.

example:
```
<script>
  var str1 = "How are you feeling today?";
  var result = str1.split("o");
  document.write(result);
</script>
```

Result displayed in alert box:
H,w are y,u feeling t,day?

In this example, the **separator** parameter value is "o". The string is separated everywhere an "o" appears, plus the separator value is not included as part of any of the return array elements. The separator value is never included in the return array.

example:
```
<script>
  var str1 = "How are you feeling today?";

  var result = str1.split(" ");
  document.write(result[0] + "<br>");
  document.write(result[1] + "<br>");
  document.write(result[2] + "<br>");
  document.write(result[3] + "<br>");
  document.write(result[4]);
</script>
```
Result displayed in alert box:
How
are
you
feeling
today?

In this example we again use a blank space as the value for the **separator** parameter. As in a previous example, this results in an array with 5 elements being returned. Instead of displaying all 5 elements at once, we access each element individually and display each value on a separate line in the browser window.

example:
```
<script>
  var str1 = "How are you feeling today?";
  var result = str1.split(" ");
  for(i = 0;i < result.length;i++) {
    document.write(result[i] + "<br>");
  }
</script>
```

This is the same as the previous example except that we use a **for** loop to loop through the array and display each element individually on its own line in the browser window. (See section 7.2, pages 293-297 for information on **for** loops)

Result displayed in alert box:
How
are
you
feeling
today?

example:
```
<script>
  var str1 = "How are you feeling today?";
  var result = str1.split(" ");
  var i = 0;
  while (i < result.length) {
    document.write(result[i] + "<br>");
    i++;
  }
</script>
```

Same as above but use a **while** loop instead of a **for** loop. (See section 7.3, pages 308-311 for information on **while** loops)

Result displayed in alert box:
How
are
you
feeling
today?

example:
```
<script>
  var str1 = "How are you feeling today? I hope you're OK.";
  var result = str1.split(" ");
  var i = 0;
  do {
    document.write(result[i] + "<br>");
    i++;
  }
  while (i < result.length);
</script>
```

Same as above but use a **do/while** loop instead of a **for** loop. (See section 7.3, pages 321-325 for information on **do/while** loops)

continued on next page

Result displayed in alert box:
How
are
you
feeling
today?
I
hope
you're
OK.

18.1.2 substr ()

The **substr()** method extracts parts of a string, beginning at the character at the specified position, and returns the specified number of characters. To extract characters from the end of the string, use a negative start number. The **substr()** method does not change the original string. If the length parameter is not specified, the entire string from the start position will be extracted.

Syntax

```
string.substr(start,length)
```

Parameter Values

Parameter	Description
start	Required. The position where to start the extraction. First character is at index 0
length	Optional. The number of characters to extract. If omitted, it extracts the rest of the string

examples of the substr() method:

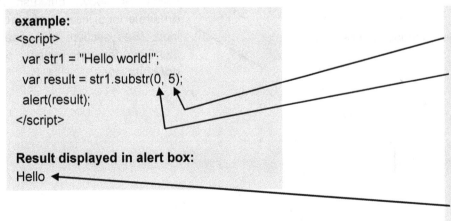

example:
```
<script>
 var str1 = "Hello world!";
 var result = str1.substr(0, 5);
 alert(result);
</script>
```

Result displayed in alert box:
Hello

In this example the **substr()** method is used to extract 5 characters starting at character position 0. The **start** parameter is set to 0, so, the character extraction begins at "H". The **length** parameter is set to 5, so, 5 characters, starting with "H" are extracted. This results in "Hello" being returned by the **substr()** method.

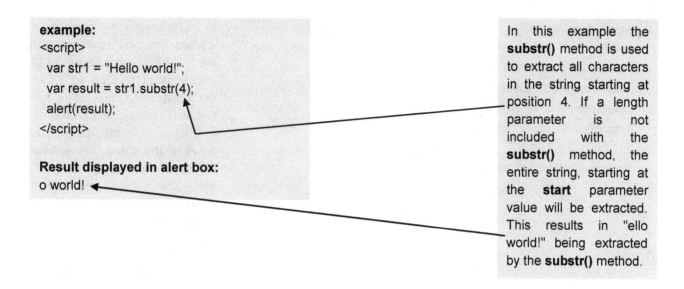

example:
```
<script>
 var str1 = "Hello world!";
 var result = str1.substr(4);
 alert(result);
</script>
```

Result displayed in alert box:
o world!

In this example the **substr()** method is used to extract all characters in the string starting at position 4. If a length parameter is not included with the **substr()** method, the entire string, starting at the **start** parameter value will be extracted. This results in "ello world!" being extracted by the **substr()** method.

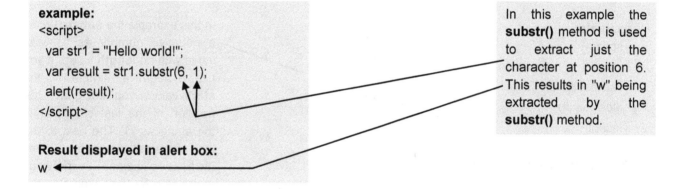

example:
```
<script>
 var str1 = "Hello world!";
 var result = str1.substr(6, 1);
 alert(result);
</script>
```

Result displayed in alert box:
w

In this example the **substr()** method is used to extract just the character at position 6. This results in "w" being extracted by the **substr()** method.

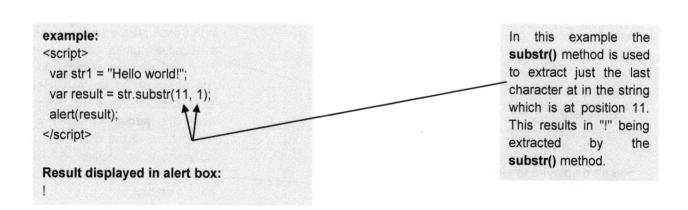

example:
```
<script>
 var str1 = "Hello world!";
 var result = str.substr(11, 1);
 alert(result);
</script>
```

Result displayed in alert box:
!

In this example the **substr()** method is used to extract just the last character at in the string which is at position 11. This results in "!" being extracted by the **substr()** method.

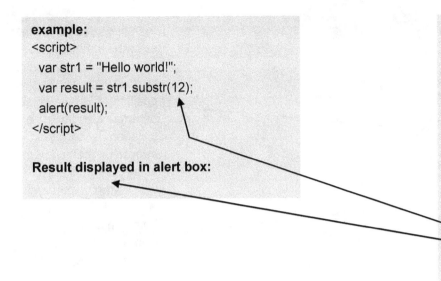

example:
```
<script>
 var str1 = "Hello world!";
 var result = str1.substr(12);
 alert(result);
</script>
```

Result displayed in alert box:

In this example the string being worked on by the **substr()** method begins at position 0 ("H") and ends at position 11 ("!"). If the **start** parameter value in a **substr()** method is positive and is greater than the last position value of the string, the **substr()** will return an empty string (""). SInce the last character position in **str1** is 11 and the **start** value for the **substr()** method is 12, the **substr()** method will return an empty string ("") and nothing will be displayed in the alert box.

example:
```
<script>
 var str1 = "Hello world!";
 var result = str1.substr(-1);
 alert(result);
</script>
```

Result displayed in alert box:
!

In this example the **substr()** uses a negative number as its *start* value with no **length** value. If you use a negative number as the **start** value, you designate the position of the last character in the string as -1. The next to the last character would be -2, etc (just as explained in previous methods). In this example, the extraction starts at the last character position in the string, The result is that "!" is displayed in the alert box.

example:
```
<script>
 var str1 = "Hello world!";
 var result = str1.substr(-6);
 alert(result);
</script>
```

Result displayed in alert box:
world!

In this example the **substr()** uses a negative number as its **start** value (-6) with no **length** value. The character at position -6 is "w". Since there is no length value, the **substr()** method will also extract all the characters in the string after position -6. The result is that "world!" is displayed in the alert box.

example:
```
<script>
 var str1 = "Hello world!";
 var result = str1.substr(-6, 3);
 alert(result);
</script>
```

Result displayed in alert box:
wor

In this example the **substr()** uses a negative number (-6) as its *start* value and 3 as its *length* value. The character at position -6 is "w". Since length value is 3 , the **substr()** method will extract 3 characters startng at position -6. The result is that "wor" is displayed in the alert box.

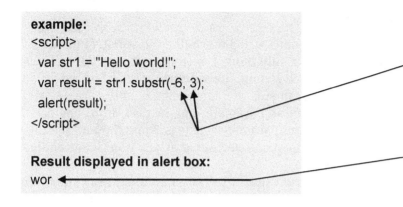

example:
```
<script>
 var str1 = "Hello world!";
 var result = str1.substr(-12);
 alert(result);
</script>
```

Result displayed in alert box:
Hello world!

In this example the **substr()** uses a negative number (-12) as its *start* value and no *length* value. The first character in the string ("H") is at position -12, so, in this case, the **substr()** method will start at "H" and extract the entire string. The result is that "Hello world!" is displayed in the alert box. Remember that if the **substr()** method uses a negative number as its **start** value and doesn't have a **length** value, the entire string from the start position forward will be extracted.

example:
```
<script>
 var str1 = "Hello world!";
 var result = str1.substr(-50);
 alert(result);
</script>
```

Result displayed in alert box:
Hello world!

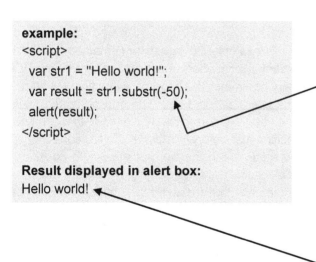

If a negative **start** value is used in the **substr()** method that has a greater absolute value than the negative character position of the left-most character in the string, the entire string will be extracted. In this example, the left-most character in the string ("H") has a negative character position of -12. The negative **start** position that were using in this example (-50) is greater that the negative character position of the left-most character in the string, therefore, the entire string is extracted. This results in "Hello world!" being displayed in the alert box.

18.1.3 substring ()

The **substring()** method extracts the characters from a string much like the **substr()** method. But instead of having a **start** and **length** parameter, the **substring()** method extracts the characters between two specified indices, and returns the new sub string. The **substring()** method extracts the characters in a string between a required **start** parameter and an optional **end** parameter. The extraction doesn't include the position indicated by the **end** parameter but, instead, stops one position before the **end** parameter value. For example, if the **start** parameter value is 3 and the **end** parameter value is 7, the **substring()** method will extract the sub string beginning at position 3 and ending at position 6.

If the value of the start parameter is greater than the value of the end parameter, the **substring()** method will swap the two arguments. For example, **str.substring(4,1)** would be replaced with **str.substring(1,4).** If either the value of the **start** parameter or the value of the **end** parameter is less than 0, it is treated as if it were 0. The **substring()** method does not change the original string. The **substring()** method cannot use negative numbers to designate the characters to be extracted as the **substr()** method does. If the *end* parameter is omitted, the entire string, starting from the **start** position will be extracted.

Syntax

```
string.substring(start,end)
```

Parameter Values

Parameter	Description
start	Required. The position where to start the extraction. First character is at index 0.
end	Optional. The position (up to, but not including) where to end the extraction. If omitted, it extracts the rest of the string.

examples of the substring() method:

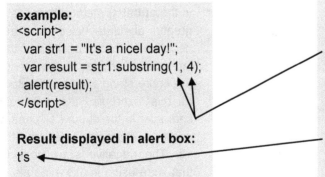

example:
```
<script>
 var str1 = "It's a nicel day!";
 var result = str1.substring(1, 4);
 alert(result);
</script>
```

Result displayed in alert box:

t's

In this example the **substring()** method is used to extract 3 characters from **str1**. The value of the **start** parameter is 1, so, the extraction will start at character position 1 ("t"). The **end** parameter value is 4, so, the extraction will end at the character position just before position 4. This means that the extraction will occur from position 1 to position 3. This results in "t's" being displayed in the alert box. Remember that the extraction doesn't include the position indicated by the **end** parameter but, instead, stops one position before the **end** parameter value. For example, if the start parameter value is 3 and the end parameter value is 7, the **substring()** method will extract the sub string beginning at position 3 and ending at position 6.

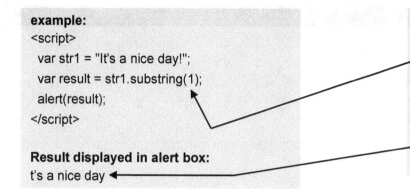

example:
```
<script>
 var str1 = "It's a nice day!";
 var result = str1.substring(1);
 alert(result);
</script>
```

Result displayed in alert box:
t's a nice day

In this example the **substring()** method is used to start the sub string extraction at character position 1. Since no **end** parameter is given, the **substring()** method will also extract all of the characters in the string after the initial start position. This will result in "t's a nicel day!" being displayed in the alert box.

example:
```
<script>
 var str1 = "It's a nice day!";
 var result = str1.substring(7, 11);
 alert(result);
</script>
```

Result displayed in alert box:
nice

In this example the **substring()** method is used to extract 4 characters from **str1**. The value of the **start** parameter is 7, so, the extraction will start at character position 7 ("n"). The **end** parameter value is 11, so, the extraction will end at the character position just before position 11. This means that the extraction will occur from position 7 to position 10. This results in "nice" being displayed in the alert box.

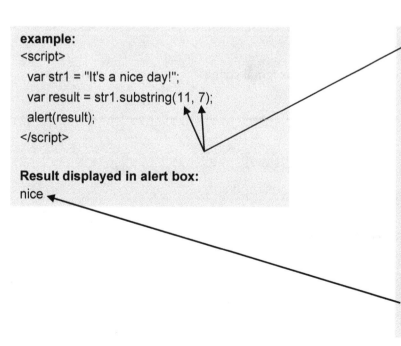

example:
```
<script>
 var str1 = "It's a nice day!";
 var result = str1.substring(11, 7);
 alert(result);
</script>
```

Result displayed in alert box:
nice

In this example the **start** parameter value is greater than the **end** parameter value so the **substring()** method will automatically swap the 2 values so that we end up with the same problem as in the above example: **str1.substring(7, 11).** After the swap is completed by the **substring()** method, the extraction will start at character position 7 ("n"). The **end** parameter value is 11, so, the extraction will end at the character position just before position 11. This means that the extraction will occur from position 7 to position 10. This results in "nice" being displayed in the alert box.

SOLVED PROBLEMS

18.1 The **split()** method is used to do what?

a) split a string into 2 substrings of equal length
b) split a string into an array of substrings
c) split a string into 3 substrings of varying lengths

Solution
b

18.2 How many parameters does the **split()** method have?

a) 2
b) 1
c) 3

Solution
a

18.3 What are the names of the **split()** method's 2 parameters?

a) *start, limit*
b) *separator, limit*
c) *start, end*

Solution
b

18.4 Does the **split()** method make any changes to the original string?

a) yes
b) no

Solution
b

8.5 Is the **separator** parameter optional or required?

a) required
b) optional

Solution
b

18.6 Is the **limit** parameter required or optional?
a) required
b) optional

Solution
b

18.7 What does the **separator** parameter specify in the **split()** method?
a) how many substrings are contained in the returned substring array
b) an integer that specifies the number of splits that are made in the original string
c) the character, or regular expression, to use to indicate where the string should be split

Solution
c

18.8 What does the **limit** parameter specify in the **split()** method?
a) how many substrings are contained in the returned substring array
b) an integer that specifies the number of splits that are made in the original string
c) the character, or regular expression, to use to indicate where the string should be split

Solution
b

18.9 Are any characters after the final split, as indicated by the **limit** parameter in the **split()** method, included in the returned array of substrings?
a) yes
b) no

Solution
b

18.10 Which one of the following is the correct syntax model for the **split()** method?
a) *string*.split(*limit, separator*)
b) split(*string, separator*)
c) *string*.split(*separator, limit*)

Solution
c

18.11 What is returned if no parameters are included with the **split()** method?
a) the entire string will be returned
b) an error message will be displayed
c) nothing will be returned

Solution
a

18.12 What is returned by the **split()** method?
a) an array of strings of equal length
b) an array of strings that are split off from the original string at each point where the *separator* value occurs in the original string
c) an array of strings that are split off from the original string at each point where the *limit* value occurs in the original string

Solution
b

18.13 Is the **separator** value included as any part of the returned array with the **split()** method?
a) yes
b) no
c) sometimes

Solution
b

18.14 What is an array?
a) a group of strings with similar names
b) a variable that can be used to store a maximum of 10 values
c) a variable that can be used to store multiple values

Solution
c

8.15 How many values can a regular variable hold?
a) 1
b) multiple
c) 10

Solution
a

18.16 Each individual value in an array is called an:
a) index
b) string
c) element

Solution
c

18.17 How is each individual element in an array referenced?
a) by index numbers starting with 0
b) by index numbers starting with 1
c) by even numbered index values starting with 2

Solution
a

18.18 The 3rd value stored in an array will be referenced by what index number?
a) 3
b) 4
c) 2

Solution
c

18.19 The 1st value stored in an array will be referenced by what index number?
a) 0
b) 1
c) -1

Solution
c

18.20 Write the code to accomplish the following:

1) Create an array called **directions** that has the following 4 elements:

Index	Element
0	North
1	East
2	South
3	West

Solution

```
<script>
  var directions = ["North", "East", "South", "West"];
</script>
```

18.21 Write the code to accomplish the following:

1) Create an array called **lastNames** that has the following 4 elements:

Index	Element
0	Smith
1	Jones
2	Miller
3	Williams

Solution

```
<script>
  var lastName = ["Smith", "Jones", "Miller", "WIlliams"];
</script>
```

18.22 Write the code to accomplish the following:

1) Create an array called **fruit** that has the following 3 elements:

Index	Element
0	apple
1	grape
2	banana

2) Display each individual element on its own line in the browser screen

Solution

```
<script>
  var fruit = ["apple", "grape", "banana"];
  document.write(fruit[0] + "<br>");
  document.write(fruit[1] + "<br>");
  document.write(fruit[2]);
</script>
```

Result displayed in browser:

apple
grape
banana

18.23 Write the code to accomplish the following:

1) Create an array called **beer** that has the following 4 elements:

Index	Element
0	Corona
1	Miller
2	Heineken
3	Bud

2) Display the length (the number of elements in the array) of the array in an alert box in the following way:

       "This array contains \<length of array\> elements."

Solution

```
<script>
  var beer = ["Corona", "Miller", "Heineken", "Bud"];
  alert("This array contains " + beer.length + " elements.");
</script>
```

Result displayed in browser:

This array contains 4 elements.

18.24 Write the code to accomplish the following:

1) Create an array called **cars** that has the following 4 elements:

Index	Element
0	Toyota
1	Ford
2	Nissan
3	Chevrolet

2) Use a **for** loop to display each element of the array on its own line in the browser window. Use **i** as the loop variable.

Solution
```
<script>
  var cars = ["Toyota", "Ford", "Jaguar", "Chevrolet"];
  for(i = 0; i < cars.length; i++) {
    document.write(cars[i] + "<br>");
  }
</script>
```

Result displayed in browser:
Toyota
Ford
Jaguar
Chevrolet

18.25 Same as problem **8-197**, but use a **while** loop.

Solution
```
<script>
  var cars = ["Toyota", "Ford", "Jaguar", "Chevrolet"];
  var i = 0;
  while(i < cars.length) {
    document.write(cars[i] + "<br>");
    i++;
  }
</script>
```

Result displayed in browser:
Toyota
Ford
Jaguar
Chevrolet

18.26 Same as problem **8-197**, but use a **do/while** loop.

Solution

```
<script>
  var cars = ["Toyota", "Ford", "Jaguar", "Chevrolet"];
  var i = 0;
  do{
    document.write(cars[i] + "<br>");
    i++;
  }
  while (i < cars.length);
</script>
```

Result displayed in browser:
Toyota
Ford
Jaguar
Chevrolet

18.27 Write the code to accomplish the following:

1) Create a string variable called **str1** with the value "Is it hot out today?"
2) Use the **split()** method with just a separator parameter to create a return array that contains each word in **str1** separated by a comma.

Solution

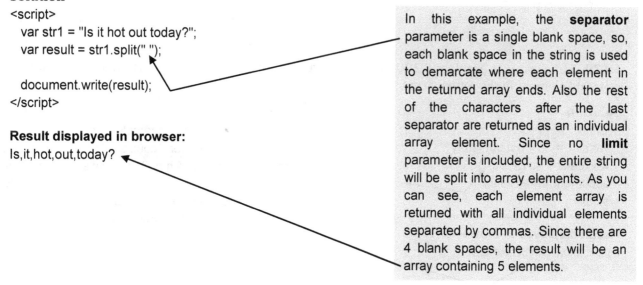

```
<script>
  var str1 = "Is it hot out today?";
  var result = str1.split(" ");

  document.write(result);
</script>
```

Result displayed in browser:
Is,it,hot,out,today?

In this example, the **separator** parameter is a single blank space, so, each blank space in the string is used to demarcate where each element in the returned array ends. Also the rest of the characters after the last separator are returned as an individual array element. Since no **limit** parameter is included, the entire string will be split into array elements. As you can see, each element array is returned with all individual elements separated by commas. Since there are 4 blank spaces, the result will be an array containing 5 elements.

18.28 Same array as problem **8.200** but use a limit parameter value that keeps the last word of **str1** from being returned in the return array.

Solution
```
<script>
  var str1 = "Is it hot out today?";
```

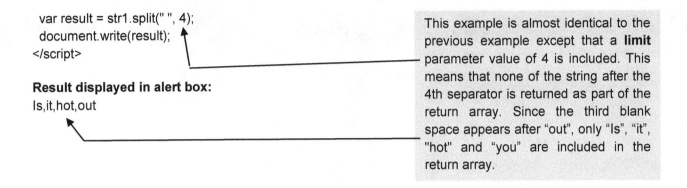

```
 var result = str1.split(" ", 4);
 document.write(result);
</script>
```

This example is almost identical to the previous example except that a **limit** parameter value of 4 is included. This means that none of the string after the 4th separator is returned as part of the return array. Since the third blank space appears after "out", only "Is", "it", "hot" and "you" are included in the return array.

Result displayed in alert box:
Is,it,hot,out

18.29 Same array as problem **8.200** but use the **split()** method to return the entire original string as the only element in the returned array.

Solution
```
<script>
 var str1 = "Is it hot out today?";
 var result = str1.split();
 document.write(result);
</script>
```

In this example, the **separator** parameter has been omitted so the entire string is returned in an array with only 1 element – "Is it hot out today?"

Result displayed in browser:
Is it hot out today?

18.30 Same array as problem **8.200** but use the **split()** method to return every character in **str1** as a separate element in the return array.

Solution
```
<script>
 var str1 = "Is it hot out today?";
 var result = str1.split("");
 document.write(result);
</script>
```

In this example, the **separator** parameter consists of 2 quotation marks with nothing between them. This causes every character in the string to be returned as a separate element in the return array.

Result displayed in browser:
I,s, ,i,t, ,h,o,t, ,o,u,t, ,t,o,d,a,y,?

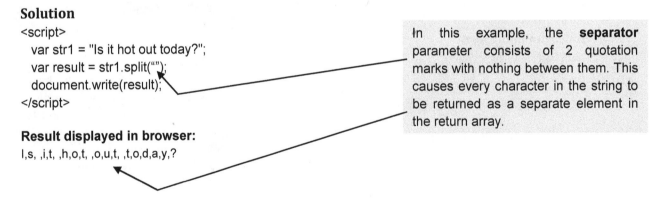

18.31 Same array as problem **18.30** but use the **split()** method to divide all of **str1** into several elements that are separated at the letter "o" with the separator value "o" being left out of the return array.

Solution
```
<script>
 var str1 = "Is it hot out today?";
```

```
  var result = str1.split("o");
  document.write(result);
</script>
```

Result displayed in alert box:

Is it h,t ,ut t,day?

18.32 Same array as problem **18.30** but use the **split()** method to display each word in **str1** on a separate line in the browser window.

Solution
```
<script>
  var str1 = "Is it hot out today?";
  var result = str1.split(" ");
  document.write(result[0] + "<br>");
  document.write(result[1] + "<br>");
  document.write(result[2] + "<br>");
  document.write(result[3] + "<br>");
  document.write(result[4]);
</script>
```

Result displayed in alert box:

Is
it
hot
out
today?

18.33 Same array as problem **18.30** but use a **for** loop to display each element in the returned array on its own separate line in the browser window. Use **i** as the loop variable.

Solution
```
<script>
  var str1 = "Is it hot out today?";
  var result = str1.split(" ");
  for(i = 0;i < result.length; i++) {
    document.write(result[i] + "<br>");
  }
</script>
```

Result displayed in alert box:

Is
it
hot
out
today?

18.34 Same array as problem **18.30** but use a **while** loop to display each element in the returned array on its own separate line in the browser window. Use **i** as the loop variable.

Solution

```
<script>
  var str1 = "Is it hot out today?";
  var result = str1.split(" ");
  var i = 0;
  while(i < result.length) {
    document.write(result[i] + "<br>");
    i++;
  }
</script>
```

Result displayed in alert box:

Is
it
hot
out
today?

18.35 Same array as problem **18.30** but use a **while** loop to display each element in the returned array on its own separate line in the browser window. Use **i** as the loop variable.

Solution

```
<script>
  var str1 = "Is it hot out today?";
  var result = str1.split(" ");
  var i = 0;
  do{
    document.write(result[i] + "<br>");
    i++;
  }
  while(i < result.length);
</script>
```

Result displayed in alert box:

Is
it
hot
out
today?

18.36 What does the **substr()** method do?

a) it extracts parts of a string, beginning at the character specified by the *start* parameter and returns the specified number of characters

b) it divides a string into substrings at the specified separator value

c) it returns each character in a string as a separate element in an array

Solution

a

18.37 Can you use the **substr()** method to extract characters that are referenced from the end of the string?

a) yes, by using a negative number

b) no

c) only under special circumstances

Solution

a

18.38 Does the **substr()** method make any changes to the original string?

a) yes

b) no

c) sometimes

Solution

b

18.39 How many parameters does the **substr()** method have?

a) 0

b) 1

c) 2

Solution

c

18.40 What are the 2 parameters of the **substr()** method?

a) *start, end*

b) *separator, limit*

c) *start, length*

Solution

c

18.41 Is the **start** parameter required or optional for the **substr()** method?

a) required

b) optional

Solution

a

18.42 Is the **length** parameter required or optional for the **substr()** method?

a) required

b) optional

Solution

b

18.43 Which of the following is the proper syntax model for the **substr()** method?

a) *string*(*start, length*)

b) *start.string*(substr, *length*)

c) *string*.substr(*start, length*)

Solution

c

18.44 What does the **start** parameter in the **substr()** method indicate?

a) the number of characters to extract

b) the position where to start the extraction

c) the value of the first character to be extracted

Solution

b

18.45 What does the **length** parameter in the **substr()** method indicate?

a) the number of characters to extract

b) the position where to start the extraction

c) the value of the first character to be extracted

Solution

b

18.46 What happens if the **length** parameter is omitted from the **substr()** method?

a) an error message is displayed

b) the rest of the string after the *start* character position is also extracted

c) only the character indicated by the start parameter will be extraced

Solution

b

18.47 What characters will be returned and displayed in an alert box as the result of the following code:

```
<script>
 var string1 = "Two plus two is four.";
 var result1 = string1.substr(0, 8);
 alert(result1);
</script>
```

a) Two plu

b) Two plus

c) wo plus

Solution

b

18.48 What characters will be returned and displayed in an alert box as the result of the following code:

```
<script>
 var string1 = "Two plus two is four.";
 var result1 = string1.substr(4);
 alert(result1);
</script>
```

a) p

b) Two

c) plus two is four.

Solution

c

18.49 What characters will be returned and displayed in an alert box as the result of the following code:

```
<script>
 var string1 = "Two plus two is four.";
 var result1 = string1.substr(9, 2);
 alert(result1);
</script>
```

a) tw
b) wo
c) t

Solution
a

18.50 What characters will be returned and displayed in an alert box as the result of the following code:

```
<script>
 var string1 = "Two plus two is four.";
 var result1 = string1.substr(25);
 alert(result1);
</script>
```

a) <nothing is displayed>
b) T
c) Two plus two is four.

Solution
b

18.51 What characters will be returned and displayed in an alert box as the result of the following code:

```
<script>
 var string1 = "Two plus two is four.";
 var result1 = string1.substr(-5);
 alert(result1);
</script>
```

a) Two p
b) f
c) four.

Solution

b

18.52 What characters will be returned and displayed in an alert box as the result of the following code:

```
<script>
  var string1 = "Two plus two is four.";
  var result1 = string1.substr(-5, 2);
  alert(result1);
</script>
```

a) or
b) fo
c) four

Solution

b

18.53 What characters will be returned and displayed in an alert box as the result of the following code:

```
<script>
  var string1 = "Two plus two is four.";
  var result1 = string1.substr(-21);
  alert(result1);
</script>
```

a) <error message>
b) <nothing will be displayed>
c) Two plus two is four.

Solution

c

18.54 Write the code to accomplish the following:

1) Create a string variable called **originalString** and give it the value "To be or not to be".

2) Create a string variable called **extractedString**. Use a **substr()** method to extract "To be" from originalString. Use a **start** and **length** parameter. Put the value returned by the **substr()** method into **extractedString**.

3) Display the value of **extractedString** in an alert box.

Solution
```
<script>
 var originalString = "To be or not to be";
 var extractedString = originalString.substr(0, 5);
 alert(extractedString);
</script
```

Result displayed in alert box:
To be

18.55 Write the code to accomplish the following:
1) Create a string variable called **originalString** and give it the value "To be or not to be".
2) Create a string variable called **extractedString**. Use a **substr()** method to extract "To be" from **originalString**. Use a **start** and **length** parameter. Put the value returned by the **substr()** method into **extractedString**.
3) Display the value of **extractedString** in an alert box.

Solution
```
<script>
 var originalString = "To be or not to be";
 var extractedString = originalString.substr(0, 5);
 alert(extractedString);
</script
```

Result displayed in alert box:
To be

18.56 Write the code to accomplish the following:
1) Create a string variable called **originalString** and give it the value "To be or not to be".
2) Create a string variable called **extractedString**. Use a **substr()** method to extract "or not to be" from **originalString**. Use only a **start** parameter. Put the value returned by the **substr()** method into **extractedString**.
3) Display the value of **extractedString** in an alert box.

Solution
```
<script>
 var originalString = "To be or not to be";
 var extractedString = originalString.substr(6);
 alert(extractedString);
```

</script

Result displayed in alert box:

or not to be

18.57 Write the code to accomplish the following:
1) Create a string variable called **originalString** and give it the value "To be or not to be".
2) Create a string variable called **extractedString**. Use a **substr()** method to extract "not" from **originalString**. Use a **start** and **length** parameter. Put the value returned by the **substr()** method into **extractedString**.
3) Display the value of **extractedString** in an alert box.

Solution
```
<script>
 var originalString = "To be or not to be";
 var extractedString = originalString.substr(9, 3);
 alert(extractedString);
</script>
```

Result displayed in alert box:

not

18.58 Write the code to accomplish the following:
1) Create a string variable called **originalString** and give it the value "To be or not to be".
2) Create a string variable called **extractedString**. Use a **substr()** method to extract the last character from **originalString**. Use only a **start** parameter. Put the value returned by the **substr()** method into **extractedString**.
3) Display the value of **extractedString** in an alert box.

Solution
```
<script>
 var originalString = "To be or not to be";
 var extractedString = originalString.substr(9, 3);
 alert(extractedString);
</script>
```

Result displayed in alert box:

not

18.59 Write the code to accomplish the following:
1) Create a string variable called **x** and give it the value "You are so beautiful!".
2) Create a string variable called **y**. Use a **substr()** method to extract the first character from **originalString**. Use a **start** and **length** parameter. Put the value returned by the **substr()** method into the variable **extractedString**.
3) Display the value of **extractedString** in an alert box.

Solution
```
<script>
 var x = "You are so beautiful!";
 var y = x.substr(0, 1);
 alert(y);
</script>
```

Result displayed in alert box:
Y

18.61 Write the code to accomplish the following:
1) Create a string variable called **x** and give it the value "You are so beautiful!".
2) Create a string variable called **y**. Use a **substr()** method to extract the last character from **originalString**. Use a negative **start** and no **length** parameter. Put the value returned by the **substr()** method into the variable **extractedString**.
3) Display the value of **extractedString** in an alert box.

Solution
```
<script>
 var x = "You are so beautiful!";
 var y = x.substr(-1);
 alert(y);
</script>
```

Result displayed in alert box:
!

18.62 Write the code to accomplish the following:
1) Create a string variable called **x** and give it the value "You are so beautiful!".
2) Create a string variable called **y**. Use a **substr()** method to extract the "beautiful!" from **originalString**. Use a negative **start** and no **length** parameter. Put the value returned by the **substr()** method into the variable **extractedString**.
3) Display the value of **extractedString** in an alert box.

Solution

```
<script>
 var x = "You are so beautiful!";
 var y = x.substr(-10);
 alert(y);
</script>
```

Result displayed in alert box:

beautiful!

18.63 Write the code to accomplish the following:
1) Create a string variable called **x** and give it the value "You are so beautiful!".
2) Create a string variable called **y**. Use a **substr()** method to extract the "beautiful!" from
   originalString. Use a negative **start** and a positive **length** parameter. Put the value returned by the
   substr() method into the variable **extractedString**.
3) Display the value of **extractedString** in an alert box.

Solution
```
<script>
 var x = "You are so beautiful!";
 var y = x.substr(-10, 10);
 alert(y);
</script>
```

Result displayed in alert box:

beautiful!

18.64 Write the code to accomplish the following:
1) Create a string variable called **x** and give it the value "You are so beautiful!".
2) Create a string variable called **y**. Use a **substr()** method to extract the "so" from
   originalString. Use a negative **start** and a positive **length** parameter. Put the value returned by the
   substr() method into the variable **extractedString**.
3) Display the value of **extractedString** in an alert box.

Solution
```
<script>
 var x = "You are so beautiful!";
 var y = x.substr(-10, 10);
 alert(y);
</script>
```

Result displayed in alert box:

beautiful!

18.65 Write the code to accomplish the following:
1) Create a string variable called **x** and give it the value "You are so beautiful!".
2) Create a string variable called **y**. Use a **substr()** method to extract the the entire string from **originalString**. Use a negative **start** parameter and no **length** parameter. Put the value returned by the **substr()** method into the variable **extractedString**.
3) Display the value of **extractedString** in an alert box.

Solution
```
<script>
 var x = "You are so beautiful!";
 var y = x.substr(-10, 10);
 alert(y);
</script>
```

Result displayed in alert box:
beautiful!

18.66 What does the **substring()** method do?

a) it works exactly the same as the **substr()** method
b) it extracts the characters between 2 specified index values
c) it divides a string into substrings based on the value of the separator parameter

Solution
b

18.67 What are the **substring()** method's 2 parameters?

a) *start, end*
b) *start, length*
c) *length, separator*

Solution
a

18.68 Does the extraction performed by the **substring()** method include the character at the position indicated by the **end** parameter?

a) yes
b) no (the extraction stops 1 position before the character position indicated by the *end* parameter)

Solution
b

18.69 If the **star**t parameter is 2 and the *end* parameter is 5 in a **substring()** method operation, what characters will be extracted?

a) the characters at positions 2, 3, 4 and 5
b) all the characters after position 1
c) the characters at positions 2, 3 and 4

Solution
c

18.70 What happens if the **start** parameter is greater than the **end** parameter in a **substring()** method operation?

a) the *start* and *end* parameter values will be swapped
b) an error message will be displayed
c) the entire string will be extracted

Solution
a

18.71 If the **start** value parameter value is 6 and the **end** parameter value is 3 in a **substring()** method operation, what characters will be extracted?

a) the characters at positions 6, 7 and 8
b) the characters at positions 3, 4 and 5
c) the characters at positions 4, 5 and 6

Solution
b

18.72 Does the **substring()** method use negative numbers to extract characters that are referenced from the end of the string as many of the other string methods do?

a) yes
b) no
c) sometimes

Solution
b

18.73 Is the **substring()** method's **end** parameter required or optional?

a) required
b) optional

Solution
b

18.74 Is the **substring()** method's **start** parameter required or optional?

a) required
b) optional

Solution
a

18.75 What happens if the **substring()** method's **end** parameter is omitted?

a) the entire string, starting from the *start* position, will be extracted
b) an error message will be generated
c) the entire string, starting from the beginning of the string, will be extracted

Solution
a

18.76 What is the correct syntax model for the **substring()** method?

a) substring.*string*(*start, end*)
b) *string*.substring(*start, end*)
c) *string*.substring(*start, length*)

Solution
b

18.77 What characters will be displayed in an alert box as the result of the following code:

```
<script>
  var phrase = "Play it again, Sam!";
  var charExtract = phrase.substring(0, 10);
  alert(charExtract);
</script>
```

a) Play it ag
b) Play it aga
c) Play it a

Solution

a

18.78 What characters will be displayed in an alert box as the result of the following code using the **start** and **end** parameters that are given in a thru h following the code:

```
<script>
  var phrase = "Play it again, Sam!";
  var charExtract = phrase.substring(start, end);
  alert(charExtract);
</script>
```

a) (3, 9)
b) (8, 14)
c) (0)
d) (15)
e) (13, 9)
f) (4, 0)
g) (15, 16)
h) (13, 12)

Solution
a) y it a
b) again,
c) Play it again, Sam!
d) Sam!
e) gain
f) Play
g) S
h) n

18.79 Write the code to accomplish the following:

1) Create a string variable called **j** and give it the value "Life is but a dream.".
2) Create a string variable called **k**. Use the **substring()** method to extract "Life" from **j**. Use a **start** and **end** parameter. Put the value returned by the **substring()** method into the variable **k**.
3) Display the value of **k** in an alert box.

Solution

```
<script>
  var j = "Life is but a dream.";
  var k = j.substring(0, 4);
  alert(k);
</script>
```

Result displayed in alert box:
Life

18.80 Write the code to accomplish the following:
1) Create a string variable called **j** and give it the value "Life is but a dream.".
2) Create a string variable called **k**. Use the **substring()** method to extract "dream." from **j**. Use a *start* parameter but no *end* parameter. Put the value returned by the **substring()** method into the variable **k**.
3) Display the value of **k** in an alert box.

Solution
```
<script>
  var j = "Life is but a dream.";
  var k = j.substring(14);
  alert(k);
</script>
```

Result displayed in alert box:
dream.

18.81 Write the code to accomplish the following:
1) Create a string variable called **j** and give it the value "Life is but a dream.".
2) Create a string variable called **k**. Use the **substring()** method to extract all characters from **j**. Use a **start** parameter but no **end** parameter. Put the value returned by the **substring()** method into the variable **k**.
3) Display the value of **k** in an alert box.

Solution
```
<script>
  var j = "Life is but a dream.";
  var k = j.substring(0);
  alert(k);
</script>
```

Result displayed in alert box:
Life is but a dream.

18.82 Write the code to accomplish the following:
1) Create a string variable called **j** and give it the value "Life is but a dream.".
2) Create a string variable called **k**. Use the **substring()** method to extract "but" from **j**. Use a *start* parameter and an *end* parameter. The *start* parameter should be larger than the *end* parameter. Put

the value returned by the **substring()** method into the variable **k**.
3) Display the value of **k** in an alert box.

Solution
```
<script>
  var j = "Life is but a dream.";
  var k = j.substring(11, 8);
  alert(k);
</script>
```

Result displayed in alert box:
Life is but a dream.

18.1.4 toLowerCase ()

The **toLowerCase()** method converts a string to lowercase letters. The **toLowerCase()** method does not change the original string. The **toLowerCase()** method has no effect on non-alphabetic characters.

Syntax
```
string.toLowerCase()
```

Parameter Values

Parameter	Description
None	

examples of the toLowerCase() method:

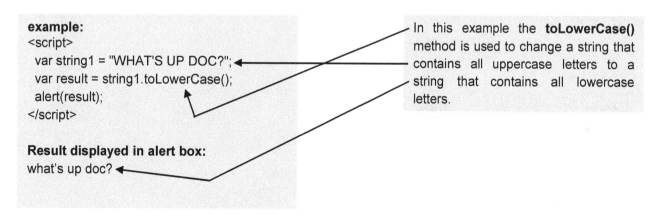

example:
```
<script>
  var string1 = "WHAT'S UP DOC?";
  var result = string1.toLowerCase();
  alert(result);
</script>
```

Result displayed in alert box:
what's up doc?

In this example the **toLowerCase()** method is used to change a string that contains all uppercase letters to a string that contains all lowercase letters.

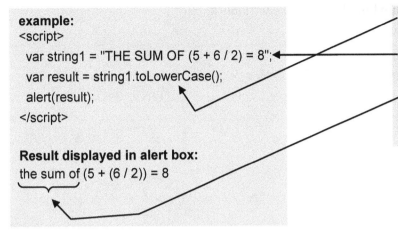

example:
```
<script>
  var string1 = "THE SUM OF (5 + 6 / 2) = 8";
  var result = string1.toLowerCase();
  alert(result);
</script>
```

Result displayed in alert box:
the sum of (5 + (6 / 2)) = 8

In this example the **toLowerCase()** method is used to change a string that contains all uppercase letters and some non-alphabetic characters to a string that contains all lowercase alphabetic characters and the original unchanged non-alphabetic characters.

example:
```
<script>
  var string1 = "THE SUM OF (5 + 6 / 2) = 8";
  var result = string1.toLowerCase();
  alert("string1 = " + string1 + "\nresult = " + result);
</script>
```

Result displayed in alert box:
string1 = THE SUM OF (5 + 6 / 2) = 8
result = the sum of (5 + (6 / 2)) = 8

This example is identical the one above except that we display both contents of **string1** (the original string) and results of the **toLowerCase()** method in **result**. Remember to use "\n" in an alert box to force a new line. (See problem 2.3 in chapter 2). This example shows us that the contents of the original string are unaffected by the **toUpperCase()** method.

18.1.5 toUpperCase ()

The **toUpperCase()** method converts a string to lowercase letters. The **toUpperCase()** method does not change the original string. The **toUpperCase()** method has no effect on non-alphabetic characters.

Syntax

```
string.toUpperCase()
```

Parameter Values

Parameter	Description
None	

examples of the toUpperCase() method:

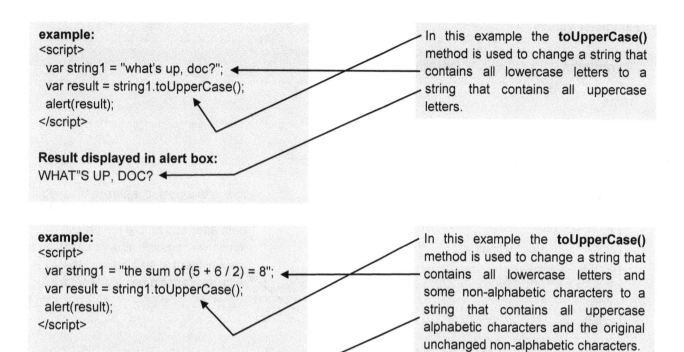

```
example:
<script>
 var string1 = "what's up, doc?";
 var result = string1.toUpperCase();
 alert(result);
</script>
```

In this example the **toUpperCase()** method is used to change a string that contains all lowercase letters to a string that contains all uppercase letters.

Result displayed in alert box:
WHAT"S UP, DOC?

```
example:
<script>
 var string1 = "the sum of (5 + 6 / 2) = 8";
 var result = string1.toUpperCase();
 alert(result);
</script>
```

In this example the **toUpperCase()** method is used to change a string that contains all lowercase letters and some non-alphabetic characters to a string that contains all uppercase alphabetic characters and the original unchanged non-alphabetic characters.

Result displayed in alert box:
THE SUM OF (5 + (6 / 2)) = 8

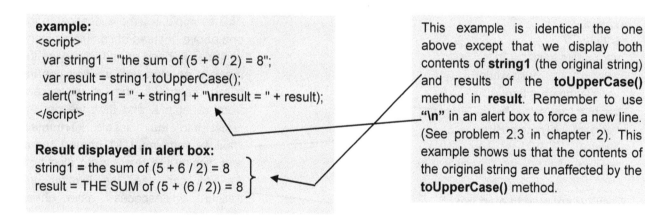

```
example:
<script>
 var string1 = "the sum of (5 + 6 / 2) = 8";
 var result = string1.toUpperCase();
 alert("string1 = " + string1 + "\nresult = " + result);
</script>
```

This example is identical the one above except that we display both contents of **string1** (the original string) and results of the **toUpperCase()** method in **result**. Remember to use **"\n"** in an alert box to force a new line. (See problem 2.3 in chapter 2). This example shows us that the contents of the original string are unaffected by the **toUpperCase()** method.

Result displayed in alert box:
string1 = the sum of (5 + 6 / 2) = 8
result = THE SUM of (5 + (6 / 2)) = 8

18.1.6 trim ()

The **trim()** method removes whitespace from both sides of a string. The **trim()** method does not change the original string.

Syntax

`string.trim()`

Parameter Values

Parameter	Description
None	

examples of the trim() method:

example:
```
<script>
 var j = "He said: ";
 var k = "      'Hello world!'      ";
 var m = " to me.";
 var n = j + k + m;
 alert(n);
</script>
```

Result displayed in alert box:
He said: 'Hello world!'   to me.

In this example, the phrase in string variable **k** has 8 empty whitespaces both after and before the phrase. When we combine all 3 variables and display them in an alert box, the whitespaces can be clearly seen.

example:
```
<script>
 var j = "He said: ";
 var k = "      'Hello world!'      ";
 var kTrimmed = trim(k);
 var m = " to me.";
 var n = j + kTrimmed + m;
 alert(n);
</script>
```

Result displayed in alert box:
He said: 'Hello world!' to me.

This example is almost identical to the one above. Instead of combining string variables **j**, **k** and **m** and displaying the result in an alert box, we first use the **trim()** method to trim all whitespace from variable **k** and then we put the result into the variable **kTrimmed**. Next we combine, **j**, **kTrimmed** and **m** and display the result in an alert box. As you can see, the leading and trailing whitespaces have been removed.

SOLVED PROBLEMS

18.83 What does the **toLowerCase()** method do?

a) it converts all uppercase letters to lowercase and all lowercase letters to uppercase

b) it converts all alphabetic characters in a string to lowercase letters

c) it converts all alphabetic characters in a string to lowercase letters

Solution

b

18.84 Does the **toLowerCase()** method make any changes to the original string?

a) yes
b) no
c) sometimes

Solution

b

18.85 What does the **toLowerCase()** method do to non-alphabetic characters?

a) nothing
b) it converts them to the lower case version of their alphabetic equivalents
c) it removes them from the string

Solution

a

18.86 How many parameters does the **toLowerCase()** method have?

a) 1
b) 2
c) 0

Solution

c

18.87 What of the following is the correct syntax model for the **toLowerCase()** method?

a) *string*.toLowerCase()
b) *string*.toLowerCase(*start, end*)
c) toLowerCase(*string*)

Solution

a

18.88 What will be displayed in an alert box as the result of the following code?

```
<script>
   var str1 = "NOW IS THE TIME";
   var displayValue = str1.toLowerCase();
   alert(displayValue);
</script>
```

a) now is the time
b) Now is the time
c) <nothing will be displayed>

Solution
a

18.89 What will be displayed in an alert box as the result of the following code?

```
<script>
   var str1 = "NoW iS tHe TiMe";
   var displayValue = str1.toLowerCase();
   alert(displayValue);
</script>
```

a) nOw Is ThE tImE
b) now is the time
c) <error message>

Solution
b

18.90 What will be displayed in an alert box as the result of the following code?

```
<script>
   var str1 = "EDMiller@Yahoo.Com#";
   var displayValue = str1.toLowerCase();
   alert(displayValue);
</script>
```

a) EdMiller@Yahoo.coma
b) edmiller2yahoo.com3
c) edmiller@yahoo.com#

Non-alphabetic characters such as "@" and "#" are not affected by the **toLowerCase()** method since they have no lowercase equivalents.

Solution
c

18.91 What will be displayed in an alert box as the result of the following code?

```
<script>
  var str1 = "The Product of 42 * 5 =  210";
  var displayValue = str1.toLowerCase();
  alert(displayValue);
</script>
```

a) the product of 42 * 5 = 210

b) The Product of 42 8 5 4 210

c) <error message>

Solution

a

18.92 What will be displayed in an alert box as the result of the following code?

```
<script>
  var str1 = "5A * 6B = 30AB";
  var displayValue = str1.toLowerCase();
  alert(displayValue);
</script>
```

a) 5A * 6B = 30AB

b) 5A * 6B = 30ab

c) 5a * 6b = 30ab

Even when the alphabetic characters are part of a mathematical equation they're still affected by the **toLowerCase()** method since they're string characters that are part of a string variable

Solution

c

18.93 Write the code to accomplish the following:

1) Create a string variable called **x** and give it the value "WHEN in the course of HUMAN events.".

2) Create another string variable called **y** and use the **toLowerCase()** method to assign it the same value as variable **x** but change all alphabetic characters to lower case letters.

3) Display the value of **y** in an alert box.

Solution

```
<script>
  var x = "WHEN in the course of HUMAN events";
  var y = x.toLowerCase();
  alert(y);
</script>
```

Result displayed in alert box:

when in the course of human events.

18.94 Write the code to accomplish the following:

1) Create a string variable called **x** and give it the value "WHEN in the course of HUMAN events.".

2) Create another string variable called **y** and use the **toLowerCase()** method to assign it the same value as variable **x** but change all alphabetic characters to lower case letters.

3) Display the value of **y** in an alert box.

Solution
```
<script>
  var j = "The Result of ((10 / 5) * (6 + 4)) IS";
  var k = j.toLowerCase();
  alert(k);
</script>
```

Non-alphabetic characters such as "(", ")", "*", and "+" are ignored by the **toLowerCase()** method beccause they have no lowercase equivalents.

Result displayed in alert box:

the result of ((10 / 5) * (6 + 4)) is.

18.95 Write the code to accomplish the following:

1) Create a string variable called **x** and give it the value "WHEN in the course of HUMAN events.".

2) Create another string variable called **y** and use the **toLowerCase()** method to assign it the same value as variable **x** but change all alphabetic characters to lower case letters.

3) Display the value of **y** in an alert box.

Solution
```
<script>
  var phraseOriginal = "HOW ARE YOU?";
  var phraseAltered = phraseOriginal.toLowerCase();
  document.write("The original phrase is '" + phraseOriginal + "<br>");
  document.write("The altered phrase is '" + phraseAltered);
</script>
```

This code demonstrates that the original string (in this case, **phraseOriginal**) is not changed by the **toLowerCase()** method.

Result displayed in the browser:

The original phrase is 'HOW ARE YOU?
The altered phrase is 'how are you?

18.96 What does the **toUpperCase()** method do?

a) it converts all alphabetic characters in a string to uppercase letters

b) it converts all lowercase letters in a string to uppercase letters and all uppercase letters to lowercase letters

c) it converts all characters to their uppercase equivalents

Solution

a

18.97 Does the **toUpperCase()** methodmake any changes to the original string?

a) yes

b) no

c) sometimes

Solution

b

18.98 What does the **toUpperCase()** method do to non-alphabetic characters?

a) removes them from the string

b) converts them to their alphabetic equivalents

c) nothing

Solution

c

18.99 How many parameters does the **toUpperCase()** method have?

a) 0

b) 1

c) 2

Solution

a

18.100 Which of the following is the correct syntax model for the **toUpperCase()** method?

a) *string*.toUpperCase(*start, end*)

b) *string*.toUpperCase()

c) string.toUppercase()

Solution

b

18.101 What will be displayed in an alert box as the result of the following code?

```
<script>
  var str1 = "you are quite beautiful!";
  var str2 = str1.toUpperCase();
  alert(str2);
```

```
</script>
```

a) You Are QUite Beautiful!
b) <nothing will be displayed>
c) YOU ARE QUITE BEAUTIFUL!

Solution
c

18.102 What will be displayed in an alert box as the result of the following code?

```
<script>
  var str1 = "YoU aRe QuItE bEaUtIfUl!";
  var str2 = str1.toUpperCase();
  alert(str2);
</script>
```

a) yOu ArE qUiTe BeAuTiFuL!
b) YOU ARE QUITE BEAUTIFUL!
c) You AreQuiteBeautiful!

Solution
c

18.103 What will be displayed in an alert box as the result of the following code?

```
<script>
  var str1 = "FrankSmith@google.COM/#@$";
  var str2 = str1.toUpperCase();
  alert(str2);
</script>
```

a) FRANKSMITH@GOOGLE.COM/#@$
b) FrankSmith@GOOGLE.COM/324
c) franksmith@google.com/324

Solution
a

18.104 What will be displayed in an alert box as the result of the following code?

```
<script>
  var str1 = "The result of ((8 * 4) + (9 / 3)) is 35";
  var str2 = str1.toUpperCase();
```

```
    alert(str2);
</script>
```

a) The Result of ((8 * 4) + (9 / 3)) Is 35
b) <error message>
c) THE RESULT OF ((8 * 4) + (9 / 3)) IS 35

Solution
c

18.105 Write the code to accomplish the following:
1) Create a string variable called **a** and give it the value "PARTING IS SUCH SWEET SORROW".
2) Create another string variable called **b** and use the **toUpperCase()** method to change all lowercase
   letters in a to uppercase.
3) Display the value of **b** in an alert box.

Solution
```
<script>
  var a = "Parting Is Such Sweet Sorrow";
  var b = a.toUpperCase();
  alert(b);
</script>
```

Result displayed in the browser:
PARTING IS SUCH SWEET SORROW

18.106 Write the code to accomplish the following:
1) Create a string variable called **x** and give it the value "thinking makes it so".
2) Create another string variable called **7** and use the **toUpperCase()** method to change all lowercase
   letters in a to uppercase.
3) Display the value of **x** and **y** on separate lines in the browser window as follows:
        The original string is '<value of x>'
         The altered string is '<value of y>'

Solution
```
<script>
  var x = "thinking makes it so";
  var y = x.toUpperCase();
  document.write("The original string is '" + x + "'<br>");
  document.write("The altered string is '" + y + "'");
</script>
```

Result displayed in the browser:

The original string is 'thinking makes it so'
The altered string is 'THINKING MAKES IT SO'

18.107 Match the following method names with their descriptions:

a) charAt()

b) charCodeAt()

c) fromCharCode()

d) concat()

e) index)f()

f) lastIndexOf()

g) replace()

h) search()

i) slice()

j) split()

k) substr()

l) substring()

m) toLowerCase()

n) toUpperCase

o) trim()

a) joins 2 or more strings and returns a copy of the joined strings

b) searches a string for a value and returns a new string with the value replaced

c) extracts a part of a string from a start position through a specified number of characters

d) returns the Unicode value of a character at the specified index position

e) converts a string to lowercase letters

f) returns the character at the specified index position

g) removes whitespace from both ends of a string

h) extracts a part of a string and returns a new string made up of the extracted substring

i) extracts a part of a string between 2 specified positions

j) converts Unicode values to characters

k) returns the position of the first found occurrence of a specified value in a string

l) searches a string for a value and returns the position of the match

m) splits a string into an array of substrings

n) returns the position of the last found occurrence of a specified value in a string

o) converts a string to uppercase letters

Solution
a) charAt()

b) charCodeAt()

c) fromCharCode()

d) concat()

e) index)f()

f) lastIndexOf()

g) replace()

h) search()

i) slice()

j) split()

k) substr()

l) substring()

m) toLowerCase()

n) toUpperCase

o) trim()

Appendix

Testing Your JavaScript Programs

There are three methods you can use to test the JavaScript and HTML code and programs found in this book:

METHOD 1
The first way is to use an online JavaScript testing website. The following four websites are some of the most popular but you can find others if you do a Google search on "JavaScript testing websites".

Website Name	Website Address
Web Toolkit Online	http://www.webtoolkitonline.com/javascript-tester.html
JSFiddle	https://jsfiddle.net/
JSBin	https://jsbin.com/
JS.do	https://js.do/

Each site will contain its own instructions, but, basically you paste your JavaScript and HTML code into the appropriately marked areas, click on **RUN** and see the results instantly appear on your screen.

METHOD 2
The second way to test your **JavaScript** (and **HTML**) code is to put the code into an **.htm** (or **.html**) file and then execute it with **Internet Explorer** (or some other web browser). This is done as follows:

Step 1: Launch **NotePad.**

Step 2: Write some **JavaScript** and/or **HTML** code.

Step 3: Save the page as an **.htm** (or .html) file. Give the file any legal file name. For example, **practice.htm**, **index.htm**, **testCode.htm**, etc. Save the file anywhere on your computer.

Step 4: There are two ways to run the file and see its results in **Internet Explorer** (or any other browser):

   1) Go to the location where you saved the file; right-click the file; left-click **Open with** and select **Internet Explorer** (or whatever browser you prefer). The **HTML** and **JavaScript** code in the file will be executed and the results will be displayed in your browser, **OR**

   2) Put the address of your file in the address box of **Internet Explorer**. For example if your file is named **testPage.htm** and is found in the **C:** directory, put the following address into the **Internet Explorer** address box:

     C:\testPage.htm

   and launch the page.

If the **HTML** code on your page runs OK but the **JavaScript** code doesn't execute and you get the following message:

   "Internet Explorer restricted this webpage from running scripts or Active X controls",

do the following steps to enable **JavaScript** in **Internet Explorer**:

   1) Select **Tools --> Internet Options** menu from the **Internet Explorer**.

   2) Select the **Advanced** tab from the **Internet Options** box. Go to the **Security** section of the

Settings window and check the box that says: "Allow active content to run in files on My Computer"

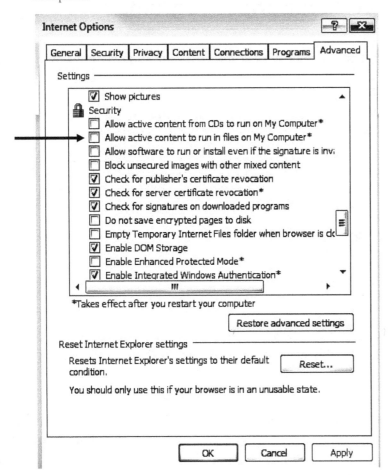

3) Click **OK** to save the security settings and close the **Internet Options** dialog box.

Your **JavaScript** code should now execute in **Internet Explorer**.

METHOD 3

The third way to test your **JavaScript** and **HTML** code is to install a web server on your computer. Installing a web server on your computer will allow you to access your **JavaScript** and **HTML** files as if they were part of a real website. All computers that host websites must have web server programs. A web server is a program that uses **HTTP** (Hypertext Transfer Protocol) to serve the files that make up a website to users who request access to that website. This process is an example of the **client/server** model.

The primary function of a web server is to store, process and deliver web pages to a client. The communication between client (computer requesting access to a website) and server (computer that the website resides on and which sends web pages to the client) takes place using **HTTP** (**Hypertext Transfer Protocol**). The pages delivered by the web server to the client are usually **HTML** documents, which may include images, style sheets and scripts in addition to text content.

Web servers (and client computers) are identified by **IP** addresses. The **Internet Protocol Address** (or **IP** Address) is a unique address that computing devices such as personal computers, tablets, and smart phones use to identify themselves and communicate with other devices connected to the **internet** either directly or through an **Internet service provider**. Any device connected to the **IP** network (the Internet) must have a unique **IP** address within the network.

A website name is not enough information to enable a client computer to communicate with a website residing on a web server. An intermediate server (a server that exists between the client and the web server) called a **DNS** (**Domain Name Server**) is needed to translate a website name into an **IP** address which directly locates and identifies a website.. **Domain Name Servers** (DNS) are the Internet's equivalent of a phone book. They maintain a directory of domain names and translate them to **Internet Protocol** (**IP**) addresses. This is necessary because, although domain names are easy for humans to remember, computers need an **IP** address in order to access a specific website.

When you type in a web address, for example: **www.mywebsite.com**, your **Internet Service Provider** checks the **DNS** associated with the domain name, translates it into an **IP** address (for example **212.173.138.95** is the **IP** for **www.mywebsite.com**) and directs your Internet connection to the correct website.

The point of all this is that if you load a web server onto your own computer you can access this server by putting the following name into the address box of your Internet browser:

http://localhost/

http://localhost/ always identifies the web server that resides on the your computer. Instead of going to a **DNS** server to find out the **IP** address associated with the name "**localhost**", your computer always translates the name "localhost" to the **IP** address **127.0.0.1**. **IP** address **127.0.0.1** always identifies and points to the web server on your computer. In other words, when you enter "**http://localhost**" or "**127.0.0.1**" into the address box of your web browser you will be connected to the web server running on the same computer. This allows you to create a website file on your computer and to access it with your web browser without actually going outside of your own computer and connecting to the **Internet** and an external **DNS** server.

The most widely used web server on the Internet is the **Apache** web server. This is because, not only is **Apache** flexible and powerful, but it's also very easy to get up and running. The easiest way to install the **Apache** web server on your computer is to download it as part of **WAMP** server which is a **Windows Web development environment** that includes **Apache**, **MySQL** and **PHP**. The following instructions will walk you through the process of downloading and installing **WAMP** server:

1) Download the **WampServer** installer from: **http://www.wampserver.com/en/**

2) Step through the installer wizard.

3) Once the installation is complete, you should see an entry for **WampServer** in your **Start** menu's **All Programs** section. In that menu, click the start **WampServer** entry. When the **WampServer** starts, left-click the icon in the **System Tray** to see the menu :

From this menu, you can start or stop the services and gain quick access to the server's configuration files. If you have any problems with the installation and how to use the WampServer menu, do a Google search on "WampServer instructions".

When WAMP server is loaded it will automatically set up the following folders and file on your **C:** drive:

c:/wamp/www/index.php

If you put the address **c:/wamp/www/** into your web browser's address bar, the Apache server will automatically execute the **index.php** file. In this case, **index.php** is the website's **index page**.

An **index page** is the web page that appears when someone visits your website without specifying a particular file name. For example, if someone visits **http://www.chevrolet.com/**, the web server will need to choose a default page, because the **URL** address doesn't include a file name.

The way a Web server chooses a default page to display is simple: When it receives a request that doesn't include a file name, it consults a list of default file names (such as **index.php index.html, index.htm**, etc.) and displays the first matching file it finds (that is, the first file named index, regardless of the file type) that it finds.

That means that if you have a file named **index.php** at the top level of your website, these two addresses will work identically:

http://www.mywebsite.com/
http://www.website.com/index.php

Both addresses will cause the file named **index.php** to be executed and displayed. The first **URL** address does this because the server looks through a list of default file names and finds the first file named **index**, regardless of its file extension, and the second **URL** address does this because the **URL** address of the request directly tells the server which file to load (**index.php**).

To make sure your website works when a visitor goes to **http://www.mywebsite.com/** without specifying a page name, you should be sure that the **top level** (first file listed in the **www** folder) of your website contains a file named **index.htm** or **index.html** (or one of the other default file names shown below). The file must be at the top level; the Web server won't be able to find the file if it's inside a folder or a directory inside or outside of the **www** folder..

Examples of index file names:

    index.htm
    index.html
    index.php
    index.php5
    index.php4
    index.php3
    index.cgi

Index

For more information or questions about the *Web Programming for Beginner's Series*, please contact the author, Randall Robertson, at:

rrobertson1914@yahoo.com